PARTING THE CURTAINS

INTERVIEWS WITH SOUTHERN WRITERS

Doug Marlette, Allan Gurganus, and Kaye Gibbons
April 4, 1994

Lee Smith, Susan Ketchin, and Clyde Edgerton
April 16, 1994

Reynolds Price and Eudora Welty
May 17, 1972

Parting the Curtains

Interviews with Southern Writers

Interviews by Dannye Romine Powell

Photographs by Jill Krementz

JOHN F. BLAIR, PUBLISHER
WINSTON-SALEM, NORTH CAROLINA

Some of these interviews originally appeared in
abbreviated form in the *Charlotte Observer*.

The interviews with Eudora Welty and with
Eleanor Ross and Peter Taylor originally appeared
in an abbreviated form in *The Mississippi Review*,
Volume 20, Numbers 1 and 2.

DESIGNED BY DEBRA LONG HAMPTON

PRINTED AND BOUND BY R. R. DONNELLEY & SONS

ALL PHOTOGRAPHS © 1994 BY JILL KREMENTZ

*The paper in this book meets the guidelines for
permanence and durability of the Committee on
Production Guidelines for Book Longevity
of the Council on Library Resources.*

Library of Congress Cataloging-in-Publication Data
Parting the curtains : interviews with
Southern writers / interviews by Dannye Romine Powell ;
  photographs by Jill Krementz.
          p.   cm.
    Includes index.
    ISBN 0-89587-116-5 (alk. paper)
    1. American literature—Southern States—History
and criticism—Theory, etc.
    2. Authors, American—Southern States—Interviews.
    3. Authors, American—20th century—Interviews.
    4. Southern States—Intellectual life—1865–
    5. Southern States—In literature.
    I. Powell, Dannye Romine.   PS261.P38   1994
810.9'975—dc20   94–24853

For my mother,

Elma Gibson,

who taught me to wonder,

and in memory of my father,

Dan Gibson,

who taught me to listen

Contents

ACKNOWLEDGMENTS

During the writing of this book, I became enamored of photographs. In particular, the photographs of Jill Krementz of New York, who returned my call for permission to use one of her photographs and ended up offering to come South to photograph the authors in this book. "Your favorites," she said, "are my favorites."

I am enormously indebted to Jill for her time, her energy, and her remarkable gifts. Her work past and present takes this book to a level I had neither anticipated nor imagined. I am thrilled, and I thank her from the bottom of my heart.

This book would not have been possible without the support of the editors of the *Charlotte Observer*, whose interest in and admiration for Southern writers over the last two decades prompted them to send me to the "four corners" in search of these authors. In particular, I would like to thank the editors who worked with me on these interviews: Caroline Beyrau, Gary Nielson, and Steve Snow.

I would also like to thank *Charlotte Observer* publisher Rolfe Neill, who encouraged me to interview Alex Haley, and former *Observer* features editor Tom Tozer, who discovered a five-

hundred-dollar surplus in the 1988 budget, which financed my trip to Gainesville, Florida, to interview Peter and Eleanor Ross Taylor.

I'm enormously indebted to former *Observer* editor Rich Oppel and current editor Jennie Buckner, whose permission to use these interviews in another form made this book possible.

Special thanks are due *Observer* assistant managing editor Bob De Piante and newsroom systems coordinator Dick Van Halsema, whose extreme tolerance for the strain these interviews often caused the computer system was invaluable and greatly appreciated.

I'm indebted to my present editor, Cheryl Carpenter, whose enthusiasm radiated. I am most grateful to Hank Durkin and Jeff Durkin for their assistance in transcribing the material onto disk, and to my colleagues Elizabeth Leland, Jerry Shinn, Richard Maschal, Polly Paddock, David Perlmutt, Paige Williams, Gigi Guyton, Mark Sluder, Ed Williams, Al Phillips, Mary Newsom, and John Vaughan, who brainstormed with me and sustained and encouraged me.

Norman Welch deserves a special thanks for saving me hours of labor by transcribing the tapes of Shelby Foote, Doug Marlette, Doris Betts, and Maya Angelou.

Without the fine ears and eagle eyes of my beloved Monday Night Poetry Group—Harriet Doar, Lucinda Grey, Judy Goldman, Susan Ludvigson, and Julie Suk—there would be weaker verbs, flabbier sentences, and clunkier rhythms.

I am also indebted to Anne Hogan, whose keen interest in Southern authors has for years inspired me.

I am grateful to former *Observer* colleague Frye Gaillard, who kept after me until I wrote to Carolyn Sakowski at John F. Blair, Publisher, to see if there was interest in this book.

And I am especially indebted to Carolyn for her expanded vision of this book, broader and deeper than I had imagined, and for her gentle prodding when energy flagged.

The entire staff at John F. Blair, Publisher—Debbie Hampton, Anne Schultz, Margaret Couch, Judy Breakstone, Sue Clark, Lisa Wagoner, and Heath Simpson—was a delight to work with, encouraging and professional. Editor Steve Kirk is a suggester and intuitor, blessed with a low emotional temperature.

A special thanks to Patti Black, Susan Chappell, Hal Crowther, Frank DeLoache, Deborah Dickey, Susan Ketchin, and Frank Ward, who well know their value and how much they helped.

There were people along the way whose kindness, generosity, and understanding smoothed the edges of hectic and sometimes frantic days of photographing. These include my cousin Sandra Fowler and my aunt Florence Noonan, both of Sullivans Island, South Carolina, who furnished Jill Krementz and me warm beds, good food, cheerful company, and many a valuable and wise assist. Thanks are also due Colleen Goddard, who kept tabs on the weather and the mail; Beverly and Katherine Webb of the Hillsborough Inn, who offered ease and elegance; Melinda Marlette and Anita Finch, whose calm sweetness and grilled salmon nourished us; Pat Hutzley of Dusty's Air Taxi, whose good humor prevailed and prevailed; and Eugene Norris, who kindly sorted out my phone messages and helped bring about the interview with Pat Conroy.

I would also like to thank my dear mother, who has believed in this book since before I was born, a woman wise in the ways of literature and of artists, a woman who has been telling me for years which details to look for, which to remember, and which never to repeat.

And my sons, Hugh Romine and Patrick Romine, great readers, great appreciators, young men who make me proud.

Last, my husband, Lew Powell, who has walked in my footsteps throughout this book, sympathetically, objectively, subjectively, skeptically, bucking me up, cooling me down, offering excellent advice and always, always a tireless shoulder and ear. I love him and thank him for it all—his fine wit, his exacting eye, and his patient and sustaining love.

PREFACE

At five o'clock one October morning in 1976, I interviewed Alex Haley in his hotel room in Atlanta. He was there to promote his book *Roots*, and I was there on assignment as book editor of the *Charlotte Observer* to write about him.

That Haley's book became a bestseller a couple of weeks later was cause for excitement and celebration. But the deeper excitement for me was listening to Haley talk that dark morning, before he was a household name, about the process of writing.

When words failed him, he told me, he would abandon his typewriter for the kitchen. He'd crack eggs, sift flour, pour the batter into a cake pan, pop the pan into the oven.

Then Haley would perch on a stool in front of the glass-fronted oven and watch as bubbles rose in the batter, watch as batter congealed into substance, the process moving inexorably toward completion.

That's what happens in writing, Haley said. Ingredients bubble and cook. Material becomes substance.

The image took hold. For the next eighteen years, I traveled the Carolinas and the South asking writers about that mysterious process whereby material bubbles into art.

I discovered writers to be an expressive and articulate group. Their minds are keen, their language zesty. They exaggerate, lie, contradict. They bare and share their souls. And, like me, they never tire of examining the creative process.

I do not offer this volume as a compendium of the best Southern writers or, in every case, the most well-known Southern writers. There are glaring omissions. The writers included here are ones with whom my path happened to cross during the twenty-year period from 1975 to 1994.

Yet there's more than coincidence at work in this book. Those included are writers who affected me deeply, either on the page or during the course of our conversations.

I fell in love with Pat Conroy one hot May afternoon in 1976, soon after publication of *The Great Santini*. With larger-than-life flourishes of humor, he described in that interview how his father would line his seven children up against a wall and shout, "Who's the greatest of them all?" The children, Pat said, were trained from an early age to answer, "You are, O Great Santini. You are."

Was Pat exaggerating? Maybe. I didn't care. As I watched him, I sensed behind his laughter an edgy, raw sadness. I knew I'd be back for more. Like Barbra Streisand as the psychiatrist in the movie *The Prince of Tides*, I was after what lurked beneath the jokes.

In June 1980, I drove to Highlands, North Carolina, to interview Walker Percy. I had just finished his latest novel, *The Second Coming*, which I had underlined furiously, like a schoolgirl. Reading Percy always sent fresh enzymes rushing into my bloodstream, and this novel was no exception.

Percy's answers to my questions were clipped and matter-of-fact until I complimented him about a particular sentence: "The darkness sprang back like an animal." He relaxed, and my bucket finally hit water as he described in detail the horror of sitting in front of a blank page of paper.

In the late spring of 1983, while vacationing at Pawleys Island, South Carolina, I lost my heart to Josephine Humphreys. I spread my towel on the sand, opened her just-released *Dreams of Sleep*, and drifted into her obsessive tale of a Charleston wife betrayed.

In Charlotte's Douglas Airport in 1985, I opened T. R. Pearson's first novel, *A Short History of a Small Place*, and read about the Epperson sisters, who had "distinguished themselves in the minds of the Neelyites by going from reasonably normal to unquestionably insane without ever pausing at peculiar." I knew I had to talk to the man whose genius bounced like a tumbleweed through that hilarious and rambunctious book.

On a gray December afternoon in 1986, as I waited to leave for the funeral of a friend's father, I began Kaye Gibbons's first novel, *Ellen Foster*. Her opening sentence captured me: "When I was little I would think of ways to kill my daddy."

It was April before I interviewed her in her duplex in Raleigh. She told me she heard Ellen's voice, then began to write. "How did that feel?" I asked her.

"Sometimes I feel like all art and good things flow in an underground stream. And I feel that the important authors have been able to drill a hole down there and hit it," she said. "I felt like I had hit it, and it scared my pants off."

All of these writers are in the business of drilling holes, and no matter how they describe it, they're joined in a common endeavor.

Eudora Welty talks about scenes of a novel floating from her subconscious while she drove a familiar route day after day. James Dickey talks about tuning into poetry the way you'd use a cat whisker to tune into a crystal radio. Gail Godwin talks about following a trail of crumbs deeper and deeper into the story's own reality.

Two authors in this collection—Doug Marlette and Simmons Jones—may at first seem unusual choices.

Marlette is best known as a political cartoonist and the author of the comic strip "Kudzu." He has not yet written a novel. I wager he will. I include Marlette because he understands the creative process and knows well the artistic temperament. "I think of artists as emotional tea bags," he says.

I include first-novelist Simmons Jones for his inspiration, as well as for his remarkable talent. Jones had written fiction off and on for years. But he knew that until he dealt with his alcoholism, he would have neither the discipline nor the control to become a published novelist. At age fifty-nine, he joined Alcoholics Anonymous. At sixty-five, he plowed back into his novel-in-progress, *Show Me the Way to Go Home*, which was published when he was seventy. Jones's perseverance and enthusiasm are powerful beacons.

I have chosen to keep the interviews in the present tense in order to capture as much of the time and place of each occasion as possible, and to reflect the abidingness of the writers' creative spirits.

It probably goes without saying that I have become vastly attached to this particular flock of writers, each of whom braves his or her way onto the blank page day after day, trusting the subconscious, believing in the power of language to lift us out of ourselves, to transform us, to bring us tidings of love, and of great joy.

PARTING THE CURTAINS

INTERVIEWS WITH SOUTHERN WRITERS

April 4, 1994

MAYA ANGELOU

December 1, 1993

Sunshine spills into every corner of Maya Angelou's white-columned house on Valley Drive in Winston-Salem, North Carolina, gilding the bouquet of fresh flowers in the living room and burnishing the African masks on the walls.

Hanging boldly in the two-story entrance hall is the Maya Angelou Quilt, created by Faith Ringgold and commissioned by her good friend and TV talk-show host Oprah Winfrey for Angelou's sixtieth birthday.

Angelou, now sixty-five, is the author of the best-selling *Wouldn't Take Nothing for My Journey Now*. She also wrote and delivered President Clinton's inaugural poem in 1993.

Yet Angelou, Reynolds Professor at Wake Forest University, is best known for her 1970 autobiography, *I Know Why the Caged Bird Sings*, which she dedicated to her son, Guy Johnson, and "all the strong black birds of promise who defy the odds and gods and sing their songs."

Angelou herself has defied the odds. Born Marguerite Johnson to parents who soon divorced, Angelou lived most of her childhood with her paternal grandmother in Stamps, Arkansas. It is this beloved woman, Annie Johnson Henderson, her portrait hanging in Angelou's breakfast room, who made the difference in her life. She taught her granddaughter to honor her height by standing tall. And she taught her to honor her gifts by reaching high and believing deeply and by striving to be more than she was.

In this interview, Maya Angelou talks about that grandmother, about her mother, about her marriages, and, most important, about her writing life.

INTERVIEWER

Your autobiography, *I Know Why the Caged Bird Sings*, came out in 1970, when you were forty-two. Your descriptions of your neighbor's sexual abuse of you, and your mother's boyfriend's abuse of you at age seven or eight, must have been among the first such descriptions in our literature. What gave you the courage to speak out?

ANGELOU

Well, at first, I thought I was going to write a book of my whole life in one book. I was asked by Random House to do it, and I thought, "Oh, this is a piece of cake." But once I started writing, I realized that I had to be writing for black girls, all black girls. Because there are so few books saying, "This is what it is like to grow up." There's Louisa May Alcott and others, but not . . . And then I thought, "I'd better be writing for black boys, too." And it was so difficult, I thought, "Oh, wait. I'd better be writing for white girls, too. And white boys, too."

Within the first three chapters, I realized that I had something to say, and I had to make a decision that I would tell a truth which might liberate me, and might liberate others.

As a result of that book, many books have come out describing the varying kinds of abuse. I have a file in my office filled with letters from women and men, mostly women, who read *Caged Bird* and somehow felt liberated enough to tell their mothers, or to confront their fathers or their uncles or their brothers, as grown women, and to say, "This was cruel, what you did to me."

INTERVIEWER

An evening you spent talking until 3:00 A.M. with James Baldwin, Jules Feiffer, and Feiffer's first wife, Judy, led to your writing *Caged Bird*. What happened that night?

ANGELOU

Well, Jimmy took me over to Jules and Judy's house. And all three of them were full of fabulous stories. And, as the Cockneys say, I had to fight for the right to play it good. I told my stories from time to time. I'd insert myself into the conversation.

And the next day, Judy Feiffer called the man [Robert Loomis] who became my editor, and still is my editor. She asked him if he knew who I was, and he said he kind of vaguely knew I wrote poetry. And she said, "If you can get her to write a book about her life, you really would have something."

So he phoned me. I said, "Under no circumstances. Never. No." He called about three times. And then he called with the *pièce de résistance*. He said, "Well, Miss Angelou, I suppose it's just as well that you say no to writing this book because to write autobiography as literature is almost impossible. Almost no one can do it."

I said, "I'll do it then."

He punched the right buttons.

INTERVIEWER

Your perfectionist button?

ANGELOU

It is. It is. And also the reaction to a larger

society saying to me in so many ways, explicitly and implicitly, "You can't do that because you're black." Or, "You can't do it because you're female. You can't do it because you're six foot tall. You can't do it because you were born poor. You can't do it." All those. And each time, I'm still not beyond jumping when that button is pushed.

INTERVIEWER

Early in your writing career, you took yourself very seriously, renting hotel rooms where you would go and spend the better part of the day writing. I'm fascinated by your description of what would sometimes happen to you physically. Your eyes would swell. Lumps would appear on your hands. What was going on? Were the physical reactions a metaphor for something internal?

ANGELOU

I think so. I'm not beyond that.

INTERVIEWER

What's going on in that process?

ANGELOU

I don't know. I don't know. I just don't know. I'm very fortunate, here in my town, to have a hotel which I use. And everyone there, from the clerks, the counter people, the reservations people, the maids and the janitors and so forth, everyone says they don't know me.

People call or come by and say, "Is this the place where Maya Angelou is?" And they say, "Maya who?"

INTERVIEWER

That's wonderful. What time do you go to the hotel?

ANGELOU

I go in usually around five-thirty.

INTERVIEWER

A.M.?

ANGELOU

Mm-hmm. I try to be in and have kind of shuffled off the outside by six.

INTERVIEWER

Do you take any coffee or anything with you?

ANGELOU

I used to. And occasionally I will get up in time to make a pot and pour it into the thermos. But usually I break at about nine, and then have coffee. But I don't know. Sometimes, you know, it's not wise to look a gift horse . . . You shouldn't put everything under the microscope. I know it works. That's all I do know.

INTERVIEWER

But what made you, in the beginning, be able to take yourself seriously enough to do that? That's a thing that many writers can't allow themselves.

ANGELOU

But it costs so much to write a decent sentence. It's a very serious matter. And so I noticed at home—I lived in Sonoma, California—

and I noticed that when I would set myself up in a room—I always have art, and I have a serious collection—I would look up, and I'd think, "Where did I get that? Now, did I buy it outright? Oh, yeah. No, I paid for that for over two years. Oh, yeah. I wonder, where is that artist? Is that hanging straight?" And there goes my concentration.

Now, at the end of a day in the hotel room, I may have done two pages that are acceptable. But I have been trying. But at the end of a day if I am at home, if I have done two pages, it's nothing.

So I thought, it costs everything. So I'd better treat it seriously.

INTERVIEWER
I want you to tell me what it feels like to shut that hotel door behind you and drive home. I suspect it feels wonderful.

ANGELOU
I don't think I feel anything then. Unless I've had one of those rare days that comes like maybe five times in a year. One of those days when every word is just right. I just flow.

And even those days when it's gone stultifyingly and stalled—even those days—I'm grateful. But I'm hardly there. I drive home and I have to be very conscious, because I could have an accident. So I am very conscious. I put myself on alert, and I drive home.

And I come in and have a shower. I will have had a shower at five, but by the time I come home, I need another shower, because working, writing, it's just as if I'd been digging ditches or cutting logs. And then I try to come into my house, and I plan a dinner. And I look in the fridge and I decide, "Oh, yes. I will do this."

INTERVIEWER
Because you've earned it.

ANGELOU
That's right. Then I go [grocery] shopping. I pretend to be there. I pretend. It's all pretend. But it's to try to get away from that [writing].

INTERVIEWER
What are you pretending?

ANGELOU
I pretend I'm sane. I pretend that I really care whether I'm having veal or chicken, vegetable soup or something. And it works. But it is pretend. Because that whole period, I'm neither meat nor fowl nor good red herring. I'm really not there.

INTERVIEWER
So you're pretending yourself back into a life.

ANGELOU
Into a normalcy. I put on my clothes, I brush my teeth, and say, "How do you do?" and all that. I operate in the familiar. That's all. But I'm not there.

INTERVIEWER
You've been married . . .

ANGELOU
A few times.

INTERVIEWER
A few times. Have you learned something new about yourself through each relationship? Are you married now? Do you want to be married again?

ANGELOU

Um, I've learned something new, yes, with each relationship. I learned something which is still true, so maybe I'm relearning it every time. And that is although I've married many times (I don't admit to the number because a number of people think that's frivolous; it's not frivolous), I bring everything I know—all my energy, my humor, I'm an excellent cook, I keep a beautiful house, I have a normal sexual appetite. I think it's normal, anyway. I don't know. [Laughter.] And I'm respectful and cheerful—so I bring all of that to a relationship.

Now, if the relationship doesn't work, I will not stay there and be a masochist for the sake of home, for the sake of the villagers, for the sake of tradition, for the sake of the church. I have to live. The man has to live. It is better for me to free myself and free him. He may find who he really wants somewhere else. My mother used to say, "A lot of people marry other people's husbands."

INTERVIEWER

I don't get it.

ANGELOU

For instance, you marry Mary's husband. Mary lives in Des Moines, Iowa. She never even met him. But that's her husband. You thought he was yours, but that's her mate, who she's compatible with.

INTERVIEWER

Now I get it.

ANGELOU

You see?

April 4, 1994

INTERVIEWER

You just got crossed up.

ANGELOU

Got crossed up.

I am happy to say, the men with whom I have lived, married or whatever, we're still friends. We have great respect. Neither has treated the other shabbily. In one marriage, we just wore the marriage out. It's like you wear a pair of shoes out.

INTERVIEWER

Would you like to be married again?

ANGELOU

I would love to be, if all things were equal.

And that's a big if.

ANGELOU

That's a big if. It's very lonely, though, not being married. And I will not . . . I come from a school where it's just not acceptable to live with someone, you know? And I have a friend. I don't think he's the one.

INTERVIEWER

You speak so sweetly and admiringly of your mother. And even though you were apart for nine years during your childhood, you seem to have had a wonderful relationship with her, and she was very nurturing.

ANGELOU

Yes, she was. You see, I have a theory that there is a parent who can be a great parent of small people, of infants and toddlers. They're the cutest little things, and doodley-doodle. They have the little shoes and the little socks and the little dresses. But as soon as that person gets to be about twelve or thirteen, they don't know what to do with them. So they say, "Shut up! Sit down! Go over there and sit down! Get out! You want to go to Europe? Here, go!"

Then there are parents who are great parents of young adults. My mom was in the latter group. I am so grateful that I got sent [early] to my grandmother, who just flooded me with love and lessons. But my ma, once I was able to talk to her, and she saw that I had some sense, and that I was going to be a good woman . . .

We'd walk out and down the San Francisco hills, and she had . . . Do you remember silver fox furs? Where the mouths of one reach over the tail of the other? She had that, and she had diamonds and makeup. She was a little woman. And we got to the corner, and I wouldn't ride with her. I rode the streetcar. I was a woman. So we got to the corner, and she said, "Baby, you know, I think you're the greatest woman I've ever known."

I looked down at this pretty little woman with her diamonds and her furs, and she said, "You're very intelligent. And you're very kind. And those two virtues don't always go together. Give me a kiss."

So I gave her a kiss on the lips. She walked across the street that way and got into her beige and brown Pontiac. And I went across the street that way, and got onto the Number 22 streetcar. And I remember it as if it was today. I remember the sun on the streetcar. I remember where I sat. I remember everything. And I thought, "Suppose she's right? Suppose I really am somebody. Just suppose . . . She's very intelligent, and she's too mean to lie. Just suppose . . . "

But that's what a parent can give to a child or to an offspring. And she gave it to me all the time.

When she was very sick, three years ago, in San Francisco, I flew out there every week. And finally the doctors told me that she might live three weeks. At the most, two months. She was so sick, she couldn't hold her head up. So I asked her, "May I bring you home? May I bring you to North Carolina?" She said [whispers], "Yes."

So I came home. I had one room turned into a hospital room. And I brought her to Charlotte. And she couldn't make the transfer to another plane. So I had a limousine go there and pick her up and bring her in and put her in the room. That was June. By Thanksgiving, she helped me to cook the Thanksgiving dinner.

INTERVIEWER
I don't believe it.

ANGELOU
Helped me to cook the Thanksgiving dinner!

INTERVIEWER
My word, what did you do to her?

ANGELOU
[Whispers.] Love.
Love liberates everything. Everything.
So when the cancer returned in May, she was not feeling very strong. I had been asked to come to be distinguished visiting professor at the University of Exeter, with lectures at Plymouth and all over in Britain, and I told her, I said, "I can't go." She had lung cancer and emphysema. She said [breathes deeply], "Go. [Breathes deeply.] Show them you spell your name [breathes deeply] w-o-m-a-n. Go."
Too fantastic. Too fantastic. So I wrote a book called *Double Stitch*, in which I talk about her.
While I was writing it, she was tied to blue plastic tubes, fighting cancer for her life. And I hoped that when it came time, I would be able to liberate her. She would expect that of me. She would expect me to be that much woman.

INTERVIEWER
Did she die here?

ANGELOU
Yes.

INTERVIEWER
Aren't you glad you brought her home?

ANGELOU
Oh, boy.

INTERVIEWER
You've said over and over that the popularity of your work is not important to you, but what's important is the work that's yet to come. The work that remains to be done. Do you still feel that way, or at sixty-five are you more willing to feel satisfaction for the work that has been done?

ANGELOU
I'm grateful. I don't mean to seem ungrateful for the work which has been done. I'm very grateful for it. I'm grateful for the inspiration and the energy and the hard work I put into it. I'm grateful for its reception. I don't mean to seem ungrateful.

INTERVIEWER
But it's not as important to you as the work ahead.

ANGELOU
That's right. The work yet to be done has to be more important. Otherwise, I mean, you would sit down on your fist and rear back on your thumb.

INTERVIEWER

Who taught you not to be satisfied?

ANGELOU

Life. I can't think of any particular person or incident, but life.

INTERVIEWER

In your new book, the best-selling *Wouldn't Take Nothing for My Journey Now*, there's a poignant essay about the beauty of planned pregnancies. Your pregnancy at sixteen was not planned. Do you regret not having had a planned pregnancy at some time later in your life?

ANGELOU

I did want other children, and I did try with marriages. I went in Germany and in London and in the States to the gynecologists. And they said, "There's nothing wrong." But I never conceived again. And I never used any protection. So it just wasn't for me. But then we are a very small family. I mean, I think our fertility may lie in being able to talk a lot or write or cook or . . .

INTERVIEWER

Aren't you glad you got pregnant when you did?

ANGELOU

I sure am. Oh, that's the best thing. My monument, it's my son.

INTERVIEWER

Did you feel honored when President Clinton asked you to write his inaugural poem? And was it hard for you to write on command?

ANGELOU

Yes. Both. Yes. It's almost impossible. There's no such thing. I mean, a public poem is a contradiction in terms. But I was delighted and pleased to have done it.

INTERVIEWER

In a recent *Esquire* article, *New York Newsday* cartoonist Doug Marlette took your inaugural poem to task, implying that the national inability of white people to feel makes us suckers— I'm quoting now—"for phony emotion, for grand hysterical displays, emotional bullies and manipulators, like Miss Angelou." He went on to say that you played "us and the new President like banjos." He said that white folks anesthetize ourselves to emotion and then "seek out exotics who seem to feel, who have access to the primitive gods and soul and feeling." He meant "exotics" like you. What do you make of this?

ANGELOU

I've never even heard that. My secretaries would never bring that to me. My sister friends, my man, would never, because usually, I can hardly stand it. But I like that. The primitive gods . . . What gods aren't primitive? Aren't all gods primitive? And, my dear, played the white community like a banjo! Oh, God! Oh, dear! Oh, I wouldn't have thought. I hadn't seen that. There may be some truth in some of it, I don't know. But if I played anything, I played myself. I played myself. Like a good bass fiddle.

INTERVIEWER

Your original name was Marguerite Johnson. Early on, your brother Bailey started calling you Maya. How did you come up with the name Angelou?

ANGELOU

Well, I married a man named Anastasios Angeloupolous—Tash Angeloupolous. And he told me when the Greeks shortened their name, the female got the *ou* ending, and the men got the *os* ending. So they cut off the *polous*—it was Angeloupolous—and it just became Angelou.

INTERVIEWER

You latched onto a beautiful name.

ANGELOU

Thank you.

INTERVIEWER

You really got raked around in March 1993 by the *Wake Forest Critic*, which described you as a "phantom professor." The alternative campus newspaper said, among other things, that you taught no classes, that you collected an annual salary well into the six figures, that your office doesn't return calls, and that when you do teach your classes, they're by invitation only. What interests me most about all this is, are your classes by invitation only?

ANGELOU

What does that mean? I don't know what that means.

INTERVIEWER

Do you ask to see their work before they get into the class?

ANGELOU

No. I look at their transcript. Sometimes, sixty or seventy people sign up for my class. I look to see who they are, or how hard they want

to work. I am supposed to take fifteen or sixteen—I have twenty-seven students—and I teach every Tuesday. This year, I missed one Tuesday. I gave them a reading day, which they wanted. I never not teach.

He's [the *Critic* writer, John Meroney] taking a slam at me again, saying now that I plagiarized this [inaugural] poem. It made me very sad. But, anyway, my students laugh like everything when they hear that I don't teach. Because when I meet them, the first thing I say to them is, "I feel sorry for you." And they laugh. And I say, "Some of you have chosen to be in my class because you've read a book of mine or two or you've seen me on television. Let me tell you: You will never work as hard again in your life as you will work for me. On the other hand, you will never be quite the same—ever—when you've come through a class with me. And I'm your professor forever."

INTERVIEWER

The course is called?

ANGELOU

The Philosophy of Liberation.

INTERVIEWER

Last questions. You say you've invented yourself as an actor invents a character. If the invention is successful, are you afraid of losing the real Maya Angelou or the real Marguerite Johnson?

ANGELOU

No, that is the real. And when I say "invent," I don't mean I'm other than myself. But I have got the courage to try to be more than I might be—to be more courageous, more kind, more

INTERVIEWER
Tell me about the real Maya Angelou.

ANGELOU
The desire to be better is who I am. Not the construction, because I miss by more than a mile all the time. But I want to be it.

INTERVIEWER
And you've had something in you since you were a child, haven't you, that wanted to be better than you were, that wanted to be more than you were?

ANGELOU
I really wanted to be the person my grandmother wanted me to be.

INTERVIEWER
And more?

ANGELOU
Oh, if I could ever be that.

INTERVIEWER
What did she want you to be?

ANGELOU
Kind. Deliberate. Soft-spoken. Gracious. Generous. Forgiving. *Forgiving*. That's what she wanted me to be. And I'm still trying.

The second child and only daughter of Bailey and Vivian Baxter Johnson, Maya Angelou was born Marguerite Johnson on April 4, 1928, in St. Louis, Missouri, and was raised by her paternal grandmother in Stamps, Arkansas. In 1940, she graduated from Lafayette County Training School in Lafayette, Arkansas, and in 1945, she graduated from Mission High School in San Francisco.

Her early career included working as a Creole cook, a streetcar conductor, and a madam. She also sang and danced in private clubs in San Francisco. From 1954 to 1955, she appeared in *Porgy and Bess* on a twenty-two-nation tour sponsored by the United States Department of State. In 1957 and 1960, she appeared in the off-Broadway plays *Calypso Heatwave* and *The Blacks*. In 1960, she produced and performed in the off-Broadway musical *Cabaret for Freedom*.

From 1963 to 1966, Angelou served as assistant administrator of the School of Music and Drama at the University of Ghana's Institute of African Studies in Legon-Accra, Ghana.

In 1973, she made her Broadway debut in

Look Away, and in 1974, she directed the film *All Day Long*. In 1976, she directed her play, *And Still I Rise*.

She served as a lecturer at UCLA in 1966 and as a writer-in-residence at the University of Kansas in 1970. In 1974, she was a distinguished visiting professor at Wake Forest University, Wichita State University, and California State-Sacramento.

In 1982, she received a lifetime appointment as Reynolds Professor of American Studies at Wake Forest University.

Her autobiographies include *I Know Why the Caged Bird Sings* (1970), *Gather Together in My Name* (1974), *Singin' and Swingin' and Gettin' Merry Like Christmas* (1976), *The Heart of a Woman* (1981), *All God's Children Need Traveling Shoes* (1986), and *Wouldn't Take Nothing for My Journey Now* (1993).

Her poetry collections include *Just Give Me a Cool Drink of Water 'Fore I Die* (1971), *Oh Pray My Wings Are Gonna Fit Me Well* (1975), *And Still I Rise* (1978), *Shaker, Why Don't You Sing?* (1982), *Now Sheba Sings the Song* (1987), *I Shall Not Be Moved* (1990), and *On the Pulse of Morning* (1993).

Angelou is also the creator of the screenplays *Georgia, Georgia* (1972) and *All Day Long* (1974).

She is the author and producer of *Three-Way Choice: Afro-Americans in the Arts*, and she directed the play *Moon on a Rainbow Shawl* (1988).

She writes for Oprah Winfrey's Harpo Productions, including a segment of the TV series "Brewster Place."

Her awards and honors include a Chubb Fellowship Award from Yale University (1970); a Rockefeller Foundation scholarship in Italy (1975); Woman of the Year in Communications, awarded by *Ladies' Home Journal* (1976); the Matrix Award (1983); the American Academy of Achievement's Golden Plate Award (1990); the North Carolina Award in Literature (1987); Woman of the Year, awarded by *Essence* magazine (1992); the Horatio Alger Award (1992); the Women in Film Crystal Award; and the Spingarn Medal for black achievers (1994).

She was invited by President Bill Clinton to write a poem and read it at his inauguration in 1993.

Angelou has received honorary degrees from Smith College, Mills College, and Lawrence University.

In 1952, she married Anastasios Angeloupolous.

In 1973, she married Paul Du Feu.

She is the mother of a son, Guy Johnson, born in 1944.

Maya Angelou lives in Winston-Salem, North Carolina, where she is working on a memoir about her mother.

April 4, 1994

DORIS BETTS

November 1, 1993 Doris Betts's directions to her Pittsboro, North Carolina, house are precise, including the spot in the road where, if you're not careful, you're likely to get broadsided.

What the prizewinning novelist and short-story writer does not prepare you for when she says, "Come through the woods," is this tunnel of leafy, golden shimmer that winds its way, eventually, to her three-story, blue salt-box in the middle of a small field. The lane is as much transition from the dusty highway as it is magical meander, reminiscent of the route the mind takes on its way to invention.

In the clearing beyond the fence are the Arabian horses that Betts and her husband, Lowry, began raising in the early 1980s. And from the side door of the house three dogs bound—Bear, an Akita and Rottweiler cross; Maxine, a "wandered-in" dog; and Lily, a Norwegian elkhound.

Something of the girl lingers in Doris Betts, a grandmother and Alumni Distinguished Professor at UNC-Chapel Hill. For one thing, she's slim. For another, she wears her auburn hair long and tied back.

"I tried wearing it short once," she says, "and I'd see my reflection in store windows, and looked like every bourgeoisie housewife in Chatham County."

Her study—computer, files, books—is on the third floor. But here in the sunny den, its windows giving onto a cluster of mimosa trees, Doris curls up to read.

She has just completed the novel *Souls Raised from the Dead*, about a North Carolina family facing life-and-death decisions. She's free now to spread out her notes for a novel-in-progress about the nineteenth-century Donner party in Nevada. For this novel, *The Sharp Teeth of Love*, Betts enters information into a notebook according to category—ghosts, nervous breakdown, cannibalism, landscape.

This afternoon, Doris Betts talks about her Calvinistic upbringing, about talent, faith, cheerfulness, marriage, and the vast differences between writing the short story and writing the novel.

You and Lowry Betts married in 1952, after your sophomore year at Woman's College, now UNC-Greensboro. While Lowry was finishing law school, you were finishing your first collection of stories, *The Gentle Insurrection*, which won the first Putnam UNC prize. My question is this: What was it about you—a twenty-one-year-old product of the North Carolina Piedmont—that prompted that kind of commitment before women were routinely taking their talents seriously? I have to add that the book-jacket photo of you, with the bare shoulders and single strand of pearls, makes you look like someone who could easily not take herself seriously.

BETTS

I think that was actually my engagement photo. [Laughter.] Well, part of it is that I had always been loved and I had never—I had *never*—been told that I couldn't do things. Although deep down, all my family—which is not a very bookish family—thought I'd get over this business about writing when I got married and became pregnant. They thought, well, that life had caught up with me, I suppose.

I do think, though, as I look back, there were two big influences. One is that Statesville, which was a town at the time I hated and wanted to escape from, but I think I had a phenomenal series of schoolteachers there. Most of them unmarried. All of them rather stern and strict. I can't say that I loved them at all. They were very demanding teachers, who when they found me idle in school, gave me extra things to do with-

out even a smile. And, I think, took me seriously. So I think that's one influence.

The other has to be having been reared in a very fundamental and earnest ARP [Associate Reformed Presbyterian] denomination, where it was honestly taken for granted that you owed something for being here. And that if you had any ability at all, it was a gift, and you were expected to make some kind of use of that.

Which is, in fact, what Flannery O'Connor said once about why she wrote. She said that she took seriously the parable of the talents. That she had always believed it. And I know now it's customary to think of that as hokey and simplistic.

But I think if you grow up believing that, it makes you take everything seriously. Almost humorlessly. There's something about a background in Calvinism that says that you only have so much time. Mortality is always coming. Work, for the night is coming. I just soaked that up from the skin. And I do not regret it. I think it has been a very useful tool. I can see that it can run away with you. But I do not regret it. I think it has been a very good goal—goal being a push.

INTERVIEWER

So, given all that—good schooling and a vigorous work ethic—put yourself back in that room where you, a bride, soon pregnant, were working on your short stories, and try to recall what you were thinking of yourself.

BETTS

All I thought about, really, was making this

story better than the last story. When I entered the contest, which was then at UNC with Putnam for that book, I honestly thought I had a good chance of winning. It seems presumptuous now. But I thought, "Oh, well, that seems good. Yes, I'll try that." And I don't think I had the kind of doubts that experience has now impressed upon me.

INTERVIEWER

You've been teaching at UNC since 1966, and many of those years you served as director of the creative-writing program. What have you learned over the years about the nature of talent in students, and the nature of talent when coupled with determination and perseverance?

BETTS

Well, the second part of the question is almost the answer to the first. There's much more talent than I once thought. I believe much more than I once did about the flower that blossoms unseen and wastes its sweetness on the desert air. Because without that second thing—determination—plus a kind of good fortune, a great many people give up. And it wasn't because they didn't have the talent. It was because they weren't willing to keep going back and failing. Or it was because life was hard to them.

When I look back at my writing class, for example, it was very small, and I was *not* the most gifted person in the class. The most gifted person in that class spent some years being treated for alcoholism, etc., etc., and many years went by before she wrote again. I mean, it's not the

sort of thing you think of when you are in college, but life is getting ready to take you seriously, and to many people it is much harsher, and their talent can simply be snuffed out, like a candle.

I'm not sure that that isn't the only thing, maybe, that writing classes can give students—perseverance. Because the talent you're not going to alter very much. You're going to teach some techniques and some skills and some habits. And, in the long run, that's what gets people through the very difficult times. If I were God and could measure the talent on some sort of divine scale, I'm not sure I would see any difference whatsoever between the quick publishers and the ones that took ten years.

INTERVIEWER

What would you call talent? You know it when you see it.

BETTS

Actually, you don't know it as much as the eighteen-year-old thinks you do. It's not instantly recognizable. They really believe it's like having a mark on the forehead of some kind that makes you say, "Aha! You, in. You, out." Whereas you really see only something that is distinctively original in the way they use language. Beyond that, everything else, it seems to me, develops. But if they don't care much for the language, then there's no need to talk about plot or character. Aristotle said metaphor was the one gift that couldn't be taught.

INTERVIEWER

Metaphor.

BETTS

Yeah. I love that. And I know what he means. What it really means is not so much that you make the metaphor, but that you are able to *think* metaphorically. That you are able to see that this thing is like that thing. Because I think the whole creative process in some way is putting opposites together into something that wasn't there before. And some really do just have that. Or are getting it. You know, you can feel them getting it. Because they'll make a lot of bad ones. That doesn't make too much difference, if they make bad metaphors, so long as they're in love with making them.

INTERVIEWER

Peter Taylor once said that what can't be taught is insight.

BETTS

That's very close, too. But the thing about insight is that I don't think it comes that early. Insight is something you grow and you mature into. You may have little insights, but it's a process. Peter was one of my teachers.

INTERVIEWER

Yes. He told me that and bragged on you.

BETTS

He was a wonderful teacher, and yet he's a totally different teacher from me, and when I look back on those classes, I will think, "What

was it Peter did?" Because most of what he did was read to us things that he was appalled we had not read already. He read them out loud. He was not a particularly dramatic reader. But I don't know that I'd ever been read to that much except in church.

INTERVIEWER

Did you have Randall Jarrell as a teacher?

BETTS

I did not. He taught mostly poetry. I occasionally got the chance to sit in on his class. And the same was true of Lettie Rogers, whom I did not have. I had Robie Macauley, who went on to be a fiction editor, I guess at *Playboy*, and published a novel and a wonderful book on writing called *Technique in Fiction*, with George Lanning. And then I had Frances Gray Patton. So I mean that's pretty wonderful for only having been there the sophomore year.

And also, they brought wonderful people to campus. And again, that's an influence, too. Just being able to see people who are "real" writers. And see that they are human, and that they do talk to you. I had a story, as a sophomore, criticized by Katherine Anne Porter. I've never remembered what she said. That didn't matter.

INTERVIEWER

Just the fact that she was reading—paying attention to—your work.

BETTS

That's right. That's right. And if you come from one kind of a background and you really have never met any writers, they are all like knights and ladies, you know. They are fictional creatures, almost. Until you actually meet some and they are no different from you and me.

INTERVIEWER

I've heard you say that your students often think an idea for a story comes in outline form, and that really it comes in a flash. Describe how your own short stories come, and if you know at the beginning what will happen and how the story will end.

BETTS

In a way, this is back to metaphor. I think what happens is that you are kind of ready for a story, but you don't know it. You are in a sort of a dissatisfied mood. Somehow, as long as you are in equilibrium you don't get any good ideas. You know, you just sort of vegetate and become bovine. But as soon as you are either dissatisfied with something you're doing or writing or whatnot, then what will happen is that something occurs that sparks you.

Sometimes, it's a first line that pops into your mind because of something you see, or you'll be reading something, and it—I don't know—collides with something else in your head. Nobody would ever think that that was the cause of it, because there's no resemblance. But it's a matter of being open to those moments.

INTERVIEWER

Almost like being fertile.

BETTS

It's like being a child, because children can't tell what's important and what's unimportant, so they have to pay attention to everything. Well, writers are like that, I think. They are always just kind of—I don't know—watching and listening, and you just can't tell what you're going to use.

INTERVIEWER

Do you ever know the end before you know the middle?

BETTS

I usually do not know. Occasionally, I will know the last line and nothing else. Which is usually, for me, a suspicious beginning, because it's apt to freeze the story to get it to a punch line, a kind of anecdotal quality. And I don't know how many opportunities you close off when you know the end. It's like slamming doors down the hall.

But usually, I only have a character and a situation and the sense that it's pulling forward. But I haven't been writing many stories, and that's a little bit different from writing novels, although novels for me, too, are sparked off in that way. And I don't think that's nearly so efficient [the sense that it's pulling forward], because you've got such a long haul not to know where it's going.

And I've gotten better at having at least a looming sense of the shape of a novel, or at least of the theme. I know, kind of, where it is heading. But I don't want to outline. I don't want to freeze it. I've had too many spark moments en route that I wasn't expecting, where suddenly there's a new character in there that you didn't plan to introduce and are glad you didn't miss because you had this outline which didn't provide for that person.

INTERVIEWER

You tired of the short story, didn't you? It became—you probably won't agree with this—too easy for you.

BETTS

No, I will agree with that. I think it did become too easy. Not that I was having a huge success at publishing that many, but I do think the short story is like rhymed poetry or anything that has a kind of preset pattern. That after you've learned how to do that, then the next stage it'll be like painting by numbers. And you will be able to do it quite competently because you've done a hundred before. But you cease to get into a story form. Although some writers can do this, I couldn't. I couldn't get into the short-story form the things that I had learned by being middle-aged and older.

INTERVIEWER

So maybe the form is better for younger writers?

BETTS

I think it does suit the young. It's quick. It's intense. It's a powerful emotion, usually. You don't linger over it. It shimmers. But the older

you get, the more the experiences you are having day-to-day are less and less like that, and they are more and more this sort of accretion of barely digested experiences. That's what I feel, I guess, in reading Proust, is that sense of that drop-by-drop accretion. I can't imagine he would have ever wanted to write a short story.

INTERVIEWER

And yet, no matter how old or how mature, there are those who will never be novelists.

BETTS

That's right.

INTERVIEWER

And why is that?

BETTS

I think there's a very real difference in the cast of mind. If you think about the number of writers you know who have been equally good at the novel and the short story, that's a very small number.

INTERVIEWER

Especially equally good at poetry and the novel.

BETTS

That's right. Again—and poetry I think is much closer to the short story—you do come closer somehow to grasping it whole, even if you don't know how it's going to end. It will turn out that your first page has a lot to do with your last page. Just as, in a poem, the first line has a lot to do with the last line, even though you didn't know what it was going to be. It is a small cluster circle.

Novels go out in a linear way. And they are much more contradictory. They are less neat. There's a difference in the scale of the prose. And that's the hardest for me, when I go to novels. I'd gotten so used to the very condensed prose of the short story that for me to stretch out a little bit and linger is almost . . . It's as if I have to give myself permission to do that. I have a tendency still to want to, you know, get it all into five thousand words, or to write the kind of novels that have chapters that are like short stories. That's the other risk that you run. I hope I'm getting better at that. It has something to do with being able to think along a bigger scale.

INTERVIEWER

Many poets envy the novelist. I've heard them say how wonderful it would be to have a novel to write, to have something to return to day after day that you didn't have to scratch up from the beginning.

BETTS

Oh, they're out of their minds.

INTERVIEWER

How come?

BETTS

I'd say, "How wonderful to be able to finish and have the whole thing right then." Then you can tinker. But how to keep going on with this thing which may be succeeding or failing, and

you can't tell when you're in the middle of it? And where you think it's going. How many more pages do I have to write? One hundred? Two hundred? I don't know.

INTERVIEWER

And tinkering is harder to do, isn't it, in the middle?

BETTS

Much harder. Because until you get through, you're not sure what you're going to have to change. It may no longer fit the whole. So you've widened your choices, but you've also widened the likelihood that 90 percent of them are bad.

The other thing that is harder about a novel is that life and work do not often supply you with the chance—I heard Shelby Foote talking about this, too—to get up a head of steam and keep it up. So that today you stop at a point while you're still going pretty well and tomorrow you will pick it up. Well, if tomorrow you have to go in and teach, and you don't get back for five days, that page is cold by then. And that's very hard.

INTERVIEWER

What would be your ideal writing day? And I mean, from beginning to end.

BETTS

I really have never had one. My ideal writing day . . . Well, I was going to say it would begin with everybody waiting on me instead of the other way around. I don't believe there's a woman writer around who wouldn't say that. Which means that you don't make breakfast.

And from the minute you wake up, you have begun to allow your thoughts to drift to what you were writing about, at least in a vague sense, without interruption.

Remember Georges Simenon? When he was writing, he went up and closed his study, and his wife would come and leave a tray outside his door. I don't believe there's a woman writer alive who was ever treated in this way. And he ate when he was ready, instead of when everybody else's tummy was rumbling.

And then you would write and have a chance to look back over the work. And you would do whatever your required amount of pages were—mine would be somewhere between five to ten on an ideal day—and look back over it. And then in the evening you would probably read. And I think that would be ideal. I have never had such a day. And, this semester when I'm off, I really had the vision that I would have those days. But that's so unrealistic.

INTERVIEWER

Why haven't you? I have a poet friend who's off this semester, too. And she had a little plan laid out. And she hasn't had any time. What happens?

BETTS

Well, part of it is that she probably is the sort of person who doesn't say no very easily. Who is involved in many other activities. I mean, you can't blame the world. It's something you do to yourself. Life just simply admits of many interruptions. You do have duties to your family or to your church or to students who are not going to let you alone if you are, after all, their adviser for a graduate thesis or dissertation.

INTERVIEWER

I read an essay of yours on Anne Tyler, and in it you commented that any writer who is 60-percent tamed, even when entering her forties, is probably not vivid enough nor honest enough to make us pause in our own preference for running away to hear her home truths. I'd love to hear you expand on the tamed part.

BETTS

I suppose by tamed I mean something like what we were talking about with the short story. Having found your niche in some way, and been willing to play to it. Knowing that you could. And that you didn't have to take any more risks or write anything that might flunk. In fact, I think it's very tempting nowadays, if you're a woman, to write politically correct female fiction. If you're a Southerner, to play the games with that that every Southerner knows how to play, and that, at every cocktail party, we do play.

So there's nothing wrong with it. But it would be disastrous if you fell into that Senator Claghorn mode while you were writing, and if you weren't trying to do something beyond what you had done before.

I was thinking about Tyler because it seems to me her great risk—what she does so well—is character, and character in a family. And I think the risk that she took, which was after that essay, in fact, was with *Saint Maybe*, which I think is a fine novel and a novel on a subject that should have been really taboo. I mean, this person she is writing about is a fundamentalist Christian of the ilk that no New York reviewer could view him with anything but puzzlement, a specimen under the microscope. Not even her background . . . She's Quaker, and she loves that character. I mean, her love for that character is obvious.

And I thought that was so much better, really, than her character of Maggie [in *Breathing Lessons*], who, I think, she could do with one hand tied behind her back. But now she made herself do something harder, less popular, more apt to fail. And I think that the achievement matches that risk. And I like to think that we all keep doing that. Otherwise, we might as well quit and sit on a wall.

INTERVIEWER

Speaking of achievement, my favorite story of yours is "The Ugliest Pilgrim," in which Violet Carl travels by bus to Tulsa to have her scarred face healed by an evangelist. Many have described Violet's journey as a journey of faith. What I admire so much about Violet is her unfailing sense of entitlement. Her feeling that she has a God-given right to be a beautiful woman. Do you think a healthy entitlement fits into your scheme of faith and religion?

BETTS

Yeah. One reason that's interesting is because when that story was chosen to make the film *Violet*, that's why they chose it. They weren't interested in the religious part at all. They had been looking for a female character with a little spunk. And in that decade [the 1970s], there weren't as many as there are now.

I've just had a meeting with a class at Chapel Hill that's getting ready to do an oral presentation of the story, and they were kind of upset about another story of mine called "The Story of Eve," in which a woman is raped and gets along just fine. You know, in fact, she kicks the blazes out of the guy between the legs, and her life is not ruined. And they felt I was really not giving enough consideration to the serious trauma. And I *am* giving consideration to the serious trauma.

But I think, for one thing, it's hard to write fiction about victims. Even in life, I have a hard time remaining sympathetic long with people who are unable to stand up and fight for things — and I consider that the absolute picture of anyone who really read the Old Testament, or even the New, which is gentler, and took it seriously.

I mean, Job's up there shaking his head at the sky, saying, "What are you doing?" Jacob is stealing his birthright. I mean, the kinds of people that led the Jews are all upstarts and self-starters, and they're not all even nice or pious people. But what they are not are whiners. None of them is a whiner. And it's unfortunate that part of the women's movement slid in that direction. It's understandable. And there's real victimization. I don't mean to minimize that. But whining is simply not a useful response. And it's not a pragmatic response.

So I tend to write about people who do believe, whether rightly or wrongly, that if things are not right, they ought to be, or they ought to be fixable, or if they're not, somebody ought to explain it to them, whether it is indeed the Almighty, or the people who surround them. And I can't imagine being interested for long in characters who were not feisty in that regard. I'm not interested in people in real life who aren't feisty.

It's one reason that my favorite kind of student is often not the one who agrees with me and docilely does what I suggest, but the one who will push or raise questions. And they don't have to be rude at all, they simply have to be themselves. I'm pretty sure they're going to survive.

INTERVIEWER

You've mentioned somewhere that when people are criticizing a piece of work—in fact, you mentioned it about your own work—that sometimes they will not be right on the money about what they're criticizing. They won't have it pinpointed. But the fact that they're raising questions means they're onto something, and it's the writer's job then to look more closely at those somewhat amorphous concerns.

BETTS

Also, they may tell you something you didn't know. The way someone else analyzing your dream, which you thought you understood perfectly, may suddenly open a door or a window onto it that you had kept yourself from seeing.

Also, I feel if someone totally misreads what I have written, then I didn't write it well. And that's an instructive lesson. If they get it, but they applied it in a way that seems skewed to me, I simply think they brought something different to the work.

Students really want to say that it doesn't matter what I intended, if you got something out of it. I wouldn't go that far. I think that's pretty sloppy-minded. But I think not to allow for the individuality of the reader is to deprive yourself of a dimension. Because in a way, what you are counting on is that your reader is at least as smart as you are. Maybe smarter. And that that person brings to it at least as much sensitivity and a whole different set of experiences, and that what you have written might, one, be misunderstood, but, two, be expanded in some way.

I'm much more interested in somebody's full reaction to something than I am in some kind of safe, analytical statement about it. That's typical. That's what everybody else says. That's true of poems, too, don't you think?

INTERVIEWER

Oh, yes. In our writers' group, occasionally someone will have a poem, and we'll say, "Maybe it's this, maybe it's that." We can't pinpoint exactly what's wrong. But our questions are a signal for the person to go back to the drawing board and figure it out. And it's amazing how inarticulate we can be about the problem sometimes.

BETTS

Well, the fact is, there are teachers who are very good at that. [Former UNC-Chapel Hill creative-writing professor] Max Steele is the best teacher I know at this very thing. He's much better at this than I am. He has himself a background in Freudian analysis, and he tends to direct the sort of question that drives the student deeper in a kind of Freudian way, that some may even resent. But he's always useful. It's not the way they begin by thinking about it. And it takes them one layer down. And it's not that he forces a certain interpretation. He just asks questions. They are often, I think, rather difficult questions. I used to sit in my office, and I'd suddenly hear him say to a student just what a shrink might say. He might say, "Why have three of your stories been about a very possessive mother?" And the student will sit there going, "Groooaan." And that's useful to know.

INTERVIEWER

Sure. It's useful to get it conscious.

BETTS

Get it clear. And then you may be able to do more with it than before.

INTERVIEWER

You believe the *why* of a short story is more important than the *what happened next*. Can you elaborate on that, please, especially for those people who loved Robert Waller's awful best-selling novel *The Bridges of Madison County*.

BETTS

Ooh! I just met Robert Waller. Dreadful man.

INTERVIEWER

He came to Charlotte with his videos. . . .

BETTS

I've got the *Time* magazine thing about the ol' mush-meister at work. Terrible. I felt better once I realized that what that book is is not a novel but a song. And so you keep asking it to have qualities that songs don't have. So once I understood that, I felt better.

But I think that what you remember after you have read a story is not, often, the plot. Because if you remember the plot, you have no reason to read it again.

INTERVIEWER

I'm almost incapable of remembering plot.

BETTS

That's right. And it's one reason that detective stories—which I love—pass in and out of the mind without touching, somehow. And you can read some of them over and over again, because you've forgotten what happened. But what lingers with you is precisely, really, that part of the story that touched upon something in your experience or your emotion or your questions, that you would say to yourself, "Yes, that's how it is." Even if you had never said that before. And it's not that it has told you something you didn't know. It has told you something you *did* know, but had not yet articulated.

And that's what I think great literature does to you. It confirms what you know, but in a way more beautiful and more intricate than you would have ever had time to formulate. And the amazing thing is that someone who did that five hundred years ago can still do it to you, out of another culture, maybe another language. So that in some way you kind of plug into the cross-cultural humanity that we all do feel, but so

April 4, 1994

seldom now have a chance to experience—except in reading.

I rediscovered your wonderful Graham Lecture, "Faith and Intellect," from 1982. It leads me to this question about your own faith, which you once said you tossed away upon entering college: What brought back this "natural doubter," as you call yourself? And was it a slow drift? Or more of a flash?

BETTS

It probably was a slow drift. I've just been talking about this with Susan Ketchin because she's doing a collection of interviews with Southern writers about faith, and I told her—and it turned out that she nodded because her experience was similar, but we were not specific—that I thought what really brought me back was being confronted by something that I could not solve myself. And Susan, like me, has been a . . . She's a very bright woman, and she can do many things, and you do get, if you're not careful, the illusion that you are a competent person.

And I also once thought that not to be a competent person, to admit that you needed more than yourself was, like whining, a kind of weakness. And that I didn't want a religion which only drew the cripples and the nuts and the sentimentalists.

I don't find it that way. But I do find that at some point, it is essential that there be some conviction that you are most certainly not omnipotent. That you will, and do, fail. It's what you used to call a conviction of sin or smallness, and you might phrase it differently now. But it does mean that sooner or later you find your own powers inadequate for something.

It has been a gradual change, and it is not the kind of faith I thought everybody else had when I was throwing it away. I thought that everybody else was very certain and very convinced and they believed every jot and tittle, and I knew I wasn't going to be able to do that.

Now that I have come back to what I think must be a fairly typical, a loving church here, which is the Pittsboro Presbyterian—very small, right uptown—what I find instead is that I am surrounded by many pilgrims, all of whom are on a journey, at various stages of what they are learning, and we have all made a commitment to keep going the same route together. And at various times we might disagree on interpretations of Scripture or on the answer to a catechism question or many another thing. That does not seem to be crucial.

What seems to be crucial is that you have decided to commit whether somebody is in charge of the universe or not, and whether that power is benevolent or not, and whether in the main the Christian story is the best revelation of that that we have.

INTERVIEWER

Even though it was a slow drift, there must have been a moment of choice.

BETTS

I do think there is a moment of choice, and that that's very different from growing up in a faith where you never question the pattern. Then it's like a template that's been set down by somebody else and everything fits.

But if you choose to make it, it does alter everything else that you do. And I have a character in this new novel, who is a woman who has been sort of a template person, and the death of her granddaughter just shatters the template. And she says the same thing that Madeleine L'Engle said, that she's had these episodes before, of feeling that she'd come down with the disease of atheism. But now she's not sure whether she's going to get over it. And it seems to me that if people are honest that they will say, at various times, "I believe very well." And at other times, "There's nothing to this. We're just bugs and lizards."

INTERVIEWER

I was intrigued to read somewhere that you and Lowry once joined a square-dance club. And it made me wonder if what seems to be a very sane marriage is a result of good luck or good management.

BETTS

A little of both. I think all marriages are probably the product of management and luck. And the fact that two people decided to manage, and not just one. Because it seems to me that a long marriage with children has just many phases to go through. And you are not always attendant, when you're at the different stages in your life. And many of my friends have been divorced, and one of my children is in this process. And it's heartbreaking. I don't care how sensibly

people have gone about it, the wounds are very deep. So I'm not sure.

I think Lowry's a pretty patient man, and rather laid-back. Quite different from me in temperament. And I think each of us needed the other's difference. I often said that if it weren't for me he'd be stuffy, and if it weren't for him I'd be scatterbrained. I mean, we each are very good for that sort of balance.

We've also each had separate careers that we were both very much involved in. And so, when we get home in the evening, it's sort of a relief to come down that road through those trees. This is very much a refuge. And there are many things that we do not do. That is, we're home most of the time when we're not at work. We don't socialize a lot. We don't entertain a lot.

I'd like to travel more, but the horses keep me . . . But after having had the children that we both shared and were concerned with, I mean, it helps to have horses and dogs and cats that you are both responsible for, and that you both jointly own in some way. You have to have something that you do together that you like a great deal.

But we're very similar in what we like when we're home. You can see that he sits over there and reads the law books and so on and so forth, and I sit over here and read the things that I am reading. The TV goes incessantly. He looks at it much more than I do. I guess what we've done is accommodate our differences. He has an excellent rational mind. He is an analytical thinker. He can save me from doing something rash, which I would be inclined to do. He has been a very serious father and comes from a home where his daddy really worked and home was it. Work and home. And is not really used to career women. His mother . . . What she mainly did was home economics. And deep in his heart, I know he wishes I did too. But, as I say, we've accommodated.

INTERVIEWER

In your newest novel, *Souls Raised from the Dead*, you said you couldn't let your hero's daughter die and have him come out of the last chapter saying the answer is so-and-so. You said in the magazine *Poets and Writers*, "I want to have some sense that, if your wounds don't kill you, they're going to heal." Is it too puritanical, do you think, to push that one step further and say, "If they don't kill you, they will make you stronger?"

BETTS

No, it's not too puritanical. It's risky to say that, I think. And I said that. In fact, I'd just come back from Union Seminary, where I'm on the board of trustees. And I like those people, and one of them was asking me about my minister here, who has come through a very hard year, his wife having had an aneurysm of the brain at Christmas. And I said, "You're going to hate me for saying this, but I will add, since you know him and care about him, that it has greatly deepened his sermons. As suffering will."

One hesitates to say it because it sounds like you're advocating hair shirts, etc., but the fact remains that everybody is going to have some suffering. And it's a question of what use one is able to make of it, if it doesn't overpower you. And I think many it *does* overpower, and they deserve nothing but sympathy and compassion. But if you are able—and if you are, it's not your strength, it's some constitution you inherited or some good grace—if you are able to transmute that in some way, it does strengthen you, I think.

INTERVIEWER

I read somewhere that you're a great believer in the trait of cheerfulness.

BETTS

Well, when I did *Heading West*, I was thinking so much about what the West represented, and the whole Manifest Destiny and the pursuit of happiness—and that seems to me now to be a very young goal, to wish to be happy, because I don't really think that's possible. I think you have moments of great happiness, but it's a kind of ripply road. But the ability to be cheerful is a trait of character.

INTERVIEWER

Inborn, you think?

BETTS

Maybe not. Partly inborn. Maybe partly what we were saying about whether suffering makes you stronger in life. Whether you come out of that still able to believe in life, warts and all. And, in fact, until then, it seems to me that it's just optimism. And maybe ill-based. But cheerfulness has already recognized that lots of things can go wrong and some of them will, and it's still good to be here. That's cheerfulness.

And that, it seems to me, is also something I see very much in Anne Tyler. If I have a connection with Tyler, I feel very much that she has not an optimism, but a cheerfulness about her characters, that they come through a great deal, but most of them love life even so.

INTERVIEWER

In *Heading West*, I saw Nancy Finch's abductor as a metaphor for the duty that had held her hostage back home. Hostage to her mother and to her brother, confining her life to the public library and spinsterhood. How have you balanced duty and freedom in your own life? Duty might have also held you captive, but somehow you didn't allow it.

BETTS

Oh, well, sometimes it succeeds, I think. That's one reason I'm interested in that theme for women. Because it has never seemed to me as simple as flinging everything away for freedom. That in itself is impoverishing, because part of duty is a part of the affection one has for other people. If there's not a commitment or a mutual serving of one another, the affection is not very deep. And if you can leave it that easily, who needs it?

So the balancing of that seems to me, in one way or another, to have been the job women have coped with always—not just in the last twenty-five years. And I'm intrigued by how well some women have done that. And I have wanted to have my cake and eat it, too. Some days I have had my cake. Some days I have eaten it. Some days I felt terribly guilty because I wasn't Super Mom and at the right place at the right time. Some days I have felt very guilty because

I knew if I hadn't had a home and children, I might have been speaking at the MLA, and that would have been great for the career. So there are trade-offs, it seems to me, constantly. I wouldn't have had it any other way.

INTERVIEWER

You believe, like Faulkner, that the art of fiction is to uplift the heart of man.

BETTS

Yeah, but it's better when Faulkner said it. When you're receiving the Nobel Prize, you can say things like that out loud. But it is true. I do believe that. And I would say something happened to me when I finally accepted that that's what I believe as a writer—that I was not going to write Ann Beattie's kind of fiction. Slice of life. Beautifully done. Like crystal. Cool. Very accurate. But that I had been spoiled by Old Testament Bible stories, and deep down, I thought that a story ought to have a point. And that essentially it was best if it could be on the right side. Now, it doesn't have to do that in a way that's obtrusive or preachy or didactic in any way, but that somehow, if you had read all of the stories that I had written, you'd pretty well know, I think, what I valued and what I thought was trivial. And that the writers I like the best also have done that, though they are not all confessed moralists. But I can tell what counts for them, and what things they would condemn or fight.

INTERVIEWER

Last question. That is, besides the uplifting of

the heart of man, what else do you hold dear? What else do you believe in?

BETTS

As a writer, I believe in the sentence. So much of my life is involved with just making the words have some correspondence to the experience that prose itself is a discipline and a reward to me.

As a person, I really value the teaching. It's as much fun for me as anything I do. And though a substitute for writing in some cases, it has been very satisfying and has brought me more children than my biological children, of whom I am greatly proud.

There are lots of things I hope to live long enough to do, and each year I want to write something I haven't written before. Something very different.

The only child of William Elmore and Mary Ellen Freeze Waugh, Doris Waugh Betts was born June 4, 1932, in Statesville, North Carolina. She graduated from Statesville High School in 1950 and studied at Woman's College, now UNC-Greensboro, from 1950 to 1953. She later studied at UNC-Chapel Hill.

She was a staff writer for the *Statesville Daily Record* from 1950 to 1951 and for the *Chapel Hill Weekly and News-Leader* from 1953 to 1954. In 1962, she became editor of the *Sanford News Leader* in Sanford, North Carolina.

In 1966, she began teaching at UNC-Chapel Hill, where she rose from lecturer to her current position of Alumni Distinguished Professor of English.

Her novels are *Tall Houses in Winter* (1957), *The Scarlet Thread* (1964), *The River to Pickle Beach* (1972), *Heading West* (1981), and *Souls Raised from the Dead* (1994).

Her short-story collections are *The Gentle Insurrection* (1954), *The Astronomer and Other Stories* (1966), and *Beasts of the Southern Wild* (1973).

Her awards include the G. P. Putnam–University of North Carolina Fiction Award (1954), a Guggenheim Fellowship (1958), the Sir Walter Raleigh Award (1959, 1966, and 1973), the Medal for Literature from the State of North Carolina (1975), and the Medal of Merit in the Short Story, from the American Academy of Arts and Letters (1989).

On July 5, 1952, she married Lowry Matthews Betts, an attorney. They have three children: Doris Lewellyn, born in 1953; David Lowry, born in 1954; and Erskine Moore, born in 1960.

Betts and her husband live on a horse farm in Chatham County, North Carolina, outside Pittsboro, where she is at work on a novel about the nineteenth-century Donner party in Nevada, tentatively titled *The Sharp Teeth of Love*.

April 5, 1994

FRED CHAPPELL

August 9, 1991

*F*red Chappell is sitting on the brick patio behind his lushly landscaped house in Greensboro, North Carolina, and he notices a small object jerking its way up a tree. He goes over to inspect, stares at the tree for a few seconds, then returns to the stone garden table.

"Just a hornet laying eggs inside a cicada," he says.

That kind of minutiae always seems to be lurking at the edge of Chappell's consciousness. Often, it makes its way into his stories. In his new collection, *More Shapes Than One*, there appear oblate spheroids, curious squiggles, swirls of ice grains, a bunched-up shadow on the wall.

Burlington Industries Professor of English at UNC-Greensboro, Chappell—the name is French Huguenot but pronounced like the church chapel—is among the notable writers, such as Reynolds Price, William Styron, Josephine Humphreys, and Anne Tyler, who studied with legendary writing professor William Blackburn at Duke University.

Poet Allen Tate once looked at Chappell and remarked, "People who dress as sloppily as Fred must have *internal* organization."

Indeed, Chappell is a study in rumpledness. During a 1980 interview, he slouched in his campus office in a green velour shirt and tossed his cigarette butts out the window.

He no longer smokes, but his laugh is still a cackle and his face boyishly unguarded.

Don't let appearances deceive you. Internally, Chappell *is* disciplined, and it shows nowhere more than when he is at his desk. In its archives, Duke University has to date eleven thousand letters written to Chappell; he has personally answered every one of those letters.

On this emerald August morning, Chappell talks about his early heroes, about finding his own grain as a writer, and about his late parents, memories of whom he says grow sweeter by the year.

When I came up the walk, I noticed you had a bunch of envelopes clipped to the mailbox. I know the mail can make or break a writer's day. But I've never asked anyone about it for publication.

CHAPPELL

It's the nicest and the cruelest thing about being a writer. A writer lives and dies by his post box. And I would've thought by now—I've been publishing books almost thirty years—I would've got used to it. But I'm always excited by the mail.

A piece of mail will make you dance around the room. It has also caused writers to commit suicide, of course. It's kind of like a daily lottery. It's fun. And you get to a place in your life where bad news is just as interesting as good news.

INTERVIEWER

How do you mean?

CHAPPELL

You've received a reaction to something you've written that you've thought about, maybe even had hopes about. And you'll read the rejection and sometimes you think, "That's what I really thought, and I was too lazy to carry it through." That's what writers do. Well, I don't think for anybody else—except for those people who win those Publisher's Clearing House prizes—the mail means so much as it does for a writer.

INTERVIEWER

Do you enjoy being part of a larger literary universe? You send things out. Someone reads them. In your reviews, you write about other writers' works. People read your novels and stories and poems. Often, these people write you letters or want to interview you. Somehow, it all seems connected, like swimming in a big ocean.

CHAPPELL

It's a privilege to be part of a community of writers and readers. Yes. That feels very good. It's no substitute for real life, because there's a way in which it's just a community of hobbyists, rather than any kind of natural community made up of neighbors and national alliances and so forth. Although the intellectual community, of course, is one of the most ancient in the world and cuts across time as well as space. I have correspondents in Estonia and places like that, as you would expect.

I think everybody in our century waits for the collapse. Sooner or later, it's all going to break down. You can see every day that it gets a little worse. Someday, it'll break down. The intellectual community won't break down. It'll survive through it somehow or another. It always has. Even through the collapse of the Roman Empire. So you're happy to be in that kind of situation. But for most people, once the external situation breaks down, there's no other life. And that's unhappy. But that's also happened to writers, too. There's no free lunch.

INTERVIEWER

There's a little couplet of yours I love. It's from your collection *River*, the first book of *Midquest*.

It says, "Each time I reach outside my skin, I just get lonesome for what's within."

CHAPPELL

Lord. I wrote that twenty-five years ago. The guy's making a diary entry. He's trying to decide on a life of action or contemplation. And he decides on a life of contemplation. He's tried the other. He's tried the hunting and fishing and—it doesn't say so in there—other kinds of adventuring around. And he finds it unsatisfactory. He will agree with Socrates that the examined life is worth living.

INTERVIEWER

And you agree with that?

CHAPPELL

I agree with it for me. I don't agree with it for everybody. I think there are lots of people that it would be disastrous for. Ronald Reagan should not examine his life. He should live a life of action rather than contemplation.

INTERVIEWER

I'm curious about your story "Alma" in this new collection. What interests me in this particular story is the heightened slyness of your female characters. Yes, their slyness is in direct proportion to their helplessness. But do you think women are inherently sly?

CHAPPELL

I think women are people, like everybody else. I wrote the story because I don't like the way women are treated sometimes. I wanted to write a story which portrayed a society in which they are ill-treated and treated like they're often treated in the world you and I know, and to show that they had found some way to get around that, that they have the ability to survive and endure.

I read the story at Greensboro College, and this nice older lady came up and said she just hated that story because she didn't think people ought to treat women that way. And I said, "I don't either. That's why I wrote the story." She made a face at me and walked away. I don't think anybody that old had ever made a face at me.

INTERVIEWER

In your essay "A Pact with Faustus," you say writers need to consider their temperaments as part of their basic writing tools.

CHAPPELL

You should know what kind of person you are, rather than trying to write against your grain all the time.

I know lots of poets who are trying to think of themselves as swingers. And really at heart they're kind of conservative, shy people who are overcompensating. If they would come to grips with that, they could probably write like Philip Larkin instead of writing very bad Charles Bukowski.

You have your own gifts, and those are the ones you should cultivate. But young people don't want to do that. They want to borrow. You've got to try on different personalities, and that's what you should do when you're young. But you should get over it as soon as you can, because your own personality is going to develop in so many ways that as soon as you can get a handle on that, the more freedom you're going to have.

INTERVIEWER

How old were you when you found the grain and kept going with it?

CHAPPELL

I was thirty-five.

INTERVIEWER

What happened?

CHAPPELL

I started writing *Midquest* [the tetralogy which includes *River, Bloodfire, Wind Mountain*, and *Earthsleep*]. It became important to me. And that became the theme of the book—to take stock and change directions a little bit. And once I decided I was going to do that, then that looked like an interesting theme, and it had the antecedents, and it fit into a literary tradition, and why the hell not? If only it had taken the three years that it was supposed to, rather than the ten years that it did. But I don't give a damn. I've never been happier than when I was working on a long project. No, I don't really care. What would I have done? Written something worse, maybe.

INTERVIEWER

You've lost both parents now. Does that make you feel at all orphaned?

CHAPPELL

By losing one parent, you get used to losing another. It's not easy. And what you feel is just a terrible, terrible loss. But in my case, over a period of years—some two or three years—the memory of them becomes a very sweet thing. You feel about them and think about them in ways you never did before. In a different light.

You may think of the same anecdotes and the same events, but the tone is very different. And there's a way for me that, both of them having died, they have not left. In fact, I feel closer sometimes to my father than I felt when he was alive. But I don't think this happens for everybody. I think very fondly of both of them. Just certain kinds of light in the afternoon or certain kinds of weather will remind me of both of them and how they were together and how the family was together, and I feel very happy, in a kind of melancholy way.

INTERVIEWER

You have been teaching for twenty-eight years, and you've recently received the highest award that the UNC system gives for teaching. What do you love about teaching?

CHAPPELL

The students. I like the students. They've been everything in the world that students are supposed to be—good and bad and all in between. But they've always been exciting.

INTERVIEWER

Have you noticed students as a whole have changed over the past quarter-century?

CHAPPELL

Students change a little bit over the years. They're not quite so secure and happy as they used to be, because now more of them come from broken families than they used to. My colleagues and a lot of people are fond of saying they don't know anything now. And it's true that they don't know quite as many books as they used to. They know other things. They know about computers and things like that.

The level of student competence hasn't really changed as far as I can see. The students haven't really changed as people. Their circumstances have changed. Most of my students now work. I would say at least 60 percent have some sort of job, on campus or off. Usually off-campus. Most students now—or a great many students—have no idea of going to college for four years and getting a degree. They're going six, seven, eight—as many years as they want to—and they may get a degree and they may not.

They're much more goal-oriented, because they have to make a living sooner. But they can't do it. Nobody's paying the bills. So many are single parents. Schools are more expensive. It's hard to make ends meet. Students have a very smart way of doing it. They're more laid-back. They take a smaller number of courses. They give them what time they can from their jobs, and they live the best they can. I admire them. It ain't easy.

INTERVIEWER

At fifty-five, your career is solidly established, your son is married, your marriage and house are in solid repair. Do the fewer distractions to your writing life make up in any way for no longer being as young?

CHAPPELL

I wasn't all that crazy about being young. I stayed young too goddamned long. I was a teenager until I was forty or forty-five. The most distraction I ever suffered was from myself— drinking too much, farting around, partying all the time. I'm kind of glad to outgrow that.

There's less distraction now, and I enjoy it. Some of the distractions I miss. It was nice living with our son. Now, he's moved on. It was nice seeing our folks, and now we don't do that.

INTERVIEWER

You were a good and dutiful son.

CHAPPELL

Growing up, I was fighting with my mother all the time. She didn't want me to write, and I wanted to write.

INTERVIEWER

Why didn't she want you to write?

CHAPPELL

She thought I would starve to death. She thought I would be in profligate company, that I'd end up like Edgar Allen Poe. That was the only writer she knew anything about. This was common in my high-school years. Everybody threatened me with being like Edgar Allen Poe. I finally read a biography of Edgar Allen Poe, and I thought that was how you did it. That sounded good to me.

INTERVIEWER

You mention the act of talking often in your poems. The pleasure of talking, the joy of talking.

CHAPPELL

Believe it or not, at this stage of the game, I don't like to hear myself talk very much. I've talked through the years. I make my living talking. I'm tired of hearing what I know I'm going to say. A lot of times, I don't know what in the hell I'm going to say. I'm tired of that, too.

INTERVIEWER

You often talk about time and writing. Once, you said that for a writer to make up for what time does not allow, you have to experience a "disciplined suffering" inside the work. You called it a "careful self-destruction." I'm wondering if the youthful drinking you mentioned earlier fits in here anywhere.

CHAPPELL

I think I meant that you try to approach a certain intensity, or even sometimes to achieve a certain intensity with your writing, and I'm speaking specifically then about the kind of writing I did when I was younger. The first and second and third novels and the kind of poetry I was trying to write then, that I never could get anything out of.

In order to push yourself to an emotional limit, you lived in all kinds of dangerous and foolish ways, and you tried to observe yourself—what was happening to you—in the midst of this kind of hysterical behavior. I don't think that's a good way to do it. I think it's a dumb way to do it.

INTERVIEWER

If there were other ways, why didn't you choose them?

CHAPPELL

Because I didn't know any better, and because I've got some romantic heroes in mind. Specifically, Rimbaud and other writers. Dylan Thomas and people like that.

INTERVIEWER

Why choose somebody like Dylan Thomas as a hero?

CHAPPELL

He was a hero for a lot of people in the fifties when I first saw him. I hitchhiked all the way from Canton to Duke to hear him read.

INTERVIEWER

He was a brilliant poet, but often he didn't show up for scheduled readings when he came to this country, and he was almost always drunk. Why make a hero of the whole person?

CHAPPELL

I didn't know much about the whole person. All you knew was that he was a magnificent reader, and a very interesting poet—at the time, he seemed the most important poet in the world—and that he lived very intensely and drank a lot of whiskey.

That's all I knew. I don't know much more than that now. I know he was a pain in the ass. They poured him onstage over at Page Auditorium. And you thought, "Oh, geez. This is not going to happen." And he gave a magnificent reading. An impossible reading. And then they poured him offstage.

INTERVIEWER

I've heard you say you're not sure you actually chose your particular form of self-destruction. That maybe it chose you.

CHAPPELL

You never know. There's always genetic basis for hard drinking. But it's something that intensifies the emotions. That's why you pursue it. And it's also the reason it's destructive. What's bad about it is that it's very deceptive. You think you're learning things that you're not really learning. And you can deceive yourself what you're getting out of it, when all you're really getting out of it is drunk.

INTERVIEWER

You're saying the opposite of what most people say about alcohol. Most people say it dulls the senses.

CHAPPELL

Oh, no. No, you drink to "grow excited with wine," in Yeats's phrase. That's the reason you drink. You drink for the excitement. To sharpen the . . . It only works for a little while. There's only an hour or a couple of hours or so that it works. After that, you're just *fthrrrzzzz*.

INTERVIEWER

Were you able actually to write while you were drinking?

CHAPPELL

No. But I remembered the level of emotions. I remembered the points that were made. I remembered people's hands and faces and the effect of their being larger than life. Of the moment being larger than life. And I tried to capture that later on.

INTERVIEWER

What would you advise your students about that kind of method? How else would you tell them to get it? And what would you tell yourself if you were starting over?

CHAPPELL

I try not to give my students too much advice about how to live their lives. I was a child too long to know that that doesn't make much difference. They're going to do what the hell they want to do, as they feel they have to do.

But you talk about specific kinds of works, generally, or I try to tell them not to put idiotic things in their bodies and expect it'll help. Just like driving a spike in the tree trunk there. It's dramatic. But it don't help the tree much. But young folks, they're theater. They like personal theatrics. And if they didn't have that kind of penchant for it, they wouldn't be writers.

INTERVIEWER

At one point while writing *Midquest*, you got to a point, you've said, where you were thinking in poetry, thinking in line lengths. You said you didn't like that. It reminded me of when Donald Hall was writing *The Ideal Bakery*, and he would stop in parking lots and try to catch on paper what was pouring out. I think I would love that.

CHAPPELL

I don't like it. It's a sense of dislocation.

INTERVIEWER

What's wrong with that?

CHAPPELL

Because you've got to do things on a daily basis. You got to answer the phone. You got to answer your mail. You got to pay your bills. And you can't do it. For me, it's not the same thing. I couldn't do the way Don does. I had to sit down and write. I rarely took notes for it. I had outlines. But I didn't take notes on specific lines.

But when you sit down and for two or three hours a day you write very intensely at poetry, you're a different person for the rest of the day. It's hard to come back. And it just gets in your blood. It's a different way of thought. And it's not a logical way of thought. It's a superlogical way of thought, or a pseudo-logical way of thought. And it causes you to be very inattentive to those around you, and what you're supposed to be doing. I find it very cumbersome.

INTERVIEWER

I read something the other day about genius and talent. It said that genius has a momentum of its own, but that talent has to rely on the har-nessing of the unconscious. I'm not sure I wouldn't think of it as the other way around.

CHAPPELL

And I'm not sure I would recognize genius in literature. You think you recognize it in painting sometimes and music. But in literature, I don't know. The one person I was ever sure of was Amon Liner [the late Charlotte, North Carolina, poet whose collections include *Marstower* and *Chrome Grass*]. I was absolutely sure Amon was a genius because there's nothing like that. Nobody ever did anything like that that I ever heard of. [Two-ply and four-ply poetry, in which an idea is approached from a number of directions simultaneously.]

And nobody was ever so alone in his endeavors and kept it up and found a way to do it under such terrible, intense pressure of the kind of horrible health he had. If I ever had to name a literary genius, I would name Amon. And I can't think of a single other one I would. And I know a lot of guys.

INTERVIEWER

I know how disciplined you are. Answering three letters a day—no more, no less—walking two or three times a day, and writing at least two hours a day. I wish you'd describe exactly how those two hours of writing go.

CHAPPELL

First, I look around the desk and see if I have any notes of any sort that I'm supposed to be using. Either other poems or pieces of poems or old scraps of paper with stuff on it that's supposed to trigger what I'm thinking about. Sometimes I do, and sometimes I don't. If I do, it's wonderful.

INTERVIEWER

And if you do have a little note, what do you do with it? And what might the note say?

CHAPPELL

I prop it up. The note might say, "She said that she couldn't." And it has a context that I've kept in memory, so that I know what it means. So the first thing I do is write that on a piece of paper: "She said that she couldn't." Just copy it down. Then try to make sense of it so that somebody else would know what in the hell that was about.

So you start somewhere. You can start with dialogue. You can start with the character "she." You can start with the place it happened. You can start with the time of day. You can start with almost anything.

And so you try to write twelve or fourteen lines. And you know that ain't right. I mean, you just know it. So you just kind of cross that out without thinking about it. And you just wait a little while, and a first line will come to you. And you write it down. It will have a rhythm to it. And it'll have a tone of voice. It will have a voice. That's the hardest thing to catch. You've got to hear the sound of it. You've got to hear the tone of it. And I actually hear it when it's right in my ear. I hear it right there. [His index finger circles close to his right ear.] And it may not be the right line. But it's the sound I want to make. I know the sound I want to make when I hear it.

And then after that, you just keep on keeping on. A good day, you can get six or eight lines, maybe. And the next good day's work you have, you'll cross them out.

INTERVIEWER

Do you enjoy being in the middle of a poem, so that the next day when you go back to write, you've got it already under way?

CHAPPELL

Yes. Yes. Thank goodness. I like that a lot. And how you start then is just the same way you write fiction. You start by rewriting what you've written.

INTERVIEWER

Do you like the feeling of writing?

CHAPPELL

I'm not in it for the money, kid. I do it because it's a wonderful feeling. It's a real feeling of having accomplished something. You're not satisfied with it. But you know you're finished. And that lasts sometimes for two or three weeks. Sometimes.

Remember X. J. Kennedy's poem: "The goose that laid the golden egg / died looking up its crotch / to find out how its sphincter worked. / Would you lay well? Don't watch."

Fred Chappell and his wife, Susan
April 5, 1994

Born May 28, 1936, in Canton, North Carolina, Fred Chappell was the first of two children of James Taylor and Ann Maye Davis Chappell. He graduated from Canton High School in 1954 and from Duke University in 1961. In 1964, he earned his master's from Duke.

He worked as credit manager for Candler Furniture Company, in Candler, North Carolina, during college. In 1964, he joined the faculty of Woman's College, now UNC-Greensboro, where he was appointed Burlington Industries Professor of English in 1988.

Chappell is the author of six novels: *It Is Time, Lord* (1963), *The Inkling* (1965), *Dagon* (1968), *The Gaudy Place* (1973), *I Am One of You Forever* (1985), and *Brighten the Corner Where You Are* (1989).

His poetry collections include *The World Between the Eyes* (1971), *River: A Poem* (1975), *The Man Twice Married to Fire* (1977), *Bloodfire* (1978), *Wind Mountain* (1979), *Awakening to Music* (1979), *Earthsleep* (1980), *Driftlake: A Lieder Cycle* (1981), *Midquest* (1981), *Castle Tzingal* (1984), *Source* (1986), *First and Last Words* (1989), *C* (1993), and *Look Back All the Green Valley* (1994).

He is also the author of two collections of short stories: *Moments of Light* (1980) and *More Shapes Than One* (1991).

Plow Naked (1993) is his collection of essays on poetry.

Chappell's awards include a Woodrow Wilson fellowship, a National Defense Act fellowship, and a Rockefeller Foundation grant (1966). He has received a literature award from the Institute and American Academy (1968); the Prix de Meilleur des Lettres Etrangers from the French Academy (1971); six Roanoke-Chowan Poetry Cups from the North Carolina Literary and Historical Society; the Sir Walter Raleigh Award (1973); the Bollingen Prize in Poetry from Yale University Library (1985); the O. Max Gardner Award, the highest honor the University of North Carolina system bestows on a faculty member (1986); and the T. S. Eliot Award from the Ingersoll Foundation (1993).

On August 2, 1959, Chappell married Susan Nicholls. They have one son, Heath, born in 1961.

Chappell lives in Greensboro with Susan, where he is at work on a novel, poems, short stories, and poetry criticism.

April 7, 1994

PAT CONROY

April 25, 1994

*L*et's go back to the fall of 1960. Pat Conroy is fifteen. Because his father is a career marine, Conroy and his brothers and sisters have lived all over the country. Always, they have attended Catholic schools. But in Beaufort, South Carolina, Conroy begs to attend his first public school: Beaufort High.

The bell has rung. The other kids are seated. Conroy remains standing.

In walks Eugene Norris, the English teacher. He faces Conroy.

"What are you doing, boy?" Norris asks. "Sit down in that seat." He pushes Conroy down.

Later, Norris calls Conroy aside: "Why were you standing up?"

"I used to go to Catholic school," Conroy tells him, "and you never sat down until a teacher said you could."

"That's the weirdest thing I ever heard, boy," says Norris. "Why would you put up with such nonsense?"

An instant friendship formed, and now, nearly thirty-five years later, Conroy and Norris are still fast friends. On Fripp Island, South Carolina, Conroy turns off his telephone as he struggles to meet his deadline for *Beach Music*. Meanwhile, in Beaufort, Norris takes Conroy's calls and drives down the coast to Fripp to deliver the essential messages.

"He always knows where I am," Conroy says.

Norris knew where Conroy was that first year at Beaufort High: A kid with a troubled home life and the makings of a real writer.

For Christmas that year, Norris gave Conroy a copy of *Look Homeward, Angel*. Conroy went berserk. He read everything Wolfe had written and became attached to Wolfe's autobiographical Eugene Gant.

The following summer, Norris drove Conroy to Asheville to see Wolfe's house. First, he showed him the bedroom where "Gant" died. Then he took him out back and showed him the apple tree from which Wolfe himself had eaten apples.

Norris plucked an apple for Conroy. "Eat this," he said.

"Why?" asked Conroy.

"Because, son, I want you to understand there's a relationship between art and life."

Conroy tells this story, then says, "Ain't he terrific? He's the greatest teacher I ever had."

This bright spring afternoon, while Conroy washes his lunch dishes, he talks about growing up rootless and alien, about the journals that are grist for his novels, and about his mother, who died ten years ago at age fifty-nine, and to whom Conroy made a promise he will spend the rest of his life fulfilling.

———

INTERVIEWER

This is an unusual interview, because you're still working on your novel *Beach Music*. I understand you're having a hard time finishing, because you must kill the mother in the book. Since your books tend to be autobiographical, this is as if you're killing your own mother. I know you hate to lose her twice.

CONROY

Yes. When I first began writing this book, what I liked about it is that my mother [the character] was in a coma, as she was when I was called back from Italy when she had cancer the first time. And the first great jump or hurdle I had in this book was when my mother came out of the coma, and she started talking. It never occurred to me I was going to have to bring her back to life and give her a resurrection scene. This took me two years.

What has been happening lately is that I realize I am now in the process of killing my mother, taking her through what was the worst thing that ever happened to my family—and certainly the worst thing that ever happened to me—my mother dying slowly of this leukemia.

I have found it very, very tough going, and several times in this book, I've wanted a doctor to rush in and say, "Great news! There's a cure for leukemia." But the credibility of the book might suffer with that. [Laughter.]

But that has been one of the toughest parts. What I realize now is that every writer has to go through the death of their parents. It's always like the creation of the world or the end of the world for all of us when this happens.

What are you willing to say about the new novel, other than it's already been sold to Twentieth Century Fox for $6 million and will be directed by Sidney Pollack?

CONROY

I don't mind giving away anything at all. We lived in Rome, Italy, for three years, and it begins in Italy with a travel writer and cookbook writer living with his only daughter, who is about eight years old when the book begins. He has renounced the South. He's never going back to the South and is in touch with nobody in the South when the book begins.

I met several Southerners like that when I was in Italy, who reeled back in horror when they found out I was from the South.

When the book opens, he is followed by a private detective as he walks his daughter to school.

Let me go back a little. I just realized something. In the first line of the book, this poor man's wife throws herself over the Silas Pearman Bridge in Charleston. She is playing "Save the Last Dance for Me" on her radio-tape recorder and a man tries to stop her—a tourist driving north from Florida. And she says a few words he does not understand before she jumps. When they fish her out of the water, they discover that tattooed on her forearm is her father's number from Auschwitz.

This is the happy-go-lucky first chapter, in which her [the wife's] parents try to take the daughter—who is about two or three then—away from the husband, saying he is responsible for the wife's suicide. This is why he flees the South.

INTERVIEWER

What's his name?

CONROY

Jack McCall. So Jack takes his daughter [to Rome], and he plans never to come back. It is these parents who have hired the private eye. They have sent their youngest daughter over. When Jack confronts the private detective, the private detective says, "The family wants to make contact with you. The younger sister is here."

And the sister says the parents want to talk to Jack, they want to reestablish communication, and they want to see their granddaughter again. And they have something to tell him, and they think they know why their daughter jumped off that bridge.

As Jack is thinking over this proposition, his brother calls from South Carolina and says that their mother is in a coma and has leukemia, and these two things converge.

And Jack returns home. And then it goes on for another two thousand pages—endless, horrifyingly long pages. And my editor wants to cut it down, of course, to the size of haiku. [Laughter.]

INTERVIEWER

And you have how many chapters to go?

CONROY

I think I have five chapters to go.

This is what's tough. Here's what the chapters are. It takes the mother of Shiloh, the woman who committed suicide, through the Holocaust. It takes the father through the Holocaust. And it also includes the death of Jack's mother. I can't think of three more depressing chapters in the world.

INTERVIEWER

You've chosen to write autobiography, which means your readers know a lot about you. What don't your readers know about you from reading your books?

CONROY

One thing they may not know is that my father's alive. I've had people not believe, when I introduce them to my father, that he's not dead. They say, "But you died. I read *The Great Santini.*"

He says, "No such luck, madam."

One thing they may not know is that I have not lived in the Low Country of South Carolina my entire life. I've lived every place. And I just pathetically latched on like a barnacle to the Low Country, because I felt so homeless in my growing up.

Not too long ago, Dad showed me the address book of every place I lived as a child. There were twenty-three addresses. There were twelve schools. Three high schools. And so by the time I got to Beaufort, when I was about fifteen . . . This poor town. They had no idea. I didn't real-

ize this at the time, certainly, but when you graduate from a high school, you belong to that town in some ways.

INTERVIEWER

Do you wish you had always been from Beaufort?

CONROY

I really do. I loved this town from the moment we drove into it. I had never heard of it before we got here. I can still remember, in the station wagon, crossing Whale Branch Bridge and seeing the marshes for the first time. I was stunned by how beautiful this was. I didn't know about salt marshes.

INTERVIEWER

Tell me about your process of taking notes. How do you take notes on a novel? And what do you write them on, or in?

CONROY

I have a series of journals. Some of them look great. I collect journals. Some are made of leather. I like to have mine on lined pages. And I always criticize myself for not doing enough journals. I feel I should do more. And, usually, when I'm not writing a novel, I do my best journal work.

INTERVIEWER

And what is your journal work?

CONROY

Certainly, if something happens or somebody says something interesting or thought-provoking, I try to write that down. I don't do my thoughts: "Today, I thought, 'Oh, Lord.'" It's not that kind of journal at all. It can be current events, what somebody said, what somebody did. Something I want to remember I do not think I'll remember otherwise.

INTERVIEWER

How does that coalesce into taking notes for a novel?

CONROY

It does in this way. One of the notes I had in the journal was "Remember the white porpoise that used to swim between Harbor Island and St. Helena Island when you first came to Beaufort." Just that note reminded me and became the basis for the white-porpoise chapter in *The Prince of Tides*.

My mother told me something once, a story I had forgotten, about the giant that had come to the door in Atlanta when my dad was in Korea. And I said, "Who's that at the door?" And it was the first seven-footer I'd ever seen. And it had a beard. And this became Callanwolde [the rape scene in *The Prince of Tides*]. My grandmother lived right behind the Coca-Cola people in Atlanta, and this guy escaped into the woods, and this became a chapter.

And what I have found is that one line or one phrase can become a chapter in these books.

INTERVIEWER

In other words, when you're not writing a novel, you're taking notes on a novel.

CONROY

No question. There's always that process going on. I just went back to the place where I keep the journals. I have lists of words. I come across words. Let me open up one of these journals, and I'll find a list of words. [Opens a journal.]

It's usually words I like the sound of.

Here's a list. I haven't looked at this. I just opened it. Here are the words: *Heart-struck. Philodendron. Cabbagy. Horoscopes. Spices. Oboes. Ginkos. Dragon-headed. Intermezzos.* And *Appliance.*

When I read, I'll read for words whose sound I like. Words that I have not used for a while or thought of for a while. Those English words that disappear from your mind. They're on the clothesline somewhere, and you just haven't pulled them in.

INTERVIEWER

So, in the process of writing the novel, you sometimes go back to the journal and see if anything will spin. Do you also keep a daily journal?

CONROY

Sometimes I'll keep a daily journal. I've got several of those here. They were very helpful for the years in Rome. Where I ate. If I ate at a restaurant, I'll know what I ate, because I'll keep the check.

And then the other kind, when you start on things like the white porpoise or a story someone told you. That begins to trigger more and more. You put that down, and it jolts something else.

CONROY

Exactly right. There was one thing that happened at the Citadel when I was there. I came across a note in a journal from a long time ago that just became the last chapter that was typed up for this book. Three cadets were lost at sea. And what I remember is, I went out in a boat looking for these cadets. We didn't know if they were going to be alive or dead. And what it ended up, they washed up three or four days later on a place—it was first time I ever heard of this place—called Daufuskie Island.

Okay. Here's something I just came across from a daily journal. And it says, "The writing in a journal is a kind of unrewarded heroism, but it does not give the accurate picture of the soul I supposed it would. When I look back over the entries, I'm surprised by how commonplace my thoughts were. Or at least the ones I chose to write down. But I think I use a journal as an aid to my memory, for it helps me to remember lost days almost perfectly, and my mind suddenly fills with the names and faces of friends and strangers I neglected to record. They spring up, a dark city of the second order, pressing around me to remember them and to put down what they said."

You know why I did this? Because what I put down often is not what I remember that day from the journal. Other things start intruding. Things that I did not realize were important that day.

INTERVIEWER

You once said that when you're writing, you have no idea where you're going. "People get married," you said, "and I didn't realize they were engaged. People die in these novels, and I'm surprised. . . . They reveal secrets to me even as I'm doing it." How does it feel to be in the midst of this mysterious process? And what is this process all about?

CONROY

Here is what happened in this book. I knew the mother was going to die when I started writing this. Okay. I knew a lot of stuff when I started writing this. I had this guy, this Jack McCall, living in Rome. I have him walking up the Aventine Hill. He's going through a rose garden, and I have him turn around in this rose garden to see if he's being followed.

I didn't know he was being followed. But that's what he did, so I went with it.

INTERVIEWER

What do you make of this whole mysterious process of something in you knowing more than you know?

CONROY

One thing this process does, it keeps me interested in what's going on. It used to terrify me.

But now I trust it. Later, I found out what that was all about. And that's part of the discovery process. It's like a lawsuit. I have to go through a discovery process before I find out what the verdict is. Especially these characters who jump alive on you. There they are.

INTERVIEWER

But what do you make of the mind's capacity to do this? It's like playing God, in a way.

CONROY

It's a fascinating process to me. I don't know what to make of it.

Some writers tell me they would simply put that [those unexpected things that happen during the writing of a novel] in another book. But I always think there's some reason. I think it is the unconscious. I have come to trust the unconscious of the writer. That voice is coming from somewhere. That voice is asking for admission for some reason. And that voice is asking for permission to be heard.

INTERVIEWER

Do you think, as in dreams, these voices are all part of the creator?

CONROY

No question. I think dreams are very important. I think dream journals are important. Extremely important. I have dreamed the ends of books. When I start dreaming about the book, I know it's now starting.

I can tell you one dream. The children's story in *The Prince of Tides* was a dream. I got up and wrote that dream down knowing it was not part of *The Lords of Discipline*, but it would be part of something.

INTERVIEWER

What was your reaction when you first saw the movie *The Prince of Tides*? And how did you bear to watch the actor who played the little boy Tom Wingo, who looks so much like you, without your heart breaking?

CONROY

I not only had the pressure of watching the movie, I had the pressure of Barbra Streisand sitting behind me watching me watch the movie. And because I'm Southern, and because I'm polite, if it had been the worst movie ever made, I would have been ecstatic: "Oh, Barbra, thanks so much! No one could have done it better." And that's the truth. She was so worried about my reaction, and so concerned about it, I wasn't about to tell her, "I have never seen such a piece of crap since *The Ghost and Mr. Chicken*."

So it has taken me awhile since I can just calmly watch it. I thought she did a remarkable job.

INTERVIEWER

What makes you a writer?

CONROY

Here's what I'm beginning to think. I became very aware when my mother was dying . . .

In fact, you got me in trouble one time. You

did not mean to. You remember when you called me up and interviewed me about Mother's Day? Okay. My mother read what you wrote. Mom was dying then, and I knew it. I made my mother sound like the second most important woman since Mary, the mother of Jesus, or possibly Athena. I couldn't have praised her more without making the readers of the *Charlotte Observer* throw up. Or you throw up.

My mother called me weeping. Not because of happiness. She was disappointed in the article. I said, "Mom, I couldn't have made you any grander if I had tried. What was it?"

She said, "You said I never went to college."

I said, "Mom, it's traditional in American families that when a mother goes to college, they reveal that fact to their oldest son."

She said, "I almost graduated from Agnes Scott. I took night courses."

And I'm thinking, "*Night courses* at Agnes Scott?" But I said, "Mom, I'm sorry. I didn't know that."

And she said, "Will you tell my husband?" [Laughter.]

So she put John on the phone, and I said, "John, Mom almost graduated from college. It slipped my memory. I don't know what got into me." And John was greatly relieved.

And you know, I thought about that later, and what that meant. Mom came from a very poor family. You remember the tornado they had in Alabama [in early 1994]? I was very moved by that tornado, because it went through the town of my mother's people. And I watched the fu-

neral on television. I didn't worry about it being my family, because the people who were hurt were Methodists, not Baptists. Then I found out there were two of my cousins who died in it. They were in their sixties—it was Vashti and Cicero. There was something wrong with them. They were mentally retarded, or autistic. And they were in this Methodist church, and they got crushed.

And I was thinking of that in connection with Mom. One thing that happens with families like my mother's is that she and her sisters got out, and they got out because they were pretty. They were beautiful girls. And all three of those girls married officers in the military. And one married a dentist. And Mom married a career marine. And so what Mom had the opportunity for that no one else in her family did was to send her kids to college.

And I think why Mother wanted so badly for me to be a writer—and this was part of her unconscious, something she would not be able to express—was simply because of this: She wanted me to be the voice of her family, especially her voice. And families like Mom's and mine are voiceless for centuries. And suddenly we go to college, and we read the great books of the world. And we look around and we realize our family has stories also.

INTERVIEWER

What have you learned about storytelling since you first began writing?

April 7, 1994

CONROY

The Water Is Wide, The Great Santini, The Lords of Discipline all take place within a school year. [Laughter.] That was the only amount of time that made any sense to me. You start school in September. It ends in June. I can take you from the first day of class to graduation, and that's about it. [Laughter.]

So one thing I've learned to do is handle time, which is a very difficult thing to do. The other thing, writing this book [*Beach Music*], I've become much more comfortable with third-person. Nan [Talese, his editor at Doubleday] made me write this one in third-person.

INTERVIEWER

Did you like it?

CONROY

Not at first. But she had a point when I wrote the first couple of chapters. She thought the first-person with me would always sound like Tom Wingo. And she said, "You've got to suppress that voice for a while." And I thought she was right. So these two thousand pages are all in third-person.

INTERVIEWER

Did writing in third-person teach you anything?

CONROY

I thought it would teach me about point of view, but it didn't. I'm one of those novelists that you could explain what point of view is, and I can't quite get it. My IQ does not go up that far. I've read everything anybody's written about point of view. It's still a mystery to me.

Here's what I understand: I was there. I saw it. This is what I'm saying about it, and this is what I'm thinking about it. And if you don't like it, you can kiss my behind. I understand that point of view. It's when you get into these little things—Eddie Fluffalo gets his version, and Betty Fluffalo gets her version—then I get very confused by all that. [Laughter.]

INTERVIEWER

But you obviously aren't confused anymore.

CONROY

I've written in that thing [third-person] so many times now, I hope I'm not confused, or I'm in for a very bad time during the editing session.

INTERVIEWER

Does writing get easier?

CONROY

No. I have not found that. And here's one thing I had to deal with in this last book that I never thought would become a problem in my writing. That is, I never thought I'd have to follow a successful book. I thought I'd have one failure piled up after another.

I was very happy with what happened to all my books. A good thing happened to all of them. So there was no abject failure. But I certainly was no household name. In fact, when I married Lenore, her father told me lovingly when I first met him, "Nobody up north I mentioned your name to has ever heard of you." I knew what he was saying. I knew instinctively what that was all about.

So what this book has introduced me to is how to follow a success. The fear that goes with that.

INTERVIEWER

And how do you follow a success?

CONROY

Tremblingly. [Laughter.] It was scary for a while, and it remains somewhat scary.

INTERVIEWER

Do you revise as you go, or revise later?

CONROY

I usually revise as I go. I hate to write a sentence down that I don't like. And since I write it by hand, when I write it down I want it to be okay. I want it to have a real chance of being what I meant to say.

INTERVIEWER

What's easy for you as a writer? What's hard for you?

CONROY

Dialogue is pretty easy for me. I thought they were giving me money for nothing when I started writing screenplays. I could write dialogue all day long. Give me a character. What do they like? I can tell you what they'll buy at the grocery store. The hard part for me is narrative. And that's what I suffer over, and that's what's difficult for me.

INTERVIEWER

How do you make that easier?

CONROY

There's no way for me to make that easier. And starting something is always the most difficult thing for me. I hate finishing this book, because that means I'll just have to think of starting another one.

INTERVIEWER

I interviewed you in Atlanta years ago, and you told me that since you had quit smoking, you had a little ritual before you started writing, and that was to work a crossword puzzle.

CONROY

I don't do that anymore. Now, I call Doug Marlette. I gave up crossword puzzles, and I now talk to Doug every day.

INTERVIEWER

But what are your rituals to start writing?

CONROY

That is one of them. I'm telling you the truth on that. And because Doug does not seem to mind, and because he's an artist, he can always jump-start me.

INTERVIEWER

What time do you call?

CONROY

About eight-thirty or nine.

INTERVIEWER

And you've been up a while by then?

CONROY

By then, I've read the paper, which also has to do with Doug, because I have to give him ideas for cartoons. [Laughter.]

INTERVIEWER

You-all seem to be so crazy about each other, and you really do seem to serve as muses for each other.

CONROY

With Doug, when he looks around, it's like he's Adam seeing the world for the first time. He has this freshness of vision I find extraordinary, and that I try to steal from.

INTERVIEWER

Without fail, you spark each other.

CONROY

He always gets me going. Also, he talks with more people than anybody in the world. He reads more magazines. He looks at more TV. He's always seeing something that is amazing to me. And he remembers this, and when he starts on ideas, it's like a bee going from flower to flower. And I find it a very stimulating way to get my own mind working.

INTERVIEWER

What is an ideal day for you?

CONROY

Okay. Let's see. I get up. I'm feeling great. I call Doug. I catch Doug on the meanest day of his life, where he is vicious about every single person and subject that comes up. And when Doug is vicious, it is poetry. And it helps me.

Okay, then if the day is really good, I will write on a chapter, and when I'm writing I get this feeling, "Yoo-hoo, boy! This is going good!" And I know it's going good, because I don't look at the clock. I get hungry and then look at the clock. And I have written into lunch.

And then I will cook some lunch. And after I eat lunch, I then will lie down, and preferably I'm reading a great book. And that's the hardest thing in the world, to get a good book to read all the time.

And maybe I'll take a nap, and then I'll go back, and I'll complete whatever I'm working on. And that's always a perfect day for me.

And then at night, my children come in and say they have made straight A's and have renounced sex. And usually at night, it's that book again. Because when I'm writing, I don't do much.

INTERVIEWER

Tom Wingo will probably long for Susan Lowenstein all his life. I heard a fiction writer say that all fiction is longing. What is the role of longing in your fiction?

CONROY

I think what it is in mine is always a longing for a better childhood. There's always a longing for the perfect mother and father. There seems to be a longing for what is unfixable. What is broken.

INTERVIEWER

If you could rewrite your childhood, or if you could fix your childhood, would you do it even if it meant you wouldn't have the wealth of material you have now?

CONROY

Yeah, I would. I surely would. I would do it for this reason. Dad and I will discuss this on rare occasions, and Dad has a line that infuriates me. He rarely admits he knocked us around. Usually he'll deny that, or that he knocked Mom around. And he even has an article in *Atlanta* magazine where he claims he never touched any of us. But one time he looked at me and he said, "Son, I should have beat you more. You'd be a better writer." And I said, "If you'd beat me much more, I'd be Shakespeare."

Because there was such pain and agony, and I found my childhood so traumatic, I don't even wish that on myself.

I remember just being totally afraid, from the time I came into consciousness as a child to now.

A couple of years ago, I went to the PEN/Faulkner thing, and they said, "What are your beginnings?" I heard Eudora Welty talk about beginnings. And Reynolds Price did this beautiful thing about a goat eating his diaper off, and Eudora saw bees and sunshine, and somebody had poured honey into her milk bottle over her mother's breast. I'm hearing all this, and I felt like I had ruined the entire thing. Because what it was was first memories that you had, and my first memory was my mother trying to stab my father with a butcher knife. I'm telling you. And Dad laughing and hitting her in the face. And here it was, "Welcome to the world, Pat. Welcome to your childhood."

And I thought about it, and that was the first scene I could come up with. And I know it was in California. I can tell you what the window looked like, the light coming through it. I can tell you everything about that scene. And somehow, I think it started over feeding the dog.

INTERVIEWER
And you kept on being scared?

CONROY

Yeah. Let me tell you, Dad was a frightening man. He was the strongest marine I ever saw walking through my childhood.

INTERVIEWER
Why do you suppose he was that way?

CONROY
I'm sure his father was exactly like that. And I'm sure no one paid it a bit of mind in the Irish-Catholic world Dad was raised in. And certainly,

no one paid it a bit of mind in the Marine Corps world I was raised in.

INTERVIEWER

You've said that being Catholic in the South reinforced your sense of rootlessness. But wouldn't you agree that a sense of alienation, in some form, is essential for a writer?

CONROY

I certainly got it. I had some great things going for me. Being Catholic in the South was the weirdest thing one could be when I was growing up. I was delighted when Hare Krishnas showed up at the Atlanta airport. I was just as happy as I could be.

I remember going into some little town in North Carolina, and some boy came up to me and said, "Are you a Roman Catholic?" I said yes, and he started running. He just ran his little ass off, looking back. [Laughter.] I still don't know what that kid thought I was going to do to him.

INTERVIEWER

What was it about being Catholic in the South? Why were there so few?

CONROY

There were very few. This starts back early in our history. I was just down in Savannah. [General James] Oglethorpe brought over Jews on his ship, but Catholics were not allowed. So this began very early in this country. But certainly in the South, it was just rampant.

My mother was a Southern Baptist, converted, and we were always the weirdest. I mean, our families could not get over the fact that we worshiped the pope.

INTERVIEWER

Did it make a difference at school?

CONROY

Dad would not send us to anything but Catholic schools. So we went to these Catholic schools all over the place. I went to Catholic school in New Bern, North Carolina, and in Havelock, North Carolina. Dad helped found the school in Havelock. [Laughter.] And up in Washington, we were in all these Catholic schools in Virginia.

And Beaufort High School, when I came down here, was the first non-Catholic high school I ever went to. And Dad went crazy. He tried to get me to go to Savannah or Charleston to go to high school.

INTERVIEWER

It must have been an experience for you, going to public school.

CONROY

Wonderful! It was the best school I ever went to. It changed my whole life. I'd never been around nice people that taught. I had these nuns and priests who were like Dad, just tearing me up in school. Then, these sweetheart teachers at Beaufort High School. I just adored them. I still see them.

INTERVIEWER

Many years ago, I read an article you wrote for *Atlanta* magazine in which you talked about losing your hearing, either during the breakup of your marriage or immediately afterward. How do you view divorce now, especially where children are involved?

CONROY

My divorce almost killed me. It was just not something I was expecting. Not something I was used to. And the one thing about being Southern and Catholic is that you have a greater capacity for guilt. I have an Asiatic capacity for guilt. Asiatic meaning as large as Asia. [Laughter.] I just suffered through that experience more than anything.

INTERVIEWER

I want to ask you about your sister Carol Conroy. I've been reading her collection of poetry, *The Beauty Wars*, and the poem "The Great Santini's Wild, Sleek Children." She mentions Skyhawk, Dauntless, Corsair, Avenger, Hellcat, Panther, and Pilot Dawn. Which one are you?

CONROY

I'm Skyhawk.

INTERVIEWER

And what does she mean by that?

CONROY

I imagine she means firstborn. I was the golden boy of that house. Now, what I hated about that poem was, I wondered why "The Great Santini's Wild, Sleek Children" wasn't called "The Great Santini's Wild, Sleek, Beaten, and Bloody Children." And I did not think she held Dad responsible for his crimes against us in her poetry. There's great beauty in *The Beauty Wars*. There's no war.

INTERVIEWER

You and your sister haven't spoken since *The Prince of Tides* came out. Do you think there's any hope of reconciliation?

CONROY

I don't think now. She quit talking to me at Mom's funeral. She's kept it up. It's been ten years.

INTERVIEWER

That's so sad.

CONROY

It is. And it is her.

INTERVIEWER

What's the problem?

CONROY

I don't know. She's never explained that to me. We were best of friends. One thing that's interesting to me about watching us all grow up—and I would not have expected this—is that the girls seem much more like Dad to me than the boys.

I never in my life could have dreamed that could happen.

I don't understand it. When I look for softness in my family, or joy, I go to my brothers. The girls, they carry that virus of meanness. I'm not close to either one of them.

My other sister, Kathy, lives in Beaufort. And I have been in Beaufort County for two Christmases, three Thanksgivings, and three Easters, and I have never been invited to her house for dinner.

INTERVIEWER

What impact did the death of your mother have on the other members of the family? I know it was devastating for you.

CONROY

I think it's been for all of us. I include the girls, too, maybe the girls especially. The girls would be talking to us if Mom were alive. She would not have put up with that or allowed it. My father likes it. Anything that causes strife.

Here is one reason why I will never forgive my sister Carol. I can understand her—I think anybody can understand a trauma in the family—and not talking to somebody because of it. I can understand why she would not talk to me or my other brothers. But I cannot for the life of me understand why she continues to talk to my father.

She knows exactly what went on. She knows precisely what went on.

INTERVIEWER

When you have seven kids, then you get more of an understanding of the family, I suppose. It's like having a little universe.

CONROY

We're great grave visitors in my family. My grandmother used to always take me around to visit graves. And my grandmother would talk to the people. "Hey, James. How're you doing? How's Jesus?" That kind of stuff. Sweet as it could be. She got me in the habit. And I always visit Mom's grave and take Mom flowers and all this stuff I can't believe I'm doing.

So I asked my brothers what they do.

And my brother Mike says he approaches Mom's grave slowly, and then before he knows it he's overtaken with sorrow and grief, and he leaps on top of Mom's grave and rolls around on his belly and his back and hurls grass and throws it up in the air and lets it float down on his face, with him weeping.

So I asked my brother Jim, and Jim says he drives miles out of the way to avoid even going by the graveyard.

And my brother Tim says he gets drunk, and then a mile before he gets to the cemetery, he floors the accelerator and goes sixty-five miles an hour, and stops drinking only when he gets by the cemetery. [Laughter.]

It affected all of us in hideous ways.

INTERVIEWER

Do you think the devastation is because she was only fifty-nine when she died?

CONROY

I think so. Mom was always young and pretty, and we were not expecting her to die.

What have you learned about your mother in the writing of this novel?

CONROY

How extraordinarily poor the family she grew up in was. And she always hid that from me, and I've been able to go back and see it now. I've been back there.

When she was dying, she asked me if I would go back with my aunt Helen, her oldest sister, to Rome, Georgia, to take a picture of the house where she was born. She was telling John, her husband—and I heard this, and I could not believe it—that they'd come from one of the richest plantation-owning families in Alabama. And I'm listening to this horseshit and I'm thinking, "*What?*"

She was telling him that they had slaves and raised cotton, and John, of course, thought Mom was wonderful and lovely, and he just loved these stories of aristocracy, and he'd married into such fine, fine stock.

And I said, "Mom, I know these people, and I'm very curious about their history. I've never heard. What happened to these people? Something terrible must have happened."

And my mother said, "The wah-uh. We were devastated by the wah-uh."

And I said, "That wah-uh must've been horrible."

And she said, "They took all the land, son. All the land. All the plantations were gone."

And I said, "What happened then? Something else horrible must've happened to that family."

And she said, "The Depression. The Depression took the rest."

And she and John agreed that the Depression was terrible.

And I said, "Mom, it must've been horrible indeed. But these people, after the Depression, why couldn't any of them read?" [Laughter.]

She was furious with me, and angry, but she sent me back with Aunt Helen, and we looked all over Rome, Georgia, for the house where my mother was born. We finally found it, and there were black people living in it—a sharecropper's cabin. And my aunt was very disappointed. Because in her mind, it was big, too. It was very nice in her mind. And my aunt said something that was very sweet. She said, "It looked so much bigger then."

And I said, "I'm sure it was, Aunt Helen."

And a guy came up the road, a man living down the road, and it was amazing. He remembered my aunt Helen. He was there the night my mother was born. He remembered the night Mom was born.

And we went into town to the library. I was going to look the family up. And my aunt is one of these people . . . She's hated my books. She never read past page 4, but she just hated them. But she's proud of me.

And we went to get gas that day. And a guy's pumping gas, and my aunt said, "Do you know whose car you're pumping gas into?"

He said, "Nah."

She said, "It's Pat Conroy. He wrote *The Water Is Wide*."

I said, "Shut up, Aunt Helen. Just shut up. I can't stand it."

She said, "He wrote *The Great Santini. The Lords of Discipline*. You would like *The Lords of Discipline*, because of all the cussing in it."

I said, "Aunt Helen, please be quiet. I can't stand that."

This gas-station attendant, he ain't heard of me, he ain't heard of my books, he ain't heard of nothing. It just humiliated me.

So we go to the library, and I'm looking up the family, and all of a sudden I'm looking around. And here's Aunt Helen with the entire library staff. Of course, Aunt Helen had told everybody.

And so the library staff says, "We've been waiting for you. We hear you're a Roman."

And I said, "My mother is a Roman."

And they have a folder on me. I'm just stunned. And so they sat me down, all this library staff, with this empty folder. And they said, "Since we heard you had a Rome connection, we've kept this folder, but we can't find anybody that knows anything about your family."

And I looked at my poor aunt Helen, and my aunt Helen says, "We were poor, but clean."

They said, "No records in churches. No records in country clubs. No records in schools. Nothing. Who was your family?"

And my aunt Helen says, "We were poor, but we were clean."

And they said, "How can a family exist in a place for twenty years and there be no record of them?"

And Aunt Helen said, "We were poor . . ."

And I said, "Aunt Helen, will you quit saying, 'We were poor, but we were clean'?"

And she said, "How do you want me to answer the question?"

I said, "Tell them we come from the family they want to know about." [Laughter.]

That's what I learned about Mom that I did not know. And that explained to me my mother's extraordinary sense of shame and her sense of pride.

INTERVIEWER
And you are repairing all that for her.

CONROY
In some way. Certainly, I feel that very strongly.

INTERVIEWER
You're the one in the family who rights the wrongs.

CONROY
When Mom was dying, she said, "I'm going to die. But one thing I'm sure of: Everybody is going to know that I was on this earth who reads your books."

———
———

Born October 26, 1945, in Atlanta, Pat Conroy is the first of seven children of Don and Peg Peek Conroy. He graduated from Beaufort High School in Beaufort, South Carolina, in 1963 and from the Citadel in 1967.

Conroy taught public school on Daufuskie Island, off the coast of South Carolina, in 1967 and 1968, but his unorthodox teaching methods prompted his dismissal.

His novels include *The Boo* (1970), *The Water Is Wide* (1972), *The Great Santini* (1976), *The Lords of Discipline* (1980), *The Prince of Tides* (1986), and *Beach Music* (1994).

Four of his novels have been made into movies, including *Conrack*, based on *The Water Is Wide* and starring Jon Voight. *The Prince of Tides* starred Barbra Streisand and Nick Nolte.

Conroy's awards include the Anisfield-Wolf Award from the Cleveland Foundation (1972).

In 1969, he married Barbara Bolling. They have one daughter, Megan.

In 1981, Conroy married Lenore Gurewitz. They have one daughter, Susannah.

Conroy's stepchildren are Jessica and Melissa, from his first marriage, and Gregory and Emily, from his second.

He lives in San Francisco and on Fripp Island, South Carolina.

March 10, 1971

May 14, 1987

"*P*eople always want to make me out as some kind of Hemingwayesque character," says James Dickey, author of the seven-hundred-page World War II novel *Alnilam*. "But what I really am is a schoolteacher."

Partly, at least, that's true. Dickey's poetry workshops and literature classes at the University of South Carolina, where he holds the chair of the Carolina Professor of English, are legion. He's a showman and dramatist, and a genius at captivating and inspiring his students.

He's also an outdoorsman: High-school football star, Clemson wingback, World War II fighter pilot, Vanderbilt track star, canoeist, archer, hunter, javelin thrower. Hemingwayesque and more.

Before he published his best-selling 1970 novel, *Deliverance*—he also wrote the screenplay and acted the part of the sheriff in the movie, which starred Burt Reynolds and Jon Voight—Dickey was an advertising writer for Coca-Cola. "It was alien to anything and everything that mattered to me," he says today.

Dickey was lucky. He had his art. And over the years, with the encouragement of his late wife, Maxine, he cleaved to it.

In 1976, he composed and read a poem on the eve of the inauguration of President Jimmy Carter.

An Atlanta native, Dickey lives with his wife, Deborah—a former student—and their six-year-old daughter, Bronwen, on Lake Katherine in Columbia, South Carolina.

Today, he talks about growing up in a house of German words, the importance of playing to win, how poetry is like listening through the static on a crystal radio, and his addiction to two drugs: Imagination and lucidity.

INTERVIEWER

You worked on this new novel, *Alnilam*, for thirty years.

DICKEY

Thirty-seven years. But that's misleading. I wrote twenty-five other books during this same period. I can only say that I started it thirty-seven years ago. I made the first few notes for it then.

Deliverance was written in a shorter time span, but it was the same way, except that I played with it and thought about it and wrote occasionally on it. But then, when you do that for a sufficient number of years—whatever the magic number may be—you see that you have all this mass of material, and that over these intermittent periods of thinking about the subject that indeed a workable story has emerged. In other words, you sit down with all this stuff you've got—you've been lugging around from domicile to domicile over the years—you sit down with it all in one place, and you look at the story, and you think the whole thing is already here. It's already here! Little did I realize it! And then you sit down and start working on it, and for the last three or four years, that's what I did.

INTERVIEWER

It must feel good to be finished with it.

DICKEY

It certainly does feel good. I don't know how the public is going to respond to it.

INTERVIEWER

Do you care?

DICKEY

I care some, naturally. But it's not all-important. The main thing is in the doing of it. *Das Ding an sich*—the thing itself. I wanted to try to make something good, something unique, and I thought I had the material to give it a pretty good go.

INTERVIEWER

Didn't you have a German grandmother who was always saying something like, "Do it right"?

DICKEY

The house was full of German words all the time I was a little boy, and that persisted in my mother. My mother didn't speak German—she spoke a kind of broken German—but her mother spoke German continually. That bust of Dante [on the hall table] came from her. Dante had always been a very big culture hero in Germany.

She was a diabetic lady who had her leg amputated because of diabetes and had to have a round-the-clock nurse living in the house. But she was a wonderful woman, my grandmother. She was very sweet, but she was very Teutonic. She died when I was in grammar school.

"Tue chtig!"—"Do it right!"—was her thing. She would say, "It's just as easy to do it right!" And it is.

My own mother was an invalid, and here I was—at least in the early part of my life—with one woman with heart disease and another who was a one-legged diabetic.

INTERVIEWER

Do you think having both a mother and a grandmother who were medically not up to par gave you a certain fascination with women and their fragility?

DICKEY

Goethe said that woman is the force that ties the man to the center of the earth, which I think is great. And he also said, as I remember, that the true woman for a man is the one who seems to be the answer to everything.

The French playwright and poet Paul Claudel, who came much later, said, "Woman is the promise that cannot be kept." That is, she seems to be the answer, but she's mortal and fragile and still subject to the same human vicissitudes man is.

Now that you've gotten me on the subject, I thought of something very funny. I was reading through the correspondence of Lord Byron, which is wonderfully good. He's so funny. He's the primary womanizer of all time, except for maybe Gary Hart. This is the gist of what he said: "In all my supposed mistreatment of women—using them for my own purposes and this, that, and the other—people have grievously mistaken my attitude. Because I believe truly that women are better than men. They have more humane qualities; they are more merciful and solicitous than men are; they are more imaginative and sensitive. Of the worst women I've ever known in my life—and I've known a good many of them as well as the good and mediocre ones—the absolute worst woman I've ever known would make quite a passable man."

INTERVIEWER

Besides the German influence in your home, wasn't there also a strong Scotch-Irish influence?

DICKEY

Yes, my father and his family connections were the ones who linked me to the north Georgia mountains. I love the place up there. I love the people. I love the folkways. Above all, I love the music. I just did a book about Appalachia. It's called *The Wilderness of Heaven*. It's a super place—Fanning County and also Union County.

My mother's father, Charles Thomas Swift, was a Confederate. As a matter of fact, I must be one of the few living people whose grandfather was in the Civil War. I'm not talking about my great-grandfather or my great-great-grandfather. I'm talking about my grandfather who was in the Civil War.

But he married in middle life, and my mother herself didn't even remember him. The only time she remembers seeing her father's face was when she was lifted up as a child to kiss him when he was in his coffin.

But my father's people—most of them, but not all of them up there in the mountains—were Union sympathizers. They didn't believe the Union should be dissolved over the question of slavery or anything else. That's why the county today is called Union County. It was a hotbed of Union sympathizers.

So my family was divided, but my natural sympathy was with the Confederacy and the Southerners. I used to pore over books of the Civil War, and my brother Tom, two years younger than I, is a very good historian, and he's probably the foremost world authority on Civil

War munitions. He's written two enormous scholarly works. He's wonderful. He's wonderful. He's built himself a house back of his house in Atlanta in which is nothing but relics that he's dug up. There're so many unexploded shells there that his mother-in-law for many years wouldn't even sleep there. He has a lot of Civil War memorabilia—all kinds of stuff—most of which he's dug up on field trips.

INTERVIEWER

Considering all your many interests—family, writing, teaching, music, canoeing, archery— what's your perspective on time and the use of it?

DICKEY

W. H. Auden—whom I knew slightly—once told me that he lived by the clock. That he did everything according to the minute hand of the clock. I couldn't do that. That's too constrictive for me. I like to have a sense of moving around and more or less the illusion of free will to do what I want at the time I want to do it.

But the problem—or the solution, I guess—is that I always want to do something. Something. Idleness—maybe because of my grandmother— idleness is something that doesn't sit well with me.

INTERVIEWER

Your doing is another man's leisure?

DICKEY

Work is relaxing to me. Here I am, sixty-four. I'm less than a year away now from official se-

nility—getting Medicare and all that other stuff, which I'll take every penny of, too—and I have to go for certain options rather than others.

INTERVIEWER

Which of your writings will you focus on?

DICKEY

Poetry! It's the best activity, and the one I like the best, and the one I do the best, I think. Although that might be argued. But whatever I do—whether it's poetry or novels or screenplays or literary criticism or essays or whatever it might be—it all comes out of the same source, which is essentially a poetic apprehension of reality or experience or whatever you want to call it. Everything comes from that.

INTERVIEWER

Do you think that instinct for poetry is in everybody?

DICKEY

Yes, a certain form of it is in everybody. The poetic instinct is nothing more than either the wish to do it yourself or the response to somebody else's having done it. To say something memorable, or to say something in a memorable way. All that poetry is is the highest refinement of that, the wish to marshal all of the expressive characteristics of language to say something memorable. It could be funny. It can be tragic. It can be whatever it wishes to be. But to say it memorably, to use language, which is the first great gift of humankind and the thing that has made everything else possible. Which has made it possible for people to record what they saw and did and learned, so that each generation would not have to begin again from scratch or at square one.

INTERVIEWER

The urge to say something memorable strikes me as an intellectual process. But the instinct to record sounds more a primitive, visceral thing.

DICKEY

Sure it is, and they're not in opposition at all. No. In fact, visceral is the beginning of giving the person what is then refined. If you shift that into the composition of poetry, you would be reminded of something that Paul Valery said: "God gives the poet one line and he's got to work like hell for the rest of it."

I think the secret of poetic craft, really, is to find what "goes with". If you have an insight, you've got to have some kind of startling verbal conjunction that casts light. It seems to require a setting. And then to invent or discover the setting that this goes into is the problem of poetic craft.

I hope you do record that, because that's the first time I ever said it, and I don't want to lose it.

INTERVIEWER

What I'd like to get recorded is your comparison of the process of writing poetry to working with a crystal radio.

DICKEY

You have some headphones and a crystal and a cat whisker. And you put that cat whisker on the crystal, and you hear static at first, and then you hear a voice. You fiddle with the crystal. The crystal is your potential inspiration, and usually there's nothing but static there. And then, occasionally, through the static, there's a voice. Sometimes it's very clear, and it says a few words that you can get through the earphones. That's the inspirational part of poetry. It is as though you were being told it from some other source, some celestial kind of voice so much better than your own voice. And then it's swallowed in static again, and you have to puzzle out what it means or what it might mean.

INTERVIEWER

It must be exhilarating to go through that process.

DICKEY

Anyone who's ever had that voice speak to them knows that there's not anything he can do with his life that would ever be as important as that is. Historically, there's an old secret as to why poets are so ruthless—why they would sell their grandmother down the river, why they betray everybody that ever supported them, why they do all kinds of things rather than have that taken away. That is the important thing to them. They know they can't be connected up with anything that important unless they hold to it and sacrifice everything to it.

INTERVIEWER

What have you had to sacrifice to be a poet?

DICKEY

Plenty of things! A good living in American business. A pretty good living in the military. A sound academic position based on what the other academics base theirs on, which is scholarship and a Ph.D. There's such snobbery in academic circles, and now there's a focus on so-and-so having a Ph.D., rather than a mere honorary degree, of which I have ten. You'd think that would be more important as indicating prestige in your field, instead of just a number of years of drudgery and a final dissertation on something that doesn't matter, such as a typographical error in a minor pamphlet of Milton's. That's an earned Ph.D.

I think it militates against the writer—the creative people—and turns them into drudges and drones. There are people who are meant to be drones, but the poets ought to be writing poetry, novels, plays, movies.

INTERVIEWER

One of my favorite poems of yours is "Falling," in which the stewardess falls out of an airplane. Didn't you get your idea from a story in the newspaper?

DICKEY

Yeah. I did. I changed everything around. I had it happen out in the Midwest, instead of New Jersey. The airline was Alleghany Airlines. The woman was French, and after the poem appeared in the *New Yorker*, a man named Andrew Sherwood wrote me from Paris, and he had been the fiancé of the stewardess, and he was waiting for her at Newark or La Guardia or some place like that for her flight to come in. And he told me something about her, and he sent me a painting by her, which I have hanging in there.

She was a girl interested in the arts, in poetry, and especially in writing songs. She was a little bit old for stewardess work, but one of the smaller airlines took her on as stewardess. But he told me she had had some psychiatric problems, and she was under treatment, and her main recurring nightmare was that she was a bird. It seems almost too coincidental.

INTERVIEWER

I notice you have several typewriters set up in your house. In fact, you've described your house as booby-trapped with typewriters.

DICKEY

I'm restless, and I like to roam around a lot. I don't like to sit for hours and write for hours. I like to work on the things that interest me right then the most. As I wander around, because there are so many typewriters here, each one with some project in it, I inevitably pass one that immediately I see something I can do with it, something I can change, something I can add, and so on. And then I sit down and work on it as long as it interests me, and then I get up and wander off for another few minutes or an hour. Everything's fluid and changed around all the time. And in an odd way, the various projects cross-pollinate one another.

INTERVIEWER

What if you had a wife who didn't want you cluttering up the house with typewriters?

DICKEY

If they're going to be married to me, they've got to know how to take things as I do—at least the things that concern me. The things that concern them, they can do their way. And I try to help them. Certainly to keep them out of my way. But I've had two very good wives. Wonderful. Wonderful.

INTERVIEWER

What are the qualities of a good wife for you?

DICKEY

Someone who understands my needs and the way I've worked out to get the poetry written and to work on the new things.

INTERVIEWER

What way have you worked out to get the poetry written?

DICKEY

I think the main thing a writer needs to determine early is to try to give as many of the individual people that he or she contains a chance to say what they want to say.

People would be hard put to imagine, for example, that the same person who wrote *Deliverance*, with all its gore, or *Alnilam*, with all its very graphic stuff, would be the same person who wrote [the children's book] *Bronwen, the Traw and the Shape Shifter*.

I think it's important that writers—not only writers, but people—try to get those facets to surface and to have their say and to do their thing.

INTERVIEWER

It seems to come naturally to you, but how do you get your students to explore their different facets?

DICKEY

The main difficulty is in having them overcome their inhibitions. Young writers are hag-ridden with self-consciousness. They don't want to be wrong. It's like tennis players, for example. Two players may have equal skills, but you can usually tell which one is going to win, because one of them is playing to win! To take it away from the other guy! And the other is playing not to lose. And the one that's playing to win is going to win.

The students who are the self-conscious ones are working not to make mistakes. I tell them to turn that around. Do something positive, and make that prevail.

You can take a poem you're working on, and by this negative approach, systematically take everything out of it that you could certify to yourself was bad. So you would end up with a poem in which there was nothing bad. It would have one drawback, though. There would be nothing in it that was any good either!

INTERVIEWER

What would you say to young people about how to make their lives more accessible to art?

DICKEY

I think anyone who's interested in writing, who's interested in words, his mind is going to gravitate in that direction naturally. That is, the reflex is going to be of that sort. He's going to have a natural and, also at the same time, a cultivated propensity to verbalize the world. And he doesn't have to do that as an act of will, although you *can* do it as an act of will. But it's going to take place as something that's more or less natural to that person, because of his own interests, his own orientation, his own physiological makeup, his own glands, his own body rhythm, whatever. He's going to do it naturally after a while.

INTERVIEWER

At one time you were into alcohol pretty heavily, and now you aren't. Why the turning?

DICKEY

I saw it for what it is. I put other things before it, and they are better than it. I remember what happened when Jean Cocteau attempted to get André Gide into narcotics—opium, I think, was his drug. Gide said, "No, I don't have any need of that. Lucidity is my drug."

INTERVIEWER

And yours?

DICKEY

Lucidity and imagination, those are the best.

One of the things that's bad for a writer as far as drinking is concerned is that it destroys your critical sense. Or at least it disorients your critical sense, so that you're likely to be enthusiastic over things that you write that are not that good. As William James said, "Alcohol is the great exciter of the 'yes' faculty in man."

INTERVIEWER

I noticed you came out pretty strongly against drugs in a recent issue of the *Chicago Tribune*.

DICKEY

Oh, Lord, yes. I've seen so much personal tragedy that comes from it. I think if this nation ever topples, it's going to be because of that. The problem is getting to such unspeakably huge proportions now there doesn't seem to be any way to deal with it.

I think all of that is linked to the way people live and what they do with their lives and how they earn a living.

I've been in American business six years, and a more fruitless, unrewarding kind of existence could not be imagined. *Could not be imagined!* The only thing that you have positive about it is that you earn money from it. But then what do you do with that?

Some of it you have to spend on upkeep, house payments, and bills. And if you have anything left over, you want to spend it on fast pleasure, something that will compensate for the drudgery which is throwing your life down the drain.

I sold soft drinks for a number of years. I could not care whether Coca-Cola outsold Pepsi Cola in such and such a month. Nothing could possibly matter to me any less than that. And yet here I was, day after day, nine to five, working on promotions. Working on radio and TV commercials, print ads. Because I was being paid to do it, to promote a product about which my inmost soul had not only no interest in, but no knowledge of. It was alien to anything and everything that mattered to me.

It was completely irrelevant, and yet most of my time every day went into it, to earn a living.

Now people feel that they're being sold short in this way. They feel that they're being picked up for nothing but a pittance. Some of the pittances are pretty good. Advertising people, the top ones, are very, very well-paid. But the essential in the person is missed. I turned to poetry, to my own art, to what I did after the workdays were over.

INTERVIEWER

And other people turn to other pleasures.

DICKEY

As much and as strong as they can get it. And as quick.

INTERVIEWER

Traditionally, what's been the substitute for art?

DICKEY

It used to be religion. But that's lost most of its strong hold. People will go to listen to Billy Graham or even Jimmy Swaggart, hoping they'll have an answer for them. But for every one who goes to church, five hundred will go to the nearest tavern.

INTERVIEWER

What's your own view of religion?

DICKEY

It's not orthodox at all. Whatever the agency was that made it all—from the smallest part of the atom and its behavior to the starry heavens—it's worthy of my attention and, if you want to call it that, worship. Nobody knows what caused anything to exist.

Science can tell us some things about how. But one question will never be answered, no matter how long things or people or matter exist. And that is, *Why?* Whatever made it is an impressive thing. Why it's made like it is, or why it exists at all, will never be known.

Goethe himself—my grandmother's culture hero—talks about the different manifestations of God in nature. And the angels say in chorus to God, "Thine aspect cheers the hosts of heaven, though what thy message none can say."

INTERVIEWER

Are you afraid to die?

DICKEY

I've died already a couple of times. At least once. It's not at all frightening to do. It's just like, you faint. You just lose it. Everything goes. But I think it's the fear of it before you die that's worse than the actual circumstance of dying. What is it John Peale Bishop says? "Long did I live consistent, lonely, proud. / Not death, but fear of death, restores us to the crowd."

August 16, 1993

James Dickey says his and wife Deborah's only serious argument recently erupted when he was trying to work out a Doc Watson solo on a twelve-string guitar, and she came in to tell him something and messed up his run on "Cacklin' Hen."

The celebrated poet and novelist was recently honored at the University of South Carolina with a "Dickey Celebration." The occasion was three-fold: Dickey turned seventy this year; he completed a quarter-century of teaching at the university where he is writer-in-residence; and his third novel, *To the White Sea*, is newly out from Houghton Mifflin.

Yesterday, a *Newsweek* photographer visited Dickey here in Columbia, South Carolina, and while they were shooting pictures in the backyard, a swarm of yellow jackets attacked them. Today, sluggish from Benzedrine, Dickey sprawls at a glass table in a glass room overlooking Lake Katherine—Deborah and their thirteen-year-old daughter, Bronwen, call this room their "Crystal Palace"—and talks in his resonant drawl about what a poet must have to write a novel, about playing football, and about aging, revision, and mastery.

INTERVIEWER

Does it irritate you that you are still described as the author of *Deliverance*—a novel you wrote twenty-three years ago—despite your poetry's considerable acclaim, and despite the publication of two subsequent novels?

DICKEY

No. I wrote it all. I did all of it. They can read what they want. I think the fact that a rather good and successful movie was made from *De-liverance* is the main thing that brought that condition about. And I don't object to that either. I wouldn't like to make bad movies. [Laughter.] I'm glad it was good, and I did the screenplay.

INTERVIEWER

And played the sheriff.

DICKEY

Yes, and I was responsible for the music. I had almost 100-percent involvement with it. I did everything but direct it, and I did a little bit of that.

I'm glad it came out like it did, and I don't feel that it really takes away from anything else I've written. As I say, I did it all: The poems and the other two novels and the criticism and the children's books and everything else.

INTERVIEWER

Your two previous novels were inspired by images. In *Deliverance*, a man standing on top of a cliff in a forest. With *Alnilam*, the vision of a man behind propellers. Did *To the White Sea* start with an image?

DICKEY

Yes. I was in a port city somewhere. I'm not sure it wasn't in Japan itself, although I don't remember, honestly, where I did see it. We were passing by those loading gantries that they have on docks, and someone said a man was supposed to have parachuted out, and his chute got hung on one of those things. What would that man do? Then that inevitably led to the next question: Who would he be? What would he be do-

March 10, 1971

ing there? And then the war came into it, and the personality for the guy began to develop.

INTERVIEWER

What a personality!

DICKEY

Yeah. I reckon.

INTERVIEWER

One thing that intrigued me about the book is that war, or survival in war, can make a beast of man. Muldrow kills like an animal, but he retains the cunning of a human. You could almost say man is the most dangerous animal on earth.

DICKEY

Yes. The most dangerous game. Game in two senses. Like game fish, big game. And the game

that's kind of like a complicated chess game. He moves here, they move there. Yes, he becomes . . . What does Pat Conroy say [on the jacket of *To the White Sea*]? "His writing makes this soldier haunted and hunted into the most dangerous man on earth." It doesn't do that entirely, because he's that way anyway. He doesn't become that under these circumstances. That just brings it out.

INTERVIEWER

In the past, you've resisted saying that *Deliverance* was a poetic novel. What about this new one? I can't imagine anyone who wasn't a poet writing this novel.

DICKEY

Everything I do comes out of the poetic part of the imagination. That's *everything* I do.

Novels. Movies. Screenplays. Literary essays. Other kinds of essays. Children's books. They're all a spin-off from the central core. At the center of the creative wheel is poetry.

I think anybody who takes the writing of poetry seriously and works at it like you have to work at it—with a great intensity and resourcefulness and an enormous expenditure of time—that person is going to find any other writing easy compared to that.

Which is good, because poetry is something you do out of love. I don't think there've been any best-selling poems or movies made from poetry. So you know that's not your motive.

INTERVIEWER

Yet so many poets try to write novels, and they can't. What's different about you?

DICKEY

I don't have any idea, except that I have a very vivid story sense. I like to tell stories. A lot of poets are lyric poets—there are very few narrative poets around—but the lyric poem is a sort of celebration of some kind of timeless moment of perception or insight, what Joyce calls an epiphany. And that doesn't have a narrative element. It's just kind of a still life. I like to have some movement through time.

INTERVIEWER

Can you think of another poet with a strong narrative drive?

DICKEY

I think there's only one other poet in Ameri-can literature who's a successful novelist and poet: Robert Penn Warren. Faulkner is a miserably, wretchedly bad poet. He's bad. And all the others who've written novels, most of them are very forgettable. Sandburg wrote an excrescence called *Remembrance Rock*, which is the worst novel I've ever read in my life—one of them, anyway. And various ones have tried to do it. To have any degree of success in both the novel and poetry is very, very rare. And I think Warren and I are the only ones who've done it.

INTERVIEWER

There's a terrible, or magnificent, grandiosity about your new hero. He's impervious to weather, to relationships, to human life. Sometimes he feels he can almost fly. Is this grandeur or folly?

DICKEY

I don't know what it is. It might be insanity. A form of it, anyway. Sort of a controlled madness. But he doesn't look at it that way. One of the things that's frightening about Muldrow is his matter-of-factness. He'll say the most curious things, and sometimes the most horrible things, as if they should be obvious to anybody. [Laughter.] Like when he sees the American airman beheaded at the air base, and then later on, he beheads this other woman and puts her head in one of the buckets. A head for a head. But he doesn't think of this until later.

INTERVIEWER

I understand originally you had a child's head in that scene.

DICKEY

A little girl. But my publisher was too squeamish for that.

INTERVIEWER

How did you feel about changing it?

DICKEY

I didn't want to do it. I wanted the reader to get a terrible shock.

INTERVIEWER

I was struck with how your hero enjoyed planning. He thought out his moves. He was precise and pragmatic. You flew more than a hundred combat missions in World War II. Did you find that planning is an antidote to the anxiety of war? Or that plotting is an antidote to the anxiety of writing?

DICKEY

Well, it might be. I do it for the thing itself, because I enjoy it. My grandmother was born in Germany, and I was raised with that sort of methodical, Teutonic way of thinking about things. It's very helpful in a lot of situations. You consider the consequences of what you're going to do. If I do this, that will probably happen. If I do that, that will probably happen.

INTERVIEWER

Like chess. But that's a pleasurable experience to you.

DICKEY

Yes, it is. My main recreation is work.

INTERVIEWER

A lot of writers would say that happily, wouldn't they?

DICKEY

I think so. A lot of people talk about how hard it is for them to write anything, how they procrastinate and dread sitting down. And there's that factor, too, because if you have what you think is a good idea, you're afraid you're going to mess it up. That's a very real fear. In other words, it hasn't been written yet, and you've got to do it. But things begin to accumulate, and one thing will dovetail into another, and it seems natural.

INTERVIEWER

And as you work, the anxiety kind of clears a path.

DICKEY

Yeah. In the face of the real creative excitement that comes up: "Now, boy, wouldn't it be good if . . . ! Now, why don't I have this happen? Let's try it!" [Laughter.]

INTERVIEWER

Often, very young writers don't realize that you have to keep trying.

DICKEY

Sure. If I have any virtue as a writer, it's in revision. Because if you get something down, if you get black on white, you can look at it and tell almost immediately what's good about it—if anything is—and what's bad about it and what's inadequate and what doesn't go with this other part.

I work on the principle of refining low-grade ore, as if I were a gold miner. I have several tons of dirt, and I work with that and extract whatever gold is in it. It's a very long and laborious process, but you have the satisfaction of knowing that the substance you end up with is just as much real as it would be if you had had to do nothing but go and pick nuggets up off the ground. It's the same stuff. It's gold.

INTERVIEWER

Many writers who shared some aspects of your lifestyle—say, Hemingway, Faulkner, Fitzgerald—were dead by now. Yet you go on, decade after decade. What's your secret?

DICKEY

I don't know. There are some writers who were better as they got older. Yeats is a good example.

But I don't like to repeat myself, and if I don't have anything to say or want to say, I don't write it. I've got to be full of the idea, especially with novels. And contrary to popular belief, I think in a certain type of talent, your creativity increases as you get older, because you can see so many options you couldn't see before.

INTERVIEWER

And your bouts of excessiveness have not interfered?

DICKEY

I don't consider myself really an excessive per-son. Sometimes, yes. Not habitually. Not somebody like Scott Fitzgerald or Hart Crane or Rimbaud or somebody like that. Or some artist like Modigliani who led some sort of excessive life of drinking and womanizing. Or somebody like Baudelaire and his *paradis artificiel*—his artificial paradise of narcotics and dissipation and so on.

It's never had much appeal to me, although I'm acquainted with it. Not as a way of life. It wouldn't be for me.

One of the things about any sort of excess for a writer, whether it's narcotics or alcohol, it destroys your critical faculty. I want to know in cold blood whether what I put down is good. I don't want to think it's good because I feel good, you know. That's a mistake. In fact, I had rather feel bad. Then if it's good, I'll know there's not any possibility of me fooling myself because of some kind of substance. I want to be as detached as I can.

INTERVIEWER

You played football for Clemson in 1942, and I understand you were pretty darned good.

DICKEY

I played in all the freshman games, although I only started the last one. We won two and lost two. We beat Presbyterian and an army team in Augusta at Daniels Field. Then the University of South Carolina beat us here at the big game, which is called State Fair, out at the fairgrounds. I was not exceptionally good, although the first two games I played quarterback. I had pretty good success with that, because I could not only pass, I did the kicking, I played safety man—they didn't have the two-platoon system then—and I was also the fastest man on the team. You don't generally get a quarterback who's the fastest man on the team. But I was, and I could run it when I couldn't find the receiver. [Laughter.]

INTERVIEWER

You've said that sex is a metaphor for you for creativity, and that there's a certain thing about the arrival of an image or a good line of poetry that has an orgasmic feel. In this new novel, there are so many fine images and so many lyrical lines, you must've felt orgasmic for months.

DICKEY

In a sense. Maybe this is sort of an intimate observation. It's not like an actual orgasm, in which your body is sort of like a machine going on involuntarily; some other kind of control takes over when it's happening. But when you have a good line or a good rhythm, it has the same effect of something involuntary about it. Something else takes it—takes it away from you—and tells you what to say. You're trying to puzzle it out, and something says to you, "No, that's not what to say. This is what you should say." And it comes from left field.

INTERVIEWER
Any accounting for this?

DICKEY

I don't have any idea. But it's been with the human race a long time. Plato talks about it. It's what most people would call inspiration. Plato

calls it "seizure." Something takes over. And you don't argue with it. The main thing, though, is that it takes us such a long time, so many years to learn what to do with it when you get it. [Paul] Valery speaks of the line *donnée* [*ligne donnée*]—the given line. God gives you one line, but you've got to work like hell for the rest of them.

INTERVIEWER

I've heard you say you are essentially a coward. That in football, you hit the guy especially hard because you were afraid of him. Is this true, that you think of yourself as a coward?

DICKEY

That's a pretty hard judgment on oneself.

INTERVIEWER
But you made it.

DICKEY

Yeah, I did. And I certainly was not cowardly during the war. I would take any mission. In fact, the C.O. had to slow me down.

INTERVIEWER
Then why would you say that about yourself?

DICKEY
Everybody thinks that. Everybody thinks that of himself. Look at Hemingway, for example. *Coward* is a hard word to use. I mean to call yourself that, or anybody else. Somebody like Hemingway has constantly got to prove he's brave, which is the essence of cowardice.

A person who's naturally brave is not going to need to prove anything. He already knows what he's going to do.

Muldrow was a brave man. One thing is, because he knows no matter how bad the enemy is or how ruthless the enemy is, they're not as bad as he is. He doesn't say he's going to do these things. He does them just as a matter of course. And it's different with different people. John Berryman, the American poet, once told me that a man can live in this culture his whole life and not know whether he's a coward or not.

INTERVIEWER

Because he's never tested.

DICKEY

That's right. And Berryman said, "I think he should know." [Laughter.] There are a lot of forms of bravery, and they're not all on the battlefield or even playing football. There are lots of different forms of it.

INTERVIEWER

At age seventy, what's your biggest fear?

DICKEY

That I'll die before Bronnie grows up and is able to take care of herself. My boys are all out in the world. They've been out in the world for years. My older son is head of the European division for *Newsweek*, and my other one is a staff surgeon at Yale Medical. I have the honor of being the father of a son who turned down a full staff position at Johns Hopkins, because they had more of what he wanted to do at Yale than at Johns Hopkins. He's a wonderful fellow. My sons are not only my sons, but they are among my best friends. [Laughter.] I just regret I don't see more of them.

INTERVIEWER

You've said mastery is the only revenge against aging.

DICKEY

It's the only compensation, I guess you could say. I'm sorry for people who are not artists, who are not striving to do something creative right up to the end. Someone who's trying—a musician or a painter or a poet or a novelist—who's trying to get that ultimate note, like the one that the great jazz trumpeter Bix Beiderbecke always felt that he could reach. It's not real high, but it's something that's not on any scale. That's what you try for.

———

Born February 2, 1923, in Atlanta, James Dickey is the second of three sons of Eugene and Maibelle Swift Dickey; the first son died before Dickey's birth. He graduated from North Fulton High School in Atlanta in 1940 and from the Darlington School for Boys in Rome, Georgia, in 1942. That year, he entered Clemson College, now Clemson University.

During World War II, Dickey joined the United States Army Air Force and flew a hundred combat missions in the 418th Night Fighter Squadron. During the Korean War, he served in the United States Air Force and was awarded the Air Medal.

In 1949, Dickey graduated magna cum laude from Vanderbilt University and in 1950 received his master's degree from Vanderbilt.

From 1950 to 1956, Dickey taught at Rice Institute, now Rice University, and at the University of Florida in Gainesville.

For the next four years, he worked in advertising in New York and Atlanta.

From 1963 to 1968, he served as poet-in-residence at Reed College; San Fernando Valley State College, now California State-Northridge; the University of Wisconsin at Madison; the University of Wisconsin at Milwaukee; George Washington University; and Georgia Tech.

He was poetry consultant at the Library of Congress from 1966 to 1968.

In 1969, Dickey joined the faculty of the University of South Carolina, where he is poet-in-residence and, since 1979, the university's first Carolina Professor.

His novels are *Deliverance* (1970), *Alnilam* (1987), and *To the White Sea* (1993).

His collections of poetry include *Into the Stone* (1960), *Drowning with Others* (1962), *Interpreter's House* (1963), *Two Poems of the Air* (1964), *Buckdancer's Choice* (1965), *The Eye-Beaters, Blood,* *Victory, Madness, Buckhead and Mercy* (1970), *The Zodiac* (1976), *The Strength of Fields* (1979), and *Puella* (1982).

His nonfiction works include *Babel to Byzantium: Poets and Poetry Now* (1968), *Self-Interviews* (1970), and *Sorties* (1971).

In 1972, *Deliverance* was made into a Warner Brothers movie starring Burt Reynolds.

Dickey's awards include the Vachel Lindsay Prize (1959) and the Levinson Prize (1982), both from *Poetry* magazine; a Guggenheim Fellowship (1961–62); a National Book Award for poetry (1966); the Melville Crane Award of the Poetry Society of America (1966); a National Institute of Arts and Letters grant (1966); and the Medicis Prize for best foreign book of the year (1971).

He was invited to read his poem "The Strength of Fields" on the eve of the inauguration of President Jimmy Carter in 1977.

In 1988, he was elected as one of 50 members of the American Academy of Arts and Letters, a branch of the 250-member American Institute of Arts and Letters.

On November 4, 1948, Dickey married Maxine Syerson. They had two sons: Christopher Swift, born in 1951; and Kevin Webster, born in 1958. Maxine died in October 1976.

On December 30, 1976, Dickey married Deborah Dodson. They have one daughter, Bronwen Elaine, born in 1980.

Dickey lives with his wife and daughter in Columbia, South Carolina, where he is working on a sequel to *Alnilam*.

April 5, 1994

CLYDE EDGERTON

*G*rowing up, novelist Clyde Edgerton didn't know that everyone in the world wasn't Baptist. He was. His family was. Almost everyone in Durham County's Bethesda community was. So Edgerton figured even boys in China went to a red brick church with white columns and felt awful if they missed Wednesday-night prayer meeting.

Edgerton is Piedmont North Carolina to the core. He's descended from two North Carolina families, the Edgertons and the Warrens, the former family related to Durham novelist Reynolds Price. North Carolinians of both the tender and twangy varieties rip through his novels, including his fifth and latest, *In Memory of Junior*.

People in small towns don't talk in abstractions, Edgerton says.

"They talk about what happens when they try to live in concert with the earth. Problems with crops and tobacco and animals are weaved in and out of stories," he says. "That kind of talk is a good habit for a fiction writer to have. If you grow up with that, I think that can make a difference."

Edgerton plays a five-string banjo, and his wife, Susan Ketchin, plays the guitar. Their Tar Water Band is making an album, *The Devil's Dream*, from Lee Smith's novel of the same name.

Edgerton has spent the morning reading and underlining Westerns in preparation for a novel set in the nineteenth-century Southwest. As another aid to research, he had lunch today with a "freelance embalmer," learning the history, secrets, and laws of the trade.

This afternoon, Edgerton sprawls in his windowless basement office to talk about small-town life, about creating characters, and about how to tell if a fellow writer will be a friend or a foe.

INTERVIEWER

You grew up an only child in the Bethesda community, outside Durham, North Carolina. Were you a lonely only child, or were there plenty of relatives around?

EDGERTON

I had twenty-three aunts and uncles. Right there. I was right under 'em. Well, there was one aunt and uncle in Greensboro and one in Florida. But most of them, I could throw an apple and hit their house. I could hit a couple more with a slingshot. And I could run to the rest of them. I had four or five boys my age nearby. Every day after school, we were in the woods playing. I never got lonely.

INTERVIEWER

I think of Bethesda when I read about the fictional Listre or Summerlin in your novels. What was it like during the forties and fifties?

EDGERTON

The community consisted of roughly, oh, two or three square miles. There was an intersection with a filling station, a general store, and a combination general store and filling station. On the fourth corner was an auto-repair shop and a grill and a house.

There was another intersection, with a Baptist church, a cemetery and elementary school, and a baseball field.

In between those two main intersections were all my relatives. We were the Edgertons. There were far more Mitchells than Edgertons.

INTERVIEWER

And you probably knew the Mitchells as well as you knew the Edgertons.

EDGERTON

I would spend the night with those people. I knew their families. I knew what their mothers cooked better than my mother did. (Not much, if anything.) I knew which aunt cooked better collards. Which one's specialty was fried okra.

INTERVIEWER

What was the tenor of the community?

EDGERTON

This was a conservative, provincial, fundamentalist, loyal, farm-based community. The people who lived there who weren't farmers were sons and daughters of farmers, almost without exception.

INTERVIEWER

Those qualities can make for comfort and discomfort.

EDGERTON

Yes. There were just beyond the block on each side of town poor black people. I was friends with one of the boys—Larry Holman—and that was frowned on by the community. That seems sad.

INTERVIEWER

I've talked to your Aunt Lila Spain—on your mother's side—and she really seemed to enjoy your particular talents and sense of humor and to be an important part of your life growing up.

EDGERTON

My mother had these two childless sisters—Aunt Oma and Aunt Lila—and there I was with three mamas. They all have a sense of humor. Lila has always been especially cosmopolitan. She left home and joined the WAVES. She's in her eighties. She's always up on current events. When I was in high school, she had a white Plymouth Fury with fender skirts and a red leather interior. She let me take it to the senior prom.

INTERVIEWER

The people in your novels—I'm thinking of Mattie Rigsbee, Raney Bell, Wesley Benfield—are these people you knew? Are they, so to speak, your people?

EDGERTON

Well, I think they resemble my people. After I start with a character, I'm walking a line between what's real and what's not.

INTERVIEWER

So you might base a character on a real person, and it will take off and become his or her own person?

EDGERTON

There are real incidents or characteristics that help me create a fictional character. Mattie Rigsbee came from an incident that my mother had when she sat through a chair. But once that fictional character is established, then in my mind as a writer, that fictional character becomes as separate from any real person as one real person is from another real person.

As my story develops, I'm led by my characters. I have to lead them in a certain way, but they become quite different from anybody I might have modeled them on. They're clearly distinct. I never see the face or body of a real person. It would be impossible for me to have a real person intrude in a fictional story.

INTERVIEWER

We've talked before about how a writer's values may end up in a story, even though that writer is not consciously trying to give any aboveboard messages to the reader. Let's talk about how the reader's values might affect his or her experience of reading the novel.

EDGERTON

When a reader reads literature—when a viewer views a painting, in other words—when the "receiver" receives art, the receiver becomes a part of the art. That receiver's unconscious goes to work on the work. The story you read between the covers of the book I wrote will not be the story the photographer reads.

If I understand the way art works, then I must understand that the reader will bring to the story that which will affect the story for better or worse. If the reader doesn't like the story, I don't have to blame myself. On the other hand, if the reader does like the story, it might mean I ought to hesitate to take the credit.

INTERVIEWER

What is it about your art you can tell other people who want to be writers?

April 5, 1994

EDGERTON

What I tell young writers is that when I see something that strikes me, I write it down. I don't ask myself, "Why is that important?" I just know it's important, because it's who I am that something seems important to me. It'll either be something I see or something I hear or something I feel inside. That may happen once a month. Or it may happen every day five days in a row. Whenever it happens, I make a note. Once, I overheard a woman talking about a boy getting a fishhook hung in his nose. I wrote it down. Later, I was able to make a scene out of that.

I write down funny kinds of things or harrowing kinds of things. So what I tell students is that the germs of stories are these little incidents overheard, or instantaneous images: Someone doing something on a street corner. Some incident or something overheard develops into a character, and that character can take me through a book.

Being a writer means paying attention to what strikes you. What you notice comes from your core. It's not going to be what other people notice. People are different from each other. In order to embrace that fact, it's important for an artist to be very sensitive to what is striking him or her.

INTERVIEWER

Am I right that soon after you received the Guggenheim Fellowship, you became more businesslike about your writing? Didn't you quit answering your phone and get an answering machine?

EDGERTON

The battle is choosing between being a celebrity and being a writer. You can either be a little bit of a celebrity and a little bit of a writer, or a big celebrity and no writer at all.

If in 1977 I could've heard myself in 1987 talking about the problems of being published, I would've been shocked at myself for having any kind of complaint. How could I go for eight years with exactly zero recognition and then complain about being recognized? But I have not found the process of being a celebrity more rewarding than being alone, writing about scenes and characters when that writing is working really well.

INTERVIEWER

What's important about not having interruptions?

EDGERTON

I need a kind of concentration which depends on a series of days and weeks in a row. For example, if I worked for a year on a piece of fiction every third day, I would accomplish far less than I would if I were writing thirty days in a row. It's a cumulative effect. A day-to-day concentration—that's very helpful when I'm writing a novel. So, on each book, there has to be a long period of uninterrupted mornings.

INTERVIEWER

How did you go about getting this kind of time?

The first thing I did was move out of my house into an office with no windows. Flannery O'Connor wrote in front of a blank wall. She would sit down there three hours a day. I don't do exactly that when I am working hard on a novel. But I do make myself sit down and work uninterrupted.

Then the next thing I did was to buy a telephone with an answering machine. I cut the ring off. But I could still hear the tape recording. So I put the whole thing in a briefcase, and then I put the briefcase in a drawer and closed the drawer. Only then could I not hear it.

In the afternoons, after I'd revised what I wrote that morning, I'd open up the drawer, get all the messages, and make the calls.

INTERVIEWER

And, finally, you hired a twenty-hour-a-week assistant.

EDGERTON

The last six months I worked on *Killer Diller*, I didn't answer any mail except for bills. I got so far behind and so bogged down in the business of being a writer—which I never dreamed would be so complicated—that I put an ad in the newspaper for an assistant.

Pat's an incredible person. She takes shorthand. She's been a courtroom stenographer. She's worked for Blue Cross/Blue Shield, so she can handle my insurance forms. She answers the phone and helps me answer the mail. She was a nun, and she's an Elvis fan. She's very well-balanced.

INTERVIEWER

During your undergraduate years at UNC-Chapel Hill, you fiddled around a bit with what you call "right-wing poetry."

But it wasn't until you were thirty-four or thirty-five and had flown jet airplanes for five years and had been involved in education that you had a solid epiphany about writing. It had to do with Eudora Welty.

EDGERTON

My wife, Susan, and I had gotten very much interested in readers' theater. We did Eudora Welty's [short story] "Why I Live at the P.O." And I had gotten very, very interested in her work and in Flannery O'Connor's work.

Sometime in here, Susan gave me a volume of O'Connor's short stories. Reading those and reading Eudora Welty was helping me see that my own background formed just as solid a base to write fiction as any other writer. This I had never thought about. For some reason, perhaps understandable, I'd always thought fiction had to be exotic, somehow. I wrote my first complete short story during the Christmas holidays, 1977.

INTERVIEWER

Then didn't you see Eudora Welty on TV?

EDGERTON

The following May—May 14, 1978—I turned on PBS, and there was Eudora Welty reading "Why I Live at the P.O." Her voice is so wonderful, and when the show was over, I said, "Tomorrow morning, I will start writing fiction seriously." I wanted to do for other people what she had done for me. Whatever that was. I can't name it.

INTERVIEWER

Did you keep your promise?

EDGERTON

The next morning, I started working on a second story. That summer, I wrote four stories, and sometime in 1979, I started sending stories out. By 1983, I had probably twelve or thirteen stories sent out—and returned 202 times. Six had been accepted, three by friends.

INTERVIEWER

From what I see and what I read, there seems to be a great camaraderie among Triangle-area writers. Maybe more so than in the Charlotte area. Why do you think this is?

EDGERTON

I think we have more confidence in our writing than y'all do. [Laughter.] The writers I know—Larry Brown, Tim [McLaurin], Jill [McCorkle], Lee Smith, Kaye Gibbons—the writers I know best who are Southern writers, most of us have something in common other than writing. We have other things to talk about. Our friendship is on a nonliterary basis. We're friends who happen to be writers, rather than writers who are trying to be friends.

INTERVIEWER

I can't imagine having friends who write and not discussing writing.

EDGERTON

Maybe it has to do with seriousness. I mean, in many ways, writing is the most serious thing in my life. It's also the least serious thing. I want to tell good stories. But sad, pain-filled writing is, fortunately, not for me. I'd rather for my writing to last only a hundred years and be pain-free than last a thousand years and be filled with pain.

INTERVIEWER

What does pain-filled writing have to do with camaraderie?

EDGERTON

Well, I think another thing. And I'm assuming we get along—make that real clear that I'm *assuming* we do. None of us asks each other opinions about our writing. We all have editors, and we use our editors, and I think we all probably believe that the best person to get guidance from on our writing is an editor, rather than another writer.

Therefore, we are not looking to each other for advice, and we avoid a certain kind of conflict, perhaps. Of course, in two weeks, we may have three writers murdered by three other writers. You can't ever tell.

I'll say one other thing: I've met quite a few writers in the last three or four years. I just met Rick Bass. We'd been corresponding for three or four years before we met each other. And I knew I would like him. I knew I would like his fiction. I also meet writers I don't like. I think the easiest way I can sum the whole thing up: It's all in the eyes. When you meet a writer, the eyes tell how competitive they might be. You can tell by their eyes whether they're interested in you. And once you feel that out and start talking about something other than deconstructionism, you have a friend. You look forward to seeing him again. It doesn't mean we avoid talking about writing. It just seems there's much more to talk about.

INTERVIEWER

From your novels, I get the strong notion you view life as both sublime and petty. Maybe lots more petty than sublime.

EDGERTON

Among other adjectives. Certainly, pettiness and the sublime are what people respond to in their own lives. I would say life is petty, and I would say that life is at times sublime. It's certainly fun to write about petty things, and it's fun to write about the sublime, if you don't do it too directly. You hope, again, that you're doing something on the page that a reader will respond to. While you can't predict exactly how a reader will respond, you can hope for a kind of response. And the main response I hope for is pleasure. After that, it gets complicated.

———

The only child of Ernest Carlyle and Susan Truma Warren Edgerton, Clyde Carlyle Edgerton was born May 20, 1944, in Durham, North Carolina, and grew up in the nearby Bethesda community. He graduated from Southern High School in Durham in 1962 and received his B.A. at UNC-Chapel Hill in 1966. In 1972, he received his M.A.T. from UNC-Chapel Hill, and in 1972 his Ph.D.

Edgerton taught English at Southern High School from 1972 to 1973 and was co-director of the English Teaching Institute in Chapel Hill in 1976. From 1977 to 1981, he taught education and psychology at Campbell University. From 1985 to 1989, he taught English and edu-

cation at St. Andrews Presbyterian College. He has also served as visiting writer at North Carolina Central University and Agnes Scott College.

Edgerton served in the United States Air Force from 1966 to 1971, piloting reconnaissance and forward air-control missions in Southeast Asia during the Vietnam War. He received the Distinguished Flying Cross.

His books are *Raney* (1985), *Walking Across Egypt* (1987), *Understanding the Floatplane* (1987), *The Floatplane Notebooks* (1988), *Cold Black Peas* (1990), *Killer Diller* (1991), and *In Memory of Junior* (1992). All his books are set in Piedmont North Carolina.

His awards include a Guggenheim Fellowship,

a Lyndhurst Prize, and the Sam Ragan Prize.

On June 21, 1975, Edgerton married writer and critic Susan Ketchin. They have a daughter, Catherine, born July 15, 1982.

Edgerton and his wife are members of the Tar Water Band. They live in Durham, where he is at work on a novel set in the American West.

April 5, 1994

May 19, 1994

SHELBY FOOTE

November 8, 1985

*F*ramed over a window in Shelby Foote's study in Memphis, Tennessee, is an envelope he says keeps him humble.

The envelope is addressed to Shelby Foote, Historian, Greenville, Miss., and it is stamped, "Return to Sender. Addressee Unknown."

The Greenville, Mississippi, native is the author of the classic three-volume *The Civil War: A Narrative*, as well as six novels. His 1952 novel, *Shiloh*, is regarded as the best Civil War novel ever published.

Foote's good friend is Louisiana novelist Walker Percy, who was a year ahead of Foote at Greenville High School, where Foote edited the school paper and Percy wrote a gossip column. The year Foote was editor, the paper won a cup for the best-edited high-school paper in the country.

Foote followed Percy to UNC-Chapel Hill, where Foote walked into the library the first day he was there, marveled at the nine stories of stacks, and ensconced himself there for the next two years.

"I'd never dreamed of so many books," he says. "Looked like hog heaven to me. I went to a few classes, but mostly I prowled the library."

Foote still can't keep his hands off a book. He'll settle with one into his favorite reading chair, fill his pipe, and pass the hours, the only noise the mellow tones of a mantel clock chiming the hour and half-hour.

This mild November Saturday, Foote talks about the diligence that was required to turn out the 1,650,000-word trilogy, about Ernest Hemingway's brain, and about how an outline can perform the same function as a good dance platform.

INTERVIEWER

I understand you're a diligent worker and that you developed a system for writing when you came back from World War II that stood you in good stead throughout the writing of your novels and your trilogy.

FOOTE

All my life, I've found out that if I lay off for one day, it'll take me two to get back to it. So it was up to me, I saw very early, to develop some very rigid work habits or I'd never get anything done.

The best system that I know of is to be thoroughly aware that you will be miserable away from your desk, so that you stay at your desk in that kind of misery rather than fall back on the other kind of misery.

I've always worked morning and afternoon. In other words, I've put in what might be called an eight-hour day. Most writers won't do that. They think two or three hours is a good, long day. And they're right. It is a good, long day if you work that way. But I work very slowly, five or six hundred words in a good day. So that I have to be there. In all my writing life, right on through *The Civil War*, I worked seven days a week.

INTERVIEWER

And the trilogy would never have been accomplished if you hadn't.

FOOTE

That's right. I didn't begin *The Civil War* intending to spend any twenty years on it. I

thought it might take two. The contract called for a short history of the Civil War. I thought it'd go on about two hundred thousand words maybe, and it would take me a year and a half, two years at the most. I knew so little about historical writing that I thought it would go much faster than a novel. It went at about the same speed, same kind of writing. I felt absolutely no different writing history from what I ever felt writing novels. Nothing pleases me more than to have someone ask me if I made up some sections of *The Civil War*. It's somewhere in one of the bibliographical notes, I said what is really true—facts made up in your head are just as respectable as facts you get out of a document. And, as a novelist, I wouldn't be false to those "facts." Nor would I be false to a fact dug out of a book. The only difference is, if you want a man to have gray eyes, you give him gray eyes. And when writing history you can't give him gray eyes unless you know he had them. But once you find out the color of his eyes, that's the way it should be. The truth's always superior to distortion. That holds true for a novel as much as it does for history.

INTERVIEWER

You've written your novels and the trilogy using ink, fountain pens, and blotters. Do you worry you won't be able to get them anymore?

FOOTE

I had some good things happen. I heard from some obscure fellow near Richmond, Virginia, who had a good supply of ink in quart bottles. So I bought a lifetime supply of that. I was prowling about in a stationery store in New York on Forty-forth Street and found my type of pen. They had about three gross of them. So I got those.

INTERVIEWER

And your type is what?

FOOTE

It's a Probate. Esterbrook. Wrote the whole *Civil War* with that thing.

The blotters were a big problem, too. It used to be, twenty-five years ago, you could go into any insurance office and get an armload of blotters. They don't exist anymore. Then there was an interview in the paper about three years ago where some woman down in Mississippi said she was pleased to find someone needed some blotters, because she had a good supply. So she sent me about, I guess, roughly two thousand. Just exactly what I needed.

INTERVIEWER

The right size?

FOOTE

Perfect. Absolutely perfect. [He shows a blotter.] Couldn't have been nicer. You wouldn't believe how hard it is to get those things. So I'm fixed for life.

INTERVIEWER

Do most people respect your schedule? Everybody you know must know you work all day long.

FOOTE

If they don't, they soon learn to, because I don't put up with any foolishness.

INTERVIEWER

Do you feel tired at the end of your eight-hour writing day?

FOOTE

Hemingway said that after a good day's work, you feel like you do when you make love to someone you really love. So you're tired, but it's not like exhaustion from running three miles. Or maybe it is, I just never would run three miles. But you feel tired in a happy way. You're glad to be that tired.

INTERVIEWER

Are you slim by nature? Or do you exercise or have to work at it?

FOOTE

I weighed 138 pounds all the way through college. And the army. I'm beginning to put on weight, and I'm up to around 160 now. And I don't have a problem with that. Although I do tend to watch it. And I had a heart incident about a year ago. Not a real attack, but a scare. And I went under oxygen. And they were real horrified to find how I lived and ate. I ate nothing but protein and fat. And never under any circumstances took any exercise whatever. It was a religion with me. But they changed my diet and told me to walk two miles every morning. And they scared me enough so that I do. And I do feel better.

What do you advise young people who want to become writers?

FOOTE

I have a standard procedure on that. I always do everything I can to discourage anybody from being a writer. And if you're successful at it, then they weren't ever supposed to be a writer. And if they are, you can't influence them.

Someone asked Flannery O'Connor if she thought the government shouldn't do more to help writers, because didn't she agree that so many people fail to be writers for lack of opportunity. She said, "Not nearly enough."

I've always felt that artistic talent, to use fancy words, is a sort of reservoir, and what direction it takes is rather an accident. I think I could probably have been a painter or a composer as well as a writer. It was just an accident that made me a writer. If I had somehow or another gotten enough interest in pictures at, you know, sixteen, I might have been a painter. It all draws on the same resources.

INTERVIEWER

Some writers know how a story is going to end, and for others the process is an act of discovery.

FOOTE

Walker said if he knew what was going to happen next, he couldn't write.

INTERVIEWER

Which is your way?

FOOTE

I know exactly what's going to happen next and even how many words I'm going to use. I get some surprises. But generally speaking I work from an outline and even a scenario.

INTERVIEWER

In both fiction and nonfiction?

FOOTE

Yes.

INTERVIEWER

But as you're drawing up your outline, how do you know it's what ought to happen? Might not a better way present itself as the work is under way?

FOOTE

In the writing of a novel, the first decision you have to make may be the most important one of all: Where do I stand to tell my story? Where's my stance? What is the tone of my voice? Where does it start?

Tolstoy went crazy trying to start *Anna Karenina*. He knew the whole story, everything he wanted to tell, he had it all straight in his mind. But he couldn't start. And he was sitting in the living room after dinner one day, looking through a book of stories, I think by Pushkin, and he read something—a very banal little statement—and Tolstoy said, "That's it!" And jumped up and ran into his study and wrote, "Happy families are all alike. Every unhappy family is unhappy in its own way." Everything was in confusion until then. And he was off.

You can't start until you feel that the tone is

right. And it's heartbreaking to rewrite. It's something I don't have anything to do with, is rewriting. Walker sits down and bangs out three hundred thousand words and then sits back and looks and sees what he's got and then goes to work. I couldn't work like that at all.

INTERVIEWER

Do you ever have writer's block? Or is that something you don't believe in?

FOOTE

Writer's block is too large a term. You have hesitations about this thing I was talking about: Where do you stand to tell the story? And God knows there's such a thing as writer's block. But usually it's a choice. A person isn't blocked because he can't help it. He's blocked, if that's the word for it, because he just doesn't want to start yet. The distinction can be pretty shaky, but in my experience, if you're blocked, it's because you don't want to write. That's kind of spooky stuff. You might not want to write because you can't, and so on. But I don't believe in writer's block the way it's usually defined. I don't believe it's something that could be cured by a psychiatrist. A really good literary critic would be more apt to cure writer's block, pointing out how he's artistically wrong.

INTERVIEWER

Do you believe you inherited your talent? Or your creative reservoir?

FOOTE

My talent—such as it is—is very hard to de-fine. It's never occurred in my family before. With one exception. I come from a long line of Mississippi planters, going back to South Carolina. Very distinguished men, in their way. But not the vestige of talent for writing or painting or music or anything else. As far as I know, not a single one of them knew there was any such thing as painting. But I do have another grandfather, my mother's father. . . .

INTERVIEWER

Whose name was?

FOOTE

Rosenstock. He was a Jew from Vienna, Austria. He came over to this country at age seventeen. And anything I have along those lines I'm inclined to think came from him. Not that he was a writer or a painter or anything, but he came from a different kind of society, a different kind of life, and I think he brought some of whatever is in Vienna with him.

INTERVIEWER

How did he happen to come, at age seventeen?

FOOTE

It's a very strange thing. He probably was trying to get away from conscription and was simply looking to make his fortune in another world. Saw he couldn't do it in Vienna. Got over here, came down the Mississippi River, got off around Greenville or a little below it. Went to work keeping books for a plantation in Avon, Mississippi. Married the daughter of the family. How the man felt about this itinerant Jew coming in and marrying his red-headed daughter, I don't know. But that's what he did. Then he became a cotton man. Made the proverbial million dollars, lost it. Got buried poor.

INTERVIEWER

I've been fascinated by that new book from Louisiana State University Press on the Percys. But one of my objections to the book is that the author leaves the women out so thoroughly.

FOOTE

Yeah, that's a big mistake, to leave Camille Percy out. Will's [William Alexander Percy's] mother. I remember her well. She was the daughter of a French baker named Bourges. She was a woman of considerable culture, by the time I knew her. She'd been everywhere. House filled with Venetian glass and everything. Had a deep voice. A very unusual, wonderful woman.

INTERVIEWER

She was the mother of William Alexander Percy, the man who raised Walker Percy and the author of *Lanterns on the Levee*. What was "Mr. Will" like?

FOOTE

I said that whatever I had in the way of talent came from my grandfather. Actually, it came from other places outside of my family. And Mr. Will is probably the single most important person, outside my family, as to developing anything in me that comes close to being an artist.

He had a quality of being able to talk to you about Keats or Browning that got you excited and made you want to read Keats and Browning. He did that thing that all the good teachers I've ever known could do. They could communicate to you their love of a subject. And once you got tuned into their love of that subject, you loved it, too.

INTERVIEWER

Which of the three elements of a novel—the stance, the characters, the plotting—intrigues you the most?

FOOTE

The plotting. The plotting is the most interesting one. See, plotting is not what most people think it is. It's not how you lay the story out. It's how you present it. That is, change of scene—chopping a scene off before it's finished and picking it up later on, and putting something in between to keep the revelation from coming at this time. That's what plotting is.

It's the last skill you ever acquire. It need not be done always consciously, as I'm sounding like I'm saying. But it's something that's right. And you may be thoroughly aware of literary criticism of all kinds, but when you sit down at that desk, you will forget everything you ever heard about that. You fly on your own. And you'd better. If you started doing things like pumping symbolism into a novel and stuff like that, you'd write a bunch of junk. It has to come naturally and of its own accord.

INTERVIEWER

Are you sympathetic to your unconscious? Do you respect the magnitude of it, and trust it?

FOOTE

Yeah. The reason I outline—it's like I was going to do a dance. I would want a good solid platform to stand on, so the damn thing didn't fall out from under me in midstep. That's all it is, is constructing a good sound thing to do your act on. It gives you freedom. To have a good, strong outline, you are free then to do whatever you want to, instead of trying to build the damn platform while you're doing the dance.

INTERVIEWER

How about these people who don't outline? Do you think that some activity is going on anyway that is constructing that platform, whether they realize it or not?

FOOTE

Of course there is. It's just, my method is my method and their method is their method. They all probably add up to the same thing. I don't think their method gives them more freedom to create than mine gives me. I think mine gives me more. But I think there's plenty of writers who'd be locked up by an outline and feel that they couldn't move. Tied up. I feel set free. Well, you can't talk about writers any more than you can talk about chairs. There are lots of different kinds of chairs. There are lots of different kinds of writers. And there aren't any rules. There are some rules. Faulkner said that. He told me once

the only rule that he had was not to write when he was tired.

INTERVIEWER

If you followed that rule it would cancel your schedule.

FOOTE

Yeah. I won't leave my desk. There are some days when I get almost nothing done. Other days when I triple that and write fifteen hundred words. But my rule is, stay at the desk and sweat it out, like a gambler and bad luck. He keeps on playing until the damn thing, the bad-luck streak, is over.

INTERVIEWER

You've been married three times. Is your wife amenable to that schedule? Did that require some adjustment on her part?

FOOTE

Well, a lot of adjustment. But you hear so many misconceptions about writing. The movies, for instance, present a writer's home life as somebody who wakes up in the middle of the night, runs back to his desk, and dashes off three thousand words. And sometimes his little wife will come in and put on a grand show and say, "I'm glad you're doing so well!"

Well, I would say, you know, "Get away! Let me alone! What in the hell is this?" I mean, I would never wake up in the middle of the night. I think probably the worst poetry and the worst prose ever that's been written is probably written under the influence of something called inspiration. That will really get in the way. It's all right to have ideas, but this inspiration stuff . . .

INTERVIEWER

You said somewhere that none of Hemingway's brain showed when he wrote.

FOOTE

Well, Hemingway was the writer [from whom] I first learned the true modern note, which is ambiguity. Take *The Sun Also Rises*. There can't be much doubt that Hemingway really despised [the character] Robert Cohn, and partly wrote the book because he disliked him so much and wanted to show him for what he was.

But Hemingway's eye was so accurate, and his impressions so good, when no thought went into it, that I think there's real good grounds for saying the only decent person in that book *is* Robert Cohn. Everybody else lives by a false code. He gets angry and breaks the code and this and that and the other. Dreadful man. But he's the only honest person. And that's something Hemingway could do. His writing eye and hand were completely accurate, no matter how fuddled he was in every other way.

A comparison to Hemingway, in a different art, is Vermeer the painter. Vermeer never has a picture that tells a story. It's just people going about household tasks, mostly. Or reading letters or writing letters or waiting for a letter or something. But there's no yearning, no mythology, except in some very early religious paintings. And yet, to me, they're the most beautiful paintings in the world, and highly dramatic. But the drama comes from where he clips off the edge of a hat or a gable of a little building and the mystery of perfection. There's that same ambiguity in Vermeer that I find in Hemingway.

INTERVIEWER

What would you advise—and we've already touched on this—young or even established writers who are looking to do the kind of things Hemingway did?

FOOTE

The first rule—and it's so simply stated that you feel ridiculous to have to state it—but the first rule is to learn how to write well. And that is done by doing it. Describe somebody crossing this room. The way his legs move, the way his head is, and the color of his eyes, and what his hair is like. Explain that. Do that so that it is—I guess *memorable* will do. So that it's real. And do it over and over and over again until you can do it so well that there's no pause between conception and execution. Your mind and your hand are hooked up to each other so that when you write, what's in your mind comes out on the paper.

You can only achieve that through very hard work, just like you'd learn how to be an acrobat or anything else. It's very hard work. A lot of rehearsal goes into being a good actor. And it's the same way. You have to learn your craft. And there are two ways to learn it. One, through reading craftsmen, and the other is through developing your craft until you get to the point where you can use it. The way William Faulkner did.

May 19, 1994

I read a good deal of Faulkner criticism, and they all ignore Faulkner's main talent, which was his ability to communicate sensation. He can tell you what it's like to be a fourteen-year-old boy and fall in a creek in Mississippi in November. He can tell you what it's like to walk across the grass out there at dawn, with the grass blades like limber icicles against your ankles. It's the use of metaphor to communicate feeling. Proust said that's the highest talent—to be able to do it through metaphor. One of my favorite modern writers is John O'Hara, who is one hell of a writer. And there's not a metaphor in all of O'Hara's fifty books. Not one.

INTERVIEWER

Do you think the gift for metaphor can be learned?

FOOTE

I think you can learn to do anything. Whether you do it well or not is something else. But it can be acquired. Hemingway is supposed to be a splendid example of a man who manufactured himself. He set out to be something that he became. He also set out and became something he didn't want to be, including a suicide. But he made himself.

There's another quality of good writers that ought to be examined more, and people pay no attention to it because they take it for granted— just like this ability to write well—and that is intelligence. There's a high intelligence in a good writer. It might not take the form of having any business sense and so forth, but he knows what he's doing, and he's got an acuteness of obser-

vation that can only come from intelligence. Faulkner was a highly intelligent man. It sounds silly to say it. But people pay no attention to it.

And a dumb fellow, a fellow who was pretty thick in the head, like Thomas Wolfe, he pays a big price for that lack of intelligence. It keeps him from being Faulkner.

INTERVIEWER

I'd like to ask about the writer and selfishness. When Hemingway and Hadley were first married, and they had very little money and most of that was hers, he rented a room in a hotel so he could write. That was a smart selfishness, I suppose.

FOOTE

No good writer would mind being called selfish. Faulkner said that "Ode on a Grecian Urn" was worth any number of little old ladies who could be sacrificed along the way.

Oh, there's a tremendous selfishness to most talented people. But it's not selfishness in the ordinary sense. He's not doing it for himself. He's doing it for what he can do. And those two might be difficult to separate, especially since he's liable to be a lousy writer who's taking advantage of that. A lot of good writers lived off their mothers and fathers. That never bothered them at all. They felt perfectly justified in doing anything. Some of them were real bastards, too.

INTERVIEWER

Tell me what you require in a room in order to write.

To feel at home there. I've never been able to write in hotel rooms or in trains or anywhere. Walker can. He can sit down and bang it out wherever he is. And D. H. Lawrence could do it superbly. Lawrence could write while talking to people. So could Keats. It's a very strange thing. Mozart. Writing the symphony down was nothing. He had it all absolutely crystal-clear in his head before he ever took the pen out. And he could chat while he was writing. But he had it all right here. [Taps his head.] He used to write, they say, at the dinner table. I swear it.

INTERVIEWER

What did you do to this room to turn it into a study? And how did you decide which room in the house you wanted for a study?

FOOTE

Because it's isolated, toward the back of things. And what I did was put in a bookcase, a desk. And made it what I wanted. That bed, I was conceived in. Look at it. It's a great heap of junk. But I guess certain things make me feel at home. That desk is about an inch and a half lower than most desks are. In fact, that table, too. But I like it that way.

INTERVIEWER

You really enjoy reading Henry James, don't you?

FOOTE

Very much. One of the best things I could advise anybody who wants to write, or even who just enjoys writing, is to pick a big writer and read him chronologically. Read his first book right on to his last book, and watch him grow. One of the richest experiences I ever had in my life was doing that with the thirty-six plays of William Shakespeare, as nearly as you can get them in chronology. And you watch that man grow, watch him get up to his peak, and then watch him stop caring.

INTERVIEWER

What about yourself and the idea of peaking and declining?

FOOTE

I don't think a writer is too aware of that. To give you another example, Faulkner wrote *The Hamlet* back in 1940. And then about 1952 or so, he began to write *The Town*. And James Meriwether, a Faulkner scholar, was able to point out a lot of discrepancies during this fifteen years or so between novels. Faulkner had forgotten, sometimes, the age or the name, the mannerisms of these people out of *The Hamlet*. So he typed up these discrepancies and handed them to Faulkner to use as a correction. And Faulkner said, "My goodness, I didn't realize how much I'd forgotten about these people. It's really quite simple, we'll go back to *The Hamlet* and change it."

Everybody was horrified, because they knew these books weren't as good as *The Hamlet*. But he thought they were. He thought they were much better. He said, "I've improved with age. These are much better."

But you don't know. And there's a good reason for that, whether you're just starting out or fixing to step into the grave. When a writer writes something and then reads it, he reads not just what's on the page. He reads what he *intended* to put on the page.

INTERVIEWER

And he reads in all the hard work the reader can't see.

FOOTE

That's right. And he thinks it's there. And it may not be there at all. You can, after say twenty years or so, read something with the eye that a stranger would have. But even then you're not too good at it. In fact, you're too mortified to read.

INTERVIEWER

I'd like you to be immodest for a minute. When you wake up in the morning and think that you wrote that Civil War trilogy, what do you think of yourself?

FOOTE

Well, it's like getting fat or anything. You were there the whole time. And it seemed like a perfectly natural thing to you. And in some kind of larger sense I do feel like a man who somehow managed to swallow a cannonball. But in the very largest sense I don't see how I or anybody else ever did it. No research assistant. No real library facilities. No training for history. So it does seem rather incredible. But I don't think of it that way. I think of sitting down and working seven hours a day until I'd written 1,650,000 words, and that was the end of it.

INTERVIEWER

Do you expect that at some point along the way, some editor at some publishing house will say it's time for the new history of the Civil War? Shelby Foote's history is outdated, or it needs a new look, or something? Or do you think you've put the lid on it for a while?

FOOTE

No. I fervently hope they'll do that. And what's more, I think they could do it. All Greek literature came out of the *Iliad*. And the Civil War is our *Iliad*. And it's inexhaustible. And it should be rewritten certainly once a generation. There are insights that were not available to me in the sixties and seventies. Yes, it ought to be done over and over again. And I expect, and fervently hope, that it will be done. It should be. It's an ongoing thing. It doesn't take away from me. If you'll allow an outrageous comparison: Horses are all the time breaking Man O' War's running records. It doesn't diminish Man O' War in the slightest. There are boxers who could probably punch Dempsey silly in one round. But it doesn't ruin Dempsey's accomplishments.

INTERVIEWER

Speaking of accomplishments, can they get in the way of writing?

FOOTE

I think to be twenty-three or twenty-four years old and to be on the cover of *Time* is extremely destructive. You are subject to . . . not to temptations, but to certain flatteries. To give interviews and things like that are serious interferences. They require you to take stock whether it's time for you to do it or not. They require you to formulate things that probably ought not be formulated. But that's only part of it. The other is, your privacy's shattered. I'm not talking about just intrusion. I'm talking about the notion of you that's floating around the country. It may be satisfying to your vanity, but it's not satisfying to your notion of yourself.

You sit down, as I did a few months ago, and read a book about you, biographical and critical. And it's all so petty. You say, "My God! Is that what I did? That's the barest little *edge* of what I did. And nobody's ever going to know what I did." And that's okay, but it's probably better not to have read it in the first place.

INTERVIEWER

When do you think this new novel, *Two Gates to the City*, will be finished?

FOOTE

I have no idea. Might not even finish it. And I don't particularly care about that. There's a wonderful urgency, you see, about writing, when you're going good. You wake up in the morning glad to wake up and get back to your desk. Wolf down your breakfast and come back. That's good. Course, it's also nice to mow the lawn.

INTERVIEWER

Do you have writer friends in Memphis?

FOOTE

I don't have a single writer friend in Memphis. I guess you'd call them society people. Empty-headed chatterers. The truth of the matter is, I don't have any hobbies and really don't have any friends. Most of the friends I have are friends I had when I was fifteen years old, and there are very few of those.

January 26, 1994

The mantel clock in Shelby Foote's study no longer strikes, but the wooden double bed where he was conceived is still there, as well as the black Eames chair with matching five-legged ottoman he bought as a reward when he completed the Civil War trilogy.

"We all get old," he says, "including clocks."

The fact is, Shelby Foote, born in 1916, does not appear to get old. In 1990, Foote advised Ken Burns on his eleven-hour landmark documentary on the Civil War, in which Foote appeared eighty-six times, giving the television audience cogent analysis and insider glimpses of the action.

During the five-night series, Foote's mellow charm and boyish good looks made him enormously popular, inspiring proposals of marriage from strangers, by mail and phone.

Does he like being our country's Civil War sex symbol?

Not particularly. To him, it's a lot of foolishness.

But he's not going to allow it to make him take his name out of the Memphis phone book, where it's been for the last fifty years.

Proposals aren't the only calls.

"Five men will be in a drinking contest arguing about whether Lee or Grant was the greater general," he says, "and they'll call me to settle the argument."

This January morning, Foote talks about what a historian can learn from a novelist, his friendship with the late Walker Percy, and what he discovered about William Faulkner when he took Faulkner on a tour of the Shiloh battlefield.

INTERVIEWER

I've been struck by the vividness of your writing in the trilogy. Here are two examples I particularly like. You were talking about the Anaconda, and you said this: "This 3,000 mile coastal portion, belly and crotch of the continent, bisected by the phallic droop of the Florida peninsula . . ."

And in describing a man named Slidell, you wrote, "His companion Slidell was five years older and looked it, with narrowed eyes and a knife-blade nose, his mouth twisted bitterly awry and his pink scalp shining through lank white locks that clamped the upper half of his face like a pair of parentheses." Nothing dry about this.

FOOTE

That is what makes me the kind of historian I am. I believe historians have a great deal to learn from novelists. Henry Adams, in fact, was a nov-

elist and a historian. And Tacitus. He's a very great historian and a true favorite of mine.

My favorite historians do two things. First, they know the value of descriptive writing that will nail a thing down in people's minds. And they know how to organize their histories the way a novelist organizes a novel—with a beginning, a middle, and an end, and various connections inside. That's narrative history. I maintain it has many virtues. What you really want is for people to understand some stretch of American or other history.

In addition to that, a good novelist knows that in handling characters, he won't do a very effective job if you spend your whole time running down some character. The reader will even develop sympathy for him. A good historian will know that as well as a novelist. He will be able to see things from his side, give him his virtues as well as his faults. There will always be both.

Historians frequently make up their minds, and their dislike shows so plainly. George McClellan is often presented as a lousy general. And there's some truth in that. But he was also the real architect of the Army of the Potomac. If it hadn't been for McClellan's work in organizing the Army of the Potomac, then Grant would not have had that army to win the war with.

INTERVIEWER

A colleague from New Jersey says Northerners don't go around bragging about Grant the way we still brag about Lee here in the South.

This phenomenon amuses him, and he says he wonders what it's all about.

FOOTE

Everybody knows that the fights you lose, you remember. Of the nearly hundred fistfights I had growing up, the ones I remember are the ones I lost.

INTERVIEWER

This same colleague also wonders what on earth gave the Confederates the notion they'd be able to win such a war, outnumbered as they were by the Union army. He thinks it might be pure Southern male swagger.

FOOTE

Leaving the swagger aside for a moment, the Confederate soldiers had at least some good reason to think they could win: The American Revolution. Those colonies didn't have a chance against the military power of England. And yet they won. In the very darkest times of the Civil War, Southerners could look back to very dark times in the Revolution. Valley Forge.

The answer, of course, is that we won the American Revolution because France came into the war. In the first two years of the Civil War, there was the hope that England and France would come in. In the last two years, there was the hope that Lincoln would be defeated in the Northern election. His opponent was running on a peace plank.

And there was a third thing. A Southern boast.

But also sort of an American boast. You didn't say, "I give up." You didn't say, "I surrender." Until, of course, you had to. [Laughter.]

INTERVIEWER

Last time, we talked about one of your grandparents. But we didn't mention your parents. What were they like?

FOOTE

They were born in the 1890s. My father died before he was thirty-one. My mother never remarried. I don't want to echo Richard Nixon, who said, "My mother was a saint." Which she was not. And my mother was not a saint either. But she often had some of those qualities. She never hurt my feelings. She had a lot of chances to do that because I could be a real jackass. She never said, "There you go again. Here you are in trouble with the school authorities. Just look at you." She could get very angry with me, and she could give me spankings and everything else. But she never hurt my feelings.

INTERVIEWER

I think that's the nicest thing anyone could say about a mother.

FOOTE

I do, too.

INTERVIEWER

When you were advising on the Civil War documentary, I'm wondering if there was one single thing you had to keep hammering home to the film writers. Some aspect of the war, maybe, that was difficult to demythologize.

FOOTE

Yes. It's the same thing we need to hear over and over again: The whole damn war wasn't fought in Virginia. Virginia seemed to think that the real war was fought there, and there was all this large-scale skirmishing going on everywhere in the Confederacy.

For instance, what difference did it make if they lost Tennessee? Finally, what difference did it make if they lost New Orleans and the Mississippi River? The opposite [what difference if they lost Virginia?] is not true. But I believe it's closer to the truth. Lee had seven different opponents. They skirmished up and down that line between Washington and Richmond for four years.

The real reason that historians have seen it that way, the Virginia way, is that the war got not only more publicity—all the photographers were there, the big-time reporters were—it got the play in the big-time newspapers which were there.

There were more large battles in Virginia than anywhere else. Nobody wants to take away from that. What I resent is their not paying attention to what went on elsewhere.

INTERVIEWER

When I last interviewed you, you'd read Marcel Proust's *Remembrance of Things Past* seven times. How many times have you reread it in the last ten years?

FOOTE

Twice more.

INTERVIEWER

With increasing pleasure?

FOOTE

Mounting pleasure. It's a theory of mine that when people want to know whether they should take creative writing, I tell them that by reading the great writers of the past and especially by *rereading* them is how to learn to write. When you know where he's going, you can better perceive how he went about getting there. And that's what can teach you really about writing.

INTERVIEWER

You were a mentor to your good friend Walker Percy. Did you have a mentor?

FOOTE

I wasn't Walker's mentor. We were coworkers. And we differed on many things. Each of us was interested in the other's work, and we were always happy to comment on it, praise it, blame it, anything else. I had published five novels by the time he had published his first one, so I was in an advisory position about the publishing business, sort of.

INTERVIEWER

Yet I read the letter you wrote to Percy in Jay Tolson's biography of Percy, *Pilgrim in the Ruins*, in which you said to him, "Sit down with pen and paper and describe anything at all: do it again and again—either an object or an action—

until you satisfy yourself. Then try telling a story that has a beginning, middle, and end. Then tear it up and do it over, and over, and over."

FOOTE

Yeah, I said that. But I still don't think of myself as Walker's mentor. Nobody contributed to his greatness like he did himself.

INTERVIEWER

While Percy was writing his seventh novel, *The Second Coming*, you sent him Beethoven's quartets, the Fourteenth and Fifteenth. The first, you called the most beautiful piece of music ever written. Interestingly, he wrote you that the music influenced the structure of his novel. But what I'd like to hear you talk about is the joy you yourself experience in listening to good music.

FOOTE

The joy is right there on the face of it, and I don't see how anybody could not experience that joy of hearing beautiful music. Beautiful music is a lot more than pretty tunes. The really instructive thing about music is when you study it enough to know how it's made, how it's built. For instance, the sonata form. You lay it out and you develop it, and then you recapitulate it. You can use the sonata form in writing a novel. It's like they often say in an army lecture, "Tell them what you're going to tell them. Tell them. Then tell them what you've told them." That's the sonata form.

INTERVIEWER

You're really completely self-educated about music, aren't you?

FOOTE

When I first was attracted to music I was very leery of learning anything technical about it. I thought it would interfere with the pleasure. But the more you know about music, the way it's written and played, the more you can appreciate it. I finally took the trouble to learn how to read scores. I still can't play any instrument and never will play an instrument. What I discovered was, my eye showed me things my ear had not noticed until then. For instance, in playing a string quartet—two violins, a viola, and a cello—your eye is moving along the score, and all of sudden your eye is saying, "Look what the viola was doing." And then you hear it. As I say, I was very leery about getting into the technicalities of music. I thought it would interfere. It did interfere. But in a very good way. It made me understand better what I was getting pleasure from.

INTERVIEWER

You told me this anecdote once, when I interviewed you soon after Walker Percy died. But I wish you'd tell me again—how you loved FDR and Percy hated FDR and the incident about the Roosevelt dime.

FOOTE

We were driving out to Santa Fe—it was 1946—and we stopped to get gas at a filling station. He was asleep on the back seat. I went to get the gas, and when they gave me my change, there was a Roosevelt dime. I put the dime right in the hollow of my palm, and I put it right up in his face, and I woke him up and said, "Look at that!" He woke up and began to curse. I have hundreds of funny stories about Walker.

Once, we were driving—we were both awake then, he was driving—and I looked out the window and there on a fence rail beside the road was a scissortail flycatcher. It was a beautiful bird, and Walker is almost an ornithologist, and I had never paid too much attention to birds. I said, "Look, Walker. There's a scissortail flycatcher." He was indignant that I knew its name. It was like I'd overheard some password I wasn't supposed to know.

INTERVIEWER

You were like brothers, weren't you?

FOOTE

We were. Walker had two brothers, and I had none, you see.

INTERVIEWER

Could you say what the friendship with Walker Percy meant to you?

FOOTE

No. I could not. That would be very hard to say. Walker and I were never sentimental, and I don't trust myself to talk about it without falling into some dreadful form of sentimentality.

INTERVIEWER

It seems to me your friendship was close and profound and very funny.

FOOTE

It was.

INTERVIEWER

Do you think the friendships—like yours with Percy—are richer for having formed in adolescence?

FOOTE

Yes, and I have a whole theory on that that interests me very much. It's because we're not only impressionable, but the impressions really sink in. They're like writing on a blank space. What happens to you during those years stays with you forever. It's not cluttered up with a lot of other things.

I went to high school in a town of about fifteen thousand, and there were about four hundred of us in the school. In those days, that was every white child in that town between the ages of fourteen and eighteen. We all knew each other during those very impressionable years, and we were likely to spend the rest of our lives associating with each other. That was of enormous value. You got to know the son of the president of the bank and the son of the sharecropper, and you got to know them in ways you never could the rest of your life. The only way that could have been improved upon is if there were blacks in the school, and there weren't.

I claim that to the extent that I understand different classes of people, different types of people, especially girls and boys, the very foundation of everything I know about human nature, at firsthand, I learned in high school. That and the army.

INTERVIEWER

You met Faulkner a year after you left Chapel Hill, and you became friends. Later, you gave him a tour of the Shiloh battlefield. Describe that tour, if you would, and Faulkner's interest in the battlefield. Did you take pleasure in showing him the site?

FOOTE

I did. It taught me something else. I knew Faulkner was a talented man amounting to genius, and I thought that sort of stood by itself. But I found something else: His perception, his ready understanding of Shiloh, which is one of the most confusing fields in the world. I've been over the ground at least a hundred times, and I can get turned around and lost, but he immediately grasped the layout, understood what had happened and had a much clearer understanding of it than anybody I'd shown it to.

What I mean by this is a very simple statement: He was a highly intelligent man. That was hardly a piece of news. But it sort of was. Anybody with that much talent, you would think his intelligence would take a back seat. But intelligence is a quality that you usually don't factor in. It's not like perception. It's not like emotional response. But it's enormously important. And that trip over Shiloh taught me how important it is. I think most great writers had a pretty high IQ as a matter of course. You wouldn't think a highly intelligent man would become an alcoholic, but it happens all the time.

INTERVIEWER

I've been thinking about your grandfather Morris Rosenstock, who came to Mississippi from Vienna, Austria, when he was seventeen, went to work keeping books for a planter, and married the planter's daughter. It seems to me you're more like him than anyone else in your family.

FOOTE

I sort of decided that, too, on sort of factual evidence. Nowhere in my family is there any sign of connection with art, in any form. And yet he had a daughter by his second wife—my mother and her two sisters were the children of his first wife—and that daughter, whose name is Morrisse Rosenstock, turned out to be quite an accomplished painter. She lectures on art to this day—she's in her eighties—up in Pennsylvania.

INTERVIEWER

You wrote an introduction to a new Modern Library edition of Stephen Crane's Civil War story, "The Red Badge of Courage." And you wrote a foreword to Thomas B. Allen's *The Blue and the Gray*. Are you doing other such introductions and forewords?

FOOTE

Yes. I've gotten out for the Modern Library the longer stories of Chekhov's last decade. And now I'm doing two volumes of Chekhov's other stories—going back to all of the stories except those longer stories. It will be a three-volume set.

There's Walker in me again. We're both crazy about Chekhov. Neither one of us can figure out what makes him so great. He'll have a little scene that's almost nothing, and it'll bowl you over.

INTERVIEWER

You and Walker both watched the TV soap "As the World Turns." When one of you missed it, the other would fill him in. I know Olive Ann Burns finally figured out how she was going to tell her novel, *Cold Sassy Tree*, from watching soaps. Do you think a writer can learn something about writing from watching TV?

FOOTE

Absolutely. But that's such an open, all-inclusive question. A good writer can learn from anything. He can learn from a week in Hollywood, Las Vegas, or Disneyland.

INTERVIEWER

In looking back over your life, do you feel gratitude that you've been able to do exactly what you wanted to do—read and write and listen to music—and that something you created will live on?

FOOTE

Freud said that there are three reasons for an artist to do what he does. The search for fame. Money. And the love of women.

He didn't include inspiration or any of those

things. And I don't argue with that. I don't think that's an unfair estimate of the motivations of artists.

INTERVIEWER

But there's been so much more for you.

FOOTE

Of course, I can't imagine living any other kind of life. At the same time, I'm extremely grateful that I was well into my adolescence—sixteen or seventeen—before I narrowed it down to it being my main interest. I wouldn't take anything for the years I spent helling around in the Mississippi Delta, drinking and all that. It was an extremely valuable experience. I did not lead an ivory-tower adolescence.

INTERVIEWER

Nor do you now.

FOOTE

That's right. There's nothing else I really cared about once I found what I really wanted. There were other things I really enjoyed. But nothing else I cared about like I cared about writing.

———

The only child of Shelby Dade and Lillian Rosenstock Foote, Shelby Foote was born in Greenville, Mississippi, November 17, 1916. At fifteen, he formed a lifelong friendship with Walker Percy, who had moved with his brothers and mother to Greenville to live with their cousin, William Alexander Percy.

Foote graduated from Greenville High School

in 1935. That fall, he entered UNC-Chapel Hill, where he stayed until 1937, reading voraciously and attending few classes.

In 1939, he joined the Mississippi National Guard, and in 1940, the United States Army, rising to captain before he was "kicked completely out" during service in Ireland for leaving to see his girlfriend, Tess Lavery.

In 1945, he enlisted in the United States Marine Corps, where he served ten months.

He has served as novelist-in-residence at the University of Virginia in Charlottesville; playwright-in-residence at Arena Stage, Washington, D.C.; and writer-in-residence at Hollins College in Hollins College, Virginia.

His novels are *Tournament* (1949), *Follow Me Down* (1950), *Love in a Dry Season* (1951), *Shiloh* (1952), *Jordan County* (1954), and *September, September* (1979).

In 1954, Foote started work on what he thought would be a single-volume history of the Civil War. The first volume, *Fort Sumter to Perryville*, came out in 1958; the second, *Fredericksburg to Meridian*, in 1963; and the third, *Red River to Appomattox*, in 1974.

Foote has won three Guggenheim fellowships, a Ford Foundation grant, and the Fletcher Pratt Award for *The Civil War: A Narrative*.

In 1944, Foote married Tess Lavery.

In September 1947, he married Marguerite Dessommes. They have one child, Margaret Shelby, born in 1948.

On September 6, 1956, Foote married Gwyn Rainer Shea. They have a son, Huger Lee, born in 1961.

Foote lives with his wife, Gwyn, in Memphis, Tennessee, where he is working on a seventh novel, *Two Gates to the City*.

April 5, 1994

KAYE GIBBONS

April 4, 1987

"*D*ear Louis," wrote Walker Percy to Algonquin Books publisher Louis Rubin on August 29, 1986. "You're right about *Ellen Foster*. I read it once, put it down for a couple of weeks, read it again to be sure. I'm sure. It's the real thing. Which is to say: a lovely, breath-taking, sometimes heart-wrenching first novel."

Rubin had also sent galleys to Eudora Welty.

"What a delight you've let me in for," Welty wrote Rubin. "The life in it, the honesty of thought and eye and feeling and word."

Kaye Gibbons knew she'd hit on something when she started *Ellen Foster*. It "scared my pants off," she says, but she sat right down and finished the manuscript in about six weeks.

It was Louis Rubin, Gibbons's Southern literature professor at UNC-Chapel Hill, who read the first thirty pages and encouraged her to complete the manuscript.

All her life, Gibbons had dreamed of writing herself out of her environment. She grew up poor in rural Nash County and moved to Rocky Mount when she was fourteen. No one in town seemed to like the girl with the thick glasses who read all the time. Gibbons's next-door neighbor called her a redneck.

Last week, Gibbons was presented the Louis D. Rubin Jr. Prize in Creative Writing for 1987, as the most outstanding fiction writer in the graduating class.

Kaye and husband Michael Gibbons, a Raleigh landscape architect, have one daughter, Mary, two and a half, and they are expecting another child this year.

On this overcast April day, Gibbons, who is battling morning sickness, talks about growing up "eating poems," about bursting into tears when Louis Rubin told her she was a writer, and about the questions she asks herself at the end of every day: "Did you have a good time?" and "Did you do anything that's tax-deductible?"

INTERVIEWER

What was it like when you discovered you and literature clicked?

GIBBONS

When I was four or five, I remember sitting on the back porch with my daddy reading the newspaper. I learned to read and to tie my mama's apron behind my back at the same time. My father was very proud of me for doing that. So that was my first stroke.

INTERVIEWER

What did you read when you were young?

GIBBONS

I liked to read meaty stuff when I was in late elementary school. It just filled me up. I also read the encyclopedias. *Child Craft Encyclopedia* had poems in them. And I ate poems for the very young. Then poems for older children. I just loved them. I remember in fifth grade in Miss Daniels' class we were sent home to memorize two poems from our textbook. And I didn't find anything in there that turned me on. So I went to the encyclopedia and looked up—under *P*—Poems.

And I went back to school, and I'll never forget sitting on the front row, and I just said, "'Let me not to the marriage of true minds / Admit impediments. Love is not love / Which bends with the remover to remove.'"

Miss Daniels had one shoulder higher than the other one. And she looked down on that low shoulder and just stared at me.

When I got through with that, I said, "'Be-cause I could not stop for death / It kindly stopped for me.' Emily Dickinson."

I felt like with the name Shakespeare and Emily Dickinson that I was somebody. I always wanted to read people I'd heard of or that I could look up in the encyclopedia. That was my way of connecting with something larger than I would ever hope to be.

INTERVIEWER

Do you suppose—growing up in rural Nash County—that language itself helped you connect with a larger world?

GIBBONS

The language of literature has always meant more to me than the plot or the character. I was always interested in why the author chose the words. Sometimes now when I read, I rewrite the sentence in a different way to see if I can do the same thing. I do that a lot with William Faulkner. But while I was reading it, I was writing at the same time. So I feel like I helped write *The Sound and the Fury*.

So my theory is that when you spend a life that deeply enmeshed in art, that it's in you and there's nothing else for you to do but write about it. I also believe we all have different ways of putting order to what goes on around us. Other people exercise to order their days. I use language to order my past. I feel like if I can get all of that in order, then I have a network for the future and everything will be okay.

INTERVIEWER

Tell me more about your childhood.

GIBBONS

We were so poor. Well, we weren't that poor. But I didn't eat in a restaurant until I was fourteen. I never remember having a baby-sitter. We just stayed at home, and I read and watched television.

INTERVIEWER

What kind of child were you?

GIBBONS

I worked very hard at not getting into trouble, because my getting into trouble would've been a distraction, and my parents were trying hard just to survive. I just did my own thing. I was terribly independent.

I have upstairs a report card from the second grade. It says, "Little Kaye knows what to do and she does it." I'm very proud of that, because I believe that's the way one should be. So when I was a child, I got along. And I used literature to help show me how to do it.

INTERVIEWER

Were there other things that helped you get along?

GIBBONS

When I was eight years old, I memorized one hundred Bible verses and was sent to Children's Bible Mission Camp at Falls of the Neuse River. I thought we were in Egypt. It seemed like the bus ride took forever. It only took an hour, but I'd never been anywhere. Oh, it was so much fun. So I went there and learned about the Lord and stuff for a week. And every year I would

memorize Bible verses and go back. I never won the big spelling bee because I misspelled *boulevard*. Stuart Lamb won.

Anytime I caught drift of a camp deal, I would join the club and go. I joined the Girl Scouts to go to camp. There was no other way to go anywhere. That was my ticket. That and the books. I joined the Woodmen of the World Rangerettes to go to their camp, and Four-H. So I got to go to four camps, and that can pretty much eat up a summer. I arranged all this myself.

INTERVIEWER

What if you hadn't been so bright?

GIBBONS

I would have been pregnant at sixteen. Married to someone who wears his undershirt at the dinner table. I would spend my days having to soak UPC symbols off the Wisk bottles, whereas now I choose to stay at home, and I don't think I could tolerate having to.

What literature did for me was to say, "There is a way out, and it's in this book." It wasn't that I dreamed about living with Louisa May Alcott. I didn't dream about living in the Puss 'n' Boots palace. I just dreamed about using language the way they did. To write myself out of it.

I think that for art to become engendered in a person, there has to be some friction somewhere. There has to be a crack for that flower to come up in.

INTERVIEWER

Where was the friction—the crack—in your life?

GIBBONS

Being poor in a community of semiliterate people. So there was a distance between my neighbor, Chicken Stew—that was his name— and the people I was reading about in *Wuthering Heights* and *Jane Eyre*. The distance between Chicken Stew's daughter, Sap Head, and Jane Eyre. That was an incredible distance!

INTERVIEWER

And there was a distance between you and your environment.

GIBBONS

I moved from the country into town when I was fourteen, and I was not only the new kid in town, but I was that new girl with the thick glasses who read so much. I was not invited to things. I was asked, "Was your mother a debutante?" I hated being ostracized. But now I am so glad, because a power has come out of it, and I think that past has given me enough momentum to last I hope a long career at my typewriter.

INTERVIEWER

You've said after you wrote the book you felt relaxed for the first time in your life. Did writing *Ellen Foster* help change your attitude about your past?

GIBBONS

I've spent a lot of time hiding from the past and not wanting to think about it or deal with what I had come from. And feeling ashamed of it. And when I started writing *Ellen*, I said, "I can use this stuff. I can use those feelings. They don't have to swirl around anymore unorganized. I can set those feelings down."

It's not that any of the details in the book are true. But all the feelings are. And the book is a girl's search for order. She likes the hedge bushes square. She likes everything neat and in a row. And in a way, that's what I was doing with my history. I was ordering everything I'd ever thought about and read. It was like all the books I had ever eaten came up while I was writing her.

INTERVIEWER

Did you know right away you were onto something good?

GIBBONS

One day I wrote a poem, and I heard Ellen's voice. And I liked her. I said, "This is strong. This is so strong." And I started [on the novel] the next day. And I was scared of it. I was as scared of it as I was the first time I read that Shakespeare poem. Sometimes I feel like all art and good things flow in an underground stream. And I feel that the important authors have been able to drill a hole down there and hit it. I felt like I had hit it, and it scared my pants off.

INTERVIEWER

What did you do when you realized you might have a novel?

GIBBONS

When I had thirty pages written, I gave it to my Southern literature teacher, Dr. Louis Rubin, because I knew that the man who'd been teaching me literature would know if I was writing it.

The day after I gave him the pages, he called me into his office. And he looked at me and said, "It's exciting. It's compelling. You're a writer."

And I burst into tears. I felt like somebody feels like when you wait for somebody to ask you to marry them. You wait all your life to hear it, and you go out to dinner, and they sit there and they ask you. And it just emptied my whole system out and filled me up with my favorite thing.

INTERVIEWER
What was that?

GIBBONS
Knowing that I was okay. When somebody asks you to marry them, it's the same thing. It's an affirmation that, yes, you are valued.

All my life, literature has been half of me. And so having my husband ask me to marry him took care of one half. Now, the other half was taken care of. And I said, "I've done it. I can do anything now."

So I just cried and cried. And my next class was Shakespeare, and we were reading about *Antony and Cleopatra*. And she was floating down the river on the barge, and he [the professor] read the part aloud where she applied the asp to herself. And that is sad, but I was sitting in the back of the class still crying. And people looked at me like, "You're real tore up over that Cleopatra."

And I thought, "It's not Cleopatra. It's *not* Cleopatra. I'm a *writer*."

INTERVIEWER
Dr. Rubin is head of Algonquin Books of Chapel Hill. Did he say, "Go ahead and finish this and let me see it when you're through?"

GIBBONS
He said, "To tell you the truth, I think you're going to need some help working with this first-person narrator." And to me, that was not acceptable. I said, "Thank you," but I knew in my head I would do it myself. That was the end of November 1985, and January 1, 1986, he had the book. I told him I was going to have it, and I didn't see the point of dragging it out.

I had spent a long time agonizing over uncompleted projects in the rest of my life. We all have dresses under the bed we've cut out. And I made myself a promise that it wasn't going to happen with this book, because I knew I had put such a store of personal faith in it that if I let myself down I'd be a severely depressed person.

INTERVIEWER
What was your method of getting this done?

GIBBONS
I developed a routine. Some people say that one can't be creative on schedule. But I think my imagination was at such a heightened point that it just came. I put Mary at the baby-sitter's, came home, got my coffee, and started my typewriter buzzing.

INTERVIEWER

You transferred to UNC from North Carolina State in Raleigh.

How did you happen to choose State?

GIBBONS

I wanted to go to Duke or Wake Forest. But there was no way. I was not competitive for that caliber of scholarship that gets one to those high-powered schools. I was not a well-rounded individual. One has to be able to afford to be well-rounded. In the South, that doesn't come cheap. You have to pay for lessons.

But I won a North Carolina Governor's Scholarship through my father's involvement with the Big One [World War II] to go to any state-supported school I wanted to. And I didn't realize UNC was state-supported. I knew that all the more affluent kids in my school were going there, and I just assumed it was not something I could do.

INTERVIEWER

You've said you're glad you can choose not to work outside the home. Why?

GIBBONS

In some ways I guess I'm a very traditional person. Michael says I like to imagine that I'm pregnant all the time. I just would like to have a lot of children, because I think that I can take responsibility for the future of society in a small way by raising responsible people. And I think I can do more good for my world by staying home and writing and raising children than by working at a university or a newspaper.

INTERVIEWER

What if you didn't have your writing?

GIBBONS

On days that I don't write while Mary's asleep, I look at my *Redbook* magazine. I'm a big coupon clipper. Michael will tell you that the days I save over 20 percent on my grocery bill are red-letter days in this house. I'm very excited, and I make him ooh and aah over it. It would be like if I'd brought in the big account for my company.

It's nice to be able to clip coupons in the morning and go a little bit crazy in the afternoon. At twelve-thirty, I put Mary down for a nap, have my sandwich, and watch "The Young and the Restless."

INTERVIEWER

Do you usually write every day?

GIBBONS

Usually, I write every day while Mary naps. But if I don't have anything to write, I certainly wouldn't do it. I don't sit down until I have the first sentence. If I have the first sentence in my head, I can go. But it's an awful feeling for me to sit down at the typewriter and tap the pencil and hold a coffee cup and look pensively out my window waiting for a thought to come.

INTERVIEWER

How do you feel at the end of a good writing stint?

GIBBONS

I feel very pleased. And I feel good to be doing something constructive and worthwhile. And I feel like I'm making up for a lot of lost time.

At the end of every day I ask two questions: "Did you have a good time?" and "Did you do anything that's tax-deductible?"

INTERVIEWER

Well, do you usually have a good time?

GIBBONS

Since I wrote *Ellen Foster* the answer generally is yes. Writing the book was a freeing experience for me, and it gave me some confidence. I used to say, "Oh, I can't do anything." Well, I can now. I can write a book. Before I wrote *Ellen Foster*, I didn't have anything. I could throw my hip out and make it pop, but that was it.

March 28, 1991

A year and a half ago, Kaye Gibbons and her husband, Michael, circled the wagons. There was a lot going on in the Gibbons household. Three daughters—Mary, Leslie, and Louise— under age four. A move to a new house. International fame from *Ellen Foster*. A second novel, *A Virtuous Woman*, completed, and a third, *A Cure for Dreams*, in the works. As well as episodes of manic-depression, which every couple of years could send Kaye to the hospital.

Something had to give. In October 1989, the Gibbonses made a decision. Michael would quit his job and become Mr. Mom.

Today, Kaye reports that life just keeps getting "sweller and sweller."

It's a life she's earned. At age ten, the Nash County native lost her mother to suicide and her father to alcoholism. She was shuffled from relative to relative until 1979, when she enrolled at North Carolina State University in Raleigh.

When she began to fictionalize her traumatic childhood, the heart-tugging *Ellen Foster* was born. At last, Kaye was doing what she was born to do.

This month and next, Gibbons is touring the country to promote *A Cure for Dreams*, set in the Carolina Piedmont.

Today, she talks about her writing, her parents, and her manic-depression, which she manages, in part, "by being true to myself."

INTERVIEWER

In April and May, you'll travel to twenty-three cities promoting *A Cure for Dreams*. Do you enjoy this end of the publishing business?

GIBBONS

Writing is so lonely, if I didn't have this going on I would never see humanity except at Harris Teeter. But it's not glamorous at all. A twenty-three-city book tour is a forty-six-cheeseburger trip. I get in town too late to get anything good for lunch. So I say, "I'll just have a cheeseburger." I come back after room service is closed. So I say, "I'll just grab a cheeseburger." Rudolf Nureyev, the dancer, just did a sixty-four-cheeseburger tour. Maybe we'll meet in Denver at McDonald's.

INTERVIEWER

Are you a good shopper and packer for these trips?

GIBBONS

I used to take everything I owned. Then I realized I had to carry this stuff myself. Now, I take just a couple of knit dresses. I can get away with that. A writer can be eccentric and look sloppy. I've got my hair cut and bleached. I'm blond now. I just mousse and go.

INTERVIEWER

Has your writing schedule stayed pretty much the same?

GIBBONS

I start about 9:00, after the "Today" show, then I work until 12:30 P.M. My office is at home. Now, I have a MacIntosh computer that I love. Over my computer, I keep a story Mary has written for me. It says, "My Mom is a writer. She writes boox and she plays with us." I've boiled life down to writing books and playing with my family.

INTERVIEWER

Your three novels are only about 150 pages each. Now, you're writing a big book, a sequel to *A Cure for Dreams*. You say this one could be 350 pages. What happened?

GIBBONS

I don't know. Maybe now that the children are getting older, and I'm secure and settled down, I can stretch out into a longer format. I never

know how to write. Every book I make up a new way and say, "This is the way to write."

INTERVIEWER

When we first talked, four years ago this month, you said little about your family background. Then, about two years ago, at the American Booksellers Association convention in Washington, D.C., you told a reporter your mother had committed suicide and your father was an alcoholic. Are you glad now you made these things public?

GIBBONS

I'm glad I did. I felt so bad about lying about it. Lying about it is a form of denial. I think that by working with the Adult Children of Alcoholics group, I was able to see that my family background is not a reflection of my character at this time. It has informed my personality development, but I should be able to get beyond it. I think that I could only tell the truth when I had enough self-esteem to do it.

For a while, that's all people wanted to talk about. But that was to be expected. Now, I'm able to talk about my work without curiosity seekers. Recently, I've been able to talk about being manic-depressive.

INTERVIEWER

What really held you back?

GIBBONS

For a long time, I was very embarrassed for anybody to know. I was acting as if mental illness were a stigma. But it's not. Manic-depression is just like diabetes. As long as I take a medication every day, it's a managed illness.

I have breakthrough episodes about every other year [when hospitalization is required]. I wouldn't give anything for the time I've spent in the hospital. I've met wonderful people. It's not uncommon to be in a restaurant or at the state fair and see my ex-hospital roommates.

INTERVIEWER

Have you ever experienced a surge in creativity during a "breakthrough"?

GIBBONS

I wrote *Ellen Foster* on one of the creative loops of the manic-depressive cycle.

INTERVIEWER

Were you aware of that at the time?

GIBBONS

Yes. I was afraid I would crash after I wrote it, and I did. I went to my doctor while I was writing the book and sort of kept a rein on it. It's hereditary. My mother suffered from major depression before lithium and before Prozac and before the enlightened medications that are available now. I feel horrible for what she must have gone through.

If you look at manic-depression on a scale of zero to ten, with zero being the doldrums and ten being uncontrolled mania, when I am working at about six and a half, I'm very productive, and I think that I'm very alert. Anything after that, I start to get confused, and I start to lose my judgment about my creativity.

INTERVIEWER

How do you manage your illness other than with medication?

GIBBONS

Principally by remaining true to myself and honest with myself. Being a writer is a dangerous profession for a manic-depressive because so much of the success of being a writer now feels unreal. It has a fantasy quality to it. But I try to read the reviews, and then throw them in the file box, and then get on with real life.

I think that trying to see myself through my children's eyes—and sometimes it's not a very pretty picture—chastens me. It keeps me on the straight and narrow.

INTERVIEWER

You seem to understand your illness very well.

GIBBONS

I am one of the very, very few people with that sort of illness who's able to stay in charge. And I feel lucky. I feel lucky that my husband understands the early warning signals. If I say, "I feel like if I sat up all night for a few nights, I could finish this book," then he says, "Uh, have you had your level checked?"

INTERVIEWER

You're hooked on the afternoon TV soap "The Young and the Restless." What's the appeal?

GIBBONS

I've been watching it for fifteen years. I know

everybody. I know them well. I know Victor Newman like I know my husband. I can remember when Nikki was a stripper at the Bayou.

When I was a little girl, I used to sit in the beauty shop with my mother every Friday, and she would watch "The Secret Storm." I probably associate watching the "stories," as she used to call them, with my mother. There's so little that I have left of her, this is one way I can keep up a connection.

INTERVIEWER
Your next novel, *Eagle Avenue*, is set in

April 5, 1994

Alameda, California, during World War II. Your parents lived on Eagle Avenue in Alameda during that time. I understand you have someone scouting for letters from that period. Are these letters a way of re-creating your parents' lives?

GIBBONS
I really think it is. When I was writing *A Cure for Dreams*, I kept saying to myself, "This is the relationship I wanted to have with my father."

My aunts can tell me things about my mother: She was clever, she was witty. But those things feel superficial to me. So [by writing] I can pretend that I had a mother who continued to live, and this is my way of knowing her.

INTERVIEWER
And what about the relationship with your father in this new book?

GIBBONS
This time, my father is [the character] Herman's father. This way, I'm working on my father and making him into the man I wanted him to be.

INTERVIEWER
You've accepted the way he was?

GIBBONS
He was a brilliant man, and he could do anything he set his mind to. He was a Renaissance farmer. I want to, more in my writing, explore the good points of his personality, which were there and which some members of my family choose to neglect.

If you had stayed in Nash County, if you had married young and hadn't become a writer, where would those writing energies have gone? Lottie in *A Cure for Dreams* reminds me of someone who might have been a writer if someone had shown her the way.

GIBBONS

I think it would have gone into being the queen bee of Bend of the River Road [where Gibbons grew up]. I probably would have run rummy games out of the back room of the store. I'd have been secretly in charge of my household. There's no way I can be secretly in charge of this house. My husband is too in charge. If I try to pretend I'm in charge, he catches me. He exposes me. If I had stayed in Nash County and married a nice boy from my school, I could've been in charge and probably not have gotten caught.

INTERVIEWER

As precisely as you can, describe what it's like for you when your writing is going well.

GIBBONS

I've begun to compare it to looking out a window. It's a very clear window, and I can see everything that's going on out there. And even though the window's down, I can hear everything. It's like a scene played in my imagination, and I listen and I write it down.

March 23, 1994

In 1992, the Gibbonses moved to California. There, the marriage came apart, and Kaye returned to Raleigh with the girls and started divorce proceedings. She fell in love with Raleigh attorney Frank Ward, whose book reviews in the Raleigh *News and Observer* she had admired for years. When they married in Raleigh's Christ Episcopal Church in September 1993, she wore a long-sleeved ivory gown with a damask skirt. "It's a Laura Ashley," she said. "Just go ahead and put that in the paper. People wonder."

The evening before, at their rehearsal dinner, Frank toasted Kaye, quoting a contemporary of Sir Walter Raleigh's, who described Raleigh as "one that fortune had picked out of purpose . . . and tossed him up and out of nothing, and to and fro to greatness."

"It is my good fortune," said Frank Ward, "to have been tossed up to the strong sweetness of Kaye Gibbons. And that—to steal the last line of *Ellen Foster*—will always amaze me."

Since *Ellen Foster*, Kaye Gibbons has matured as a person and a writer. She talks freely about her mother's suicide, her father's alcoholism, and her own and her mother's manic-depression.

As a writer, she no longer feels that locating her novels in a specific place signifies provincialism. Her fourth novel, *Charms for the Easy Life*, originally called *Eagle Avenue* and set in California, is set specifically in Raleigh.

Kaye is also systematic about the study of her craft. She knows exactly which novels to turn to for learning what she needs to learn for her own novel-in-progress.

Today, Kaye has accompanied Frank to Hickory, North Carolina, where he is deposing a man who believes he is God. Frank has left her at the Holiday Inn Express with her laptop computer and an afternoon's supply of Diet Cokes. Wearing Frank's shirt and daughter Mary's socks, Kaye Gibbons talks about her reading journal, about her daily struggle with whether to write or watch the soaps, and about the difficulty of deciding some days whether she's merely happy or heading for another manic episode.

INTERVIEWER

At the beginning of *Charms for the Easy Life*, you thank several people, including your brother, David Batts. He took you in, you wrote, dusted you off, and showed you the virtues of an honest day's work. Tell me about your brother.

GIBBONS

We were estranged for a long time, through no fault of his, while I finished growing up. Now, as an adult, with my own children, I realize what a tough time he had being twenty-three and twenty-four years old with a ten-year-old moving in with him. The fact that I turned out okay and am not robbing Zip Marts is due in great part to my brother. He has remarkable perseverance, which he taught me. He also taught me the value of a dollar. I think I would have been thrown thoroughly off track by money if he had not raised me.

INTERVIEWER

Why by money?

GIBBONS

From going from having nothing to having some. He made me work for what I got. I never take anything for granted because of him. He taught me how to set priorities and goals.

INTERVIEWER

He took you in to raise after your parents died?

GIBBONS

I lived with aunts, and then I moved in with him. He had just gotten married, too, and he was strict, and he was really the only parent model that I remember besides June and Ward Cleaver. I have based my parenting on the way he raised me. The children seem to be turning out.

INTERVIEWER

I read that you're doing a book of essays about your mother. You said you were going to interview family members who knew her, because you have such an intense desire to know what she was like.

GIBBONS

I always think I can do two things at once, but I can't. I'll be through with this book in about three months, then I can get back to something like that. I'm very curious also about her manic-depression. That's also one of the reasons I'm eager to get back to it.

INTERVIEWER

Your mother is certainly your subject.

GIBBONS

The book I'm finishing right now is about the effect of childhood on a woman's adulthood. She's abused by her husband, and she needs to figure out why she let that happen to her for fifteen years. And she has to tell herself her life story. And she has to get at her relationship with her mother. And she said that she had to untangle it with a needle, the way the mother teases a knot out of a child's necklace. That's what this book is. Every chapter is a knot.

INTERVIEWER

I'm very interested in the reading journal Frank's mother started you keeping. You said it has also become an emotional journal.

GIBBONS

It's no different from hearing "Louie Louie" and remembering where you were in 1968. Those Proustian-Madeleine feelings rush forward. When I wrote down [in the journal about] the Ethan Canin book of stories *Emperor of the Air*, ten years from now I'll remember everything about this time in my life during these two weeks.

I've started so many diaries, and I work on them for about three days, and then I tear the pages out because I worry about dying and being found with a diary and a pen in my brassiere strap.

Now, I have transferred mine into a larger notebook, and I have reading sections for my daughters and for Frank also.

INTERVIEWER

Give me an example of what you might say in your journal about one of Canin's stories.

GIBBONS

"Remarkable. Line by line and story by story. So much better than his novel. He should write stories only." I make other writers' thoughts and books my business. It's a little private book-review column.

The children do the same thing when they read. Leslie, who is five, read *Little House in the Big Woods*, and I asked her what she thought about it. She said, "I do not like outside books."

So my children are like me. Now, I realize I've trained them to admire around-the-house and in-the-yard fiction, stories of domestic life. I read a chapter or two out loud to her and bored myself silly. So now she's reading E. B. White.

INTERVIEWER

And how is the journal an emotional journey?

GIBBONS

I went back to [Saul Bellow's] *Humboldt's Gift*, and that is about a great manic-depressive character in literature [based on Bellow's friend, the poet Delmore Schwartz]. The mother in my new book is manic-depressive, as am I. I will remember the pain and elation of this recent episode of my illness when I look back ten years from now and read this journal. [Bellow's] *Herzog* is a compilation of human neuroses, and I will remember that I was in a hotel room in Hickory with *Herzog* by my bed and wondering if I was going to watch soap operas this afternoon or write.

Will you talk about the elation of this recent episode?

GIBBONS

I have found that I write best in what is called hypomania, which is halfway between being normal and being full-blown manic. Last week I wrote thirty pages, and I was hypomanic, and it felt dangerous. It was like living without a net, and sure enough, over the weekend I was crazy as a loon. I take twenty-seven pills a day, and sometimes I feel it really does no good. These are anticonvulsants which are now used primarily in the treatment of manic-depression.

I don't take lithium. It flattened me out and made me feel a desire to join the Junior League. I had no brain-wave activity at all. It was not unlike being lobotomized, so I wouldn't take it.

INTERVIEWER

There really does seem to be a connection between the manic phase and an exceptional ability with language.

GIBBONS

There's a new book called *Touched with Fire: Creativity and Manic Depression* that explores this topic. When I am depressed, I can't see the scenes, I can't hear the language. All I want to do is sit and cry and moan. And I feel so worthless that what's the point of writing? What's the point of any human activity if all I'm doing is barely hanging onto being human?

During mania, my thoughts are very disorganized and incoherent, and if I write anything at all while I'm manic, it sounds as if I'd written it drunk, and it's not a good idea to write drunk.

In that in-between state, it's like looking out of a very clear window and seeing the story on the other side. I have a hypersensitivity to language, and my thoughts come easily in an organized, patterned way. The thoughts run wide and deep in this state. But I can be like that and work nonstop for five days, and then I can't work for a week. I can't do anything for a week. That's when I read, which is what I'm doing this week.

INTERVIEWER

But that state can lead up to a full-blown episode.

GIBBONS

Right.

INTERVIEWER

Or not.

GIBBONS

Right. If I take my "trampolizers," which is what my daughter calls them, I can calm myself down. But I have taken so much medicine for so long, I've learned how to manipulate my right-brain activity with pills. I had brain mapping done recently, and it showed an almost bizarrely high level of activity in my language center. I had myself mapped in one of those hypomanic states and realized I was wasting my time. I needed to get home and write. And if I can't write when I feel that way, I feel very thwarted and unhappy.

INTERVIEWER

So you know to take advantage of that state.

GIBBONS

I could use Ian Hamilton's biography of Robert Lowell—chapter 4—and see what I'm going to do next. Lowell talks about walking around campus feeling too good. Sometimes I will realize I am feeling too good, and I have to get myself somewhere and calm myself down, because the feeling is like being in a fast car without brakes heading toward a wreck.

There's sadness also. Every time I start to feel good, I don't know if I'm happy or if I'm going crazy. Am I happy, or am I going to be sick next week?

INTERVIEWER

One thing I liked so much about *Charms* was the wonderful blending of fact and fiction. You must have had a good time researching the 1940s. I'm wondering, did Churchill really call Mussolini a hyena, and did Mussolini call him one back? Was jitterbugging actually outlawed at Duke? And did the fattest lady in the world die in Florida?

GIBBONS

Yes, jitterbugging was outlawed at Duke. Yes, about Mussolini and Churchill, and the fat lady did die in Florida.

And the first draft was top-heavy with details. So then I rewrote it and put people in it, and I built some room around the characters and gave them space to move around. I actually created a plot, though now I couldn't tell you what it is.

INTERVIEWER

What about Margaret's future mother-in-law, who wrote the political column for the Raleigh *News and Observer* called "Under the Dome"? Was she based on someone real?

GIBBONS

I made that family up. But I had them living in a house called Mount Vernon in Raleigh. That's right across the street from me up on Hope Drive. I visualized that they were there. So now it's nice to look out my window and see where my characters live. In the book I'm writing now, I've set it in my hometown, Rocky Mount, and the mother goes to Duke to the hospital, and she comes to Raleigh a lot to shop at Ellisberg's. I didn't want to do this. I wanted not to set my novels anywhere. I didn't think that my little postage stamp of space was worthy of literature. I thought, "Where am I going to set these books?" *Ellen Foster* was set nowhere. *Charms* was the first book with a somewhere to it, and people bought it, so I'll do it again.

I found that it makes no difference in Poughkeepsie if my book is set in New York or Raleigh. A reviewer in the Boston paper opened the review by saying, "Who would have cared to know anything about Raleigh, N.C.? But now we do."

I equated setting books in North Carolina with provinciality, and I just had to outgrow that. That's an adolescent view. Once I outgrew it, I was fine. My children in a few years are going to think I'm nerdy. They'll outgrow that, too.

INTERVIEWER

I'm wondering where you got the anecdote about the mother who wouldn't let her children ride a live animal, but as soon as an animal died, she let her children crawl up on it until it was hauled away. You incorporated that anecdote very smoothly.

GIBBONS

That came from a WPA book of interviews called *Gumbo Ya-Ya*. And she was a landlady who also ran a livery stable of sorts. It was fun to start with a little cube of information like that and build a character around that and have her visit her son at the VA hospital. That's when I love what I am doing. That's when I think that I'm going to be doing this when I'm ninety-five.

INTERVIEWER

Is it the love of discovery and connection?

GIBBONS

There's something of a Southerner's love of the grotesque in there. I've still got some of that love of Flannery O'Connor's freaks in me. I don't think I'll ever outgrow that. Then there's the love of language. A delight in language, which I share with my husband. A love of absurdity. And I think my mind when I'm manic wanders so much and makes so many connections that seem almost supernatural that I'm prone to do this in my writing. I'm prone to bring together incongruities, and I try to surprise readers.

INTERVIEWER

And also yourself?

GIBBONS

Yes. From the first draft of *Charms* until it was published, I had to read it between fifteen and twenty times. And if I didn't like it, I would have been miserable. So I needed to write something I didn't mind reading over and over again. That's how I know when my writing is not of a good quality. When I can't stand to read a chapter several times, I just delete it. If the surprise and the delight isn't there, I delete it without mercy.

What I have just sent off to New York yesterday is about a woman during a manic delusion who believes Robert Kennedy is in love with her. She thinks all men are in love with her. She thinks [the character] Bob Hughes on "The Guiding Light" is in love with her. Harold Robbins. Leon Uris. David Niven.

There have been times I have believed Prince Andrew was aware of my presence in the universe, and he was looking for a girl like me, waitress though I was. And if the king who married Wallis Warfield Simpson could go from being First Lord of the Admiral to second hand on an American tramp ship—that's not original—then surely Prince Andrew would come to me, and he would find his way to Chapel Hill, and he would take me away from that barbecue restaurant.

I spoke with great authority when I wrote about the mother's belief that Anthony Quinn was aware of her presence, or that she ran out of *Who's Afraid of Virginia Woolf?* screaming, "I don't care how good looking he is, he's not going to talk to me like that."

It's quite fun to write manic delusions, but I couldn't write them when I was manic. I had to write them with the distance of sanity.

INTERVIEWER

It must feel so good to get that down on paper exactly right.

GIBBONS

Nothing feels any better. I believe that if I were not manic-depressive I would be an architect. I would be using a different part of my brain. I have a curse and a gift, and I have to endure the episodes to write.

INTERVIEWER

You've mentioned what you call "outtakes," paragraphs you simply had to write to move on to the next paragraph, and which you removed from the novel-in-progress. What do you do with your "outtakes"?

GIBBONS

I have a file in my computer called "Decent Outtakes," and I throw everything in that. And so far with this novel I've had 175 pages, and I have 65 pages of "Decent Outtakes." Some are barely decent. I could edit the "Decent Outtake" section and come up with two sections.

But Dr. Rubin at Algonquin taught me never to throw anything away. It can be plowed under. When I can't create, I open my "Decent Outtake" section, and I grab a page and figure out how to work it into what I've already done.

I still feel like I get paid by the hour, and that if I don't work each day, I'll get fired, or that I'm going to run out of sick days. I have a work ethic that my brother gave me.

I'll probably blow the afternoon with this struggle about whether to watch soap operas or write, and I'll tell myself, "Look, you looked at 'The Young and the Restless' two months ago. Nothing's changed." I'd like to know if Nikki's baby does belong to her half-brother, but someone can tell me that. I need to work.

And I've found as far as craft goes also, there's nothing like the doom of impending penury to focus the mind wonderfully. I tend to finish a book about the time I run out of money. And I find not many writers will admit that. It's amazing how much I tend to work there toward the end. The day after the bank statement comes, I'll work fifteen hours.

INTERVIEWER

What have you learned about the craft of storytelling since you wrote *Ellen Foster*?

GIBBONS

I feel that the first layer of writing is art. The surge. The second layer, I come behind myself and craft what I have written. And I learn as I go from other writers. For example, right now I've kept reading Saul Bellow's *Herzog* to learn how to do density. This book that I am working on needs a weight and volume to it unlike I've had before. The weight cannot pull the story down. The anecdotes cannot be tangents that would have been better cut out and saved in the computer for another day.

I have to learn how to make all the elements of a dense story work, and Bellow is the one to teach that. Bellow and [Gabriel] Garcia Marquez do this. And I can learn how to quickly draw a character, a secondary character, from reading writers like Dominick Dunne. He does it beautifully. Five years ago, I would have been too much of a snob to read Dunne. But he can draw character and back away.

INTERVIEWER

How do you find the writers you need? How do you know who you need?

GIBBONS

I met Dominick Dunne and started reading his book. And I've always known, because of years of studying literature, where to go to find what I need. It's learned acquisition.

It's learning how to get myself out of my chair and say, "I'm losing my way in this plot. How am I going to manage this?" And that's when I'll read an old Anne Tyler book, for example, and I'll see how she creates a plot around a simple domestic story. Or Alice Hoffman.

But I wouldn't go to Alice Hoffman for a quickly drawn character. I'd go to Dunne. In the process of writing one book, I'll use ten writers, because that's about how many elements of craft there are in a novel.

I think that's the mistake writing programs make, churning out MFA students who think they've learned to write. I don't think anybody's telling the students you need to relearn it every time you start a book.

And I find that I'll write thirty pages at one time, and then I need to go back and move everything around.

And the hardest part for me as far as the craft goes is figuring out the best structure for the story. Should it be told in a contrapuntal fashion? I think it's interesting that Bach, who developed contrapuntal theory in music, was manic-depressive. It doesn't work a great deal of the time. It hasn't worked since *A Virtuous Woman*, and I resort to chronological order, and I thank God that chronology is available to me. There's nothing like a clock or a calendar to set one's scrambled novel in order.

INTERVIEWER

To me, one of the most fraught passages in *Charms* is when Margaret's mother, Sophia, and her fiancé, Mr. Baines, are out there on frozen Lassiter Mill Pond and Sophia is gliding around in a chair. Margaret, who's watching, says, "The exhilaration my mother felt came to me, it seemed, in a correspondent breeze of the sort Wordsworth wrote about. It filled my chest, all my mother's happiness blown directly into me." Do you remember trading happinesses with your mother?

GIBBONS

No, I don't. And I think one of the reasons I write about it is to create that experience. Another reason I write about mother-daughter relationships is because of my daughters. It occurs to me as if for the first time that my daughters are being raised in a household with a violently manic-depressive woman, and I look at myself through their eyes. And I have looked at my pain through their eyes. The pain attendant with any divorce, no matter how supposedly amicable. The grief there that they felt.

Then watching me so joyful with the marriage to Frank. I've tried to see myself through [a] child's eyes. So the narrator in the new book could be any one of my daughters when she's thirty-five years old. And it's quite an education to look at myself through my adult child. It has made me get out of bed and stop being depressed—like stopping a car on a dime—on days I didn't think I could move. That vision of myself through my child's eyes has put me in motion and has helped with the illness more than the twenty-seven pills a day.

———

The second child and only daughter of Charles Bennett and Alice Dorothea Gardner Batts, Kaye Batts Gibbons was born May 5, 1960, in Rocky Mount, North Carolina. She graduated from Rocky Mount High School in 1978 and entered North Carolina State University in Raleigh on a scholarship in the fall of that year. In 1980, she transferred to UNC-Chapel Hill, where she began writing her first novel, *Ellen Foster*.

Her novels are *Ellen Foster* (1987), *A Virtuous Woman* (1989), *A Cure for Dreams* (1991), and *Charms for the Easy Life* (1993).

Ellen Foster won the Sue Kaufman Prize for first fiction from the Academy of Arts and Letters, a Special Citation from the Ernest Hemingway Foundation, and the Louis D. Rubin Writing Award from the University of North Carolina.

She has received a grant from the National Endowment for the Arts, a 1990 PEN Revson Award for the best work of fiction published by a writer under thirty-five, the Heartland Prize for Fiction from the *Chicago Tribune*, and the Sir Walter Raleigh Award for best fiction. She also won the University of North Carolina Distinguished Alumnus Award.

In 1984, she married Michael Gibbons. They are the parents of three daughters: Mary, Leslie, and Louise.

On September 25, 1993, she married Frank Ward, a Raleigh attorney. He is the father of two children by a previous marriage: Frank Jr. and Victoria Ward.

Gibbons and Ward live in Raleigh, where she is at work on a fifth novel, about a woman who is manic-depressive.

April 15, 1994

GAIL GODWIN

September 4, 1987 When novelist Gail Godwin and composer Robert Starer built a new house recently in Woodstock, New York, an artist presented them a painting of a moon coming up over fields. Godwin and Starer hung the painting over the mantelpiece and invited the artist for dinner. They situated him on the sofa—before the fire—so he could admire his work. "But I noticed that as he was looking at his painting, he became more and more unhappy," says Godwin. "Finally, he said, 'You know, that fire is so alive, and it changes every minute, and it makes my painting look so dead.'

"'But that fire will go out,' I told him, 'and your painting will still be there.'

"That's the way my fiftieth birthday affected me. At fifty, you really understand that you are going to die one day. But it's not at all unpleasant. You kind of look around and see all the things that are going to outlive you, like the stars and the moon and this beautiful view out my study window.

"This view makes my poor little life seem very finite by comparison."

After graduating from UNC-Chapel Hill, Godwin worked as a reporter for the *Miami Herald*. She was productive, but her flair for dramatic detail—which in at least one case once included a bit of pure fantasy—got her fired. Afterward, as she likes to say, "I hurled myself across the sea" to London, where for several years she worked "as a glorified receptionist" for the United States Travel Service. The long, slow hours there gave her the opportunity to begin writing fiction.

Later, she earned her Ph.D. at the University of Iowa. *A Southern Family* is Godwin's sixth novel. It is set in Mountain City, North Carolina, a thinly disguised Asheville and also the setting for Godwin's 1982 novel, the best-selling *A Mother and Two Daughters*.

Godwin talked recently from Woodstock about turning fifty, about Thomas Wolfe, and about the fine line between fiction and autobiography.

INTERVIEWER

Your mother worked as a reporter in Asheville during World War II. I've heard Thomas Wolfe's mother would frequently call your mother to say, "I've just remembered one more thing about Tom."

GODWIN

Her main beat was to go out to Oteen, where they had the military hospital, and interview servicemen who were recuperating. Her other thing was anything about the Tom Wolfe legend. And Mrs. Wolfe would call the paper, like she was bestowing another gem, and Mother would go over there to hear what she had to say.

INTERVIEWER

What did you think about Wolfe, growing up?

GODWIN

My grandmother and I would be out walking, and she'd point to some old geezer and say, "That was so-and-so in Tom's book." I would want to know who it was. I guess that's when I first realized that old people had once been young.

INTERVIEWER

Did you read Wolfe when you were young?

GODWIN

I would read a little bit, and then just a longing to have done what he did would rise in me. There were certain things—when he describes October in the mountains, and when he describes a train trip—and I would think, "Oh,

now that's gone. He's taken that." I never really read him like you read a book.

INTERVIEWER

You once wrote an article about how your grandmother aligned herself with the stove, and her daughter, your mother, aligned herself with the typewriter. How did you choose the typewriter?

GODWIN

I certainly got a lot of encouragement from my teachers. I was real fortunate to go to this excellent Catholic school in Asheville: Saint Genevieve's. They [the nuns] had so much time to devote to us. If I wrote something, not only did my mother devour it, but I had all these other "mothers," and they would all read it. We weren't allowed to talk on the school bus, but we could read. The nuns rode the bus, too. I would give a nun something I had written, and she would read it, and then she would nod and smile and mouth the word *good*. I had a lot of encouragement.

INTERVIEWER

And your mother was writing fiction as well as working at the newspaper.

GODWIN

Yes, she would come home and write stories. It was very natural of me to want to do the same thing. She talked about her stories, and she worked them out. If we would go for a walk, she would say, "Oh, I could use that in my story."

INTERVIEWER

You've said you have felt you were a writer for years. What were the symptoms?

GODWIN

I knew for years I was a writer, but I did not know—in fact, it still amazes me—that I'm a published writer. But the symptoms. The minute something happened—sometimes even before it happened, sometimes I even made it happen—it was being stored away in a little box and a not-so-little box. And I saw people's lives as stories, and I repeated moments according to their dramatic value.

When I was younger, this got me in a lot of trouble. If things were going along too well, I had to change the course. I remember breaking an engagement. I was ironing with the boy's mother in her kitchen, and we were talking, and she was saying how nice it was for me to help him with his studying. I said, "Well, he is a bit slow."

Everything just crumbled right there in the kitchen. There was a part of me watching, saying, "I can't be doing this." It was like some demon was interfering. And that's very close to writing. If I'd been writing and had two women in the kitchen, that's the way I would've ended that story, because on a deeper level this engagement was really a matter between me and the boy's mother. She wanted me as a daughter-in-law, and I wanted her as a mother-in-law, and he *was* a bit slow.

INTERVIEWER

After learning your first novel had been ac-

cepted for publication, you got a raging tooth-ache. You said then, "There are things in us that just won't let us have too much." Are those things still in you?

GODWIN

I think they are always going to be in me. It's just that—I don't know if it's in my makeup or my history or what—I'm always extremely conscious all I have could be taken away instantly. That nothing is owed me. I don't understand the universe, and I want very much to play my part in it. When something really good happens, I tend to reflect. But I no longer always get sick.

INTERVIEWER

I've heard that one of your favorite bookstores in the world is Malaprop's in Asheville. What makes it special to you?

GODWIN

I came to Asheville one time, and my mother said, "There is this wonderful new bookstore. These girls have a great idea. They serve coffee and pastries downstairs, and there's music." It's in a real run-down building, with creaky floors, which makes it lovely.

A recent time I went to Malaprop's, and I was really depressed. I had just given the commencement address at UNC-Greensboro, and I was thinking, "Life is over, and I'm old." And they had the new Saul Bellow book [*More Die of Heart-break*], and I said, "I'm going to buy that." And then I thought to myself, "Well, I'm buying his book and reading it, but he'll never read me."

When the owner got it off the shelf, she said, "Look at this picture of Saul Bellow on the back. He's pointing to his bookshelf, and look which book he's pointing to." He was pointing to *A Mother and Two Daughters*. And it just made my day! I loved him all the more. I went down the rickety stairs and got myself a cup of coffee and just sat there and read.

When you're young, you want to sit in public places and be seen reading. And then when you're older, you're really reading. And I was both. I was really reading, and I was being seen reading.

INTERVIEWER

Many of your novels and stories draw on events and locales in your own life. How do you draw the line between fiction and autobiography?

GODWIN

They are not the same. In fact, the longer I write, the more I think that even if I sat down and said to myself, "Now, Gail, you're going to write your autobiography," before the first sentence was over, I'd start changing things. One example—which is kind of central to *A Southern Family*—I was trying to evoke the character of a certain young man who had died. This was, of course, a real person. But I had given myself the right at the very beginning of the book to make up anything I needed which would lead me not to the literal truth—I'll never get to that—but to an imaginative truth I could live with. So I had to find the right experiences for

him, which would reveal his personality and that would've shaped his personality.

In the book, his father is a builder. At the time I was writing the book, I was having an upstairs study built for myself, and one of the workers—a young worker—fell through the Sheetrock twice in one day. And the builder was so mad and so embarrassed. When I got home, there was a thin layer of white dust all over my dresser and my perfume bottles. The builder rushed down, and he said, "I have to explain what this clunk has done." That scene just got deeper and deeper into the book, and it's told through the father's eyes.

If something in real life passes by and you see that it would be right for your characters, you put it in. It's like a little bird making its nest. The more you do it, the more you get stickier fingers.

INTERVIEWER

Do you think by writing about the fictional Theo in *A Southern Family* you were trying to get at the imaginative truth of your brother's suicide, as well as your father's suicide?

GODWIN

God, yes. That's probably one of the things that not only fueled my writing but got me through it. But to have this kind of loss twice! And in both cases not to really have known them very well. It's just like the mystery going down for the last time. I hope there are no more of these. And trying to imagine the person, and not only the person but the kind of person, the kind of figure those real people represented . . .

INTERVIEWER

You studied under Kurt Vonnegut at the Iowa Writers' Workshop. What effect did he have on your writing?

GODWIN

He was just like that nun on the bus. He was somebody whose writing I admired. He was a literary figure, and there he was sitting alone with me in a room with his big feet up on the desk, reading my writing and saying, "Wow!"

INTERVIEWER

Describe your writing schedule.

GODWIN

The first thing is to get up out of sleep. This is a very important transition. The other morning right before I woke up, I had a second long dream. I was running for some kind of political office, and our plumber said, "But what is your platform?" I thought for a minute, and I said, "My platform is constructive sorrow."

The other day I was real depressed, and I said to no one in particular, "What am I? What am I supposed to do next?" I've had this feeling lately that I'm changing into something else. And then I had the platform dream.

It's moments like that—when you are told something, or you allow yourself to tell yourself something that you couldn't have known on an ordinary, mundane level. It may set the tone for what I write next.

INTERVIEWER

After that waking transition, do you spend the rest of the morning writing?

GODWIN

Then I have some coffee, and if I'm working on a book, I get up and go to the study. I've been without a book for about six months, and I've been writing a lot in my journal about what I want to do next.

I'm trying not to do anything now. I don't want to force anything. But there are images that are interesting, and I'm flirting with those. This week, I've been going through some old journals, which is a nice way to get used to the new study. I have a view that is just beautiful. It really competes with my poor little finite life.

INTERVIEWER

I've heard you mention some philosophers you like to read.

GODWIN

When I was moving my books, which was quite an operation—I packed them all myself because I wanted to have them in a certain order when I placed them on the new shelves—I realized I had more books on religion, psychology, and philosophy than any others.

I do have some people I go to again and again. I started with Jung and his view of the collective unconscious. That I liked, but I couldn't accept that everything was determined.

I read everything that James Hillman has written. He wrote *Healing Fiction*, about how, if you tell yourself the right fiction, if you see yourself in the right kind of story, you can heal yourself. He's a Jungian analyst, and he now does quite a bit of lecturing. There's a groundswell around him. He does workshops. I don't even want to meet him. He's an older man. I found him through Malaprop's.

Another one is Edward Whitmont. He wrote a book, *The Symbolic Quest*, and every time I thought I was going to have to go into New York and go into analysis, I would read this book instead. I have his number, and if I really need to I'll call him. Now, he's written a new book which is the best of the goddess books. It's called *Return of the Goddess*, and the reason I like it is that it's based on solid stuff, and not wishy-washy.

There's a wise man right up in the hills in Asheville: Father Gale Webb, a retired Episcopal minister. He wrote *The Night and Nothing*, which Harper & Row had published, and it had been out of print for years. Scott Peck was staying in a monastery in Asheville, and he found this book, and he had to have it, so he stole it, and then he wrote to his publisher to see if it could be reprinted.

Father Webb also wrote *The Shape of Growth*. It's trying to tell people who still want to go to church ways to look at it so you can still go. The changes in spiritual consciousness. I read *The Night and Nothing* first. I have three copies in different rooms. It talks about acedia—that's my favorite sin—sloth and despair and giving up and all that.

Then I wrote him [to ask] if he had anything more, and he referred me to a nineteenth-century book by Bishop Francis Paget, *The Sorrow of the World*.

INTERVIEWER

Why do you need so many philosophers?

GODWIN

Very early on, I realized that I wasn't going to be sold on organized religion, and it made me sad, because I knew I wasn't the biggest thing in the universe. But I had to find my own way, and I did it mainly through books. When we moved, I treated myself to a bedside table that has three drawers in it. But after just two months, all three drawers are filled up with books. And I was going to put dainty little things in there, like handkerchiefs.

INTERVIEWER

You turned fifty in June. Did that have an impact?

GODWIN

It's interesting. I have this feeling that I am turning into something else. Now, you can take that on various levels. You can say, "Well, of course. You're turning into an old person." But I think I'm breaking up. I'm not as tight. I'm breaking into particles. And maybe that's what death is. You just break up into particles.

For years, my personality thrust has been forward. I've been aspiring. I've been trying to be a writer, trying to make enough money to live. I've been climbing and aspiring. Suddenly, I am not. I'm not an ingenue anymore, not an aspirer. It's time to go on to something else.

I was writing in my journal about this woman who had come to see us. She's an older writer, someone I have long admired. But she came in, and she was very egocentric. She was not as good as her books. After she left, I thought, "If, after a certain age, a woman fails to become motherly—if she denies that motherly part of herself—she can only be bizarre."

Here I am fifty, never having had children, but I think I'm going to be more motherly in my attitudes toward the world. This year, I saved a little maple tree. I transplanted it and put sticks around it, and it's growing. So I think my consolation prize for being fifty is that I'm going to make a lot more things grow.

March 4, 1991

When Gail Godwin finished her last novel, *A Southern Family*, a best-selling tale of love and murder set in Mountain City, North Carolina (a.k.a. Asheville), she dreamed she was running for office and that her platform was "constructive sorrow." With her latest novel, *Father Melancholy's Daughter*, Godwin's "constructive sorrow" platform is transformed into reality.

The new novel, her seventh, is the poignant story of a young girl's longing for her absent mother. It is also the story of the girl's struggle to grow up while she cares for her aging, melancholy father, an Episcopal priest in the fictional town of Romulus, Virginia.

Godwin has written often about her mother, the late Kathleen Cole, who wrote short stories and reported for the Asheville paper during World War II. On December 30, 1989, Godwin's mother was killed in a car crash on her way to the Asheville airport.

Like her mother, Godwin is an inveterate journal writer. Each morning, she has toast and coffee in bed, then writes in her journal before getting up.

On a recent morning, after writing in her journal, Godwin talked about her new novel, the nature of art, the sensuousness of grieving, and the benefits of longing.

INTERVIEWER

You've written a lot about mother-daughter relationships. In this novel, the poignancy of six-year-old Margaret's feelings for her absent mother is powerful. Did the intensity of Margaret's longing surprise you even as you created it?

GODWIN

It did. It must have come from some deep part of myself, because my mother certainly didn't run away. We had a rather close relationship. I think that it has to do with the fact a daughter can never completely know her mother, and that's what fascinates her. I touched on that longing to know the first woman in your life—the other woman, the other who is also you.

INTERVIEWER

In the Fall 1988 issue of *Antaeus*, there's an excerpt from your journal in which you write about being annoyed with the *New York Times* for not having selected one of your books for its "Notable List." You mention the "cantankerous pleasure" of getting older and skilled at what you do, and how you are becoming less and less part of "their world" and more of your own. Is this a natural process of maturing as a writer?

GODWIN

It's certainly been true for me, because my best pleasure to do with my writing comes from what I discover as I make the book. I love the whole process: The search, finding out what I don't know. But then comes this period in which your spiritual search is turned into a product. That's what I'm in now, which, I must say, as I get older and older, I hate more and more, and am less willing to put up with the nonsense. I no longer want to get up at six to wash my hair for second-rate photographers.

INTERVIEWER

Once again, please describe your writing schedule.

GODWIN

I write about three hours at the most. It could be nine to twelve or ten to one. I feel I should write more, because it's my job, and most people who have jobs work eight hours a day. But three is all I can do. If it's gone well, it's about two word-processor pages, with justified margins. That's on a good day. On a bad day, it's a page.

INTERVIEWER

Do you dress before you write?

GODWIN

Oh, heavens yes! I have to get myself all psyched up. I clean my face. Do my whole routine: Baking soda and peroxide for the teeth, flossing.

INTERVIEWER

One of your characters, a playwright, says *Lovely* is the art of pleasing others, while *Art* is about pleasing yourself. Do you agree with her?

GODWIN

Art is pleasing yourself. That's one of the things art does. But you can please yourself and it won't be art. Art is having the mastery to take your experience, whether it's visual or mental, and make meaningful shapes that convey a reality to others.

INTERVIEWER

But many of the characters in your novels are artists, and many of them are extremely selfish. Do you believe selfishness is an artistic necessity?

GODWIN

You have to put it first, and that poses a lot of uncomfortable moral dilemmas. For instance, you may hurt the feelings of people you write about or that you use as models. I have found that I have a sampling tendency. I pounce on somebody and kind of extract all their juices, and then I'm stuck with the loyalty aspect. I've pounced, and now I can't just abandon this person. As I get older, I'm better about that. I don't just drop them and never call them up again.

INTERVIEWER

Say more about this pouncing.

GODWIN

You're attracted to some problem in the novel that you're writing, and your antennae then perk

April 15, 1994

up and go looking for examples in life, people around you who might embody something. Then you seek them out and try to make yourself congenial to them so that you can get to know their life.

Once in a blue moon, this leads to a wonderful, lasting friendship. But sometimes—and this is the monster part—you realize they were kind of a hook, and you hung your coat there for a while, and then you took it and went on. And there's the poor, naked hook waiting there that got used to your warmth.

INTERVIEWER

You say intriguing things about grief in this novel, especially about the departure of grief's ache. Ruth's daughter Margaret says, "You don't want the ache to go away, because as long as it's there, so are they."

GODWIN

Exactly. The last part of this book was written after my mother was killed. I had her blue Ultrasuede coat I'd given her. One of her handkerchiefs was in it. For the first few weeks, I could smell her particular smell. It was a blend of her perfume—Tabac Blond—and the smell of bread, although she never baked bread. I would smell it every day. It made me so mad when it started to fade. Grief is sensuous. You keep them alive through strange little rituals.

INTERVIEWER

You pay attention to your dreams, don't you? And you record many of them in your journal.

GODWIN

I do. I do. I seem to be dreaming more and more. It may be the kind of life I lead. It's a quiet life. Some of the dreams are continuations over the years, and finally they change. Finally, after dreaming for years that I miss getting to a math test, I finally in a dream have the wit to go up to the teacher to say I missed it and ask if I can make it up. And she says, "Yes, you can make it up."

INTERVIEWER

You've described your mother as an "elusive presence I've been studying all my life." Did that elusiveness perhaps fuel this new book?

GODWIN

I think it did, because I have always known this feeling, in relation to my own mother, of wanting to know more than she would or could tell me. And yet she told me quite a lot. Yet there was an essence of her—a part of her personality—that was stubbornly mysterious, almost as if she couldn't help herself.

INTERVIEWER

Your mother left you forty-eight of her journals. You must be finally getting to know her better now.

GODWIN

Yes. And she had some very interesting dreams, too, at the last. She dreamed of going to this big party. She was always kind of shy. She worried, as we all do, "Am I wearing the right dress?" She was at this big party and everyone approved of her. There was a lovely pool, and she wanted to swim. Someone said, "No married women are allowed in that pool." She said, "But I'm not married." She was suddenly clothed in the right outfit to go swimming, and she swam in the pool.

INTERVIEWER

You've said her last years were among her happiest.

GODWIN

I think she was beginning to know what her myth was: She was an igniter. She wrote in her journal that she had not become the great novelist she had wanted to be, or the playwright or many other things. But she realized she was able to ignite others and excite them about ideas and how to get things done.

INTERVIEWER

What was her attitude toward life near the end?

GODWIN

She was killed on the 30th of December, 1989. On December 19, she wrote, "Please, Lord, a little more time on this beautiful green earth I am learning to appreciate and love, and through that and by grace, learning to love thee more."

INTERVIEWER

In the novel, Margaret talks about longings. She says, "Certain people pass through our lives and have a gift to give us by arousing intense longings." How is longing a gift?

GODWIN

That's just been my experience, through the study of others and the study of life and reading and experience. Longing's a great gift someone can give you, if you know how to use it.

INTERVIEWER

How do you use it?

GODWIN

Well, different ways. I mean, there may be a chance to grab that person and marry them. Or it may be more of a Dante [and his idealized love for Beatrice] thing. You see someone, know someone, and you realize this person is teaching you about love and is a messenger. I more and more believe that love is the whole philosophy. That that's what the Gospels have been saying for a long time. If you can't love, you're not truly alive.

February 21, 1994

Gail Godwin is lying on her king-size bed, two cats, journals, and books spread out around her, windows open. During the interview, she will watch the fog roll in from the mountains until it completely swathes her house.

Godwin is keeping an ear out for the Federal Express truck, because she's eager to mail her editor a cassette of herself reading aloud a section of her new novel, *The Good Husband*.

Godwin's editor is Linda Grey, also president and publisher at Ballantine. Godwin calls Grey "truly the mother of this book," a woman who "lured me into technology with audio tapes."

"She started having cassette tapes made of her authors' list," Godwin says, "and she sends them to booksellers, so that when they get in their cars, they can stick this cassette in and just listen."

As Godwin taped herself, she learned that her voice is downbeat. So she pepped it up by keeping time with her fingers, as if she were conducting an orchestra. She also provided theme music to open and close the reading.

"It taught me something about selling myself through my voice and through the selection of material," she says.

Always, Godwin is learning something. She's a perpetual student of human nature, who like her new character Magda probes every nuance of relationship and memory for meaning.

In Clorox-stained brown polo shirt, gray sweatpants, and faded blue Ralph Lauren socks "with the little rider turned outside," Godwin talks about the sadness of the successful woman, learning to live in the moment, and how to "dresse and undresse" the soul.

INTERVIEWER

Let's go back many years, before you were famous. You were twenty-nine, divorced, and a fact-checker at the *Saturday Evening Post* when an uncle died and left you five thousand dollars. You knew exactly how you wanted to use the money. You sent off a short story to the Iowa Writers' Workshop, and they accepted you. It was the right thing at the right time, wasn't it?

GODWIN

It was right technically. It was also right that it fit into my myth: I was flying off into nothing. My suitcases got lost, and because there was a snowstorm, they couldn't get my luggage to me for days. I landed on a blank page. I was so grateful to be there and to have the fact-checking and my marriage behind me.

INTERVIEWER

Before that, you'd been frustrated because you didn't feel that what you had in you—the ability to become an accomplished writer—was getting out. You didn't know where to start. What would you tell an aspiring writer today about the frustration of where to start?

GODWIN

I'd say, first of all, when you start feeling that way, sit down and relax and just say, "You have time." And what is most important is to develop your power of gathered attention. Paying attention and then gathering it up. If you can do this, it becomes a force.

You have to sit still, or be still long enough to just look out and look in and see what's happening. See what *you* see happening. Not what you've read that's happening, and not what someone has told you is happening. What *you* see happening: "At dusk, the world really does turn blue." It could be something that simple. It could be that when some people say, "I love you," they screw up their faces in a way that says just the opposite.

These are precious details. And write them

down. That's so important. You forget details. You remember long swaths of indeterminate material. But you don't remember specifics.

INTERVIEWER

I have a friend who wants to write a novel. She's published eight collections of poetry, but she just can't seem to break that barrier that allows her to get the prose out.

GODWIN

That's such an interesting problem. I was just thinking about it. This sounds like a detour. Saturday, Robert [Starer] and I went to an art show of a recent friend of ours, a man in his late thirties. And he's got AIDS, and he's supposed to be dead by now. But he started painting two years ago—he was a hairdresser and never had an art lesson in his life—and here on the wall were these paintings that are life transfigured, nature transfigured, nature with a glow behind it.

I thought, "It would be the easiest thing in the world to paint these." But I screw myself up, and I make little barriers around me. It's almost as if he has nothing to lose now, and all this could come pouring out. He's got his death sentence, and he lives and sees. I said, "How on earth? Where does this come from?" He said, "I'm just a vessel. It just comes out."

In my daylight hours, I'm so inhibited. It makes me sad. There's still so much I know is in there, and I have to catch myself off-guard to let it come out.

INTERVIEWER

I'm wondering if you don't catch yourself off-guard as you revise, because I recently read that you said, "The more I revise, the more my novels come alive." What happens during the revision?

GODWIN

They're not so inhibited. At first, they're very sparse, and then the more I work on them, the more I put things in. I start off with a broad line, and as I go along, I put in all those details. I have to do the line first.

INTERVIEWER

Does the line go from A to Z?

GODWIN

No, the line goes from A to A-and-a-half.

I guess I write like an ant pushing a big crumb along. I go a little bit. Then I zigzag and go a little more and go back and put in some more details. The computer has made my writing life happier, but not one bit faster.

But not to revise is an inexcusable carelessness. Not to revise is like looking through a pair of binoculars and not bothering to adjust them to your particular eyesight. You can be looking at green burrs and brown sticks and blue and white in the background. You adjust them, and you see you're looking through a gorgeous stand of pine trees, and on the hill behind is a very interesting house perched up there.

INTERVIEWER

Your half-brother's suicide in 1983 triggered

A Southern Family. What triggered *The Good Husband*?

GODWIN

Two things. One, during the spring before I began *The Good Husband*, I was party to a man's dying. It was a friend's friend, a man in our church. And he was told he had cancer. He was a professor. They told him there was very little they could do. He decided to forgo all the chemotherapy and staying in the hospital. He simply went home.

I'd go over a lot. He was a witty professor, and words meant a lot to him. I watched his mind, one could say, deteriorate. He went into a fantasy world. But he would talk and say things that made perfect sense to him. And some of them were so touching, I actually ended up using them on Magda.

He was the first person I ever got to watch die. My father committed suicide. My mother was killed in an accident. I think it's very important to watch someone die. It isn't depressing, especially when this person who is doing it is going toward it like a journey.

INTERVIEWER

And what was the second thing?

GODWIN

The other thing took a couple of years to come to fruition. I had read an article in a book—I was in England—and it upset me so much I left the book in my hotel room. It was about the sadness of the successful woman, and it was written by June Singer, who is a Blakeian and a Jungian, and she described how many women who've become successful get terribly depressed. She found that the antidote was to imagine in great detail your own deathbed.

Ah. No, you can't pay your bills anymore. You can't clean the house. You can't fight your way up the ladder. All you can do is lie there. You think about your life, what's important, whom you've loved, who has loved you, what's important to you, what it's all been about.

I had a great revulsion to this book, and I left it in the room, but it followed me and followed me.

INTERVIEWER

So a part of you is the successful, high-achieving Magda, on her deathbed, who hasn't yet learned to smell the roses. The part of you June Singer was talking about. I would think the other characters represent parts of you, too.

GODWIN

As one keeps writing, all characters are parts of oneself.

[The testy, pugnacious novelist character] Hugo Henry is a part of me. In fact, a woman writer, Rob Dew, read this character and joked, "I don't want anyone to read this book. They'll know you based Hugo on me."

Hugo is all "Why didn't I get what so-and-so got?" It's not very attractive, but you kind of love him.

[Magda's husband, mild-mannered househusband] Francis gets a great deal of pleasure in taking care of the moment, gardening, pulling up weeds, and doing one thing at a time.

I had one reader tell me how disappointed she was in Francis. She said, "I found it so appalling that he hasn't done anything with his life."

"First of all," I said to her, "let's think of the centuries of women who 'haven't done anything with their lives.'" There's that. And there's this whole American notion that to do something with your life, you have to get dressed in a suit in the morning, pick up a briefcase, go up an elevator, wield your power, come home, collapse, and get drunk.

INTERVIEWER

Now that you're onto that side of yourself that Magda represents, how do you deal with the depression that maybe comes when you don't enjoy the moment?

GODWIN

I don't know if I do deal with it. I had been deferring my gratification ever since I was about four, telling myself, "You've got to make something of your life, and later you can enjoy it." So this went on—I was twenty-four, thirty-four, forty-four, fifty-four—then suddenly, you know, I reached the point where I realized I had not developed my pleasure-taking powers very much.

Robert and I would go to Pawleys Island [South Carolina] and stay a month, and we'd pack up our car with music and my typewriter, and we'd already rented a piano, so that it would be ready to be delivered to the cottage. We'd get there and unpack and then go to a giant food store to get food for a month. And one year we got down to Pawleys and unpacked, and rushed

around getting organized, and then I burst into tears and said, "But this isn't fun!"

I'd gotten very good at deferring my pleasure, and I couldn't seize it. We had just built this beautiful new house on top of a hill with an indoor swimming pool, and I had beauty all around me, and I felt something was keeping me from it.

INTERVIEWER

What have you done about it?

GODWIN

I haven't done anything about it.

INTERVIEWER

I'm impressed by the amount of knowing in this novel. There's the knowing of what it's like to be dying. The knowing of what it's like to give birth to a stillborn child. The knowing of what it's like to be in seminary. The knowing of what it's like to be thirty-five years old and giddily in love. The knowing of what it's like to be a pugnacious man who's blocked on a novel. How do you go about getting all this knowing? And do you know more than you think you know?

GODWIN

We all know more than we think we do. We sometimes hamper ourselves by thinking we have to overresearch. I had to do research. God help me, I've never had cancer. I haven't ever given birth, much less to a stillborn child. I've never been in a seminary, but seminaries are one of my abiding loves and fascinations.

My assistant did all the medical research on ovarian cancer, and I read several books. Once I have satisfied myself that I've been given permission to write about birth, once I've talked to people who've done these things, then I can allow myself—if I have the outline and know what the events were—to feel it from the inside and imagine.

INTERVIEWER

There's another kind of knowing you have, too. A deep knowing about relationships.

GODWIN

I wonder if I haven't always had that. Someone told me recently—who knew me as a child—that when I was little I would go to church and lurk on the sides of conversations and listen to what older people were saying.

INTERVIEWER

Every writer I've ever talked to has told me that they never got enough of adult conversations when they were children.

GODWIN

It was that wanting so much to know what they were saying and what their relationships were to each other and watching their faces. I'm glad to hear it wasn't just one nasty little girl.

INTERVIEWER

Those wonderful woodcarvings that illustrate this novel—misericords, Francis's passion—where did you learn about them?

GODWIN

We were in Wells Cathedral in England and a very personable lady, Linda Lyall, was giving us a tour, and she told us to look under the seats. You don't see them unless you pull back this creaky wooden seat from the thirteenth century, and underneath is a glorious carving, maybe of lovers, or some animal. The purpose of the seats was so that monks and priests could look like they're standing up and still rest themselves.

Here's what triggered it. She said, "It's a little bit like God's mercy. Things we do that only God sees." I thought, "I've got to have that somehow."

INTERVIEWER

Did you have a floor and yard plan for Francis and Magda's house?

GODWIN

Not a good drawing, but I had to know where all the rooms were. I had to know where the road was, so that when Alice and Hugo drove by at night, I had to make sure Alice could see his room. I have to know where the rooms are and what they look out on.

INTERVIEWER

Let's talk about writer's block. Shelby Foote says he doesn't believe in it. Neither does Allan Gurganus. William Styron says writer's block is nothing more than having insufficient mastery of the material. You once spent a whole summer writing a hundred pages of a novel that never saw light. One day, you realized what you'd written wasn't salvageable, and that night, you went to bed disconsolate. But somehow during the night, you let go of your terror and woke refreshed, with the first chapter of a new book in mind. Was that writer's block?

GODWIN

Maybe there are two kinds of writer's block.

An awful kind would be to feel the need to express something, and not know what you wanted to express, and have these kinds of inward knockings, and not be able to let anything out.

I've had several kinds. One is, I start with it, and I realize it's dead material. Dead to me. Either my motives for writing it weren't connected to me—my central core—something really genuine in me. It was more, "Oh, hey, this is a good idea." It's very disappointing when it's dead, especially for someone who hates to waste time.

The kind I'm most familiar with is having a need to tell about certain people and then having to wait. I am learning to wait. Ha-ha. Not very much.

It's having to wait or just not knowing how to organize the material so it will reach others. It swirls around in my head. I have to organize these scenes, and I have to let the reader know who these people are, and I have to make pictures. So it's not so much a block. I've always thought when somebody says "writer's block," you're just silenced. I haven't had that ever happen so far. Please, God.

INTERVIEWER

You told me once that you must say to your unconscious, "I know you're down there. I want all the help you can give me. But I don't want you take me over." You also said you thought we each have a creature who lives inside us trying to become conscious. "It's full of ideas," you said. "It's got lots of pep. It's not conscious, and that's the danger. If you're not in control, it'll set you on fire and you'll burn."

GODWIN

I would only amend that to say creatures, plural. I can feel those little creatures scurrying for cover now. I can't grasp it in retrospect. It happens in process. *You know how it feels.* I have all these things I have to do before I can start to write. I set up my space.

Toni Morrison was interviewing me on a Canadian TV program, and she and I got into talking about that at the very end. Little rituals we had that set up our space as a sacred space. One hoped.

And hers was that she had to start writing before the sun came up. She would get up and light a candle.

Then mine was that I have to go to my study, close the door, light the incense, and there's a little medallion my mother gave me. I always touch that after I turn on the computer. The green "NUM lock" light comes on. I turn it off. And then I touch that little medallion. It's keeping in touch with an impetus. I sometimes write little notes to myself before I begin. I write them on the computer, and they're expunged as the work goes along. I often try to catch that moment—the moment between when I know nothing and the moment that comes fifteen minutes to an hour later, and I have done something.

I look at what I have done, and I go back and

remember when it was blank, and I try to figure out what happened. It is as if you make the step of faith, of doing these mechanical things and starting with whatever you have, and someone will throw you little nuggets.

When you had Hugo Henry getting off the plane in South Carolina, you knew something was going to happen to give him an idea or the confidence he needed. So what does happen between the not knowing and the knowing? In your mind, you make a step of faith. But what is your body doing?

GODWIN

I started with Hugo getting off the plane. I rewrote that sentence over and over and over again, until I knew he would be broadsided by the heat and humidity—when you're coming from the Catskills, you're broadsided in the South.

From there, I was able to know that he would want to whip out his handkerchief, and he didn't, because he was already imagining his welcoming committee.

Now I had a trail of corn, and I simply followed it. You have to have a little trail of corn to lead you into the character's feeling.

Then he sees his reflection in the window, and then he is imagining the snooty ladies waiting for him. And of course it's something different.

That's where my angel comes in the room. Hugo walks into the airport, and the first thing he sees is a replica of his dead father—a skinny, sharp-chinned old geezer in a cheap, white see-through shirt, with his father's exact posture. And that gave me the key to the whole chapter.

It is through acknowledging his father's illiteracy that he is saved, and he gets his next book. But I had to follow the line of what he would be doing.

INTERVIEWER

So you stayed in the moment with the character.

GODWIN

There's this great book about depression through the ages, *The Sorrow of the World*, by the English bishop Francis Paget. I copied this down in a fit of despair: "Through humbly and simply doing what we can, we retrieve the power of doing what we would."

That is what happened in the Hugo chapter. It does come from the unconscious, if you humbly and simply do what you can, you sometimes get the power of an insight.

INTERVIEWER

Two of your characters are into "ordering their loves"—that is, putting in order the ideas and things and people they each knew would always be part of them. Magda does it because she is dying. Alice does it after her divorce, and it brings her clarity and a solitary happiness. Do you think "ordering your loves" is valuable before you know you're dying?

GODWIN

That's what *The Divine Comedy* is all about. That's what life is all about. That's the big question on the final exam. It's not easy to do, and you can't always consciously say who and what you've loved most.

But it reveals itself to you through dreams. In my case, it will probably reveal itself over the decades through the recurrent themes of my work.

But I think you should make an attempt.

INTERVIEWER

What's the first step?

GODWIN

I would make a list and look at it and see where you're lying.

There are things in people we want to love the most and we don't, and then there are things in people we do really love whether we should or not.

In my lowest moments of depression, what keeps me going is a kind of competitiveness with my fellow writers. At the bottom, maybe what I've loved most is ambition, striving. I'd be sick if that were the truth. But there it is.

But if love is the thing that invigorates and stimulates us, that's something we'd want to admit.

On the other hand, when Magda makes her lecture at Francis's seminary, she says that sometimes suddenly loving someone can be like a flash of God. Look how Beatrice set fire to Dante's poetic spirit. The memory of this little Florentine girl that maybe he saw three times inspired the whole *Divine Comedy*. Through loving her, he could find out something he loved most.

INTERVIEWER

So romantic love may inspire ambition, a passion sometimes more passionate than romantic love?

GODWIN

I've been a believer in that. There's something perverse about artists. They will go seeking the stimulus of love. I don't consciously go out and seek to fall in love and look for pain. But you seek an emotion that will jolt you so that you will write.

I saw this movie about Proust. He would literally drag himself up from bed about once every six months and get dressed and go out to some gathering. He says, "I have to go fall in love so that I'll have something to write about."

INTERVIEWER

I love the quotation you used from George Herbert's collected poems: "Summe up at night what thou hast done by day; / And in the morning, what thou hast to do. / Dresse and undresse thy soul; mark the decay / And growth of it; if with thy watch, that too / Be down, then winde up both, since we shall be / Most surely judg'd, make thy accounts agree."

GODWIN

George Herbert was a clergyman for only three years in England, and then he died of TB. He wrote all these poems in these last few years.

I visited the tiny little church in Bremerton where he was — the church is lovingly kept — and in one of the windows they had this verse typed out. They put it in a plastic sheath. I just loved the part, "Dresse and undresse thy soul; mark the decay / And growth of it." And watch the final exhortation, which is also a warning: "Winde up both, since we shall be / Most surely judg'd, make thy accounts agree."

I read this in September of 1991, and I began the book October 1991. It didn't take long.

This novel is really about taking stock, which you seem to be doing in your own life. I wonder if taking stock includes going back and finishing things—which is what Alice does, and Francis and Hugo. Are there things you'd like to go back and finish so that your "accounts agree"? Or do you do this through your fiction?

I do it through my fiction. But, yes, there are things I'd like to go back and finish. They're not tasks. They're the very opposite of tasks. They're like going back and finishing loving people I didn't love well, going back and finishing enjoying things I didn't enjoy well. Maybe I can still do some of that.

The only child of Mose Winston and Kathleen Krahenbuhl Godwin, Gail Kathleen Godwin was born June 18, 1937, in Birmingham, Alabama. She attended Saint Genevieve of the Pines in Asheville, North Carolina, from second through ninth grades. She also attended Hannah High School in Anderson, South Carolina, and Norview High School in Norfolk, Virginia. In 1955, she graduated from Woodrow Wilson High School in Portsmouth, Virginia. She attended Peace College in Raleigh, North Carolina, and graduated with a B.A. in journalism from UNC-Chapel Hill in 1959. In 1971, she received her Ph.D. in English from the University of Iowa.

She worked as a news reporter for the *Miami Herald* from 1959 to 1960 and as a research assistant for the United States Travel Service in London from 1961 to 1965. In 1966, she was an editorial assistant at the *Saturday Evening Post*. She has taught at the Iowa Writers' Workshop, the University of Illinois, Vassar, and Columbia University.

Her novels are *The Perfectionists* (1970), *Glass People* (1972), *The Odd Woman* (1974), *Violet Clay* (1978), *A Mother and Two Daughters* (1982), *The Finishing School* (1985), *A Southern Family* (1987), *Father Melancholy's Daughter* (1991), and *The Good Husband* (1994).

Her short-story collections are *Dream Children* (1976) and *Mr. Bedford and the Muses* (1983).

Her awards include the Thomas Wolfe Memorial Award, presented by the Lipinsky Endowment of the Western North Carolina Historical Association; the Janet Heidiger Kafka Award from the University of Rochester; two National Endowment for the Arts grants; a Guggenheim Fellowship; and the Award in Literature from the American Academy and Institute of Arts and Letters.

In 1988, she was made a Distinguished Alumna at UNC-Chapel Hill. She has been awarded honorary degrees from UNC-Asheville and UNC-Greensboro. In October 1994, she received a Doctor of Letters, *honoris causa*, from the University of the South in Sewanee, Tennessee.

In May 1960, she married photographer Douglas Kennedy of Miami, Florida.

In July 1965, she married Dr. Ian Marshall, presently a practicing psychiatrist in London and Oxford. They later divorced.

She lives with composer Robert Starer in Woodstock, New York, where she is at work on a new novel.

April 5, 1994

ALLAN GURGANUS

*A*t a desk covered with clocks in a rent-controlled Manhattan apartment, Allan Gurganus worked seven years on his first published book, the 712-page comic novel *Oldest Living Confederate Widow Tells All.*

Gurganus grew up in Rocky Mount, North Carolina, where at nine he was the Fannie Gorham Grammar School correspondent for the *Rocky Mount Evening Telegram.* He graduated from public school but says he failed algebra once and French twice and was never accepted into accelerated English.

In 1965, at age eighteen, Gurganus enlisted in the navy and served four years on the aircraft carrier USS *Yorktown.* He spent spare hours educating himself in literature — Russian, French, German, and English.

"All the most interesting people I know are the ones who are self-taught," he says. "I had the good luck to discover literature without having anybody leading me to it."

Later, Gurganus attended the Academy of Fine Arts at the University of Pennsylvania; Sarah Lawrence College, where he studied with short-story writer Grace Paley; and the Iowa Writers' Workshop, where the late Pulitzer-winning short-story writer John Cheever became his mentor.

Gurganus is writing and illustrating a collection of stories called *White People,* and he will soon return to work on an earlier novel titled *The Erotic History of a Southern Baptist Church.*

He talks today about his character Lucy Marsden, the Civil War, the AIDS epidemic, and the abidingness of life's ordinary people — the ones who leave the porch lights on.

INTERVIEWER

About seven years ago, you discovered a *New York Times* item about Confederate widows and their pensions. When your eye fell on the phrase "the oldest living Confederate widow," I understand you rushed home and wrote the first thirty pages of *Oldest Living Confederate Widow Tells All*, starring ninety-nine-year-old Lucy Marsden. What clicked?

GURGANUS

I'd been looking for a perspective from which to consider the South. What I really wanted was one life, one voice, one person who would embody everything that had happened to the Old South and the New South. She'd have to be old so she could have seen all the changes, all the alterations. And suddenly the phrase gave me a domestic situation. The beauty was, I immediately got Lucy's voice. I got her voice as if it were beamed to me on shortwave radio. I typed for four hours.

INTERVIEWER

What was it like writing in the voice of a woman?

GURGANUS

It seemed natural to me. The best talkers I know are women. I grew up with black women and white women telling stories, justifying themselves. Everybody knows the South is a matriarchy and the women are in control. The idea that men are in control is just a myth everybody agrees to pretend to.

INTERVIEWER

In 1965, you were an eighteen-year-old navy man stationed temporarily in Long Beach, California. One day you were browsing in a library when you discovered a stack of dusty ledgers. Those ledgers turned out to be a set of the federal census for 1790. When you opened the North Carolina volume, you discovered your ancestors had owned slaves. You were shocked. Did this novel—or some form of it—begin cooking inside you that minute?

GURGANUS

Oh, absolutely. I identified with the slaves themselves. Here I was on a ship, as the slaves had been. Here I was being shipped to Asia to do work that I didn't want to do for people I didn't respect. I was just a number, as they were. I was in a uniform, as they were. I felt tremendous identification. The fact that my [family's] name was on the [census] list made me feel completely and utterly implicated. It was like being a rabbi and discovering your mother's maiden name was Adolf Eichmann or Josef Mengele. You feel you are both things at once.

INTERVIEWER

In your novel, in 1899, President William McKinley visits the fictional town of Falls, North Carolina. Did he actually visit in the area that year? And did Sherman rip through on April 7, 1865, burning houses along the Tar River, as he did in your book?

GURGANUS

The dates and factual details are all true. What

I do with them is something else altogether. I used facts like the frame for a loom. The frame has to be symmetrical, and then you can weave over that and hope that what you weave can be symmetrical, too.

INTERVIEWER

You used a Montgomery Ward catalog of 1899 for much of your research. What else did you use?

GURGANUS

I looked at everything I could get my hands on. My own family's history is in the book. The shortbread recipe at the end of the book is my grandmother's, which she brought over from Scotland in the 1880s. It's full of whatever I could find by hook or crook, including privately published memoirs by veterans.

I have a very, very good memory. I never wrote down anything. My kind of research would be considered impressionistic to a real scholar. But I got a letter from Shelby Foote saying I got it all right.

INTERVIEWER

In the novel, you poke gentle fun at some of the customs, peculiarities, and traits of small Southern towns. But it seems you have a deep affection for the little town of Falls, where the novel is set, and which is loosely based on your hometown of Rocky Mount.

GURGANUS

Enormous affection. I can't imagine any luckier thing for a writer than to grow up in a town of twenty-four thousand on a main rail connection, that is a bird sanctuary, where the grandfather owns a farm and the father owns a business, and the family is mildly prosperous but not rich. The rich people have to stay, because they're bribed into promises of the family business, and I got away.

INTERVIEWER

I'm fascinated by the solitary chimneys that still stand sentinel over the ruins of those grand old pre–Civil War houses. Did the inspiration for Captain Marsden's family home, The Lilacs, spring from your own fascination with burned grandeur?

GURGANUS

The curious thing about lilacs is that they tend to like carbon in the soil. They're enormously stubborn plants. For me, the idea that lilacs would still come up around the stainless steel is a great testament to the stubbornness of things.

Growing up in the South is really like growing up in ancient Greece. If you see the ruined temples all the time, you have to wonder what the culture was. Northerners don't live with the reality of the war, because they haven't lived with ruins the way we have. The losers always feel the war more than the winners.

If every grandmother who said she buried the silver behind the barn had buried the silver behind the barn, we would not have lost the war for lack of money, and people with metal detectors would be out twenty-four hours a day digging up treasure troves. The losers always feel the war more than the winners.

INTERVIEWER

In your novel, Baby Africa is the name of a neighborhood in Falls where blacks lived early in the century, and where they had probably lived since emancipation. You create an awareness of how close blacks were to the events of their lives—namely, freedom, then bondage, then a freedom they were ill-equipped to handle. On the larger scale of history, we're prone to forget how recent those events are.

GURGANUS

It's enormously recent. American history is so short it's easy to forget how fresh all these things are. When Walt Whitman was a baby, he was put in the arms of Lafayette when Lafayette was visiting this country. That is going to the very roots of the culture.

INTERVIEWER

I'm also struck by how much impact a young man's death in the Civil War can have on the next two generations. Are we naive today about how much the events of the Civil War still affect our lives, especially our emotional lives?

GURGANUS

I think we only have to look at the most recent war—Vietnam—to understand how much we lost, what a terrible mistake it was. It's perfectly in keeping with the Civil War. The very people who are terribly prowar are now trying to cut back veterans' benefits, cutting out the counseling services, and are economizing at the expense of the veterans.

We don't even have to go back to the Civil War to see the terrible implications of what a war does to us. At every shopping mall in America there are these clusters of Vietnam veterans, just as the Civil War veterans were in town squares from the 1870s to the 1910s. So it's a continuous kind of problem. As the Bible says, "The sins of the fathers are visited unto the second and third generations."

INTERVIEWER

Your main character, Lucy Marsden, says early on in the book, "A person's life, it's just about a week." At forty-two, you seem to have an uncanny sense of life's brevity.

GURGANUS

I think part of it is serving in a war. I was enlisted during the war in Vietnam, and I became very conscious at eighteen I might be killed.

And what's gone on in the AIDS epidemic. There's a very real connection between the war in Vietnam, the AIDS epidemic, and the Civil War. In all three there are young men who are dying for causes and reasons beyond their control and beyond their help.

I've lost some of my best friends and some of the most interesting minds and some of the hugest talents in this country [to AIDS]. I've seen people age fifty years in six months. You see people lose a couple of pounds every day, which means the aging process is hideously speeded up.

Lucy in the novel was ninety-nine, and I'm only forty-two. And I've lost lots more of my contemporaries than my grandparents did.

INTERVIEWER

Your use of the language is yeasty and bright. How do you see your relationship to words and language?

GURGANUS

I'm a great believer in well-made things, and I don't really make a distinction between high art and a beautiful, beautiful table. I think my relationship to language is like a carpenter's relationship to wood. I didn't invent the twenty-six letters of the alphabet any more than a carpenter invents the trees. The goal is to take that material and make something beautiful and lasting, decorative and enduring. I'm very conscious of making a table that will not rock or be rickety or buckle with wear. I'm very interested in writing books that will last longer than I will. I think of literature as a note in a bottle that you seal up as best you can and throw out in hopes somebody on another shore will find it and nod over or smile over.

INTERVIEWER

You and John Cheever discovered each other early on in your career. What does it mean to have had such a mentor?

GURGANUS

I feel very, very lucky. He was one of the few people in the twentieth century who answered mail the day he got it. I understand now what a co-respondent was. It was like tennis. You write a letter; you get a letter back. Immediate response. Only now at this advanced age do I realize how generous he was to stop what he was doing and look at what I was doing.

He was a snob and sort of a Brooks Brothers fashion plate. But he was also a self-made man and a person who took enormous pleasure in the domestic life. His fiction is full of the joys of meals in the evenings, front porches and tennis and an orderly lawn.

It was my good luck in being the student of Grace Paley, Stanley Elkin, and Cheever. The greatest writers are the most generous. It's only second-rate writers who are competitive and jealous. They never said, "I'm worried you'll be good someday." They were absolutely thrilled to think there might be something in the world that had not been there before.

INTERVIEWER

You wrote a first-person piece in the May 1989 *House and Garden* about the clocks on your writing table. Why so many?

GURGANUS

A combination of things. One is they are real reminders of mortality. Another is I like to know what time it is. I like the sound of the ticking. I read my work aloud a lot. The clocks serve as a metronome, a pulse rhythm. Habitual sounds become very comforting.

INTERVIEWER

I read a description of your rent-controlled New York apartment. You said it was like living in a file drawer.

GURGANUS

I live in a lower-middle-income housing project for people who make twenty-five thousand dollars or less. They don't throw you out when you start making more—five hundred is the lid on rent—but people ask me if I'm moving. My friends are still my friends and my apartment is still my apartment. If the mailman delivers a box to my door, my neighbors take it in. It's not what your average North Carolinian thinks of as New York.

I always had a dream when I was a kid that the most fun place to live would be a kind of puppet workshop with a refrigerator in it. That's pretty much what I do. I have a drawing table and a writing table, and everything is sort of set up for me, so I don't have to put it away and take it out again.

INTERVIEWER

You seem to have a deep appreciation for the abidingness of life, even its ordinariness, in much the same way novelist Walker Percy does. In fact, Lucy says, "All a small town's joys and grief, child, live in the four words—Tonight was no exception."

GURGANUS

Well, it seems to me that we've read novels about upper-class people and novels about lower-class people. I've always thought that the serious American literature that's required is about that unnoticed middle. The joys of middle-class life. Not just the Riviera and not just the trailer parks. But the kind of household I grew up in—mildly prosperous, beautifully organized, and well-run. That was a great pleasure.

It's easy to write about people who want to climb the Himalayas. I wanted to take the most apparently mundane material in the world—like a woman making potato salad—and to make that in some way as dramatic as climbing the Himalayas. That has been my goal: To honor those people who stay home, pay the bills, and leave the porch light on at night.

INTERVIEWER

Where is home for you?

GURGANUS

Home is where my friends are, where I'm working. The joy is, I now have a portable computer, and I have friends everywhere, so home is just about everywhere I go.

I love travel and love being in motion. I'm also a homebody, and I always take a few of my precious objects with me. I have a marble nineteenth-century copy of a small Roman god that weighs about five pounds, a German windup toy, and a crystal paperweight my brother shoplifted for me from the Belk-Tyler in Rocky Mount. I take those with me, and I put those things down on the desk, and within an hour I'm working on a story in the computer.

My real psychic home is North Carolina, and my material is very much related to the place.

Even in my next book, *White People*, many of the people in the collection are natives of Falls, North Carolina, so I think that my ambition is to write a series of books—a whole shelf of books—about people from Falls. I know who's in every house on the street in Falls. I hope I live long enough to write as many of the stories as I can.

A phone is ringing in Chapel Hill, North Carolina, and Allan Gurganus is not answering. When he calls back—"mortified"—he explains that at the time for the interview, he was in a church basement investigating a set of 1860 Gothic windows he hopes to acquire for a Victorian house he's restoring in Hillsborough.

A friend, Melinda Marlette, happened to be on the spot when the four-thousand-square-foot bungalow in Hillsbourgh's historic district came on the market. She stood by as the broker called Gurganus in Chapel Hill. Within a week, he'd bought the house.

"It's on an acre of property," he says. "It's next door to the eighteenth-century town cemetery. William Hooper, who signed the Declaration of Independence, is buried ten feet away. I'm thrilled."

Gurganus is in the process of converting the kitchen, which faces east and is flooded with light, into his writing studio. He is also in the process of writing a "magical letter" to the vestry of Hillsborough's St. Matthews Episcopal Church, offering to have the Sunday-school building painted at his expense in exchange for the Gothic windows.

Gurganus bought the house, coincidentally, as he was finishing his story "Preservation News," about a man's search for the perfect historic house to restore.

With the forthcoming publication of two collections of stories—*Angels Are Among Us* and *Preservation News*—Gurganus talks this clear winter morning about obsession, energy, intuition, homosexuality, and the absolute necessity of looking for beauty in the world.

INTERVIEWER

When we last talked, you were living in Manhattan. Since then, you've moved back to North Carolina, bought a house in Chapel Hill, and are now restoring a Victorian house in Hillsborough. Do you feel at home here?

GURGANUS

I'm a double-dipping North Carolinian, as if I were ever anything but. It's wonderful to be back. The way these Gothic windows just came to me through phone conversations, through friends of friends, through the detective work of small-town gossip. All that convinced me this was absolutely the right move. When you get to be in your forties, you really want to be stationary and to have a garden and be rooted and be responsible to one place instead of two.

I feel I've found the perfect spot for that.

INTERVIEWER

Y'all have really developed a community of writers in Hillsborough and Chapel Hill and Raleigh and Durham.

I think of us as refugees from elsewhere who started in North Carolina and had to go a long way around and about to come back successfully. There's a way in which you're born into a hometown without any choice in the matter. There's a moment when you decide to choose what was assigned to you in the beginning. This is really what I write about. I write about community and people who are in love and in battle with their neighbors and their family. So it seems to me I'm going back to the well, going back to the source.

The metaphor of a dilapidated house being brought back is prophetic in some way. The day I finished the story "Preservation News," Melinda [Marlette] and the broker called up and said, "Here's your house." You write about the quest for a perfect house. All the mystical components are in place. You can read the signs very easily.

What about the writers?

The writers here—Kaye Gibbons, Lee Smith, Daphne Athas, Max Steele, and Elizabeth Spencer—it really is different from the more rivalrous feelings that a lot of New York writers have for each other.

Part of it is that we realize that the tradition we're working with is so rich and is so various that there's room in it for all of us. We're all in some ways telling the same story, but from different parts of the choir loft. There's a kind of joy in the success of other people. It complicates and enriches my own sense of how loaded the community is with stories waiting to be told.

How much of the talent you evidence in your work is raw, and how much of it have you learned by apprenticing yourself to the study of writing?

The exciting thing for me is that I feel that I'm really at the end of my apprenticeship, and I'm just getting down to the work I'm meant to treat.

I think there's a way in which, when you get to your middle years and you realize how complicated everything is, you want to break out of the single strokes you used when you were younger. They need to be held up to the light and turned and honored.

One of the things I'm trying to do in both these new pieces is to honor the facts of the case. A lot of the material is really autobiographical. My great-grandmother really did have a streetcar accident in Chicago. That's completely out of my family history.

I'm moving closer to facts in some ways, with all the equipment of fiction and all the elaboration of fiction, and I want to bring that equipment to bear on three or four different questions that recur over and over in my books. It's been a very rich time. I feel especially with [the forthcoming novel] *The Erotic History of a Southern Baptist Church* that I've really sort of turned into an ecclesiastical historian. I feel on the brink of doing my best work.

Let's go back and talk about raw talent.

GURGANUS

First of all, most people think that talent is an excuse not to work. And in fact talent is an imperative to work. A lot of people would think that if you had 70-percent talent, you'd only need 30-percent perspiration to put it all together. So they think the lucky people are the talented people.

The really serious artists I know are the ones who know that if your God-given talent is 100 percent, you have to return the favor by giving it 100-percent work. There are no shortcuts. The greatest artists understand that and have to work harder.

There's a rule that says you can have 50-percent talent and 50-percent character. But in fact your talent and your character have to be of the same scale or you'll never achieve anything beautiful or lasting.

You can have 70-percent character and 30-percent talent. But if you get down to 29.4-percent talent, it's not enough.

It's a strange sort of Faustian bargain. You have the voice, but you also have to have the kind of intelligence, and the kind of political intelligence, that allows you to get out of the Methodist church choir and onto the stage of the Metropolitan Opera. It doesn't happen by accident. It takes enormous concentration and daily energy. And it has to be a kind of obsession.

Sometimes people say, "Oh, I admire you so much because you get up every day and work, and you don't have any boss supervising you."

That's like praising a kleptomaniac for stealing. It's an obsession, and obsessions are not admirable or repellent. They're obsessions. The word obsess means "to sit before." So an obsession means you are a pilgrim bowing before the mecca. You are a small thing sitting before a large thing and worshiping it and concentrating on it. Sacrifices have to be made.

My love life and my erotic life are less concentrated and obsessive than my work life. Yeats talked about the choice: Perfection of the life or perfection of the art. In most cases, I've chosen perfection of the art. It's a kind of priesthood. It's a calling.

INTERVIEWER

Without obsession, most writers—novelists especially—couldn't sustain the energy required.

GURGANUS

That's really what it comes down to: How much energy you can put on an individual page. Energy that's transferred to the reader. Energy that energizes the reader. It's like creating immense Eveready batteries, batteries that the reader can plug into and feel rejuvenated and confirmed.

I got a letter from a woman in Israel who told me that her nine-year-old daughter had a brain tumor, and she was reading *Oldest Living Confederate Widow* in waiting rooms during her daughter's surgery and during the whole nightmare process. And she told me that the courage and energy of Lucy Marsden, who had endured everything and remained standing, had become a kind of model for her and had got her through the process.

She said, "I know you would want to know that my daughter recovered and graduated from high school yesterday." Of course I wanted to know, and that means so much more to me than TV rights and limos and all the perks most people would concentrate on.

It means you've done something right. You've sensed some kind of true energizing thing and made a vessel and put it out into the world so that other people can cling to and stay afloat by holding onto it.

INTERVIEWER

Your story "It Had Wings" was twenty-two pages in raw form. You boiled it down to three. That kind of work, which the reader never sees, reminds me of what your narrator says in "The Practical Heart": "Carelessness oh so hard won."

GURGANUS

It's work. I think my attitude toward it is as complicated as everybody's attitude toward work. Most people feel they would prefer not to. Given their choice, if they had unlimited means, they would go fishing, write a poem, make a pie, or make love. And so it never stops being work in that strange way that work is finally the noblest impulse. It contains everything you value.

And it's a painful process, because it's a process of giving beautiful things up. Cutting twenty-two pages is like cutting a field of flowers to get one bottle of perfume. It's a service to your readers. It means that your readers can read fewer pages and have more emotion.

And the great line from André Gide: "I rewrite

to be reread." That's what all writers want. Not to be read once and digested and eliminated. But to be reread. To make a kind of polar north on somebody's compass that they can go to in moments of doubt and depression and find some kind of solace and direction and amusement.

INTERVIEWER

Do you think of yourself as a comic writer?

GURGANUS

I do, though I deal with very dark subjects. The ability to make people laugh at difficult and impossible human situations. That's what I think the subject of fiction is—complication, pain, and

April 5, 1994

the difficulty of just living a life, especially of trying to live an ethical life.

In some ways, the seemingly lucky ones are the ones with no scruples, who do exactly what they want. It's those of us who try not to hurt people's feelings who inevitably end up hurting people's feelings. Our very act of seeking to protect sometimes wounds them.

Because I'm turning my kitchen into a study, I have a stove and a refrigerator that I don't need. I called somebody up to offer the stove and refrigerator. And this person says, "I can afford a stove and a refrigerator." So I wind up apologizing. So now I'll give it away to the Salvation Army. And I know he can't afford a stove and a refrigerator.

That's where the comedy becomes beautiful and meaningful. I think people would prefer to do the right thing. Sometimes it's too difficult to do, but I think it's what they would prefer.

My characters are those who try to do the right thing and in the process get it wrong. By laughing at this impulse, we forgive ourselves our virtue. It's not the crimes you have to forgive. It's your own earnest virtue.

That's one thing in my work that's bringing me so many readers: It appeals to a kind of deeply well-meaning person who has made a mess of things and who identifies with my character.

INTERVIEWER

In "Preservation News," you write about a man involved in restoration and preservation. In "The Expense of Spirit," you write about a woman who wants to have her portrait painted by John Singer Sargent. Both characters yearn. Is yearning at the base of fiction?

GURGANUS

You have to know what a character wants on some ultimate level. And if you can identify that, then the next question is, what will the character do in order to get the thing that he or she wants?

Then the next question is, what's standing in the way of the action that's required to get the desired object or the desired sensation? If you put those things together, including the compromises that must be made in order to get what we want, then we have a story.

For me, the stories that have a moral component—a character who's aware and holds dear certain rules of human behavior—become the most interesting of all stories.

We're all caught in what we've been told we should do and what we deeply, deeply long for. And the tension between those two impulses is the tension fiction grows out of.

INTERVIEWER

You've said storytelling is inherently curative. And you mean for the writer as well as the reader?

GURGANUS

That's right, for both. I think it's a cure that requires two participants, just as the act of lovemaking requires two participants. You can't tickle yourself. You have to have someone else to break your electrical field and make you giggle.

I feel a kind of a suspense until I've heard from certain people who've read my work.

INTERVIEWER

Who are those people?

GURGANUS

Other writers. And increasingly friends who have day jobs and who live regular lives who will tell me honestly what worked for them emotionally, what they considered unbelievable, where I lost their interest, what could be sacrificed. You have to be very ruthless about your reactions in order to be completely effective and efficient.

INTERVIEWER

You've used images from your dreams in your work. I'm thinking specifically of "It Had Wings" in your collection *White People*. But you've spoken of another function that must come in to govern the dream life. You've called it a "sidecar on the motorcycle."

GURGANUS

Listening to a stranger's dreams may be interesting in a surreal way for a short time. But until you know the person and know their dilemmas, you can't interpret the dreams.

And for me it's that interpretation that makes the dream most interesting. It's not weirdness for the sake of weird, but strangeness for the sake of meaning that interests me most.

The other thing—it sounds simple but is profound—dreams are meant to be mysterious. One of their functions is to mystify us and therefore to interest us. One of the functions of fiction is to mystify us. Fiction writing is alternatively deeply intuitive and profoundly intellectual. But never at the same time.

INTERVIEWER

How do you mean that?

GURGANUS

I mean that I flood out an image without analyzing it or justifying it, because it feels good. And then a day later, I go back and look at it and see how it pertains. If I analyzed it as I was writing, I would probably contract—tighten up—around it.

You have to be both first very instinctual and then very cool and smart. You go from very hot to being very cool.

A lot of people never know what they've done. But you can hit on huge, mysterious questions without having the answer. If the question is big enough, it can engage any number of readers.

What's difficult, and what makes very good writers so rare, is that it's very unusual to be both deeply intuitive and deeply intellectual in the same body.

That's why there are so few college professors who are great novelists. Because they are smart, and you have to be a little stupid to be a great writer. You have to be a kind of a peasant, because you're asking such simple questions over and over and over again: Why can't I have what I want? Why doesn't love last? Why must I die? Why can't I be sure there's an afterlife? Why do bad people so often succeed? Why are good deeds so often punished?

You have to keep asking them. Smart people ask hard questions and come up with one answer for a lifetime. That's an efficient way of operating.

But if you're writing in the voice of a character, you have to ask the same question in the voice of that character. That requires a kind of godlike patience with your own creation. It's like a child asking, "Why is the sky blue and why is the grass green?" You want to say, "Because it is. Now, let's go to your trumpet lesson."

But good parents are like good novelists. You have to answer every single question.

You have a hyperdeveloped on-off switch, which is the hardest thing to practice and evolve. You stop being smart and start being emotional, and then you stop being emotional and start being smart.

INTERVIEWER

What writers do you think do this best?

GURGANUS

Chekhov, whom I admire immensely. And Henry James. Flannery O'Connor.

To have the greatest work, you have to have both components. You know how you cool hot milk: You pour it from one container to the other. The distance between one cup and the other cup is what cools off the milk. One cup is intellect and one cup is emotion. The most beautiful work moves constantly back and forth between the two.

INTERVIEWER

Some of your writing sounds so real it has al-most a documentary feel to it. Your fiction is very convincing.

GURGANUS

One way you make things real is to be completely alive to the five senses. What I would like to do on every page, I would like to document a scene in terms of what is visible and what can be touched, what can be heard and tasted and what can be smelled. Smell is very important. So that if you are attuned to all five senses—not just the eyes, which are the most conventional, if not the most profound—but to the texture of the world, then you can make anything true.

INTERVIEWER

But there's something else that's very convincing, and that's your voice.

GURGANUS

I'm a great believer in narration. In the last twenty years, with the advent of minimalism, a lot of writers have lost faith in the convention of the narrator.

The word *narrate* is from the Greek word *gnaurus*, to know. And so a narrator is a knower. And narration is a knowing. But what's beautiful is, the narration always knows more than the narrator. I may not know the end of the story, but my tone has to convince my reader that I do. Or that I'm a reliable tour guide who should be listened to. And by trusting the narration, the narrator himself learns the story in the presence of the listener.

In the story "Art History," again from *White People*, the narrator says, "They could arrest me for everything I like about myself." That's an arresting statement.

GURGANUS

I think we all are secret outlaws. I guess I would say there are two kinds of people. One kind, when they hear a police siren, assume a black person is being arrested. And justifiably. The rest of us assume the police are coming for us. Unjustifiably. But we're sure we're about to wind up in jail.

My thought process is, "Guilty until proven guilty." So that if all of us secretly believe that we are monsters, and all of us secretly believe we are outlaws—that we are outside the law and the law will not protect us, the law protects the others and victimizes us—a fiction writer is immediately ahead of the game, because he understands that everybody is a victim and an apologist. And that contradiction—between what we secretly love most about ourselves and are proudest of and our own tragic sense of what can happen to a good person in the world—makes for the arena in which fiction is played out.

INTERVIEWER

You wear a moving man's zip-up uniform when you write, because you say you perspire so freely, and you say, too, that your body is the ultimate testing ground of what works and what doesn't on the page.

GURGANUS

I think in some ways the five senses are the ultimate arbiters and the ultimate judges and the ultimate supporters, if you know how to tap that knowledge. And the body is the holy of holies in human experience and in the best fiction.

And, finally, my sense of what's great in fiction is told to me by my breaths. If I read a sentence and I'm so engaged that I hold my breath until the end of the sentence, as if I'm sustaining the story by making a little sacrifice myself, then I know I'm in the presence of greatness. I know that because my intuitive body tells me.

To be able to create on the page the idea—with those twenty-six little jiggles that we manipulate to create sensation—that a real body that experiences pain and pleasure is writing, is to automatically engage the body that is reading the book. You acknowledge the body of the reader. You titillate the body of the reader with sexual sensation and with pleasure and with pain. But if there's not a body at the center of the fiction, it doesn't mean anything.

INTERVIEWER

Sometimes you get in touch with a waking dream life, and when you do, you hook up with the most readers. Another way you've described it is like getting to a preexisting map. Do you believe in Jung's collective unconscious?

GURGANUS

My teacher John Cheever used to say, "Fiction is a force of memory improperly understood." Which I think is a very elegant way of saying it. What it really means is that if you provide enough convincing detail for yourself and the reader, there is a strange quantum leap of the imagination. It doesn't come from nowhere. It comes from a million serious and intelligent decisions that prepare you for it.

We don't dream in algebraic equations. We dream bacon and eggs equal parking ticket equal mother. We're using the stuff of our own experience as a means of our own salvation. So this quantum leap doesn't happen abstractly. It comes from reality. And then you step into what can only be called hyperreality.

If you're an intelligent writer and reader, you allow yourself to be carried along into this cathartic, extreme moment of truth. And terror sometimes. The question is being answered.

INTERVIEWER

Can you give me an example?

GURGANUS

When I was writing *Widow*, I had never been to Charleston, South Carolina, but I had read about it. I created it in my head without any kind of documentation: A circular slave auction house with galleries on the sides and a big circular building with stalls outside, very close to the dock so that slaves could be brought in and fattened up, have tar rubbed into their wounds to make their skin look better, and to have their teeth whitened.

When the book came out, I was on a publicity tour in Charleston, and I was in a cab riding to the hotel, and I passed a circular building at the center of town. I said, "Stop the car." I got out and I recognized this building I had made up in my head.

I was confused, because in my hyperreal memory-slash-fantasy of this building, the dock was only seventy-five feet from the circular building. I asked at the hotel and discovered that around the turn of the twentieth century, a landfill had been put in, and that the water line was rerouted. Very, very strange. Totally unexplainable.

You do feel when you hit on these things, you're getting a sign you're doing something right, and doing it crucially, as a service occupation.

INTERVIEWER

A service for other people?

GURGANUS

It's a service that I provide for myself and other people. It's not about ego. It's not about self-praise. It's not about how different I am from other people. When it's really working, it's about how each of us contains all other people, if we only have the heart and imagination and time to honor them and consider them.

INTERVIEWER

Your character Tad Worth in "Preservation News" finally got his weight down to where he wanted it and enjoyed being fifteen pounds lighter. You're slim. Do you stay that way naturally or by obsession.

GURGANUS

I think it's obsession. I think I tend to burn

up immense amounts of energy, and I think that a lot of this is genetically determined. But I always think of myself as being lumpy. I'm like those thirteen-year-old girls who look in the mirror and see Jabba the Hut. In fact, they look like Audrey Hepburn.

INTERVIEWER

Do you ever suffer writer's block?

GURGANUS

If you don't believe in writer's block, you don't get it. I don't believe in heaven, but I don't believe in writer's block either. People are their own worst enemy. Look at Ava Gardner. I once saw her in a white swimming suit and a white bathing cap in Rocky Mount. It was a life-changing experience. That beautiful Indian—Native American—skin.

But she interfered with herself. She could have been a great actress, but she never believed she was a great actress. So in some ways she wasn't.

I think of myself as a survivor. I survived Vietnam. I'm a gay man who lived through the AIDS epidemic in New York, and I guarantee you it wasn't because I was home behaving like a priest. If you live through a certain number of cataclysmic experiences, you learn not to waste your time and not to interfere with yourself. You don't have to import pain. Pain will find you.

INTERVIEWER

And, unlike Ava Gardner, you believe in yourself.

GURGANUS

Don't forget, she was drafted into Hollywood when she was eighteen. She became other people's idea of what an actress was.

I'm self-invented, the way all artists are.

The people who are orthodox—the people who stayed home and inherited the family business and did exactly what they were told—are inherently less interesting than those who gave it up and found it again.

I was very lucky because my family was well-off in Rocky Mount, but not so well-off they could bribe me into staying there. We belonged to the country club, but there was no huge threat to keep me in that reality.

I was too restless to stay. Some of my friends are still there. Rich, and leaders of the town. And they envy me. They don't know what I've done is on the basis of work and immense determination. They think it's luck. They have to think that.

And what's interesting, they are my subjects. I am not my subject. I love them on the page.

INTERVIEWER

I've heard people say being gay allows a male writer to enter more easily into the mind of a woman in fiction. Yet gays aren't women. Does being gay have any effect at all on your writing?

GURGANUS

It does. For one thing, it means that everything you do erotically is illegal. And it also means that you are deprived of the standard rituals of human life. That is to say, you get married, you have babies, the babies grow up, the babies take care of you in your old age, you die and have a funeral. And all that you're guaranteed as a gay person is a funeral.

So what you have to do if you want to think well of yourself, and I do and so do my friends, is invent alternative rituals and create alternative families and find a way to value yourself in a society that considers you illegal and unnecessary and immoral.

So if you can survive—again, it comes back to survival—if you can survive living in a culture that does not respect you and does not consider your choice an appropriate one, then you are stronger than the people who've never had to question, who assume the wedding and the christening and the funeral is everybody's God-given right. And it's not.

So there's really more imagination about gender.

Most people would be very confused if they were asked to write the autobiography of their spouse in the voice of their spouse. It would be very painful and very embarrassing for many Americans to say "I" and mean "she" and to say "mine" and mean "hers."

Being gay entitles you to realize how arbitrary gender identity really is and makes you understand how it can be elevated to a kind of art form. It makes you understand that all gender is a form of disguise, just as all clothes are costumes.

And so in some ways, if you can survive these different questions and forge answers that are true for yourself, then you're in a better position to create people from other genders.

INTERVIEWER

In a 1989 interview in *Poets and Writers*, you said you hadn't been tested for AIDS, and not knowing made you want to pack in every possible thing in *Confederate Widow*, because you didn't know whether you'd live to write another book. Have you now been tested?

GURGANUS

Yes. The news is good. Thank God.

Part of it was just the exhaustion of not knowing. I felt that I was a better nurse for not knowing, because I could more identify with the people I was caring for. If only as a courtesy to your lovers, you need to know. And partly because medicine caught up, so that it became medically beneficial to know. For a long time, it didn't matter whether you knew it or not. It was an existential question.

Knowing that I have a prospect for a long life—and I come from a long-lived family—has been a beautiful reprieve.

INTERVIEWER

What's an ideal writing day for you?

GURGANUS

What it means for me is getting up earlier and earlier, before offices open at ten o'clock, and to have quiet time and very strong coffee when I'm nearest to a kind of dream state.

I love the way the world looks in the

morning, and my ideal day would be to work uninterrupted from six-thirty in the morning to one-thirty in the afternoon. To have the answering machine with its bell turned off so I don't know how many calls are coming in, and to go so far into the fiction that I freely surprise myself and make myself laugh and cry.

And then at one-thirty, I can enter the world and deal with banking questions and grocery questions and philanthropic causes and friends with a kind of double strength, because I've had a citizenship in two worlds in one day.

It's a great extra gift that artists are given—to have a world that you can control, and this world which none of us can control. To have art is to have your hand on the emergency brake all day. You can't really stop the world, but you can re-direct it. It's a great hidden bonus.

Part of my ethical sense as an artist is never to ask for an exemption because I'm an artist. I pay my taxes, and I ask after the health of the dry cleaner's children. I pride myself on being the same kind of good citizen I might have been if I were an insurance adjuster. Sarah Bernhardt said, "Artistic is a disease that afflicts only amateurs."

The joy of having this double citizenship is all the joy I ask.

I don't want people to take care of me because I'm helpless. That's part of the bargain: To be as completely in this world as I am in the world of fiction.

INTERVIEWER

In the story "The Impractical Truth," the narrator says, "There is always something embarrassing about love. All of it. That's because there's always something wrong with the beloved." What's that about?

GURGANUS

It's about the impossibility of beauty in the world, the absolute necessity to look for beauty everywhere.

There's a great line in [Samuel] Beckett in which he says, "Continuing is impossible. I continue."

And for me, the thing that's so rich about this life we're living is precisely how much pain we can live with while still expecting pleasure and order and perfection.

And I try in my work never to give easy answers. Always to honor the citizenship of pain, because we're all card-carrying members of that community.

No matter how entitled, no matter how much money you have, your parents die, your loved ones die, and you die.

And yet that doesn't prevent any of us from getting up every day and striving and trying and yearning.

And that's the heroism of every day. Which is the realest kind of heroism. Not done for medals. Done for a deep sense of self-worth, which is the only thing that saves any of us.

Allan Gurganus was born June 11, 1947, in Rocky Mount, North Carolina, the first of four sons of M. F. and Ethel Morris Gurganus. He graduated from Rocky Mount Senior High School in 1965 and attended Monterey Language School in Monterey, Mexico, and Radioman and Cryptography School in San Diego, California, both in 1966. He attended the University of Pennsylvania and the Pennsylvania Academy of Fine Arts, both from 1966 to 1967, and Harvard University from 1969 to 1970. He graduated in 1972 from Sarah Lawrence College and received an MFA from the University of Iowa Writers' Workshop in 1974.

From 1966 to 1970, Gurganus served as message decoder on a United States Navy aircraft carrier.

From 1972 to 1990, Gurganus taught fiction writing at the University of Iowa, Stanford University, Duke University, Sarah Lawrence College, and the University of Iowa Writers' Workshop. He is on the permanent faculty of Sarah Lawrence College.

His novel is *Oldest Living Confederate Widow Tells All* (1989).

His short-story collections are *White People* (1991) and *Preservation News* (1994).

Gurganus has won two grants from the National Endowment for the Arts, a Danforth Fellowship, and an Ingram Merrill Grant. *Oldest Living Confederate Widow Tells All* won the Sue Kaufman Prize for the Best First Work of Fiction, an award from the American Academy and Institute of Arts and Letters, and the Sir Walter Raleigh Award from the North Carolina Literary and Historical Association. He also won the *Los Angeles Times* Book Prize for the best work of American fiction. In April 1994, Gurganus's short story "The Practical Heart" won the National Magazine Prize for *Harper's*.

In May 1994, CBS aired *Oldest Living Confederate Widow Tells All*, with a cast led by Donald Sutherland, Anne Bancroft, Cicely Tyson, Blythe Danner, Diane Lane, Gwen Verdon, and E. G. Marshall.

Gurganus lives in Hillsborough, North Carolina, where he is working on a second novel, *The Erotic History of a Southern Baptist Church*.

September 23, 1976

ALEX HALEY

October 1 and 2, 1976

When Alex Haley enters the Atlanta TV studio, his name is not yet a household word. It will be in another week, when *Roots: The Saga of an American Family* vaults to number two on the bestseller list.

Haley, born in Ithaca, New York, and raised in Henning, Tennessee, moves into the WSB-TV studio as unassuming and silent as a shadow. But under the bright lights, his energy begins to uncoil. He talks about how he picked through the slim clues that led him from this country, back across that ocean "which every one of us here in America crossed," and into deepest Africa.

It was in Gambia, on the outskirts of a village, that Haley heard from the chief Griot—a man whose meticulous memory is trained to span generations of oral history—the same story he had heard since childhood: The story of his four-times great-grandfather, Kunta Kinte, who went out of the village to chop wood one day in 1767 and was never heard from again.

"In that miraculous moment of discovery," he says, "I was really rendered almost mute and dumb. There are just no words to convey that emotion."

Now, Haley is transformed from researcher into evangelist.

"Go with all possible haste to the oldest people in your families," he urges the TV audience. "They may be holding in their heads some of your most precious gifts. They may be holding in their heads the clues to your own roots.

"And family reunions. We have got to start in this country a return to family reunions. There's a magic moment when the chairs are lined up and the oldest members of the family are sitting in the softest, easiest chairs holding those wriggling babies, and all the middle-sized people are standing up. And the camera goes click, and everybody who was there walks a little taller because they were there and they know the beat of their family, and they know who they are."

Haley's schedule is jammed. The only time he can sit for an interview is at five o'clock in the morning in the Atlanta Hilton Hotel. Here, night easing into day, Alex Haley talks about learning to write, about cranking microfilm to find his ancestors, and about his love for his own roots, lovingly nurtured in the little town of Henning, Tennessee.

INTERVIEWER

During your 20-year tenure in the Coast Guard, you rose from cook—with a time-consuming hobby of writing love letters for your shipmates to their girlfriends—to the official position of chief journalist. What did you learn during those years about the difference between writing letters and writing articles and books?

HALEY

One night, there was a book around that I'd read pieces of off and on. And I just picked up that book and propped it on the typewriter, and I began with just the pure, capricious intent to type a chapter of this book onto this piece of paper.

Well, I started, and I tell you what happened. Around the second paragraph, I began to feel, for the first time in my life, what good writing felt like in a typewriter. It was disciplined, it was sharp with clarity, every word was necessary, the sentence structure was beautiful.

That thing grabbed me. It just simply did. I wanted to somehow make my writing feel like that. And I set out in that direction.

INTERVIEWER

You've said that when you'd get stumped writing, you'd go in the ship's kitchen and mix up a cake and pull up a stool to the windowed oven and sit there with your head in your hands watching that thing bubble and seethe. In fact, you've compared that process of the cake baking to the process of writing.

HALEY

I would look at that cake batter in the pan, and it would look as if it would ever be thus. Then, miracle of miracles, a bubble makes its appearance in some unexpected place. In another second, another bubble makes its appearance in another location. And another will do the same. And then, you know, what you start watching is that absolutely miraculous process of something being created from raw material. And what is being created is really quite different from the raw material. And that is a very similar thing to the process of writing. You have your notes and your memories and your feelings, and those are your ingredients. But that thing that happens in your hands and in your head—when you do it well—creates another thing entirely.

INTERVIEWER

When you got out of the Coast Guard in 1959, you decided to pursue writing as a career. You headed straight for Greenwich Village, rented yourself a basement apartment, and, as you've said, "prepared to starve."

HALEY

One time, I was down to eighteen cents: A nickel, a dime, and three pennies. In my little cupboard I had exactly two cans of sardines. And I just did something crazy and capricious and dumped them all in a little box.

Well, I carried the little box around with me for years, and it wasn't until much later that I had enough money to have the two cans and the eighteen cents framed. I have them right over my mantel today in California, and they symbolize for me the "hanging in there" when I didn't know I could make it.

INTERVIEWER

Your writing was selling regularly, but you wanted to hit bigger markets.

HALEY

I wanted desperately to write for *Playboy*. I was given an assignment by them to do an interview with Miles Davis, but he wouldn't answer my questions with anything but a yes or a no. So I wrote an expository lead and put the rest into question-and-answer format, and *Playboy* liked it so much they decided to continue that format.

You might say that the *Playboy* interviews evolved by accident.

INTERVIEWER

You interviewed Malcolm X for *Playboy*, which led to your coauthoring *The Autobiography of Malcolm X*. That book earned you your first real writing money and some leisure. What did you do next?

HALEY

I was kind of in a vacuum period after the book was finished, and the time was in the sixties, and there was a lot of talk then about blacks and about Africa. And I had all these stories in my head that my grandma and her sisters had always told me. About how they were born in Alamance County in North Carolina on Master Tom Murray's plantation. They just talked about it repetitively until those stories were like Biblical parables I learned in Sunday school. I just sort of knew the name Alamance County like I knew the name Bethlehem.

INTERVIEWER

And then there was that day in 1965—before the world had ever heard of your four-times great-grandfather Kunta Kinte of Gambia, Africa—when you went to the National Archives in Washington and asked to see the 1870 census records for Alamance County. They brought you eight rolls of film, and you turned that crank, watching the names "march in stately tread" until you got to the fourth roll. Then there came that moment that galvanized you, that stopped you cold.

HALEY

I saw Tom Murray, blacksmith, wife's name Arrena, and listed below were the names of my aunts. There was Aunt Vinnie. And there, for God's sake, was Aunt Liz. The Aunt Liz who sat on the porch with long gray hair, and these census records showed my Aunt Liz was only six [in 1870].

I came out of there bewildered. The more I kept thinking about it, the more my mind kept going back to childhood, where I had first heard the story of "the African" who had been chopping wood when he was kidnapped.

INTERVIEWER

Your emotions must've been a choppy sea that day.

HALEY

There were times when I felt like walking back through history swinging an ax. I began to find something in me, some fury. But fury is something that at best can immobilize and at worst can destroy you.

People have asked me if delving into the past like this is going to stir up trouble again for blacks and whites. I say, "Hell, no!" We've spent so long cosmetizing and hiding. Let's get it out there and look at it and deal with the legacy.

Most white folks don't know much more than black folks about where they came from. Black folks all think white folks can trace their families back to William the Conqueror. I hope we've transcended that feeling. I want to be evangelistic about this particular thing. I want to spread

this concept, this awareness of a sense of our own roots, throughout the country.

INTERVIEWER

You worked on *Roots* for ten years, often returning to the sea for extended writing stints. Why the sea?

HALEY

After about three days in a ship's stateroom, you feel like you're in a womb, and you can just write like crazy.

INTERVIEWER

You've had two failed marriage. Maybe your obsession with writing doesn't mix well with domesticity.

HALEY

It was my life to learn to write, and that just didn't make me very domestic. I just simply was married to what I was doing, and I freely admit it. In some kind of way, I don't feel a whole lot of guilt about it. I just couldn't help it.

INTERVIEWER

You're writing a book now about how you discovered your roots—the book behind the book. Then what?

HALEY

I want to write a book about that dusty, sleepy little town of Henning, Tennessee. It is said, and properly said, that anytime a small town in America dies, a little bit of America dies with it.

And Henning is symbolic of every small town in America. Every emotion a human being can feel is evoked in it. I feel I have that book like a lollipop in my mind.

It's very meaningful to me that I just sort of came out of Henning, and I've seemed to retain its values. It's like although I now live and operate within a big-city context, deep down inside, I'm still small-town, and I'm not too sure about all of the city slickers, really.

———————

Born August 11, 1921, in Ithaca, New York, Alex Palmer Haley was the first of three sons of Simon Alexander and Bertha George Palmer Haley. He grew up in Henning, Tennessee, and graduated from high school at age fifteen. He attended Elizabeth City Teachers College in Elizabeth City, North Carolina, from 1937 to 1939.

From 1939 to 1959, Haley served in the Coast Guard, retiring as chief journalist.

From 1959, he worked as a freelance writer, selling articles to *Reader's Digest, Harper's, The Atlantic*, and *Playboy*, where he initiated the *"Playboy* interviews."

Haley's works include *The Autobiography of Malcolm X*, written with Malcolm X (1965); *Roots: The Saga of An American Family* (1976); *My Search for Roots* (1979); the novella *A Different Kind of Christmas* (1988); *Queen* (1993); and *Henning* (1994).

In 1977, Warner Brothers made a twelve-hour ABC-TV miniseries based on *Roots*.

In 1993, CBS made a miniseries based on *Queen*.

His awards include a special citation from the National Book Award Committee (1977) and a special citation from the Pulitzer Prize Committee (1977).

In 1941, Haley married Nannie Branch. They had two children, Lydia and William.

In 1964, he married Juliette Collins. They had one child, Cynthia.

In 1978, he married Dr. Myran Lewis and was divorced.

Alex Haley died of cardiac arrest at Swedish Hospital in Seattle, Washington, on February 10, 1992.

April 7, 1994

JOSEPHINE HUMPHREYS

August 20, 1987

"*J*o, you live in your own little world!" Josephine Humphreys's mother chided not long ago.

"It was supposed to perturb me," says Humphreys. "But I just lit up and ran and put it in the novel."

That novel, *Rich in Love*, set in Charleston, South Carolina, and nearby Mount Pleasant, is the result of Humphreys's most recent sojourn in her creative world.

Humphreys believes her mother is only partly right about that world. "I do live in my own world. But it isn't little. And if things go right in that world, I hope a lot of books can come out of it."

So far, things have gone extremely right. Her first novel, *Dreams of Sleep*, was welcomed with a chorus of praise and won the 1985 Ernest Hemingway Foundation Award for most distinguished first book of fiction.

But writing fiction was a long time coming for Humphreys. When she graduated from Duke University in 1967, she turned down money from the Mary Duke Biddle Foundation to write a novel. Instead, she accepted Woodrow Wilson and Danforth fellowships to study English literature at Yale. After earning a master's degree there in 1968, she transferred to the University of Texas, where she wrote half a doctoral dissertation and quit.

Humphreys realizes now that academia cut jaggedly across her grain. But it took acute chest pains—and a fierce determination to reorder her priorities—to return her to her creative world.

The windows of her writing studio on Broad Street in Charleston look out onto cobblestoned Chalmers Street, usually thick with tourists. Her doorway, by contrast, opens onto the lush solitude of a historic courtyard.

"I like to be on that edge," she says, "between those two worlds."

It was from this office that she talked about the despair she felt before she began to write her first novel, about her "on-purpose" hallucinations, about the parallel between bird-watching and writing, and about the transforming power of love.

INTERVIEWER

You were about thirty-three when you started writing your first novel, *Dreams of Sleep*. What prompted you to start?

HUMPHREYS

Absolute despair. I was working too hard. I managed to give birth during school vacations [while teaching English at Charleston's Baptist College]. I was driving twenty miles to work, and breast-feeding. I made my mother drive my first child all the way up to Baptist College at eleven o'clock every day so I could breast-feed him. And I ended up in the doctor's office with chest pains. I mean terrible pains. I went to a cardiologist. After lengthy tests, he told me there was nothing wrong with me.

While he was out of the room, I looked in his folder, and he had written down, "Anxiety reaction." I decided I wasn't going to go down in anybody's book that way.

So it was a point of taking stock. In a matter of months, I quit work and quit everything and decided I would decide what was important, and the children were number one. And so I was going to do stuff with them and write a novel.

I started with a thirty-three-year-old woman who is terribly despondent. I couldn't have the reason for her despair be that she hadn't written her novel. So I was forced to invent a plot to explain her feelings.

INTERVIEWER

That was about nine years ago, and since then you've continued to keep your life simple. You no longer entertain or teach Sunday school or coach your sons' soccer team. What have you gained by giving up these things?

HUMPHREYS

I've gained time. If I made time for all those things, I wouldn't have the mental energy for writing. I have to protect myself from minor interests I could spend my whole life happily doing.

INTERVIEWER

Such as?

HUMPHREYS

Cooking. I love to cook, and I don't do that too much anymore. Bird-watching could become an obsession with me. I try not to get out in the woods too much, because it could take over. I know a lot of writers who are obsessed with bird-watching.

INTERVIEWER

What's the connection there?

HUMPHREYS

I think the connection is that in both writing and bird-watching, the dullness and monotony of ordinary life crack open, and there is always the possibility of something wonderful coming over the horizon. There's always the chance you're about to see some rare and beautiful thing you've never seen before, and that maybe no one else has seen before either.

INTERVIEWER

What have you lost by being so focused?

HUMPHREYS

I have lost friendships. I regret that. I've gained some friends. I have some real good friends who are writers, and the friendships are by correspondence or telephone, and these are probably the best friends I've ever had. They're very helpful. My old friends . . . I don't have the time to do the things you have to do to maintain friendships: Go out to lunch, go to someone's house at night for dinner. It just becomes an ongoing rush of activity, you know. Sometimes I worry because of the traditional understanding that a lawyer's wife is responsible for social contact, which I just don't do. But it's perfectly okay with Tom. But about once a year, I worry about that.

INTERVIEWER

In both *Dreams of Sleep* and *Rich in Love*, you use Charleston and environs as a setting. Have you encountered any problems doing this?

HUMPHREYS

The problem is that I don't feel any compunction at all to stick to the truth. In both books, the geography is not accurate. One real spot is not next to the other real spot in the book. That's the way I have to do it. I want to have a combination of a real place and an imaginary place, with the feeling of the real, but the essence of the imagined, which is more important to me.

That's very difficult for people who live here. If they're reading along and come to something that's not right geographically, they get thrown off.

INTERVIEWER

What do you like about Charleston and the South, assuming you do like Charleston and the South?

HUMPHREYS

First of all, it's the physical appearance. It's the age and beauty of the buildings and streets and surrounding countryside, especially maybe the surrounding countryside.

There are really no Charleston institutions I'm crazy about. And history itself has never appealed to me. I'm not a history buff. I don't know anything about the Civil War or the things you're supposed to know, partly in rebellion. There's so much of it here, I didn't want to be part of it.

INTERVIEWER

Edmund Wilson said once that Northerners do not grasp the state of the Southern mind. Do you agree with that?

HUMPHREYS

To be most honest, what I like best, and what I think I see, as a common quality of the Southern mind, is a sense of humor. All the Citadel cadets were from New Jersey or New York, and we always went out with Citadel cadets. And I remember thinking when I was going out with them that their sense of humor was completely different—if they had one. Most of the time, they didn't. They were very serious and very success-oriented. Sort of rigorous people. Whereas the Southern boys were much funnier. Their conversation was always more interesting, because of the possibility of a laugh now and then.

INTERVIEWER

In *Dreams of Sleep*, the main male character was a doctor, and a doctor is a minor character in *Rich in Love*. Is that a coincidence?

HUMPHREYS

I've always been fascinated by doctors. My grandfather, who brought my seventeen-year-old grandmother to South Carolina from Amarillo, Texas—even sent her to Ashley Hall to be "finished," then later divorced her—was a doctor. In fact, he became president of the Medical University of South Carolina and eventually president of the American Medical Association.

After their horrible divorce, my parents steered cleared of doctors. When they did need to take us to the doctor, they always picked the scuzziest-looking doctors in the worst part of town. They thought the less money the doctor was making, the better the doctor was, because that meant he wasn't in it for the money.

I was never really conscious of it, but I know that's where all that came from. I think when you're a child, you try to gloss over the really weird parts of your life and pretend they're okay and there's nothing terribly wrong. That's the great talent of children, and why they survive—they have this drive to make everything okay in their heads.

INTERVIEWER

You never saw this grandfather until after you were married, yet you grew up in the same town with him. As a child, did you think it unusual that you didn't know your mother's father?

HUMPHREYS

No. But it annoyed me, in a minor way, that he was rich and we weren't, or that my grandmother wasn't. I thought that was especially unfair. I had a romantic sense that maybe someday there would be a reconciliation. But I knew there wouldn't be, because my mother had convinced me—and rightly—that he was a bad man.

As an adult, I went to a wedding, and at the wedding, my husband pointed out to me my grandfather. He had met him as a lawyer. My sister was with me, and we treated it as a joke, and we sneaked around the yard and looked at him from behind trees.

INTERVIEWER

Did your relationship with your grandmother play any part in your becoming a writer?

HUMPHREYS

Oh, yes. She and my mother together started me as a writer simply by fiat. They said, "You will be a good writer."

My grandmother was a part-time sculptor and had a studio with the [nationally known] artist Elizabeth Verner. She went there every day. It was on Tradd Street, and we'd go and play around. She didn't stay long. She really never accomplished a whole lot. But one day I had written a story, and she took me down to her studio and asked me to read it aloud to Elizabeth Verner. I was flattered by the comments, and I liked hearing her tell her friends that I was a writer. I was about seven then.

Now, I understand the importance of what you say to your children. They take it to heart. It sinks in. Children are constantly making their idea of what they are.

INTERVIEWER

What about your father?

HUMPHREYS

I don't think my father ever understood what a writer does. And he still doesn't. He doesn't like to read novels. He thinks they are fairly useless. A novel is not a book you'd keep around on a shelf and open and consult, which is the kind he likes.

INTERVIEWER

Do you think your choice of a college—Duke—affected your writing career at all?

HUMPHREYS

Only in one way, but that was huge. Reynolds Price was teaching there, and William Blackburn, and they were probably the really most important, serious influences on my becoming a writer—a real writer. They were great teachers, and I think both of them became more important to me in my imagination than in real life.

I never went out to eat with them or to their homes, except later. Each was the kind of person who appears to a college kid and shapes up a kind of vision about what life is like, and what you can do with yourself, and what's important.

I hate the word *mentor*, but that is what it is. An older person who appears at a crucial time in a younger person's life and is an inspiration. And I think they influenced my writing, not by any specific advice they gave, but because I loved them so much I ended up writing for them. That's what a great teacher is: Somebody you write for.

INTERVIEWER

You graduated from Duke, then took a master's at Yale, then went to the University of Texas for doctoral work. But you never completed your Ph.D. dissertation. Why not?

HUMPHREYS

I was working on my dissertation around 1970, and I was at a point where I'd been teaching for a while at the Baptist College. I had two children. I had not done any writing for—oh, gosh—five years, maybe, so it was the early seventies. I felt that I was working on something simply because it was there. I was working toward a degree that wouldn't even help me in my job. I liked my dissertation topic— William Cowper, the eighteenth-century Methodist fanatic–British poet, who was insane and wrote not-very-good religious poetry and some sort of interesting preromantic poetry. He was an odd person, and I became very interested in his character—the person—which was really not what I was supposed to be writing about. I got sidetracked by the curiosity of this man, and I realized that I was up the wrong creek. And I just stopped.

INTERVIEWER

You've said that a place to write is very important to you. What's your office on Broad Street like?

HUMPHREYS

Well, I have a small room in the old Confederate Home, and it's got everything I need in it and very few distractions. Nothing to play with. I don't really even have many books here—just a word processor and typewriter. I have three windows, two of which look out onto Chalmers Street, which is the old cobblestone street. The office opens onto a colonnade that goes onto a beautiful courtyard, right next to Washington Park. St. Michael's tower is over the next wall. I have a combination of pure solitude and a view onto busy humanity, which I really love.

INTERVIEWER

How does your work go in that office?

HUMPHREYS

I need blocks of time where I can sort of . . . I think of it in terms of going under. I can write almost anywhere. But it's best for me if I can have four or five hours of steady writing, uninterrupted.

I didn't know this at first, but the way I get things done is similar to meditation, or a kind of on-purpose hallucination. Which sounds too wacky to be believed. But it really works that way for me.

INTERVIEWER

Please elaborate.

HUMPHREYS

All you have to do is start, and the writing feeds the writing. I don't believe in the inspiration of the muse. I think it's a habit of your mind that you can get into.

I don't meditate, but people who do don't think of it as divine inspiration. I think they think of it as a state of mind that they know how to get to. An exercise. The seventeenth-century poets had a lot of the same notions. They did think of it as divine inspiration, but also a practice—a meditative exercise—that could lead to revelations.

INTERVIEWER

How do you think of it?

HUMPHREYS

I think of it as something akin to schizophrenia or a disorder. It's a good thing that there's such a thing as writing as a respectable activity, because if there weren't, people like me would be locked up. I'm not competent to live a normal life. I absolutely can't keep a house clean. There are some people who are unable to be in a room without trash accumulating, and that's one of my problems. I'm distractible. Anything that comes along attracts me and interests me so much that I want to do that, and I don't want to be doing the things I'm supposed to be doing.

During that time I wasn't writing, I had a great interest in mental patients, and I did a lot of volunteer work on the psychiatric ward of the county hospital. I was extraordinarily interested in the visions of the people, the things that they could see that we thought were crazy, but weren't necessarily.

I never got obsessed with teaching, but I got real involved in counseling students and in helping students who couldn't read. I think that is the problem. I just go off in strange directions and wander away.

INTERVIEWER

You have created two dreamy, solitary characters—Alice in *Dreams* and Lucille in *Rich in Love*—and in both cases it is love, both physical and emotional, that brings them to themselves and into the world. Do you personally think of love as a powerful catalyst?

HUMPHREYS

Yes. I think it's the only catalyst. I don't think there are very many things that are strong enough to change human laziness and habit and blindness. But that's one, and it's a real powerful one.

April 7, 1994

April 25, 1991

Usually, a hush fills the historic tree-shaded courtyard at the Confederate Home in Charleston, where novelist Josephine Humphreys rents a writing studio. But today, even by long-distance, you can hear power saws buzzing, readying exhibits for the annual Spoleto arts festival.

Humphreys's third novel, *The Fireman's Fair*, is set in Charleston during the aftermath of Hurricane Hugo. As in her previous novels, love storms through lives, creating new landscapes in her characters' hearts.

This cool, rainy day, Humphreys—settled on the wicker sofa in her studio, drinking Cuban coffee—talks about disorder, domesticity, self-doubt, and creativity.

INTERVIEWER

You dedicated this new book to Reynolds Price, with whom you studied as a Duke undergraduate. You once said you write for Reynolds Price and another Duke teacher, William Blackburn. Is this still true?

HUMPHREYS

They were so inspiring. I still look back on those years with such a sense of excitement, and I don't think I would've ended up doing this if it hadn't been for them. They made writing seem like the most important thing that I could do. And, personally, they were so wonderful—in different ways.

Blackburn was a gruff, difficult man, and I don't know why so many people were so absolutely in love with him. But we adored him. He was somebody you have to fall for, and everybody did, even though his class [Renaissance literature] was incredibly difficult. We'd panic and get sick before exams, because his exams were so hard. But everyone wanted to take the course.

Reynolds was in his early thirties, and he was

absolutely magical. Magical. And so handsome and so funny. When we were in his class, we were mesmerized for an hour every day.

When I graduated from Duke, Dr. Blackburn offered to get me some fellowship money to spend a year writing fiction. I turned it down, because I was scared to do it. Then, several years later, he died. So when I was writing *Dreams of Sleep*, it really was for him. It was a delayed gift. And I was very happy to be able to send that book to Reynolds later, when I had finished it. Dr. Blackburn had been Reynolds's teacher also at Duke when he was an undergraduate there, and they were very close.

INTERVIEWER

When people talk about Charleston, they often talk about fitting in. In your new novel, one character fits in so well he's called "Mr. Charleston." Yet another—a native with a degree from Yale—doesn't. You're both a native and the great-great-granddaughter of George Trenholm, the Confederacy's secretary of the treasury. And sometimes even you say you feel you don't fit in.

HUMPHREYS

One interesting thing about a so-called aristocracy is that once you start making those distinctions among people, you can go on forever. Within an "in" group, there are further distinctions. That's why I think it's not an ideal community when you have a setup like that. My guess is that very few people actually feel they are the inner circle, because they learn to become attuned to these supposed qualifications. And nobody has them all.

INTERVIEWER

In *The Fireman's Fair*, you describe Charleston as "a place where people continually run into each other in spite of rifts and irreconcilable differences. Divorced partners find themselves in the same grocery aisle twice a week; men who have cheated each other in business drink together at cocktail parties. No one seems to mind." Is this an approximation of the truth?

HUMPHREYS

I think so. And I think it's kind of a nice thing. It makes for some odd situations. But, you know, I think any close-knit community would be like that. If it's a stable community and people stick around after calamities, then they will see each other.

INTERVIEWER

The Fireman's Fair is set in the aftermath of Hurricane Hugo. But you began the novel before Hugo hit.

HUMPHREYS

I had finished my first draft. I had just finished it, as a matter of fact. I wasn't pleased with it, and one of the reasons I wasn't happy with it was because the story is about someone who feels this pressing need to change his life, but there was no real reason for him to do so—no initiating spark. Then all of a sudden this thing happened to all of us here that seemed to dramatize our lives. I think there was a process of clarification for a lot of people. It became clear to us that you could lose all your material possessions, and that wouldn't matter very much.

INTERVIEWER

You mentioned recently that you were planting flowers at your house on Meeting Street. I know you love domestic things. Do you indulge yourself in domesticity when you've finished a novel?

HUMPHREYS

Yeah, I do. I don't love all domestic things. I do not love making up beds, washing dishes, or cleaning up. I love cooking, gardening, painting, and I love to iron. I like all the things where you feel like you're making something happen, or making something exist. But maintenance is not my cup of tea—where you do something like make up the bed, and eight or nine hours later it's messed up again.

INTERVIEWER

You talked about maintenance in Charlotte earlier this spring. In fact, you said that to be wife, mother, and novelist, you had to give up achieving any kind of order around the house. Is this really a major problem?

HUMPHREYS

It's major. It's a problem to me because it's embarrassing with respect to my husband and children. I feel terrible that I don't keep a neater house. They don't complain, and they help, and the boys know how to iron and run the washing machine. Now and then, I try to reform and spend a couple of days madly cleaning up—to no lasting effect.

To be honest, I think I would've been like that even if I weren't writing. There are some people who are pathologically messy, and I've always been one of them. My mother says it's just laziness, and that may be. Except that I work really hard on other things.

INTERVIEWER

What's your mother like? Is she a good housekeeper?

HUMPHREYS

Mother has an alien streak herself. Her house, if she told the truth, is not highly organized. It's better than mine. I can see maybe an inherited gene there.

She's just great. She is a real supporter. My mother reads a lot. She's real smart, too, and has always been interested in a lot of different things. We had our rough times when I was a teenager—a lot of pitched battles. But she says she doesn't remember any fights.

INTERVIEWER

You speak of your two sons—Allen, age seventeen, and Willy, sixteen—very lovingly.

HUMPHREYS

They are wonderful. They are so much fun to be around and to talk to and do things with. I'm so proud of them. The thing is, they're better than I am. I really admire them. They are more

honest, more generous, more fair-minded than I am, and so it's a funny feeling to have children that you look up to.

INTERVIEWER

Are there differences in you during the long haul of writing a novel and when you're not?

HUMPHREYS

When I'm writing, I feel as if I'm really engaged and really buried in this story. And when I'm not writing, I feel guilty that I am out of that trance and not working.

I think when I'm not writing, I'm more prey to anxieties and worries about regular life. When I'm writing, I don't fret too much about normal, everyday things. If I don't have that [writing] to focus on, then troubles can attack me. I'm really quite a worrier. I can work myself up into incredible false fears. Things like termites, the bank balance, children.

INTERVIEWER

When you're writing, is it that you notice things more acutely?

HUMPHREYS

Yes. You notice everything, and everything seems to be full of meaning and directly centered on the thing you're writing about. I heard E. L. Doctorow say something like that—that when you're writing, all experience seems to organize itself around your themes, which can give you some really strange feelings of coincidence and ESP. You start to think you're onto the secrets of life.

INTERVIEWER

Can you imagine yourself ever not writing?

HUMPHREYS

I didn't write any fiction for eleven years, between college and age thirty-three. So I can imagine it. In fact, when people ask me what my hopes are, they expect me to say prizes and movies. But my real and only hope is that I can keep doing this. Anything that threatens my future work is really scary to me.

INTERVIEWER

You've said the way you write is akin to a trance or an "on-purpose" meditation.

HUMPHREYS

Well, it works best when I'm really writing hard, putting in long hours every day. It's actually easier to do that intense imagining writing by pen than it is with the computer. But I do have a computer. I go back and forth.

Sometimes I like to write lying down. I have a sofa in the office, and I lie down on it and put my paper and pencil on the floor. It sounds uncomfortable and awful, but that works sometimes. Who knows why?

INTERVIEWER

And the trance?

HUMPHREYS

It's like watching a movie or a TV story and writing it down. Writers often use metaphors that suggest they're not in control. They talk about the characters writing this novel. Those are only metaphors, only a description of the way a writer feels at the time. That's not really what's happening. But when I feel that way, that's when it's going best.

Reynolds [Price] says that writing depends on the subconscious, and I think that's true. It comes often from the part of the brain that you're not in touch with on a daily basis, and that's why it can be so surprising to the writer. The things that happen in a story can actually surprise the person who's in charge of the story. In a way, it's like dreaming. It comes from your own brain, but you have the sense that it comes to you from somewhere else.

INTERVIEWER

Do you ever get to a point when you're writing and you know you're too tired to write? Or do you ever feel you've expended too much energy on other things? In other words, are there things which affect your best ability to write?

HUMPHREYS

Yes. Physically, I have to watch out, because I get tired. And traveling, which is something I used to love to do, is more and more difficult for me, because it just exhausts me. After I come back, it takes me a long time to recover.

INTERVIEWER

Do you require a lot of sleep, and do you think sleep affects creativity?

HUMPHREYS

I have always needed a lot of sleep. I go to bed at about eight o'clock every night. And I don't get up early either. I go to bed at eight and get up about seven. I think sleep is truly restorative. I was talking to Kaye Gibbons recently, and she said she'd gotten in her nightgown at five-fifteen one afternoon.

INTERVIEWER

Do you find you dream less when you're deprived of sleep?

HUMPHREYS

That's true. I'm just remembering now that towards the end of writing *The Fireman's Fair*, every night I was dreaming not about the story but about how to tell a story. They were the strangest dreams I've ever had, sort of a searching for the ways in which these characters could work out their own lives. They were not concentrated on the events of the book, but rather on my own thinking. It was very strange. I called them "fiction dreams." The dreams were about pure fiction, not about the story. They were about making fiction.

INTERVIEWER

I read an interview with you in which you said it's good for writers to have self-doubt.

HUMPHREYS

It seems to me that maybe the essential stance of a writer has to be that of a questioner, because if you're writing fiction, you're creating a reality. But you're also questioning reality and questioning the status quo, and that has to be the writer's whole way of thinking.

INTERVIEWER

But what does that have to do with self-doubt?

HUMPHREYS

If you have constant self-doubt, you're always sort of wondering if you're right or wrong, wondering if you're seeing things clearly or not. Also, I think people who are happy and healthy don't write.

INTERVIEWER

Why is that?

HUMPHREYS

They just live. Why should they write? They just go ahead and enjoy life and do the best they can, and there's no reason to sit down and write poetry or fiction. I think people who sit down and write poetry and fiction are not sure of things, but are trying to find out. They're not sure of themselves either, and they're trying to find that out.

INTERVIEWER

I have to ask. Do you still manage not to entertain?

HUMPHREYS

I haven't had anyone over for dinner in years. Now and then, we find ourselves having a sort of big party—big by our standards, anyway. During the College of Charleston Writers Conference, all the writers came over for dinner, and it was really fun.

INTERVIEWER

What did you feed them?

HUMPHREYS

Shrimp and pasta salad.

INTERVIEWER

This is your third novel in which love has been the agent that brought a character to him or herself—to their best selves. Do you, in real life, believe that love has the power to transform? To take us from haziness into focus?

HUMPHREYS

Definitely. It can also take us from focus into haziness. It's just a very powerful thing in all its forms. It's a clarifying force or a mystifying force. But in the long run, I think the tendency would be towards clarity.

———

The first of three daughters of William Wirt and Martha Lynch Humphreys, Josephine Humphreys was born February 2, 1945, in Charleston, South Carolina. In 1963, she graduated from Ashley Hall in Charleston, and in 1967 from Duke University, where she majored in English. She received her master's degree from Yale University in 1968 and enrolled at the University of Texas to begin work on her Ph.D., which she did not complete.

From 1970 to 1977, she taught English at Baptist College of Charleston.

Her novels are *Dreams of Sleep* (1984), *Rich in Love* (1987), and *The Fireman's Fair* (1992). All her novels are set in Charleston and Mount Pleasant.

Her awards include a Guggenheim fellowship, the Ernest Hemingway Award for *Dreams of Sleep*, and the Lyndhurst Prize.

Rich in Love was made into a Richard and Lili Fini Zanuck film, starring Albert Finney as Warren Odom.

Humphreys married Charleston lawyer Tom Hutcheson on November 30, 1968. They have two sons: Allen, born July 13, 1973; and William, born December 24, 1974.

She and her husband live on Sullivans Island, South Carolina, where she is at work on her fourth novel, set in the past. She is road manager for a twelve-member, Charleston-based black gospel group, The Brotherhood.

April 16, 1994

SIMMONS JONES

"*A* most unsatisfactory child" is how Charlotte's Simmons Jones describes himself in early youth. A boy who preferred ballet lessons to football. A boy who turned the side porch of his home into a theater for productions he wrote, directed, and starred in. A boy who considered it a treat to be sent to his room, where he could play alone and in peace with his beloved marionettes.

Son of Charlotte's own Scott and Zelda Fitzgerald—Morehead Jones and Cornelia Dowd—Jones grew up going against the grain. After graduating from the Virginia preparatory school Woodberry Forest, he entered UNC-Chapel Hill, where he was twice asked to leave.

When his friends were entering banking, Jones was living on the Left Bank in Paris. When his friends were marrying and starting families, Jones was playing summer stock in New York and establishing himself there as a fashion photographer.

Now, as his friends settle into retirement, Jones emerges with a brand-new career and a first novel, *Show Me the Way to Go Home*.

Meet the man who has covered the walls and ceiling of his entrance hall with hand-painted clouds, because, at last, he has found the right perch in the right tree house, this celestial condominium in the historic Poplar Apartments, his first real home.

Listen as the inimitable Simmons Jones talks about art, alcohol, age, and the writing life.

INTERVIEWER

With your background, how could you not be a writer?

JONES

How could I not be a mess? Which I'm delighted to be.

INTERVIEWER

Why do you compare your parents to Scott and Zelda Fitzgerald?

JONES

You know, back then in the 1920s, parents didn't come apart. They were born married. Children at school had said they had read in the paper that my mother was divorced. Anyhow, she went to Reno and got divorced. And my father, on the day of her divorce, sent her a telegram saying, "You're nobody's baby now."

INTERVIEWER

Let's talk about Woodberry Forest. How did you like it there?

JONES

For the first time, I was away from home, and I was away from my mother, whose companion I was, and I had never had friends. And I had friends, and they liked me.

INTERVIEWER

Why hadn't you had friends?

JONES

Oh, I had the children of my mother's friends. And I still have them. And we love each other.

And we have a lot more fun than we did then. Then, they were all doing the right things, and I was unsatisfactory and growing more so every day.

But I was very satisfactory at Woodberry, except I refused to do athletics, which was the first time in history anyone had refused, and they didn't know how to cope. So they finally just said, "Well, what you do is sign a slip saying you were present on the campus."

INTERVIEWER

And you loved it because you were intellectually stimulated.

JONES

Yes. I had no father, you see, and it was a school full of fathers and brothers, and no mothers.

INTERVIEWER

Between semesters at Woodberry Forest, you worked for the now-defunct newspaper the *Charlotte News*, which your mother owned. For a while, you wrote obituaries.

JONES

And I thought it was bullshit. I didn't believe in death whatsoever.

INTERVIEWER

Did you learn anything about writing from your work at the *News*?

JONES

I thought it was way beneath me. I don't mean

the obituaries, I mean the whole scene. And I was a duty to everybody on the paper. Very unsatisfactory. And Brodie Griffith, who was the city editor, just had to bear with me.

I got to write features, and they were very artistic. Very artistic. When I finished writing them, they would go straight to my uncle Edward Dowd, who was at that point the editor, and he would come down and make it better, and then he'd give it back to me. And I'd recorrect it and go back and turn it in.

INTERVIEWER

By recorrect, you mean you put all the things back in that your uncle had taken out?

JONES

I put it all back just the way it was. And they would print it that way, much to my uncle's surprise and dismay. So anyway, they put up with me. And I went to a lot of movies. I went to the courthouse with a man called Tim Pridgen, who was, of course, a marvelous journalist, and I'd sit in court and just be enthralled with these dramas.

INTERVIEWER

At the end of your first year at Chapel Hill, you were asked to leave. Why was that?

JONES

You had to attend 75 percent of the classes, and I hadn't done that. I had better things to do. In the first place, of course, I found out that you could drink beer until your allowance ran out. I had a lot of friends who also drank beer, but they went to classes. Anyhow, I would have milk shakes to calm down during the day. So they asked me to leave, and I left. And they said, "You can come back and do better." And so I went to summer school.

INTERVIEWER

Then you worked at the *News* for a year before you went into the army.

JONES

Yes. I had a poetry column. You don't know what an authority I was. It embarrasses me now. The authority of the press. These people would send in their poems, and I would say, "They're absolutely marvelous!" or "You ought to forget poetry." And I knew nothing. Nothing.

Then I was drafted into the army, to everybody's consternation and my despair. I was nineteen. And after I got over the first terrible, terrible nightmare of being in this enforced situation and going through basic training, I found something that was absolutely invaluable. I learned that I could exist under any circumstances.

I wouldn't give anything for having had that experience, to know that I could cope with anything and make friends, no matter where and with no matter whom.

These boys were from the streets of Brooklyn and the Lower East Side, and they were tough as nails, and they said things I had dreamed of but never thought you mentioned—but you did.

And after they learned me and I learned them,

it was just absolutely a situation that I would never exchange for anything. I never had better friends than they were.

INTERVIEWER
What was your job in the army?

JONES
It's hard to believe. I was in the beginning a corporal machine gunner, until they saw the error of their ways and made me company clerk and put me behind a typewriter. I went through the war that way and ended up thirty miles from Berlin in the company of a typewriter.

And my brother was killed in the Battle of the Bulge, which was the great tragedy of my life. And I went back to Chapel Hill, and I was there a few years, and they asked me to leave again. Not enough going to class.

INTERVIEWER
Back up a second. That was your beloved younger brother, Morehead Jones.

JONES
Yes. We were attached to the 102nd Infantry. He was killed not far away.

INTERVIEWER
And the impact on you was devastating.

JONES
It was devastating, because we were like opposite sides of the same coin. We adored each other, and it was unquestioned love, and I've looked for it all through my life, to find another

friend like that. Of course, it was when we were young.

INTERVIEWER
How were you opposites?

JONES
He was the child everybody wants. He was perfectly beautiful and didn't know it. He was an athlete. He would walk into the room, and that was it. No matter the tricks I played and the talking I did, he got the attention. I, of course, was the unsatisfactory child. He was six-foot-two and very impressive physically. And sweet. He was one of the gentlemen of the world. It never occurred to him to be mean to anybody.

INTERVIEWER
And you still dream about him.

JONES
He visits. And they are not always happy dreams. But they are very, very moving always. We even have quarrels. It's wonderful. And so I don't think anybody really dies.

He was absolutely unjudgmental of me. Whatever I did was perfection. And you run into that never. He probably would have changed. He had the signs of the alcoholism. Of course, he was so young. I keep forgetting how it is to be young.

INTERVIEWER
In a way, it sounds as if he's still with you.

JONES
I live with his presence. I see his face many

April 16, 1994

times in other people on the street, in photographs of utter strangers. And the fact that I keep looking for that same kind of friendship, which is, of course, a dream. It's an emptiness and yet a great joy to me, because it demands that I retain my youth. I have to be young to speak to him. And so that's a lovely thing.

He had a very mysterious look in his eyes, because he was nearsighted. And they didn't want him in the army, but he insisted and used his pull and went into the infantry and had exactly the end he would have chosen. He's still in Epinal, France.

INTERVIEWER

Let's get back to Chapel Hill. You attended those classes you liked: Lyman Cotton's class on T. S. Eliot and Dr. Hardin Craig's on Shakespeare. Have you always had an intense interest in some things and an intense lack of interest in others?

JONES

Yes, and I'll tell you, it was the mark of what I am, which is an alcoholic. I was awfully interested in being accepted by people. And I did everything you were supposed to do socially— all the dances, all that, and the fraternity [Delta Kappa Epsilon]. I think they regretted taking me in. As a matter of fact, I'm perfectly sure they did. But we had such a good time. And we talked until dawn and drank, and I thought, "This is better than going to school." It never occurred to me you couldn't make up for it tomorrow. That's typical of a drunk.

INTERVIEWER

And of youth.

JONES

Well, drunks are always young. Until the crash.

INTERVIEWER

And then to Paris, where you said you went through the family's "hunk of change"—they'd sold the *News* by now—like it was a "dose of salts." And you lived on the Left Bank next door to Bill Burney, who'd written a Broadway play called *Dark of the Moon*.

JONES

He was also a drunk. *Alcoholic*. A nicer word. My mother came over to Paris about that time with all her friends and suggested it was about time for me to come home. What was I doing? So I got a job in New York, which is how I escaped Charlotte again. I did all this thing in the summer-stock theaters, and from there I went into fashion photography. Everything I did was a fantasy.

INTERVIEWER

In all this fantasy, why hadn't you started writing?

JONES

I was vastly insecure because I had been told, "Don't write." So I didn't. "No. You can't be an artist. Don't do that. Don't be a dancer. Don't do that. Don't go into theater. Don't do that." It was a constant struggle. Inner yearning against outer obligation, is the way that Jung puts it.

And I hesitated always, because of who I might offend. Whose feelings I might hurt. What I might reveal that was hurtful.

Truman Capote never hesitated to write down what he had to say, and he felt it was good. I never had that. I know a lot of people who write, and they think they're just great, and they're not. I think what I write is great, and it might not be. So that insecurity was there. But the life of creativity—doing the theater and the fashion photography—was absolutely irresistible.

INTERVIEWER
What was so irresistible?

JONES
The people. I think it's the only life. I think scientists or artists—those are the only lives. If you miss living a part of that life, then you've missed the point.

INTERVIEWER
And when you were working as a fashion photographer, no matter how serious your drinking, no matter how haphazard and careless your life, you could turn it out. You were a talent. What are the components of that kind of talent?

JONES
I think it is wanting to explore things that you feel, things that you see, and explain them. I think it was Nietzsche who said, "We have art in order not to die of life." Now, if that doesn't make your hair stand on end! I think an artist knows that. Not here [points to his head], but in the fiber. Sometimes, they don't know what that longing is, and it's very painful. And then suddenly they're given a set of these paint-by-the-numbers things, and by God, this is what it is! And to hell with the numbers.

INTERVIEWER
You were about fifty when you returned to Charlotte.

JONES
I was drinking very heavily in New York, but I was doing awfully well in my profession. I was highly regarded, sought. And if I'd had any sense, I would've been making money, instead of just spending it or wasting it or not getting it when I should've gotten it.

But my mother was very ill. She'd been in institutions, including Highland Hospital in Asheville, and she was out and had improved. The bank was her guardian. And the bank called me and said she was very ill mentally, and they said, "You'll just have to come home." So I sold out. I pulled up stakes and I left New York. It was 1970, and I was fifty. It was time. I had left everywhere just in time.

And I came home, and it was absolute hell. Absolute hell. Well, you cannot live with a paranoid schizophrenic who does not know who you are. She didn't know who I was, and then she would know who I was. So then I left for Rome. Then my mother became very ill physically. I came home again. She died, and I moved back to Rome.

INTERVIEWER

And in 1973 or 1974, you came back to Charlotte again, as if you couldn't stay away.

JONES

I left Rome in a very bad state the second time. Because I was drunk, and because I had wasted years, and because I was doing nothing, there was really nowhere to go. You know, *Show Me the Way to Go Home*. And, of course, I had none. But mother's house was rented. And so by the happiest of circumstance I ended up here in The Poplar. Three blocks away from where I was born.

And that's where I started writing. I would take off a week from drinking [to write], then reward myself on Saturday with a drunk, which would take a week to get over. Go back to a week of writing. And then, by God's grace, AA came into my life. I had never joined anything but a party. I saw an actress friend of mine on Dick Cavett one night. She had gone to this twelve-step recovery program, and she looked marvelous. She could still sing. She could still stop a show. And I thought, "That's for me. There's something wrong in my life. Maybe that's what it is." You know, an alcoholic doesn't know that's what's causing him unhappiness.

INTERVIEWER

And you put so much psychic energy into AA that your writing took a backseat.

JONES

I was devoted to AA. That was my life for six

or seven years. And then I took up writing again. And I had a terrific agent. He declared me a genius. Then, a year later, he declared me a dud. Forget it. He couldn't sell it.

And I thought, "Well, I'm one of those people who thinks he can write. And it sounds wonderful to me. And actually it's not good."

INTERVIEWER

But finally you sent your manuscript off to a friend—head of the Drama Department at the University of Minnesota—who sent it, in turn, to a former New York editor. These people loved your novel. They restored your faith in yourself.

JONES

I read the book again and had the time of my life. It was fun. It was funny. And I'll tell you, I thought up a tacky phrase: Something funny happened on the way to the tragedy. It's always funny. Otherwise, you're dead. You can't make it. But the tragedy runs under everything. And I sent the novel to Mr. [Louis] Rubin.

INTERVIEWER

You've said that your mother's family—and your father's family—thought writing a book was the ultimate achievement. Didn't they realize you had to be unsatisfactory in some ways to write a satisfactory book?

JONES

My aunt [Louie Jones Taliaferro] did. She

said, "You don't have to play golf. You don't have to play bridge. You don't have to do anything you don't want to do. Just be Simmons."

INTERVIEWER

Does it bother you that your first novel is coming out when you're at the not-so-young age of seventy-one?

JONES

It's exactly the right time. As I told them when I went to talk to the American Booksellers Association—I just came up with this brilliant thing, of course—I told them that I had had a life of riotous research, and this is the result of it. And in a way that's true. I wouldn't have written this book without that. It isn't the Dead Sea Scrolls, you know, but it's a hell of a good book.

INTERVIEWER

When you're deep into writing, how does your day go?

JONES

I wake up about 3:30 or 4:00 A.M., and I go straight from the bed to the coffee. What's wonderful [about this early-morning time] is, it's yours. It's almost magical, because nothing of the practical world intrudes. That time of day belongs to me, and that transfer from dreams— no matter whether you recall them exactly or not—to my typewriter is just essential to me.

INTERVIEWER

You only write about two hours in the morn-

ing because of "psychic fatigue." Why is writing so psychically exhausting?

JONES

Because you have engaged your obligation of your spirit, and it takes tremendous doing.

INTERVIEWER

What do you mean by "obligation of your spirit"?

JONES

There is a demand that something makes on you to do this thing, to explain something, to get to the typewriter and see what the hell Susan is going to say next. Because then she is as much a part of your life—more a part of your life—than anybody you will see for the rest of the day.

INTERVIEWER

Why do you suppose artists create a world where another reality is going on?

JONES

I think it is like, "Why are some people alcoholics?" A major part of that comes with your birth. I think that an artist is God's gift. That is the greatest gift you can get. No matter what suffering it causes you, you have been given the chance to live that life. The failure to live the life you're given is the worst sin or lapse. Then you've missed the boat. The train came through, and you didn't get on it.

INTERVIEWER

When you've finished writing, other people are just beginning to wake up. What do you do the rest of the day?

JONES

I have to shop, and I love to have lunch with people. There are all the mechanical things of the day you have to take care of. Things that it takes to hold life together.

It's also the compulsion thing. Things have to be right. The room where I write—it doesn't look clean to anybody else, but to me it's right. It's what comes with being compulsive and an alcoholic. You've got to keep the world fairly neat—in your view, fairly neat. If it's out of order, there's a sort of desperation.

If I feel this building where I live is not properly in order, and things are not going well, and the wrong people are living here, and the walls are leaking, I lose the security of a place to work. It's your tree house. You've got to have it with the birds in it. I never had a home. I had perches. And I had beautiful perches. This is home.

INTERVIEWER

You keep mentioning compulsions. Do you believe there's a connection between the compulsion of alcoholism and the compulsion of art? Why are so many writers alcoholics? It can't be coincidence.

JONES

I don't think it is. In the recovery program, they say, "It's all right to build castles in the air. Just don't move in." An artist not only has to know how to build castles in the air, he has to move in. But there's a fever to a person who drinks—an unsatisfied thing. The alcoholic says, "I can do that if I have another drink." The writer says, "I can do that if I can write that page over again."

INTERVIEWER

Am I right that you enjoy being older?

JONES

It's lovely being older. Because if you don't like my apples, don't shake my tree. Forget it. Leave me. That's all right. It wouldn't have been all right to be rejected way back then. But now, reject me! I've got my typewriter. And the mortgage money in the bank.

INTERVIEWER

In your mind, how old are you?

JONES

I am young. I am very young. It doesn't occur to me when I'm talking to you that I'm anything but twenty-eight. Possibly even twenty-two. But it occurs to me I'd better hurry if I'm going to write five or six more novels.

INTERVIEWER

And you are?

JONES

I pray God. Because it's the only thing I can do that counts. Outside of loving people.

———

Born June 12, 1920, in Charlotte, North Carolina, Simmons Jones is the older of two sons of Morehead deBerniere and Cornelia Jordan Dowd Jones. He graduated from Woodberry Forest School in Orange, Virginia, in 1939 and attended UNC-Chapel Hill from 1939 to 1940 and from 1945 to 1948. He also studied at Pembroke College, Oxford University.

From 1941 to 1945, he served as a machine gunner and a company clerk in the United States Army.

During summer vacations while he was attending school, Jones worked at the *Charlotte News*; he was also employed there from 1940 to 1941. In 1950, he worked for various theatrical productions on Broadway as a production assistant and assistant stage manager. He worked for summer-stock theater in Myrtle Beach, South Carolina, and Memphis, Tennessee, from 1951 to 1956.

In 1956, Jones studied with New York photographer Alexie Brodovitch. For the next twenty years, his fashion photographs appeared in and on the covers of *English Vogue, Vogue Pattern, Harper's Bazaar, Seventeen*, and *Gentlemen's Quarterly*.

He also photographed the fashion collections in London, Paris, and Rome for magazines world-wide. He is the author of one novel, *Show Me the Way to Go Home* (1992).

Jones lives in Charlotte, where he is at work on a second novel, *The Skin I'm In*.

April 4, 1994

DOUG MARLETTE

December 8, 1989

*I*n Atlanta a couple of years ago, Doug Marlette and novelist Pat Conroy were swapping all the hideous stories they'd ever heard about ex-wives and ex-husbands. The stories gathered momentum. Marlette would tell one. . . . Conroy would top it. Marlette would tell another. Arm-waving ensued. Knee-slapping. Occasional collapses to the floor in raucous laughter.

Before long, the two decided to spend their Sunday mornings turning their stories into a film script. They worked for a year, called it *Ex*, and are waiting to hear if Warner Brothers will exercise its option. [In May 1994, *Ex* and Conroy's latest novel, *Beach Music*, were sold to Twentieth Century Fox for $6 million.]

The last years have held dizzying change for Marlette. In 1986, he and his wife, Melinda, became first-time parents. In 1987, he left the *Charlotte Observer*, where he'd drawn editorial cartoons for fifteen years, for the *Atlanta Journal and Constitution*, where he won a Pulitzer Prize for his cartoons in Atlanta and Charlotte. Two years later, he left Atlanta to become editorial cartoonist for *New York Newsday*, and the Marlettes moved to Manhattan's Upper West Side.

Marlette is the author of two new books: *The Kudzu Chronicles: A Doublewide with a View* and *Til Stress Do Us Part: A Guide to Modern Love by Reverend Will B. Dunn*, both based on his syndicated comic strip, "Kudzu," which appears in more than three hundred newspapers worldwide.

Over a barbecue sandwich and fried onion rings at the Old Original Barbecue House in Charlotte, Marlette talks about how the South damages its women and how to break out of your own Bypass and fly like Michael Jordan without ever leaving home.

INTERVIEWER

Your family has been in North Carolina for generations. The Marlettes were French Huguenots who settled in Orange County in the late 1700s. Who were they, and what were they like?

MARLETTE

My grandfather, Robert Earl Marlett, without the *e*, was raised in Saxapahaw in Alamance County, on cotton and tobacco farms. He worked in the mills, and he helped survey the railroads that ran to Gastonia. He was also deputy sheriff, and he used to bust stills and arrest moonshiners.

He died in 1987, when he was ninety-seven. He always voted Democrat. Once I asked him, "You were a big Roosevelt man, right?" He said, "I voted for him four times, and I'd vote for him again today if he were running."

"Why is that?" I asked. He said, "He was the only president who ever cared anything about the poor man."

I was misting up with sentimentality when he said, "Of course, the only mistake he ever made was that he should've let Hitler kill the Jews."

INTERVIEWER

You must've been shocked. But I'll bet that taught you something about the South.

MARLETTE

It brought me back to the reality of what has always been the struggle in the Southern character, particularly among the Southern populists. The poor whites, like my grandfather, always had to have somebody to hate. That kind of racism and ignorance and bigotry resided so comfortably with this populist concern and compassion for the poor.

North Carolina is the kind of state and region that can tolerate both a Jesse Helms and a Terry Sanford expressing popular, but contradictory, wills.

INTERVIEWER

You grew up in Greensboro and Durham, North Carolina; in Laurel, Mississippi; and in Sanford, Florida. Were you aware, growing up, of the South's peculiarities?

MARLETTE

The South is like my family. It's very colorful. But I didn't know that it was colorful, because it was all I knew. There's a kind of a low-grade schizophrenia that's part of the cultural landscape of the South. That also ran through my family.

My grandfather was a swashbuckling figure in his young manhood. But when I came to know him, he was living in a little house behind the big house, fifteen feet from the back door, where my grandmother presided over everything. They never talked. They never even spoke. They never acknowledged each other's existence. Yet they resided within spitting distance. I grew up with that, but I didn't realize how strange this setup was until I got away from it.

The premise of "Kudzu" is that way. I didn't realize how funny adolescence was until I got away from it. [Pat] Conroy always tells me, "You've got stories a novelist would kill for."

INTERVIEWER

You and Pat Conroy are very good friends. What makes you two click?

MARLETTE

For one thing, we fit creatively. I'm attracted to and interested in Pat's ability to elaborate and embroider. He's attracted to my ability to distill and refine. He's words and I'm pictures, although for a cartoonist I'm very verbal, and for a writer he's very visual.

INTERVIEWER

Talk about the screenplay you and Conroy wrote.

MARLETTE

It came out of our observations of ex-husbands we had known who became obsessed with their former wives' lives and began to wage war on their new relationships. We kept asking each other, "What is it that drives civilized people to such an extreme response?"

I said to Pat, "You ought to do something in your next novel." He said, "We should do a screenplay."

It was the most pleasantly creative thing I've done. We would get together on Sunday mornings and talk for a couple of hours and work for an hour or two. I'd say, "What if he did this?" Then he'd say, "Wait! What if he did this?"

That's what all writing is: "What if?"

INTERVIEWER

Did the "What if?" approach bring about "Kudzu"?

MARLETTE

My first impulse was to have a Southerner. Then I said, "Where is he from?" That's how I got Bypass, North Carolina. Then I said, "What's his family like? What is he like?" I knew he'd get his literary sensibilities from his mother and that his father would be missing.

INTERVIEWER

Why missing?

MARLETTE

I'm not sure. I think it's metaphorically true for this age we live in. My dad was in Vietnam during my teenage years. I understood absence. And then you get the mother, and the power of that relationship with the son. I knew Kudzu would be looking for surrogate fathers.

INTERVIEWER

Kudzu and his mother have a powerful bond. But it's a bond built on control and guilt. Do you think Southern boys and their mothers have a relationship distinct from Northern boys and their mothers? Do you think there's something insidious about Southern women?

MARLETTE

The first sentence of Anne Rivers Siddons's *Peachtree Road* says, "The South killed Lucy Bondurant Christian Venable on the day she was born. It just took her until now to die."

Maybe relationships between mothers and sons in the South are more "Kudzu"-like, in that women are denied power in so many ways that they have to express it through their children, in manipulation and control.

The South damages its women. Those things that happen culturally to women are more extreme and vivid in the South. And the racism, the sexism are much more socially acceptable. So women learn to make their mark in neurotic ways. They're like plants that don't get enough sunshine. They still grow, but they grow with all these brown spots.

INTERVIEWER

That relationship between Kudzu and his mother gives your strip lots of good tension.

MARLETTE

You need spark. You need conflict. If you have this guy, Kudzu, who has this literary sensibility, then he's going to want to leave Bypass. His mother wants him to stay. Kudzu's longing to get out is a universal, from Bruce Springsteen to Thomas Wolfe.

Unrequited love is another universal. Kudzu wants Veranda, and he stands no chance. And that's poignantly funny. So is her self-absorption. These are things that are painful but funny, like slipping on a banana peel. If you do it, it's painful. But watching it is funny.

INTERVIEWER

Nasal T. Lardbottom and Maurice Jackson also make for sparks. Nasal's a world-class wimp, voted the whitest white boy at Bypass High. He gives whiffy high-fives and wears a bow tie. Maurice Jackson, on the other hand, is a middle-class black boy, athletic and cool.

Maurice has soul, and Nasal has a slide rule. As Maurice would say, "What's happenin', bro?"

MARLETTE

This is something that goes on in our culture that nobody can talk about, because we're so sensitive about race. But because of their four hundred years of oppression, blacks have the green light to be natural, to be more self-involved, to slam and jam and run and gun, to be more aggressive in sports and have better hang time. To fly like Michael Jordan. To soar. To be what is humanly possible.

INTERVIEWER

So, really, you're talking about human potential. Not race.

MARLETTE

What I'm getting at in the strip is that the ability to soar has nothing to do with race. But because blacks have suffered, because there was slavery and four hundred years of oppression, it's okay for them to achieve. It's okay for them to feed the grandiosity that's present in all human beings.

Whites, because of their privilege, because of their role as oppressor, have a built-in inhibition to that grandiosity. It would be too much to be white and privileged and on top, and also to slam and jam, run and gun, and soar.

INTERVIEWER

But women, black or white, have not been on top for the past four hundred years, and they're not out there slamming and jamming and running and gunning. Does the oppression principle apply to women as well?

MARLETTE

The real opportunities to slam and jam are in motherhood, in creating healthy human beings. That's something feminists don't want to talk about right now, because they are rightfully staking their claim in society to that deferred dream. And that's important and long overdue. But at the same time, you know, we're going through a time where that basic involvement with themselves that is biologically expressed through childbearing is being played down and denied.

Women have always had all kinds of power. But a lot of times it gets expressed unconstructively. Look at Mama Dubose. When she coughs, Kudzu stays home. That's power. But it's the power of manipulation. It would be good if she could take pride in Kudzu's independence from her, in leaving her mark and letting him go. That's soaring. That's immortality.

INTERVIEWER

When you were growing up, did you, like Kudzu, long to leave home and go to New York?

MARLETTE

New York always loomed in the imagination. I always imbued those geographies I heard about on "The Tonight Show" and read about in Salinger with more realness than the reality that surrounded me. I think we all do that. I always thought that that's where life is really being lived, because things seemed so excruciatingly dull and depressing at home. I call my childhood the trailer park of the spirit. The Bypass of my life.

But that longing is what we have to outgrow. That's what Kudzu has to outgrow: His belief that the grass is always greener, that enchantment lies somewhere outside himself. He has to learn to get enchanted with what he has and with himself. That's tricky. But that's the challenge of every writer and artist and every human being.

INTERVIEWER

How do you feel about the South now that you're living in New York City?

MARLETTE

Going north, you see the differences more clearly. The South has, as Walker Percy calls it, that minuet of overture and response. People say, "Hey, sugar." They say, "Come over and visit." People don't do that in the North. In the North, you can't afford to be open like that, because your neighbor will mug you.

The South encourages a kind of community where you're taken care of. I miss that. The North is more direct and aggressive. Probably, Southerners could stand to be more direct, and Northerners could stand some of the mannerliness.

INTERVIEWER

Kudzu is left-handed, and you're left-handed. He's blond. You're blond. He has literary aspirations. He's really you, isn't he? Or a part of you?

MARLETTE

Kudzu is definitely a part of myself and part of my experience. But so is Will B. Dunn. Everything is autobiographical. There is a Will B. Dunn in every political cartoonist and in every editorial writer. But Kudzu himself is probably closer to one aspect of my personality. Like Kudzu, being able to read really set me apart in my family.

INTERVIEWER

What would you tell young people who want to "break out of Bypass" and become a writer or artist?

MARLETTE

I would tell them they don't have to break out of Bypass to do it. It's all around them. It's like being an athlete. The best athletes get the other team to play their game. The best artists get other people to see the way they see, to look through their eyes. It doesn't have anything to do with where you are. It has to do with what you see.

People now experience the Low Country of South Carolina through Pat Conroy's eyes. It's Conroy Country. He had the eyes to see it, and the words to express it. He's gotten the world to play his game.

This is the gift for artists: To be able to see that there's something dramatic going on, whether you're in Bypass or wherever. That what is going on around you is fascinating and dramatic and exciting.

INTERVIEWER

Do you use different areas of your brain for the comic strip and for the editorial cartoons? The cartoons move like arrows, and the strip like a carousel horse.

MARLETTE

It's all coming out of the same thing. I'm using the same skills in a different way.

With the political cartoons, I'm distilling down to one single image and one picture and getting across more opinions about the outside world. The characters in the cartoons are already performing in Washington. I put them in a situation and make a response to the objective world.

The strip is dealing with more enduring things, more universal things, things that don't change.

In four years, we'll have a new president. But we'll always have a craving for chocolate. We'll always have unrequited love. We'll always have strivings for power.

February 25, 1994
March 25, 1994

Doug Marlette leans against the kitchen wall in his nineteenth-century house, Burnside, in Hillsborough, North Carolina, arms folded, face suffused with pleasure. He is listening to a tape of the songs for the musical he's producing with the Chapel Hill–based Red Clay Ramblers, who most recently performed on Broadway in *Fool Moon.*

The way the musical came about is the way things often come about in the South.

Former Georgia congressman Ben Jones, a fan of Marlette's syndicated comic strip,

"Kudzu," had gone to UNC-Chapel Hill with several of the Ramblers, including Bland Simpson. Jones thought "Kudzu" and the Ramblers would be as natural as okra and tomatoes. He got the two together.

"This is the story," Marlette says. "The Japanese are buying the town of Bypass. Essentially, Big Bubba Tadsworth, Veranda's daddy, is selling. The villains are not the Japanese. The villain is Big Bubba Tadsworth. Okay?"

In 1989, Doug and his wife, Melinda, bought this three-story white clapboard house in Hillsborough's tree-shaded historic district. For a while, they commuted between New York, where his work is, and Hillsborough, where his roots are.

"I'm the only guy in Orange County I know who carries subway tokens," he says.

When son Jackson entered first grade, the Marlettes decided to make Hillsborough their year-round home. Now, Marlette faxes his political cartoons to *Newsday*, commuting to the office once or twice a month.

When Marlette talks, his hands are a Morse code of motion, flicking, flitting, punctuating. When he says, "Do you know what I mean?" he leans forward, blue eyes squinched and expectant.

Intense, funny, restless, Marlette talks this bright winter afternoon about musicals, novels, and cartoons, about being his own arbiter in the marketplace, and about the streak of inherited family rage that fuels all his work.

INTERVIEWER

It must've felt like falling into heaven when you fell in with the Red Clay Ramblers. Three of them are from Burlington, and you didn't have to explain the South or "Kudzu" or anything else to them.

MARLETTE

Not only that, but they understand [Kudzu's uncle] Dub [who runs the service station in fictional Bypass, North Carolina]. I mean, Bland *is* Dub.

INTERVIEWER

You've written a movie script, *Ex*, a book, *In Your Face*, articles for *Esquire*, and, for a long time now, a comic strip. But when you started writing this musical, you told me you discovered that a song in a musical was like a psychotic episode, that it could do things writing could never do.

MARLETTE

The songs do all the heavy lifting. And you never finish with a musical. For instance, in *A Funny Thing Happened on the Way to the Forum*, the song that made that a hit was "Comedy Tonight." And that wasn't written until the very last, just before the show was going to open.

[Stephen] Sondheim had another nice opening song, but they knew it wasn't quite what it needed to be. And they said, "We need a song that says what this whole thing is going to be about." So he wrote "Comedy Tonight," and it was a great hit. And Larry Gelbart, who wrote the libretto for it, said that song made the difference in the play being a hit or not.

INTERVIEWER

Why does a song do such powerful things?

MARLETTE

Music and pictures are those two primitive things that are the universal language. Like images, music gets under your skin. And it's real powerful. In a play or a novel, you're telling stories, advancing action, revealing character with language alone. But in a musical, the music is everything. And when the music happens, everything happens.

So it's like a psychotic episode, or it's like an LSD trip. And it not only reveals character and advances plot, but you hit hyperspace. Or what they call it in *Star Wars*, when it goes *whishhhh*! And it goes forward. You go through light years. You're way somewhere else than you would have been in the same amount of time just telling it.

In writing a musical, there aren't any rules, but you want to mix it up. You want to have big production numbers, you want to have quiet moments, you want to have a show tune that'll bring out everybody. And you want to have the love song. And you've got to have all that happening in the right mix, so it never flags.

Try writing something, and you know how hard it is to get something to happen. But also try throwing in this music element. How do you juggle all that and keep it going? You have to have what they call an eleven o'clock number, from the old days when the musicals started at eight-thirty, and they finished at eleven-thirty. Now, it's going to be a ten o'clock number, because the shows start earlier. But it's the big

show-stopping number about a half an hour before the show's over, to wake everybody up for the end.

INTERVIEWER

Has working on this musical altered the way you see your characters?

MARLETTE

So much of what you're doing is dictated by the form, and what you need in a strip is to get things happening. Bumba-bum-*bum*. Bumba-bum-*bum*. Like in a dah-dah-dah-*dah*. You can think in these kinds of rhythms. What's fun about the musical is fleshing things out more and realizing the whole world more three-dimensionally. For instance, there's a character in the show that's a real natural, and that I've always wanted, but I just haven't gotten to in the strip.

INTERVIEWER

Who imagined this character?

MARLETTE

I did, out of a necessity. It's a girl. It's a love interest for Kudzu. For the strip, for comedy, it's funnier to have things not work out for him. It's funnier to have Kudzu in love with Veranda, and Ida Mae in love with Kudzu. And it's hopeless. That's painful. And it's funny.

On the stage, we need satisfaction. We need a love interest that goes somewhere. So there's a girl character who is one of the good ol' boys in the station, who becomes the girl who blossoms. A good ol' gal named Mike. Michelle. And she's an ace auto mechanic, a better good ol' boy than Kudzu is.

So there're two love arcs, two story lines. There's Will B. Dunn, who will end up with Mama. And Kudzu, who will discover the rose under his nose. And I may also do her in the strip.

INTERVIEWER

Why do you suppose the musical popped her out of you and the strip didn't?

MARLETTE

She wasn't necessary in the strip. She was in the show. We needed love songs. You want people to care and feel something about the characters. And the closest thing we had until then is the song about Kudzu getting a letter from his daddy. That's nice. But there was no payoff to Kudzu's love for Veranda. No matter how we tweaked it, the audience will never believe they'll end up together. Nor should they. So we've got a wonderful song called "When Your Love Ain't Lovin' You Back," where Kudzu's singing about Veranda and Michelle's singing about Kudzu. And they're there in the station, closing up together. And, by the end of it, he discovers her.

INTERVIEWER

If the theater requires this emotional pull from the audience, why doesn't the strip need it, too?

MARLETTE

The strip can handle it fine. And it can be fun and funny. It's just that it works better for

humor's purposes to have Kudzu frustrated by Veranda. That's painful *and* funny. But if it were all pain or irresolution, people wouldn't feel any satisfaction leaving the theater.

INTERVIEWER

Sounds like you've fallen in love with the theater and with musicals.

MARLETTE

There are so many shows that I see where I don't care about anybody. I want to. There's never a better moment than when you're sitting there just before the curtain rises. It's all potentiality. It's really a great moment in life. The theater gets quiet, and it gets dark, and the curtain goes up. But so often, you're disappointed. So part of the motivation for us is to not have that happen. We want satisfaction. Now, whether we can pull that off . . . I think we've got the ingredients. But it's all recipe, and it's all got to be balanced. And it's tricky.

INTERVIEWER

Why is it that so many shows and plays are boring?

MARLETTE

You know that British composer Andrew Lloyd Webber? It's not that all his things are boring. It's just that there's so much reliance on spectacle and technology. And we're enamored of it. And there's so much he can do to dazzle people with. But so what?

I suspect the reason *Tommy* was a success was

because of the technological dazzle, and also the music was of this generation. There's a nostalgia aspect, where people say, "Hey, that's us. We remember those songs." But you don't like anybody in that show. You don't care about anybody.

And the same thing with *Sunset Boulevard*. I mean, I was glad when the lead character got killed at the end. I wish he'd gotten killed in the first act.

This is just little ol' me, a cartoonist going to the theater. But that's what I see, and my collaborators agree with me. There's not a lot you can take kids to on Broadway. I guess that's what makes you want to do things that entertain you. That would interest you and would be satisfying.

INTERVIEWER

In our earlier interview, one of the things you told me was that Pat Conroy had said to you, "Any novelist would kill for your material." Now, here you are writing novels.

MARLETTE

Trying to. But it's all on the back burner since I've gotten involved in this musical. Now, it's easy for me to say this, talk about writing my novel, and I could go on and not write anything and die, and I'm just a big blowhard about all this. Okay? But what you begin seeing . . . I may have to edit myself.

INTERVIEWER

No, please don't.

MARLETTE

Don't edit?

INTERVIEWER

No. Don't edit.

MARLETTE

Well, it's just like the theater. I find myself not interested in a lot of stories and novels I read. Very just . . . uninterested. I *want* to be interested. And the same thing goes for much of the theater I see. It's really bad. And I think that's part of the motivation. Over time, you start realizing that there's a lot of really dumb stuff that's taken seriously.

And for me as a cartoonist, it doesn't matter what you do and how much is in the cartoon. It will never be taken seriously. It's that old thing with comedians. I'm not complaining, like Woody Allen wanting to be Bergman—just observing.

There's something about humor and about drawings, especially. Developmentally, pictures came before words. We dream before we speak. Cave paintings came before Gutenburg. There's something older and wilder and scarier about pictures. You can't control them. You can control language. So, a cartoon is always going to be seen as child's play. No matter what's in it or what it's about.

And in a novel, you can be incredibly thick and dumb and boring and tedious and pompous, and you will be reviewed in the *New York Times*. And sometimes even get good reviews.

When I was sixteen, I didn't know if I could

draw cartoons. But I could see that there were a lot of bad cartoonists drawing. Making a living. I didn't know if I could be any good. But I knew I could be at least that bad.

INTERVIEWER

And now you're seeing that about novels.

MARLETTE

I would never say that I'm going to write a novel, because I don't know if I *could* write a novel. But I want to try it. Because I see novelists taken seriously who I know that I can at least be that bad. But I don't know if I can be any good. So that's where I am, the same place I was when I was sixteen with cartoons.

INTERVIEWER

Speaking of novels, I was fascinated by your story about being in Charlotte signing books when someone brought you a pamphlet called *The Burlington Dynamite Plot*. This pamphlet was written by your great-uncle, Walt Pickard, a leader in the biggest textile-mill strike in the country, the strike of 1934. When you read that pamphlet, you said it had the genetic imprint of your people, and you could almost hear a novel taking shape, with your uncle's voice narrating. What exactly did you recognize in his voice?

MARLETTE

Let me read you something: "Everything I'm about to put down in this little book is the good truth. I wouldn't say it any different if it were the judgment day. Six mill hands in our town of Burlington, N.C., were rounded up by the sheriff, framed by the mill owners and their detectives and stool pigeons and sentenced to serve long years in the pen, all for a dynamiting they knew no more about than you do. But it wasn't just six mill hands they were putting away in jail. It was our union they were aiming to lock up."

Just this plain-spoken voice and the directness. And the rage. You get the sense of outrageous injustice and being screwed.

A year or so before I got that pamphlet—and this is my favorite moment, by the way—I was giving a speech over at the Wilson Library at UNC, and afterwards I went with all these historian types, and they were talking about a book, [Jacquelyn Dowd Hall's] *Like a Family: The Making of a Southern Cotton Mill World*. And I said to them, "You know, my grandmother was in that book." And they asked me who my grandmother was. And I told them Gracie Pickard, and Walt Pickard was her brother. And they said, "You're related to *Gracie and Walt Pickard?*"

INTERVIEWER

She must have been the heroine of the union movement.

MARLETTE

She was bayoneted by a National Guardsman in the mill strike. They put her in the back of a wagon and paraded her around to show people what would happen if they tried to strike or unionize.

Liberals' eyes get all dewy when they hear this

April 4, 1994

about her. But as her grand-younguns knew, if you had a bayonet, you *would* use it on Mama Gracie. She passed on last year, and there was quite a turnout at the funeral. I suspect there was a kind of checking to make sure she was dead.

INTERVIEWER

So Gracie and Walt had a legitimate reason for being angry. The mills weren't paying enough. But did they also have a bigger rage? I ask because I've heard you talk about rage running through your family.

MARLETTE

I just think it's the rage that's running through Western civilization. It's the same. That's all there is out there. Tonya Harding taking out her rage on our favorite princess, Nancy Kerrigan. I look at Tonya. That's my family history. Not Nancy. It's that thwarted, seething resentment. It's hardscrabble. And then the guilty ambition. And the bitchy mother.

INTERVIEWER

But there's a metaphor here, something Gracie stands for—being paraded around in that wagon, being made a spectacle of—that causes the rage.

MARLETTE

Humiliation. That's right. Humiliation. The narcissistic injury. That's part of it. See, my grandmother was humiliated a hundred yards from this house. The county tried to take her children away from her during the Depression, up in that courthouse.

Or let's put it this way, and this is my grandmother, and this is the South, and this is our whole thing. When we were coming to look at this house back in 1990—and this was the first time I'd seen her in a few years, and it was after I'd moved to New York, and we were at a family reunion—she sat down next to me with her food, and she said, "Now, where is it you live now?" And I said, "Well, I live in New York City, Mama Gracie." And she said, "I wouldn't *put a crick in my neck* to look up to them tall buildings."

Now, what does this mean?

INTERVIEWER

What does it mean?

MARLETTE

To her, that's a narcissistic blow, those tall buildings. It's a pain in the neck. Other people's pride and success is a pain in the neck to her. And she won't acknowledge them. She wouldn't *hurt her neck* by looking up at those buildings. Because *she* wants to be up. And they should be looking up at *her*. You know what I'm saying?

It's that Southern sort of thing. Those big shots in New York. Well, screw them and the horse they rode in on.

That runs very powerfully in my bloodstream. And in every Southerner I know. And that's all part of why you want to go up there. You want to go up and burn New York down, like they burned us down. That's all the history here.

That's in my grandmother. She expressed that. So that was her way. She felt put down. So she put them down.

INTERVIEWER

Yet that rage gives you invaluable strengths as an artist.

MARLETTE

No question. In my strip. In my cartoons. The trick for artists, when there's been so much damage, is to find a way to get it all out in a constructive way. Then you can be interviewed for books.

INTERVIEWER

But getting it out has a payoff more than getting interviewed.

MARLETTE

It's therapeutic, to use that stupid word. But when people ask me why I do all this work, I answer and they laugh, but it's true: It keeps me off the streets. Or it keeps me from beating somebody up. Or stabbing somebody.

There's just too much stuff. Too much conflict inside. And it has to come out. And people find different ways of dealing with that. And, for me, and for any artist, it all seems kind of inevitable. Things couldn't be any other way.

INTERVIEWER

You still keep an apartment in New York. But you and your family are spending more and more time in Hillsborough. What's your workday like here?

MARLETTE

In Hillsborough, I get up at six or seven. And I go down and get the paper, and I read all the stuff, and I check out the TV, what's going on in the news. And I get an idea. And I try to start drawing on it by about eight or nine.

INTERVIEWER

What happens between reading the paper, watching the news, and the idea?

MARLETTE

I focus on a subject that seems promising. What people are talking about or what interests me. Then I go and sit down, and I do that process of trying to figure out how to say what I want to say, and do something funny about it. You know, something interesting about it. If I have a strong opinion . . . That's, boy! But usually it's more kind of noodling with the what's-funny-here.

I drew a cartoon recently that illustrates this kind of primitive thinking process. It was reprinted a lot. It was of Tonya Harding as Richard Nixon. Did you see that cartoon? Now, that's an unusual association. It's like, Tonya was denying this and denying that—something Nixonian about her.

It's the ability I've cultivated to free-associate across this range of material and history, and the instinct to put it together. It's an instinctual thing that goes on on some real subterranean level. The best stuff happens that way.

This kind of primitive thinking process is one of the gifts, one of the things that I do. The thing that I see as I get older is that this is an unusual thing even among cartoonists. But only a few cartoonists can do it. Not many of them.

INTERVIEWER
What other cartoonists would you say do it?

MARLETTE
[Paul] Conrad, [Mike] Peters, and [Jeff] MacNelly. I'm sure it happens in others that I just don't see. It's a primitive thinking. It's visual thinking. It's image thinking. And it's pretty instinctive, putting things together that are interesting. And those are the cartoons that are delightful. They're the ones that'll make you say, "Oh! I hadn't thought of it in that way." I mean, I can pretty much bet nobody thought of Tonya Harding as Richard Nixon, right?

INTERVIEWER
When that hit you, did something visceral happen in your body?

MARLETTE
You go . . . [Squints his eyes, presses his knees together, hunches his shoulders.]

INTERVIEWER
Could you spell that?

MARLETTE
It's kind of squeezing yourself in guilty delight. You just know that there's something good there.

INTERVIEWER
You must've known with the drawing of the American eagle shedding a tear when *Challenger* exploded.

MARLETTE
I knew it was good. But I didn't know it would get so much of a reaction. You know when something works.

INTERVIEWER
Let's get back to your workday.

MARLETTE
So I draw my political cartoon by noon. On a good day, like today. And then this afternoon, I do a Sunday page for the strip. Between the two, I do lunch. Go get something, or eat something here. And sometimes I take a little nap for fifteen minutes. I go get the mail. By about two, I start back in and work until five. Then dinner. And then not do anything.

INTERVIEWER
So is your actual workday any different from what an ideal day would be?

MARLETTE
What my ideal day would be, would be to finish all that work, finish it by noon. And then, what I really love is working on this musical.

INTERVIEWER
Don't get so quiet. I can't hear you.

MARLETTE
No, I love it when, like on Wednesdays, I finish the real pressure of the "Kudzu" deadlines. And then Thursday and Friday, I feel like it's a breeze. All I've got to do is the editorial cartoon. And I've been arranging it so that I would get time with Bland [Simpson] to work on the

223

musical. And, when I'm doing that, when I'm like driving over to his house . . .

INTERVIEWER

Are you whispering because this is off the record?

MARLETTE

No.

INTERVIEWER

Then please speak up.

MARLETTE

It's because I'm so guilt-ridden about it, I guess.

INTERVIEWER

Well, come out, because it sounds wonderful. But I can't hear you.

MARLETTE

When I'm going to work on this musical, it feels just like . . . It's like easing into a warm bath. It's just total fun. It's not work at all. It's just a pleasure. And so that would be my ideal day, then, would be to finish all this stuff by noon and spend all the afternoons and weekends doing that other stuff.

INTERVIEWER

You get a lot of work accomplished in a day. Your political cartoon and your strip. How did you learn to focus so well? I remember at the *Charlotte Observer*, you'd be busting deadline on your cartoon at six o'clock, and this was before "Kudzu" was even a gleam in your eye.

MARLETTE

I took up all the time I could, and I struggled and fought with that. And I see people, and I know what they're doing. But there's not any way you can tell anybody this.

I remember when I was twenty-four or twenty-five, and [Reese] Cleghorn was my editorial-page editor, and he would say, "We've got to get Doug to get these cartoons in earlier." And then everybody around would, of course, say, "There's no way. Please. Come on. He's an artist." What's funny is, it would have been good if I *had* been pushed to get the cartoons in earlier, but it couldn't have come through Reese's method.

INTERVIEWER

It took creating "Kudzu," and putting yourself under another daily deadline, that forced you to get your political cartoon done earlier. I remember how you would force yourself to sit still while you listened to an album all the way through.

MARLETTE

Now, it just comes down to, you want to be at a certain point, and you just do it.

INTERVIEWER

I also remember when you were drawing your cartoon, how you would get up from the drawing board and check your mail, or go to the bank, and maybe it was because you were having so much fun drawing you literally couldn't sit still.

MARLETTE

There's something probably to that, because to some degree, when I have something really good, I still have a hard time sitting down and doing it. Because it's too much. It's just too much. You're stealing fire from the gods. So you've got to go and distract yourself from it. There's also just a general difficulty with being involved with myself. It's guilt. White man's disease.

INTERVIEWER

Isn't that the same thing as having too much fun?

MARLETTE

It's the same thing.

And so the distractions were out of having to not sit down and deal with myself. And you just develop more of a tolerance for being with yourself, for making touchdowns. I used to fumble the ball as I'd go toward the goal line.

Some people have great capacities to sit for long periods of time and do that. And that's like a talent. And then some people have to develop a tolerance for it.

INTERVIEWER

That brings up a question. There's talent, plenty of it. And there's creativity. Sometimes those things dovetail. Sometimes they don't. But what is the difference between the two? Would you say that creativity fuels talent, allows talent to happen?

MARLETTE

I've always thought there were people who were better artists than I was, who had much more natural ability than I had. I remember a girl in my eighth-grade class who seemed very talented, but she very quickly did not like taking art classes. She wasn't creative in that way.

INTERVIEWER

What's missing in a case like that?

MARLETTE

That rage we were talking about. The drive. And fighting demons. The demons are driving you to, by God, *show* somebody. It's like my grandmother. They're going to *show* you.

INTERVIEWER

That show-you mentality can serve as a necessary goad. But can it also be destructive?

MARLETTE

Yeah. Sometimes, artists and writers will have a lack of compassion or empathy for themselves or for others. And sometimes, that which is off in their work is connected to that. And that's probably true in novelists. But the thing that drives people to want to succeed is sometimes also the weakness in their art.

It's the Lewis Grizzard syndrome. Someone whose talent is subverted by their own meanness. I found it poetic that he died of a heart disease. Anyone who read Grizzard over the years knew he had no heart. And he represented everything that is wrong with the South—that dark underbelly of chip-on-the-shoulder defensiveness and bullying mediocrity that is celebrated so often in this region.

INTERVIEWER

Still, can't that meanness be a first cousin to creativity?

MARLETTE

Sure. It's ambition. It's a natural part of narcissism, of putting your mark on the world. Of getting response from the environment. Or getting that gleam in the eye of Mother. There's that drive. But there's so much connected so often to rage, and it's because they didn't get that response. And then they're going to, by God, get it now. You see it in all stand-up comics. Comics are always so ticked off. I never want to look at them. I see it in myself, and it's so much a part of the drive. I *am* my grandmother. You know. My work *is* my rage. I'm bayoneting the world on her behalf.

INTERVIEWER

Before you knew you were an artist, back when you were seven or eight and getting poor-conduct grades, did you think there was something odd about you?

MARLETTE

I knew there was something different. I remember this real vividly from the first grade. We took these standardized tests in school, and when the results came back, my parents had a meeting with the teachers. And when they came back from this meeting, they treated me differently. Something had happened. I didn't know what, but it was kind of scary. Unfortunately, they didn't know how to handle this very well. But suddenly I felt pressure in some sense. Like

I was a Martian. And they said with great solemnity and gravity, "Okay, son, you can be anything you want to be."

INTERVIEWER

How'd that make you feel?

MARLETTE

Awful. Because I was made to feel I was clearly not of this gene pool. I was not of them. I'm not saying that's what they meant to convey, but that was the feeling. I'm sure that feeling was reiterated in other ways. They gave me the sense of potential that I had, but the way it transmitted was that if I made anything less than an A, then I wasn't living up to my potential, according to these standardized tests. This was something they'd never had to deal with in the Marlette family. And the drawing part I took for granted. I thought that was what everybody did until I got to school, and then people would give me things for drawing, and I would get attention for that. And then I knew that that wasn't what everybody did.

INTERVIEWER

And it must have just felt good to do it, too.

MARLETTE

Yeah. Because I can see now that it was the natural thing to do. What was unusual was that I had an eidetic memory—visual memory—and I could remember how things looked and replicate them in drawings.

INTERVIEWER

In an interview with the *Philadelphia Inquirer*, you said that if you look up the sketch of the human being in the encyclopedia, you peel back the layers and see the musculature and then the organs and then the bones. You said the artist is the one with the first layer peeled back—musculature and no skin. The artist's job, you said, is to grow skin. Not armor. I have two questions. How do you grow skin? And is it a good idea to grow it?

MARLETTE

I think of artists as emotional tea bags. Our skin needs to be a semipermeable membrane. Can you imagine walking around without skin? It would hurt. Everything would hurt. Well, that's the way artists and neurotics are. Everything gets under their skin. Everything infects them and bothers them. Gets to them. They notice things that other people don't notice.

And I think the trick for us all is to grow skin, not armor. What most people get is armor, so they don't ever feel anything.

INTERVIEWER

How do you grow psychic skin?

MARLETTE

Through insight. Through understanding. It's what I would want to teach [son] Jackson. That everybody, even those closest to us, has their own framework and way of seeing things that maybe doesn't have anything to do with us, and is not the final word on anything. There may be something to what critics say about your work.

Or there may not be. But it's up to you to decide.

I'm able to discern that now more than when I was younger. I'm able to see that sometimes, for instance, some of the very best things in my work may cause people not to like it. That doesn't mean I shouldn't do it. And you have to figure that out.

But the main thing is just being able to see that people have their own ways of seeing things. My comic strip has helped me learn that, because it does such a broad range of things. For instance, one of the things that makes it work so well for a musical may limit it in the marketplace. Because it's not about cats. And it's not focused on a gimmick relationship like a "Calvin and Hobbes."

What I do works beautifully for a musical, and it's almost like the strip was a necessary prelude to the musical. But the very things that are good about it—it's not something you can sum up in a sound bite or an ad promo—may be the very reason why an editor in, say, Los Angeles, is not going to run it.

INTERVIEWER

That takes awhile to see.

MARLETTE

I notice the kinds of people who buy cartoons are always the same tribe. Essentially, they're the last people in the world you would get to pick comic strips, right? They're humorless, literal-minded, midlevel editors. All the same tribe. And it's true at every paper I've ever been at: *Newsday, Atlanta Constitution, Charlotte Observer.*

And you realize, "Hmm. If these people were really rallying around my strip, maybe there might be something wrong."

INTERVIEWER

So you've had to learn to become your own mentor.

MARLETTE

My own arbiter. It's tricky. Trying to market my art, but be true to myself. I just have to do what I do, and let the chips fall where they may. But at least you begin seeing to trust your own instincts, not other people's.

I remember early on, certain personalities would react to Veranda. Hated it! *Hated it!* And very often they were Southern belles in denial.

Or certain personalities didn't like Kudzu's having such a dominant mother. I know one very prominent person whose mother is very dominant in his business—in newspapering—who I'd heard did not like it. And I said, "Oh, well. He *is* Kudzu. Well, no wonder." And I say, "Well, gee. I really must be hitting."

But that might interfere with me being successful in that marketplace. And that applies in screenwriting and in the office.

You've still got to go with your instincts. But you just learn over time, basically, that at least if it fails, I will go down in my own flames, not somebody else's flames.

INTERVIEWER

What other characters bring out visceral reactions?

MARLETTE

Doris [the parakeet] is another one. Over the years, I've noticed there are people who *looove* Will B. Dunn—the superego—and *haaate* Doris—the id. I mean, hate it!

[Cartoonist] Jules Feiffer is one. Jules said from the beginning, "*Get rid of the bird.*" He didn't like the bird. "*Get rid of the bird.*"

And I'm thinking, "Get rid of the *bird*?" Can you imagine me saying, "Jules, lose the dancing woman"?

Over the years, I would notice there were certain people who had exactly Jules's reaction. And I would notice they had Jules's personality, too. It was generally people who hated the animal part of themselves. Didn't like to see that they had one. Very compulsive. Very guilty.

And then there were other people, at the same time, who'd say, "I wish you'd do Doris every day." And I'd say, "Now, is this opinion more valuable than the other?"

Animals in comics—Snoopy, Garfield, Doris—give us cute, cuddly versions of the animal part of ourselves.

I told Jules once, "Of course you feel that way, Jules, because first of all, you have this dog, Pasha, who comes around humping your leg all the time. Humping. Pasha. Passion."

Anytime you visited Jules, you would always have to sit through Pasha's humping number. Pasha was Jules's way of externalizing his own id. Because if he had this dog there humping the leg, then he thought it meant he didn't have to hump people's legs. And that meant those problems were *out there*, not *in here*.

Then I said, "But, Jules, you wrote a play where in the final act someone picks up a dog and throws it out the window of a high-rise in his Manhattan apartment. Clearly, you have ambivalent feelings about that animal part of yourself, as we all do."

INTERVIEWER

When you were working on your novel, you told me you were experiencing a lot of chaos as you were putting things down in the computer. Nothing was linear. It was all coming at once.

MARLETTE

I don't write linear, and it's real hard to me, because I just put all this stuff out there, and I have to stare at it and see where things go, and it creates anxiety. And you have to have tolerance for that anxiety, for it not being finished, and for it not even looking like anything presentable.

INTERVIEWER

And particularly for you, who's used to starting and finishing something twice a day. You start and finish. Start and finish.

MARLETTE

Right. That's the big thing.

INTERVIEWER

And also, you get immediate response. You know, in a sense, where you stand every day. And here you are, thinking of a novel.

MARLETTE

Actually, I don't. I send these things off in the black hole of Long Island, and I never hear a thing about them. I get my paycheck, and I see them reprinted in *Newsweek* or whatever.

But there is something to having a sense of closure every day. As Pat [Conroy] said to me, "1972. 1976. 1980. 1986. 1994." He said, "That's when I get that moment. But every day you get that."

INTERVIEWER

But what we're really talking about is sticking with something and trusting that the original impulse will carry you through all that ambiguity.

MARLETTE

There are novelists I know who aren't troubled by these things. I'm thinking of one who not only writes linearly but who might as well be typing. He writes right off the top of his head—hut-tut-tut-tut-tut-tut-tut-tut—and he just modems it right to his publisher, and he publishes a book a year and is very proud of that. But his books don't lay a finger on you.

And there are political cartoonists like that. Like these novels, some cartoons are just pleasant distractions. Brain candy. It's fun and amusing. But they don't lay a finger on you. And there are cartoonists who dedicate their entire careers to becoming that kind of artist, the kind who will be bland enough to be reprinted in *Newsweek* or the *New York Times*.

The things that are reprinted are not necessarily the best. As a matter of fact, they may be the worst.

And that can apply to journalists, poets, novelists—anyone who lays pen to paper.

Yes. My test for a cartoonist is, Can I remember their work? Does it get under my skin? Does it tattoo my brain? Are the images indelible? When I do a drawing, I want to be awake when I finish the drawing. If you hold a mirror under my nose, I want there to be vapor. That is my goal. Those are the kinds of drawings I want to do, and those are the kinds I like to see.

Same for literature. I want to feel something about what I've read. I want it to get under my skin. I want to be awake when I finish. I want to see things differently. I want to be changed. Surprised. That's what delights me.

Don't you just love that? It's so exciting. It's the feeling I get when I come up with something new. I get it if I read a poem that startles me. Or *something*. And it seems so rare to me. And I want that. That's what I would go for, and that's what I want to write like.

The second son of Elmer and Billie Moore Marlette, Doug Marlette was born in Greensboro, North Carolina, December 6, 1949, and lived until age twelve in Durham, North Carolina. He attended Laurel High School in Laurel, Mississippi, and graduated in 1967 from Seminole High School in Sanford, Florida. In 1971, he graduated from Florida State University, where he majored in philosophy, and where his cartoons in the student daily, *The Flambeau*, began attracting widespread attention.

In 1971, Marlette became an editorial cartoonist for the *St. Petersburg Times*, and the next year for the *Charlotte Observer*. In 1987, he went to the *Atlanta Journal and Constitution* and in 1989 to *New York Newsday*.

He won a 1988 Pulitzer Prize for his cartoons at the *Atlanta Journal* and the *Charlotte Observer*.

Marlette was the first cartoonist ever to receive a Nieman Fellowship at Harvard University.

His other prizes include the National Headliners Award for consistently outstanding editorial cartoons, the 1984 Robert F. Kennedy Award, and the 1985 Sigma Delta Chi Distinguished Service Award for editorial cartoons. In 1992, he won first prize in the Fischetti Cartoon Competition, the only repeat first-prize winner in the award's history. In 1984, he was selected by *Esquire* magazine for inclusion in its Register of Men and Women Who Are Changing America.

He is the creator of the syndicated comic strip "Kudzu."

His cartoons have been collected in fourteen books, most recently *Faux Bubba: Bill and Hillary Go to Washington*. He is also the author of *In Your Face: A Cartoonist at Work*.

In 1971, Marlette married Patricia Stenstrom of Sanford, Florida.

In 1980, he married Melinda Hartley of Norwood, North Carolina. Their son, Jackson, was born in 1987.

Marlette and his wife and son live in Hillsborough, North Carolina, where he is at work on a musical production of "Kudzu" with the Red Clay Ramblers.

April 6, 1994

T. R. PEARSON

January 6, 1993

*T*he Winston-Salem, North Carolina, native who put fictional Neely, North Carolina, on the map can now open his front door and see straight down his tree-lined street to Ellis Island.

T. R. Pearson, the man Reynolds Price once said writes "with the furious dedication of ants tatting lace," lives in a brownstone in Brooklyn Heights, New York.

Often, Pearson walks from his house to the Brooklyn Bridge, then crosses the bridge on foot into Manhattan.

"It's a beautiful walk," he says. "A lot of people don't even know about it. You can look up and down the river. It's absolutely lovely."

Pearson enjoys the best of two worlds. When he's not in New York, he lives in a log cabin he built himself in the wilds of Carroll County, Virginia.

"New York is the perfect antidote to Virginia," he says. "Down there, I get my fill of doing nothing, so I come here and do everything."

Pearson is the creator of six outrageously funny novels, including *A Short History of a Small Place, Off for the Sweet Hereafter*, and *Gospel Hour*, each set in North Carolina and including such hilarious characters as the Epperson sisters, Mrs. Phillip J. King, Aunt Sister, Mr. Emmett Dabb, and Mr. Wade Shorty Glidewell.

His latest, *Cry Me a River*, is part murder story and part character study. It is the leanest of his novels, and the most poetic.

Pearson once said, "I don't really have any inclination to hang around with people who write books. I know how I am, and I wouldn't want to hang around with me." Now, he interrupts his morning schedule to talk about how he writes to amuse himself, the virtues of house painting over teaching, and the value of a long-distance marriage.

INTERVIEWER

I see a huge difference in this new novel. It's shorter, for one thing, only 258 pages, a good 100 pages shorter than most of your novels. And the sentences are tauter.

PEARSON

There is a difference. There actually is. I started with a different premise. The notion was, I wanted to write the sort of crime novel I'd like to read. Which I can't usually find. I'm not a big fan of the genre, because I'm not interested in the plot. I'm interested in texture.

I felt like it would defeat the purpose if it were too flabby. I knew I had to keep it lean, had to play by the rules. I was really stringent. I cut and cut and cut, until I had what I thought was enough to reveal character but not so much as to be distracting and troublesome.

What I was really interested in was the fact of the narrator's life eroding all around him. I wanted that to come through. That's all insinuated. That's all subtext. You have to read that into the book. It's revealed not only by what he says, but how he tells it. The superficial part of the book is the murder mystery. If it were up to me, I would've left all that out.

INTERVIEWER

You graduated in English from North Carolina State in 1977, then spent a number of years in graduate school—both at State and at Penn State—before you realized you were a writer, not an academic. Did this come to you like a bolt?

PEARSON

The only thing I remember is that I was working on a Ph.D. supposedly and not very interested in it. I was taking a bibliography course, and I was finding myself folding paper, making folios and quartos, and I thought, "This is idiotic." I'd had enough. I pulled up and left. I gave over graduate school for house painting.

INTERVIEWER

And you moved to Fuquay-Varina, North Carolina, where you lived in a rent-free house and wrote in the mornings. How did your parents feel about your dropping out of graduate school to paint houses?

PEARSON

I had to make a living. I had to make time. I couldn't help myself. It was all I could do.

INTERVIEWER

You've said that at age eighteen, you started writing stories you thought editors would like and would therefore buy. Then, sometime in graduate school, you realized you shouldn't be making a distinction between writing to sell and writing for pleasure. That if you couldn't write for pleasure, you didn't want to write. That must've been liberating.

PEARSON

I felt considerably less constrained. I didn't second-guess myself—"How is my public going to take this?"—not having a public. That's been my guiding principle. I work to amuse myself and hope for the happy coincidence of amusing other people as well. I never stop to think, "How is this going to play?" Because that would ruin me if I did that.

INTERVIEWER

I know you believe you inherited your writing gift from your paternal grandfather, who was a Wake Forest graduate and a Baptist preacher, and who, on the side, sold both shrubbery and the *Greensboro Daily News*. He wrote and published poetry and essays, and you've described him as "very peculiar."

PEARSON

He just handed the reins over to me, and now I'm the oddball.

I'm sorry to say I think writing is a semi-sick compulsion. An itch. It's not very healthy. I feel guilty when I don't write. I can remember, even as a twelve- or thirteen-year-old, sitting down and writing, and I can't even begin to tell you why. There was no prospect that I was going to win the Pulitzer Prize when I was thirteen. I don't know what I was doing.

My feeling is probably at variance with others'. But I think people who are inclined to write will write. They don't need to go to writing school. They don't need to be instructed. They'll write because they can't do anything else.

INTERVIEWER

Who's your favorite living Southern writer?

PEARSON

Probably Barry Hannah. I stay away from polite Southern fiction, of which there is quite a bit. When Barry Hannah is on, there's nobody better. He can be very lazy. Southern writers come in all sorts of stripes. Some aren't to my taste. Some books I recommend to people that I don't like myself but I know will fit the tastes of people I'm acquainted with.

INTERVIEWER

Your dedication in this latest novel is "For Stone, Max, Grace and D." Who are they?

PEARSON

Our cats, my wife, and my dog, not in that order.

INTERVIEWER

Which one is your wife?

PEARSON

Stone. She [Marian Young] has four names. I pick one at random and stick it in there. Max and Grace are our cats. D is my dog. The flatulent dog in the book is modeled on my dog. It's a good thing D can't read.

INTERVIEWER

Speaking of Marian, you met in a rather unusual way. She's a literary agent who discovered you in 1984 when she read your manuscript *Off for the Sweet Hereafter*.

PEARSON

We met through the mail. We wrote letters back and forth, and we found that we were very companionable. We overcame very long odds.

April 6, 1994

Well, I mean she was in New York, and I was in Fuquay-Varina.

We got married a couple of years ago. In Scotland. My mother thinks we got married there so she couldn't come to the wedding.

INTERVIEWER

You and Marian have worked out an unusual marital arrangement. You spend most of your time in your log house in Virginia.

PEARSON

Maybe eight months. Marian spends most of her year in New York. I do most of the traveling.

It's an ideal way to be married. It works out real well for both of us. Our natures fit, because we're both completely happy like this, and nobody feels shortchanged. We just had to adjust the formula until we got it right. Now, about the time she's sick of me, I leave. Nothing said. I just know.

INTERVIEWER

When you were painting houses, you used to write from five in the morning to about eight-thirty. Then you went to work. Now, you write from about six to ten in the morning. Since you no longer paint houses, what do you do with the rest of your day?

PEARSON

Squander my time in one fashion or another. I'm not terribly industrious. I try to stay busy. It'd be real hard to say. When I'm in Virginia, I work around the house. There's no end of stuff to do. I read a lot. I don't do anything attendant to writing. I never hold workshops or teach classes. I don't write blurbs. I'm not terribly writerly.

When I quit writing for the day, I do mean I quit. I don't mope around the rest of the day thinking what I'm going to write tomorrow. I put it out of my mind. I'm not about to let writing novels ruin my life.

INTERVIEWER
That sounds wonderful.

PEARSON
It's very nice. I found that I couldn't write and

have any kind of employment in which I had to think. I couldn't teach and write, because it was too taxing to try to teach all day. I was just too tired. Mentally tired. But painting—that was completely mindless work. My brain was empty all day.

I've also been very lucky in that I've always made just enough money in publishing to survive. I try to live on a little money, because I don't want to have to go and teach. Because primarily, I don't believe I could teach anybody to write. And who would want to write like I do? I'd feel like an absolute fraud in a classroom.

INTERVIEWER
What don't you spend money on?

PEARSON
It's nothing I don't do. I don't deny myself. I find when I'm in New York, I'm hemorrhaging money. There's nothing to do but spend money in New York. In Virginia, I get by on groceries. I cook and eat. I don't have any will power to speak of. I don't save money by saying, "No, you can't have that." I could be considerably more frugal. Usually, when money runs low, something comes along.

INTERVIEWER
Your vocabulary tickles me. You use odd, old-fashioned words. Funny words. Tricky words. But you don't talk that way.

PEARSON
I'm pretty laconic in person. People can be as-

tounded when they come to bookstores and meet me and find I don't have anything to say.

I'm not a comedian at all. Given the opportunity, there are all sorts of words that come to mind. But when I write, I have the luxury of sitting and waiting. I do a lot of waiting. In the movies, writers are riddled with inspiration, and they write at a breakneck pace. I do a lot of sitting around. I don't consider that I write a lot in a given day. Five or six hundred words—that's a lot for me. I'm a good year and a half on a novel anymore.

INTERVIEWER
One of the things I like about your writing is its rhythm. In fact, it reads as rhythmically as poetry.

PEARSON
The rhythm is very important to me. I know that some people can't hear it. Some people in publishing can't hear it. They don't pick it up. I think I read with my ear. And so I hear clunkers when I read my work or when I read other people's work. It grates on me when the thing doesn't move along in the greatest sort of clip.

What I want is the prose to be rhythmic enough to suck a reader along without being so rhythmic as to be irritating.

This particular novel is the first one I'm going to be obliged to go out and read from. I only can because it reads fairly smoothly. In some of them, the sentences are so long. You cannot read a page-long sentence out loud and still respire appropriately.

You once told me something I love to quote. You said, "When Southerners tell a story orally, they invariably start in the middle, thinking that they're starting at the beginning. Then as soon as they start talking, they realize they have left out something. So they have to go way back before they can tell you about now. This means the story has its own impetus, and so it goes forward and it goes backwards, too, and you have a story that goes in two directions at once."

PEARSON

I've changed my perspective. This is interesting to me. In North Carolina, there's a prevalent tendency for people to talk at great length, sometimes about absolutely nothing. People tend to digress. There's a lot of chatter involved in regular human commerce.

I moved to Virginia, and in the mountains there, the population is sparse and people are cut off from each other by topography. Most of the people who live there are not inclined to talk at all. I'd been used to people I couldn't possibly hope to shut up, and here I was where I couldn't squeeze two words from them if I had to. There is not much ambient chatter.

It probably is regional. In the mountains, people's natures are probably dictated by where they live. I find very few people in Virginia who are blitherers. If I do find them, they've been imported from the flatlands, almost without fail.

INTERVIEWER

Do you think you get a better grasp of Southerners writing in the North?

PEARSON

I might be a bad example. I'm not away for that long. I sort of think the South—especially as it's represented in many Southern books—is just overdone. It's good ol' boy laid on too thick. We're not all yokels, after all. I play it as straight as I can play it. I try not to make any hay from being a Southerner. I just go about my business.

INTERVIEWER

I'll say again that I think you've made a huge leap in this latest novel. Can you say what happened?

PEARSON

By the time I finished editing this book, it felt right. I can't say that about all the books I've published. Some novels work better than others. This one just worked. I can't even say exactly why. From my view, it's that I got so attached to the narrative voice. I never worked from an outline. I knew halfway through what was going to happen. Had it in my head. Knew how it was going to end. I was just in this very odd zone, and it wasn't even that difficult to write. It just came out that way.

And I'm a little less inclined than I was in the past to indulge myself. I used to go completely backwards out of sheer perversity. I wouldn't do that now. I think I can write a novel that is sufficiently fractured without driving everybody to distraction.

INTERVIEWER

Do you love to write?

I never come away tired. I reach the point where I know I'm through, where I can't concentrate anymore. It's getting harder and harder for me to concentrate for four hours.

There's nothing rhapsodic about writing. I can't say I've ever been truly inspired—the muse is on my shoulder, and I'm typing furiously. Usually, I'm sitting and waiting.

Writing books for me just gets more and more difficult. I work very hard not to repeat myself. I'm constantly trying to do something a little different to keep myself entertained.

The only son and second child of Thomas Elwood and Sara Anne Burton Pearson, Thomas Reid Pearson was born March 27, 1956, in Winston-Salem, North Carolina. He graduated from Reynolds High School in Winston-Salem in 1974. In 1977, he received his B.A. in English from North Carolina State University in Raleigh, where he also received his M.A. in English in 1980. In the fall of 1980, he entered Pennsylvania State University to begin work on his Ph.D., which he later abandoned for house painting and novel writing in Fuquay-Varina, North Carolina.

Pearson's novels include *A Short History of a Small Place* (1985), *Off for the Sweet Hereafter* (1986), and *The Last of How It Was* (1987), all set in fictional Neely, North Carolina, based loosely on Reidsville, North Carolina. He is also the author of *Call and Response* (1989), *Gospel Hour* (1991), and *Cry Me a River* (1993).

In the fall of 1993, Pearson served as the Visiting Southern Writer-in-Residence at the University of Mississippi in Oxford.

In Scotland, on September 28, 1990, Pearson married New York literary agent Marian Young, with whom he lives in Brooklyn, New York.

He spends portions of each year in his log cabin in Virginia near the North Carolina border, where he is at work on his seventh novel.

January 11, 1972

WALKER PERCY

July 2, 1980

"Walker says I'll spend a hundred dollars on groceries and not buy one bag of sugar," says Mary Bernice "Bunt" Percy, fishing in her purse for hotel sugar packets she's saved to sweeten her husband's iced tea.

The Percys, who live in Covington, Louisiana, and Walker Percy's brother and sister-in-law, LeRoy and Sarah Percy of Greenville, Mississippi, are spending July at what is referred to locally as "the brown house" on Lake Sequoia in Highlands, North Carolina. Here, Percy, whose first novel, *The Moviegoer*, was published in 1961 to wide acclaim when he was forty-five, likes to "flop, fish, and read."

He's recently completed his fifth novel, *The Second Coming*, starring Will Barrett of Percy's 1966 novel, *The Last Gentleman*, and set in fictional Linwood, North Carolina. Barrett is an expert golfer who's recently begun to slice his drives out of bounds. Thus does Percy signal us that Barrett's life is also sailing out of bounds, and that he's entering an existential crisis for which only love can provide solution.

Percy has supplied directions to "the brown house." "I'll walk out and meet you down at the bottom of the driveway," he said. "I'm a guy who's wearing yellow pants, and there ain't many other guys up here wearing yellow pants." He later points out the towering cowcumber trees which slope from porch to winking lake.

While Percy settles back in a wooden porch chair, Mary, Sarah, and LeRoy are off to Mountain Fresh Market in town for lettuce, tomatoes, cucumbers, sugar.

"We'll have lunch ready when you get back," Percy calls to his wife, a certain slant to his voice suggesting he's never fixed a meal in his life. Percy, who's wearing a checked shirt and a blue cashmere V-neck sweater, talks about novels as explorations in pathology, the trick of letting go when you're writing, and when it is that God finally takes pity on a writer.

INTERVIEWER

This is such a beautiful view. Does a beautiful view inspire you?

PERCY

I can write better in a Holiday Inn at the intersection of, say, I-80 and I-55 than in a room with a beautiful view. This [new] book is a transaction between sex and love. What better place than the Holiday Inn? The anonymity of it. The paradox works best. Imagine a man finding himself a better human being in an anonymous environment.

INTERVIEWER

Was it difficult to slip into the character of young, somewhat schizophrenic Allison in this new novel?

PERCY

Allison was a woman, and she is me. Women are not people. They are a species and a race set apart.

INTERVIEWER

Have you ever known anyone like Allison?

PERCY

There are many gifted, superior, smart girls—like Allison—who don't know how to live, who flunk ordinary living. People scared her to death. She was too tender a plant.

INTERVIEWER

Did you base the town of Linwood, North Carolina, on Highlands, North Carolina?

PERCY

No. A lot of people think Linwood is Linville, but it's not. There are no caves like that in North Carolina. But there are in Tennessee.

INTERVIEWER

How did you research building a log house like the one Allison lives in?

PERCY

I got the description of notching log cabins from reading the first issue of the *Red Clay Reader* [published in 1964 by Charleen Whisnant's Red Clay Press in Charlotte, North Carolina]. There's a whole section in there on how to build a log cabin.

INTERVIEWER

How did you choose to go to the University of North Carolina?

PERCY

Uncle Will [his poet-planter cousin, William Alexander Percy, who adopted the Percy boys after their father's suicide and their mother's death in a car wreck] had gone to Harvard, but he thought Chapel Hill was the best state university in the South. It was, and as far as I know, still is. LeRoy and I both went. Tuition was a hundred dollars, and there was no entrance requirement.

There was a placement test in English, with classes divided into advanced, average, and retarded. I had just finished reading Faulkner's *The Sound and the Fury*, and I wrote my placement theme in a Faulknerian style—no capitalization, no punctuation. They put me in the retarded English class, and the professor really thought I was hot stuff. Compared to the rest of the dummies, I guess I was.

INTERVIEWER

What was your reading experience before Chapel Hill?

PERCY

I had Uncle Will's own intellectual stimulation. He knew how to communicate the excitement of reading. And I'd had terrific reading experience even in high school—Roma Roloff, John Cristoff—and I remember reading [Douglas Southall] Freeman's life of Robert E. Lee sitting on the porch of the SAE house. It was natural to read things I really wanted. I can't imagine anyone wanting to become a writer without some other writer getting him excited.

INTERVIEWER

Except for writing a gossip column in high school, you came late to writing. In fact, you seemed to be heading down another path. At Chapel Hill, you majored in chemistry and minored in math and German. At the College of Physicians and Surgeons at Columbia University, you vacillated between pathology and psychiatry.

PERCY

I think I would've ended up in psychiatry. Pathology is the most elegant of the medical fields, and psychiatry is the most interesting. I felt more at home on the psychiatric ward than anywhere else. Maybe it takes one to know one.

INTERVIEWER

You interned at New York's Bellevue Hospital, where you performed more than a hundred autopsies. I've heard you say that autopsies are good training for the novelist of the twentieth century.

PERCY

The confrontation with death. Death is the new obscenity in our civilization. People don't like to talk about dead people. To live well, you have to talk about death.

You might say I'm a pathological novelist. Or a pathologist novelist. The natural set of pathology is of someone trying to discover the lesion. The novelist says, "What's wrong with this person?" The pathologist says, "What'd he die of?" Novels are really exercises in pathology. What's gone wrong with the best of all possible lives? What's gone wrong in the best of all possible environments?

INTERVIEWER

What about the craft of writing? Does it get easier?

PERCY

Craft gets more difficult the longer you do it. It's not like bricklaying, which must get easier. Within the craft, there are the things you make up and the things that just happen.

INTERVIEWER

How do you account for this fine sentence—among many fine sentences—in this new novel, "The darkness sprang back like an animal"? Did you make that up, or did it just happen?

PERCY

It's a small thing. But a small, good thing. I don't know how that happens. A little figure like that makes you feel good. Every now and then, things break right.

It's a matter of letting go. You have to work hard. You have to punch a clock. You have to put in your time. But somehow there's a trick of letting go to let the best writing take place.

Maybe it's a day you wake up, and you've had good dreams, and the day before you've left off at a good place. Hemingway always said, "Quit while you still have juice, and the next day the juice will still be there." Well, that ain't true. When everything's going right, you can sit for three hours and stare at a blank piece of paper.

But say everything's going wrong. It's a Monday morning, and you've had bad dreams, and you know nothing good is going to happen. But you go anyway. You go into your little office, and you look at a blank wall. And you give up. It's a matter of giving up, of surrendering, of letting go. You say, "All is lost. The jig is up. I surrender. I'll never write another word again. I admit total defeat. I'm washed up."

And you stay there, and after an hour, you say, "Oh, well. I've been cast up on an island. I'm a wreck. But here I am. Still alive. Here's a pencil. Here's the paper. There's the three-ring binder and the Blue Horse paper." And you say, "Since I'm here, why don't I write something? Life is finished. Western civilization is destroyed. I'm sitting in the rubble of Manhattan. Everything's gone, everybody's dead—except a girl. There's always a girl. Me and this girl. We'll just see what happens."

What I'm telling you is, that's when things happen.

What I'm telling you is, I don't know anything. It's a question of being so pitiful God takes pity on you, looks down and says, "He's done for. Let's let him have a couple of good sentences."

It's a strange, abject, little-understood profession. Saul Bellow says that being a writer reminds him of the mating of dogs.

INTERVIEWER

You've lived in Covington, Louisiana, since 1950, raised two daughters there, become a grandfather four times over, watched the population double to ten thousand. You've described the town, forty miles north of New Orleans, as "neither here nor there," and you say it's an "ordinary place in the pine trees and we live in an ordinary house by a bayou." You practice what you preach, don't you, about the art of staying put?

PERCY

The trick is doing what you're doing without getting the itch. The itch usually doesn't work. You move on, and it's the same thing. Repetition is one of the six great themes in literature—figuring out how you can live in the same place without being miserable. It takes a conscious cultivation of the ordinary.

March 26, 1987

W alker Percy says he's buying new shirts

and a necktie on the occasion of the publication of his sixth novel, *The Thanatos Syndrome*, a philosophical thriller set in Louisiana.

While he was performing autopsies at Bellevue Hospital, Percy contracted tuberculosis. That disease provided him a three-year, guilt-free "rest cure," which he spent reading the European philosophers and novelists, especially Sartre, Camus, and Kierkegaard.

His reading led him away from medicine and into the study of linguistics and man's alienation from himself. The latter theme wove its way into his first novel, *The Moviegoer*, in which Binx Bolling tries to flee his sense of alienation by womanizing and going to movies.

Since that time, Percy has published five more novels and two collections of essays: *The Message in the Bottle* and *Lost in the Cosmos*.

Today, before he sets off on a national book tour, Percy talks about turning ideas into fiction, about our terror of confronting ourselves, about his theory of catastrophe, and about his favorite subject—death, and how it enhances life.

INTERVIEWER

If you, like Dr. Tom More in *The Thanatos Syndrome*, had become a psychiatrist, do you think you would've also written novels?

PERCY

The answer is no. Maybe some people can, but I can't do it. I can't have two professions at once. Even when I tried teaching, I didn't have sufficient energy to write. Being a shrink would take all the energies and all the anguish you would usually spend on a novel. Unless, like Dr. More,

I was a failed shrink, and I had plenty of time. Then it might work out.

INTERVIEWER

Will you talk a bit about that leap you took in your writing whereby you transformed your philosophical ideas into fiction?

PERCY

I don't know how it came about. All I know is that I had written a couple of unsuccessful novels in the 1950s, and I was also writing articles for learned journals on psychiatry and philosophy and linguistics, even one with the fascinating title of *Philosophy and Phenomenological Research*. I was interested in ideas about language and about the French philosophers Camus and Sartre.

But then I had to support myself, and I thought I would write a couple of novels. I wrote two which were pretty bad. One was a sort of Southern Bildungsroman, about a young man who's out of sync with the world. But it had too much Thomas Wolfe influence in it, and it wasn't very good. And then I wrote a second, shorter novel about my experiences in a tuberculosis sanitorium, a sort of short *Magic Mountain*, which was pretty good and wasn't published.

Then it crossed my mind: Why not do what the French do and we Americans usually don't? That is, if you have ideas about language and philosophy, why not incarnate them, put them in novel form the way Sartre and Camus did? Americans don't usually do this.

INTERVIEWER

But Americans were hungry for it, weren't they?

PERCY

They were hungry for it. I remember we were renting a little shotgun cottage in New Orleans, and I was sitting on the back porch there one day, and I was thinking, why not take a young man who was alienated in a peculiarly American way—not like a dramatic French alienation, but in a special Southern, New Orleans way—and set him down in Gentilly, a middle-class section of New Orleans? And there I had Binx Bolling in *The Moviegoer*.

I wrote the first sentence: "This morning I got a note from my aunt asking me to come for lunch. I know what that means." It felt exactly right. I said, as they say, "I think I've found my proper voice."

I wasn't trying to use Binx Bolling to present ideas. It was that fiction was the best way to talk about the twentieth-century themes of alienation and inauthenticity and what Kierkegaard called repetition and rotation. Binx thought he could escape his feelings by moviegoing and through his girlfriends and secretaries.

INTERVIEWER

How important were those years, not long after medical school, when you were recovering from TB? Weren't you able to read almost all day?

PERCY

I've often said that getting a light case of TB was the best thing that could've happened to me. It gave me a period of enforced idleness. I was brought up with a strong Presbyterian work ethic, and there was no way I could've loafed for two or three years without guilt. But when you have TB, you are guilt-free. It was perfect for me.

I was a little bit like Hans Castorp in [Thomas Mann's] *The Magic Mountain*. There he was, stuck up in the mountain while World War I was going on, and I was stuck up in New York while World War II was going on, in this strange place with friends—some dying, some very ill—sitting around in bars, drinking and talking and doing a great deal of reading.

INTERVIEWER

What kind of reading?

PERCY

My education had been strictly scientific. Premed was a mistake. It was all chemistry and very little English.

My three years of recovering were really the equivalent of a liberal-arts education for me. It was the beginning of writing. I read a book that got me very excited. It was *Philosophy in the New Key* by Suzanne Langer, about the nature of language. I wrote a review of it and sent it off to a journal, and lo and behold it was published, and that was the beginning of my literary career.

INTERVIEWER

That idle time seemed to be essential for you, but many of us avoid idleness at all costs.

PERCY

I think that's true in the sense that one reason Americans like to keep so busy—either by being workaholics or real alcoholics or by spending eight hours a day watching TV—is the terror of confronting oneself. The worst thing that can happen is to be alone with oneself without radio or television or any diversion. That's one reason I watch [reruns of] "Barnaby Jones."

INTERVIEWER

I've read that Charles Percy, your great-great-grandfather, tied a sugar kettle to his neck and threw himself into a creek.

Do you think this legacy of suicide has anything to do with the themes of affirming life that recur in your novels?

PERCY

Yes, he threw himself in Percy's Creek [in Mississippi]. My father committed suicide, too. I suppose that legacy has made me very conscious of the availability of death. I hadn't thought about it before, but I think it influenced my method in novel writing.

I suppose it has to do with the characters' options. I usually have somebody who's depressed or overcome by her life or his life or somebody who's dying, like the young man in *The Last Gentleman*. What interests me is how the availability of death and the closeness of death—whether it be depression or the availability of suicide—there's something about the closeness of death which has the paradoxical effect of making life fresh and valuable and available.

The two go together, which opens up a whole theory of mine—which I call the theory of catastrophe—that somehow when people are in a catastrophe—war or a car wreck or a serious illness, under the circumstances of near-death—one somehow has the option of recovering life.

I think of the famous scene of a young German soldier in *All Quiet on the Western Front*. In the midst of all that slaughter and trench warfare, he sees the butterfly, and he reaches out his hand to touch the butterfly just before he gets shot.

The point is that under these horrifying conditions of near-death, he is somehow enabled to see the butterfly for the first time. He's seen butterflies all his life. But somehow his eyes are open for the first time to the beauty of being, the goodness of being.

INTERVIEWER

You've said, in fact, that to live well you have to talk about death.

PERCY

Talking about anything makes it real. I think the whole subject of art—in my case, writing—has to do with seeing things afresh and expressing ordinary experiences which everybody experiences and usually don't set much store by.

The best letters I get are mostly from young people who read my books. They'll mention a perfectly ordinary section which describes what is an ordinary situation on an ordinary Wednesday afternoon, and they'll say, "That's exactly how I felt!"

The best thing about writing is to repeat the ordinary experience, and by putting that experience into language, it makes it available to the person who reads it in a way that it hasn't been available before.

You've said life doesn't have to stop with failure. Not only do you not have to jump in the creek, you can even take pleasure in the general fecklessness of life.

PERCY

I have a whole theory about that. You hear a lot of bad things about watching TV. My own feeling is that one reason it's bad is that when you're watching TV—half-hour segments of an ongoing program or one hour of "Dynasty"—what you're watching represents one successful take out of ninety-nine outtakes which have been thrown out because they didn't work. As Thomas More says in the novel, even when somebody like Jane Fonda has a breakdown and goes crazy, the particular take they use is one that works. It's rounded off. She breaks down in just the right way.

The poor kid who's grown up on this says, "My God! That's not the way my life is. My life consists mostly of failure." So Thomas More thinks his job is to get his patients to accept that failure is the way most of life is.

INTERVIEWER

What's your writing day like?

PERCY

It's very humdrum. Writing is what I do. I wouldn't know what else to do. At nine o'clock, I pick up my three-ring binder with the Blue Horse note paper in it. I have an idea of what comes next, and so I start working. I don't have the famous terrors or the famous writer's block. I work at it, and I write a few pages. It'll go pretty well or pretty badly.

Now and then you have a piece of luck. Luck or providence. And something will go right and you know you're doing something right. Those are the good times.

My best piece of equipment is what Hemingway had—a built-in shit detector. He had the faculty of knowing when he wrote badly. He didn't at the end.

I think my piece of equipment is the same thing. I'm not a genius of a writer. I don't write naturally well, but I know when I do badly and I'll go back later and work on it.

A great many writers don't have that. A great many writers think it's all good. My only claim to excellence is I know when I do badly, so I know when it has to be redone.

INTERVIEWER

What about the rest of your life?

PERCY

My wife and I either play golf or walk a couple of miles in the afternoons. I really enjoy a quiet life. I enjoy my work, see a few friends. I have two daughters who live right here and two nice sons-in-law and four grandsons. I've got my books and my writing. What else does a man need?

I also confess to watching an awful lot of junk on TV, listening to Larry King on the radio. I eat a lot of junk food and listen to a lot of junk television.

I'm happy, except for this damn hay fever, which is about to kill me. I have to lie down flat on my back with my nose straight up in the air to keep it from running. Otherwise, I'm in great shape.

Born May 28, 1916, in Birmingham, Alabama, Walker Percy was the oldest of three sons of Leroy Pratt and Martha Phinizy Percy. When Percy was eleven, his father committed suicide, and the family lived for a time with Percy's grandmother in Athens, Georgia. Two years after his father's death, his mother died in an automobile accident. Their elder cousin, William Alexander Percy of Greenville, Mississippi, adopted the boys and raised them.

Percy graduated from Greenville High School in 1934 and entered UNC-Chapel Hill that fall. He graduated in 1937 with a B.A. in chemistry and entered the College of Physicians and Surgeons at Columbia University, graduating with high honors in 1941.

While interning at Bellevue Hospital in New York City, he contracted pulmonary tuberculosis and had to enter Trudeau Sanitorium in the Adirondacks. In 1944, he was released and returned to Columbia to teach pathology. He suffered a relapse and entered a sanitorium in Connecticut. He never practiced medicine.

His novels include *The Moviegoer* (1961), *The Last Gentleman* (1967), *Love in the Ruins* (1971), *Lancelot* (1977), *The Second Coming* (1980), and *The Thanatos Syndrome* (1987).

His nonfiction works are *The Message in the Bottle: How Queer Man Is, How Queer Language Is, and What One Has to Do with the Other* (1975), *Lost in the Cosmos: The Last Self-Help Book* (1983), *Novel-Writing in an Apocalyptic Time* (1986), and *Signposts in a Strange Land* (1991).

He won the National Book Award for fiction (1962), a National Institute of Arts and Letters grant (1967), the National Catholic Book Award (1971), the *Los Angeles Times* Book Prize (1980), the *Los Angeles Times* Book Prize for Current Interest (1983), and the St. Louis Literary Award (1986).

On November 7, 1946, Percy married Mary Bernice Townsend. Their children are Mary Pratt, born in 1947, and Ann Boyd, born in 1954.

Walker Percy died at his home in Covington, Louisiana, on May, 10, 1990.

April 4, 1994

REYNOLDS PRICE

*R*eynolds Price points to the hill outside his house in the piney woods near Durham, North Carolina, where his legs first failed him six years ago. The occasion: The May 1984 outdoor wedding of neighbors. The diagnosis: A pencil-thick, cancerous tumor on his upper spine.

It's been a year and a half since Price, James B. Duke Professor of English at Duke University, underwent the last of four operations to remove the astrocytoma. Surgery and hours of radiation left him a paraplegic—but free of cancer.

Meanwhile, Price's mind has been a literary dervish. He was halfway through what would become the award-winning novel *Kate Vaiden* when he had the first operation. Next, he completed a book of poems, *The Laws of Ice*. Then a play, *August Snow*, triggering two more plays, which make up the trilogy *New Music*. His essays from 1954 to 1987 are now collected in *A Common Room*, and he is at work on another collection of essays, *Clear Pictures*, about his youth.

His latest novel, *Good Hearts*, is a sequel to his first, *A Long and Happy Life*, which in 1962 firmly established the twenty-nine-year-old Price in the literary vanguard.

Price began teaching writing at Duke when he was twenty-five. His first year there, sixteen-year-old Anne Tyler enrolled in his writing class. At that point, Price has said, he knew no better than to expect such extraordinary talent year after year.

Price's resonant voice is melodic, his haircut rakish. Surrounded by objects he loves and photographs he cherishes, he talks about hypnosis and memory, the questions he never asked his parents, the black sheep in an extended family, and the gallery of heroes who saw him through a horrific illness.

INTERVIEWER

Your new novel, *Good Hearts*, takes up Wesley Beavers and Rosacoke Mustian at midlife. We haven't seen them since *A Long and Happy Life*, more than a quarter of a century ago. How did you happen to return to those two lovable characters?

PRICE

I have been trying for several years now to write a novel in the male first person. I made attempts to get it started in 1983, and *Kate Vaiden* broke into that.

Then, after *Kate* came along and was successful, I still wanted to go back and do this story. I started again making notes for it in 1986, and after a couple of weeks of note-making, found myself going back to the old idea I've had for so many years, of taking up Rosacoke and Wesley again.

INTERVIEWER

You wrote *Good Hearts* very rapidly, didn't you?

PRICE

Now that I'm at home so much of the time, I'm working a lot faster than I used to. So a novel of that length would normally have taken me eighteen months to write, and I wrote it maybe in about three or four—four, I think—with time out in the middle for surgery at Duke.

I've always enjoyed writing more than most people, I think. But I did especially enjoy working on this particular one.

INTERVIEWER

Is there any other reason for this new speed, other than being at home more?

PRICE

I've cut so much rival activity out of my life. Teaching and seeing my friends are the only old things that I still do. I've cut out all the chores and going for groceries, and I've cut out almost all the old going-places-to-give-readings stuff.

So I've got all that time. I've got a lot of energy, thank God, and the subject matter is coming fast. What would have happened thirty years ago if I had cut back everything very drastically? I don't know whether it would've been the same or not. But what's happening now is what's happening, and I'm very pleased about it.

INTERVIEWER

You once said you get the baby blues when you finish a piece of work.

PRICE

Since finishing *Good Hearts*, I had a small version of the baby blues—maybe a few days or a week. Then, once I'd gotten through with the teaching last fall, I started work on really what I thought at first were isolated essays about important people in my childhood. I started with a piece about my parents, then about my mother's next eldest sister, Aunt Ida. And then I began to realize that a lot more memory than I had realized was there, and it was coming back.

Do you think the more you tap those memories, the more the memories surface?

PRICE

The way it started was pretty unusual for me. Because of these four spinal surgeries I've had—three major ones and a fourth time when they had to go back in to repair an incision that had come open—so as a result of that surgery, I have a lot of chronic back pain. And drugs were not helping and were making me drowsy, and I hated that. So my surgeon suggested last summer that I should try the biofeedback program at Duke.

So I went into biofeedback once a week for an afternoon, and it helped a lot learning these sort of subliminal techniques of relaxation and so forth. It's really a form of meditation. "Well," he said, "this is working well. Would you be interested in trying hypnosis?"

So I said, "Sure." And I went to Duke Hospital's main hypnotist, Dr. Patrick Logue, and we did five or six weeks of hypnosis, in which he initially induced me, then turned me over to a cassette of his voice, then weaned me from that onto the ability to do it to myself.

And though we never attempted any memory regressions in the course of our pain therapy, we talked a lot about it as a tool for uncovering memory. And the last day I was there, I said, "You know, sometime, Dr. Logue, I might want to come back and let's do some memory regressions." And he said, "Okay." Then he said, "I won't even hypnotize you, but let's just have a little experiment now."

And he said, "Do you know where you lived when you were three years old?" And I said, "Yes, I lived on Greystone Terrace on South Elm Street in Asheboro, North Carolina." And he said, "Okay, where was the front door?" And I said, "It's in the middle of the front of the building—a two-story brick building with white trim around the windows."

And I sort of laughed and said, "God!" And he said, "What don't we know?" And I said, "We don't know if any of this is right." And he said, "The chances are that since you are responding so quickly and definitely that a lot of this *is* exact memory." That I think is what triggered me to go on and write the memory things, realizing how much more was there than I knew.

INTERVIEWER

Writers typically seem to have excellent memories. Why do you think that is?

PRICE

The wiring. I think it's pure genetics. Adults always spoke of me as being a very watchful and attentive child, and I always preferred hanging around the grownups to the children.

INTERVIEWER

It's amazing how many writers say that.

PRICE

Oh, I know. I mean, I liked my contemporaries, but I really did prefer hanging out around adults. And of course I was an only child until I was eight. So basically, my parents and I were a real triangle. I realized very early in my life that we were all married. It wasn't a question of it being a twosome. It was a threesome.

The memoir sounds very satisfying to write.

Enormously satisfying. I loved doing it. And like everyone else who's middle-aged in America, I just tremendously regret the fact that I've got all these questions which are now unanswerable. There are only one or two people alive who knew my parents intimately enough, early enough, to answer questions for me.

What kinds of questions?

About Mother's growing up. As a child, you know A and K, but you don't know B, C, D. My mother's mother died when she was about four. Her father died when she was thirteen. She never had to leave home, because an older sister, Ida, and her husband and children moved into the house. And though Ida and her husband were wonderfully kind people, there was always that sense that somebody's come into my home and taken over my parents' role. I would love to know a lot more about, really, her response and feeling to all that.

Certainly, as I said in interviews about *Kate Vaiden*, there's a lot of atmosphere of my mother in Kate—this rather rebellious, outlaw person who nonetheless was very warm and open. Mother never did anything remotely as dramatic as Kate's various runaways. But it was sort of in her soul. She never acted it out.

And then my father . . . It was only when I started writing the memoirs that I suddenly realized, "My God! My father graduated from high school when he was seventeen years old. He didn't marry my mother until he was twenty-seven!" Meanwhile, he had small, insignificant jobs in Warrenton, the hometown, and lived at home with his parents. Why was there a ten-year period in there? And Mother used to laugh about their extended six-year courtship.

She was really something else, my father's mother, and I've written a lot about her and my very few memories of her, one of which is of her slapping my mother. Well, I'm positive that it wasn't a serious slap. I can't have been more than four years old. And we went there from Roxboro for a visit, and Mother and Dad and I went into her bedroom—she's in bed—and my memory is that Mother leaned over to kiss her first, and that my grandmother slapped Mother and said, "I want to kiss my baby."

All the boys—there were three Price boys—all of them got as far away as they could get. Two of them went to Tennessee, and Dad got the least far of anybody. He was the baby boy. He was sort of the eyeballs, as they used to say.

The strange thing was, my mother always liked Mrs. Price. Kind of balance of power. She was very two-minded about my father's sisters, who were very powerful, brainy women, all of whom ended up living at home for various sad reasons of their own.

And of course my father had that serious drinking problem for the first six years of their marriage. He made this deal when I was being born. Mother and I were both in such serious trouble in labor, and he made this deal with God that if we survived in good shape, he would quit. We did, and he did.

INTERVIEWER
What sort of people were the Prices?

PRICE
The Prices were very bookish, brainy people. They were marvelous talkers. They were great wits and mimics. And there was a great deal of unhappiness in the family. My father's eldest sister ran off with her high-school principal when she was sixteen and went as far as Granite Falls, North Carolina, which in 1910 might as well have been Boulder, Colorado. She had a child. The child was not born for about eighteen months after she left home. But she was sixteen and he was forty, at least, which was just unheard of.

And then after three years of living with this old gent, she just came back home one night with the baby—it was a son—and never left again. Mr. Grant came to town once to try to persuade her to return, and she wouldn't return. She never got a divorce. He was never mentioned, and she lived on until her late eighties, certainly her mideighties, and died in the late 1970s.

The boy is now a man in his seventies. He's been living in Georgia for years. He never knew his father. When Mary Elinor, the sister in question, died, I went down for her funeral. And we were sitting in the kitchen afterwards drinking coffee, and I said to her next oldest sister, Lulie—who had lived with her there all those years—I said, "Lulie, is Mr. Grant alive?" And she said, "Oh, Lord God, he can't be. He'd be over a hundred."

INTERVIEWER
How did the family react when she ran off with Mr. Grant?

PRICE
They were not people who had any great shame about anything. They were very self-confident. I mean, the family was full of drunks, most of whom were fairly charming, cheerful drunks and were liked in the community. But there was no great attempt to paper over the cracks or conceal things.

INTERVIEWER
That's rare. How do you account for it?

PRICE
Of course, partly, in a town as small as Warrenton and Macon, you couldn't have covered it up if you'd tried. Even the CIA couldn't have managed it. I think one of the things has to be that these were people who were definitely not wealthy and were certainly not preening themselves on their aristocratic origins. But they were very, very socially secure people. They knew who they were. They had solid, respected

places in their community, in the church, the power structure of Warren County, and had since the eighteenth century at least. And they just didn't worry that if somebody went out and got drunk and ran off with somebody else's girlfriend that they were going to lose status, because they wouldn't have and did not.

So they didn't wear their hearts on their sleeves. They didn't go around moaning and groaning about the black sheep of the family. But there was certainly no great attempt at getting all the skeletons back in the closets.

INTERVIEWER

Things happen in families.

PRICE

What happens, happens. What is, is. When the sky falls down, you go back home. That's where order and retreat and protection is. And the women came home. The boys left. And of course none of us at that point in American history—even the women themselves—could consciously see that the men had so much more scope for getting away than the women did. When their marriages collapsed, there was nothing to do but come home to Mama or Daddy, which they did. And, luckily, they had a stable family home with enough money to tide them all through until they all went out and got good jobs and supported themselves and their children.

INTERVIEWER

What about your mother's family, the Rodwells?

PRICE

Mother's family were very much the other brand of Southern whites. They were extremely warm-hearted, totally absorbed in family business. They had as much trouble in their houses as the Prices did, but they were tolerant people. They weren't so hard on themselves and so demanding of themselves as the Prices.

INTERVIEWER

You've said about Warren County—where these people lived—that it's a place about which you, as a writer, have perfect pitch. Do your students know a place or a family that well?

PRICE

My writing class that I teach this semester—I've got fifteen students in it—they are wonderfully intelligent, and some of them are very gifted. But almost to a man and a woman, they have absolutely no connection with their family past. I can't get them to write about anything that happened before yesterday. There's not an older person in any of their stories. Their imaginations are very thin, and, unfortunately, in the absence of contact with extended families who had elaborate oral traditions of story, they simply substituted television as their reservoir of stories. So they've got "Sesame Street," where I've got Aunt Ida. And it's a damned poor substitute.

INTERVIEWER

In your new book, Wesley Beavers, who is fifty, seems to be looking for a substitute. At least some sort of substitute for marriage.

PRICE

I'm fifty-five, and an awful lot of my old friends have really undergone these sort of baffling breakdowns. I've seen several of my friends' marriages . . . One or the other of them simply one day just sort of announces, "I quit."

INTERVIEWER

What's that all about?

PRICE

It's very hard to look at fifty on the calendar and not begin to realize that you're hardly the cock of the walk that you once were. There's not a thing about Rosacoke that Wesley wants changed. He just no longer feels the need to be there. He feels dead, as he says. And I think an awful lot of people who are not doing something fascinating and creative do feel dead.

I mean, my God! It's hard enough to keep creativity going as it is. But what about all those people we couldn't live a day of our middle-class lives without? The people who run pinball-machine arcades? Suppose you manned the cash register at the local porno book shop? How would you keep from going just totally bananas? I mean, I'm never amazed when somebody walks into a bank or a McDonald's and shoots sixteen people. I'm always amazed that more people *don't* do it.

INTERVIEWER

Is there an equivalent for creativity in those people's lives?

PRICE

Well, that's what I look for, and so many of my books are about those kinds of people. I definitely don't scorn those people. My own parents were people of that sort, and almost all the people whom I grew up loving in my childhood were people who either farmed or worked in the daily jobs that supported a farming community.

INTERVIEWER

What kept them going?

PRICE

What kept them going in their time—the first half of the twentieth century—was basically family. The relationships between generations. The relationships among members of the family, all of whom lived within at least a thirty-minute ride of one another. The whole unending, theatrical event of family life, which had a tremendous amount of heartbreak in it, as well as an awful lot of gratification.

I think as long as the extended family worked, as long as it really was what people *did* in small-town and rural America, it was a satisfactory way to get through life.

After the Second World War in America, we began sort of abandoning the extended family for all sorts of reasons. Everybody got in their Ford and went to Nevada, leaving Ma and Pa in Virginia or Kentucky or wherever, and so the family broke down. And I'm not at all one who wants to climb on President Reagan's bandwagon and say, "Let's bring all that back." I think there are things about the extended family that are well vanished. The family, after all, was the hothouse of all kinds of neurosis and psychosis when things did not go well, and I saw plenty of the bad part of family in my own time. But it was those people's entertainment, their reward, and their hope of creativity.

INTERVIEWER

The extended family is hardly your own entertainment or your reward. Did you decide early to chuck it?

PRICE

By the time I was in high school and college, I had seen enough of that sort of feeder-and-fed culture of family life to realize I didn't want that for myself. I loved a lot of it. I loved an awful lot of the people involved. But I didn't want my entire hope of happiness and fulfillment and security to be based on what my sisters and brothers and nephews and nieces thought of me, or my parents, and what I could do for them down the road, and what they could do for me.

My family . . . Once I got this cancer and took to a wheelchair, my family's been wonderful. Several of the older members of my family, whom I had almost lost touch with, have really rallied. It's marvelous. What do you do if you live in Salt Lake City and everybody else is in Paducah, Kentucky? You can be sure as hell they're not going to walk in off the streets and start taking care of you when you're dying of radiation poisoning.

INTERVIEWER

Emma, Rosacoke's mother in *Good Hearts*, in-

terests me, because she seemed to reach a stage in life where she was very much at peace living alone. She didn't crave here-and-now extensions at all.

PRICE

She was at peace with her own very strange and very unexpected conclusions about religion and family. I don't know where that all came from in my imagination. I do remember very late in my mother's life—when my brother and I had left home and Father was long dead and she was losing her eyesight fairly rapidly—I used to feel awfully guilty if I didn't get over once every two weeks to see her.

I began, though, to realize that in the last two or three years of her life, she didn't mind at all if I weren't over there, and she wasn't having to worry about cleaning the house up and getting herself dressed and cooking supper. And I once said to her, "What are you going to do this weekend?" And she said, "Oh, I don't have any plans." And I said, "Well, who are you going to be with?" And she said, "I'm going to be with myself. I'm pretty good company."

And I got Emma somewhat out of the sense that she really had invented a way of being alone. She panicked when Father died. She was forty-eight years old, and he was fifty-four. She couldn't imagine how she could suddenly be the things she had never been before: A person who ran a family and ran a household. She really learned how to live alone. And she could have gone on till ninety if her body hadn't just given out on her.

One thing I've never done is to imagine what someone like my father would've done had my mother died first. My mother picked out my father's tie and socks every day of his life. He couldn't have made a cup of instant coffee.

INTERVIEWER

Did your parents know how much you loved them?

PRICE

I think they did. I've thought about that a lot in writing these pieces, and it sounds awfully self-congratulatory, but I think that my brother and I were very satisfactory children. We were normally rambunctious. We ran and played and had childhood friends and got into scrapes. But we were very, very close to them, and they knew that.

I've often wondered lately where my particular parents got the degree of tolerance and trust they had in us. They never once said, "Be a doctor. Be a lawyer. Be a minister." It was just, "What do you want to do?"

INTERVIEWER

Maybe it was that same security that allowed them not to hide the family skeletons.

PRICE

I think that's very true. They did not live their lives through us. They had a good marriage for the twenty-six or twenty-seven years it lasted, and when Father died [in 1954], Mother did not attempt then to continue to live her life through us. She was very interested in what we did. She loved the fact that *A Long and Happy Life* and *The Names and Faces of Heroes* were published in her lifetime. She loved reading them, and she loved seeing my picture in places. And never a word about, "Why on earth have you put a sex scene in the middle of so-and-so?"

INTERVIEWER

So you have had the freedom to write exactly what you wanted?

PRICE

Yes, and the access to my material.

INTERVIEWER

What do you mean by access?

PRICE

Let's say that my material is simply everything that's been deposited in my mind—conscious and subconscious—for the last fifty-five years. A fiction writer's—and probably a poet's and dramatist's—success is in direct proportion to his or her ability to open up direct lines to all that material. Not to be frightened by it.

I think if I had had the sort of neurotic and fearful relationship with my mother that so many of my friends have had, then I just couldn't have done a *Kate Vaiden*. I wouldn't have been able to go ahead and face the fact that my mother might have wanted like hell to run many days in her life. The fact that she didn't was rather heroic of her. But Kate chose to run, and it was very interesting to follow that on through to some kind of imaginative conclusion.

Would you say one way we assess artists is by their imaginative conclusions?

PRICE

We measure artists by really two things. We basically measure them by the capacity of their imagination: How many different kinds of things they knew, and could tell us. What they know is partly genetic, it's partly given them by their family, and it's also partly the fact that they were able to sit and accept it and take it all in. And then how they were able to externalize it, to go on and pass it on and tell it in their work.

INTERVIEWER

Four or five years ago, you had no idea you would develop cancer, endure four operations, and be confined to a wheelchair. Has living through that ordeal helped you face life with new freedom?

PRICE

I guess one of the things that that ordeal demonstrated was that I was stronger than I thought I was. But I should have known that I would be, because I came from very strong stock.

I remember thinking the night my father died—I was holding his arm when he died—I remember very consciously thinking at the time that there's nothing so scary about death. I just saw him. He just did it, and he was nobody terribly much stronger than me.

No, I haven't learned anything that I didn't know intellectually already. But I've learned it on the firing line, which is the only place that you really learn something. And I've just learned to live very much for the present. And I think that's probably one more reason why the work has come so rich and thick in the last four years—because I'm just very much here. I'm not back there or up yonder. I'm very much here, and I feel that.

And without wanting to sound like the chairman of the Epworth League, I really do feel very grateful for every day that I have. It's very good to have a sort of gallery of heroes behind you, because you can at least say, "Well, I knew Ida, and she did it, and so why can't I?" Which is one thing I really grieve that my students don't have. They have so few of the Idas back in there. All they've got is Sylvester Stallone. Imagine facing spinal cancer with Sylvester Stallone as your model. Good luck, Chuck. There's nothing to do but laugh, as my mother would say.

April 15, 1992

*I*n the robust-looking face of fifty-nine-year-old Reynolds Price you can see—lurking mischievously—the face of six-year-old Reynolds Price, which graces the cover of his recent memoir, *Clear Pictures*. That book was the result of Price's intense period of memory-gathering in 1988. Since then, he has completed two more novels: *The Tongues of Angels*, and this latest, *Blue Calhoun*, the love story of an older man for a young woman, set in Raleigh, North Carolina, in the 1950s.

On a muggy, overcast afternoon, azaleas ablaze amid the pines out his window, Price talks about writing, cravings, cancer, and prayer.

INTERVIEWER

I read long portions aloud from your new novel, *Blue Calhoun*, and its cadence was like poetry, and never let up. I don't remember such a strong and sustained cadence in your other books.

PRICE

It was literally nothing I ever for a second worked at or worked to get. I didn't sit down and think, "What are the rhythms of Blue Calhoun's voice?" I think it was simply the way it's almost always been, that a character—or at least the psychic weather of the character—had formed in my mind long before I began writing the book.

I didn't by any means know all the events of the plot before I began writing. I knew the one basic event, which was his falling in love with this girl and making a huge throw of the dice on her. But how it was all going to come out, I really didn't know when I started.

But I just knew exactly what it felt like to be him. And he's a good talker, and like so many of the men in my own family, who were intelligent, charming alcoholics, he had a wonderful sort of seductive ability to keep you sitting still while he wove his narrative spell around you.

INTERVIEWER

It was interesting the way you revealed his good looks almost exclusively through other people's description of him, particularly his mother's.

PRICE

I hadn't even thought of that. But of course if you're going to like the character, he cannot tell you he's good-looking.

INTERVIEWER

Blue Calhoun says at one point that if he'd had a son instead of a daughter, he might've been more loyal to his family—stopped drinking earlier, not run off with the beautiful Luna Absher. I've read studies that say fathers are more loyal to their families if they have sons.

PRICE

I know two alcoholics in my own family—my father and one of my mother's nephews—who were "bad to drink," as they used to say, until, in my father's case, his first son was born, which was me.

In the case of my mother's nephew, he quit when his first male descendant was born. He only had a daughter himself, but when that daughter had a son, he quit. He said, "I'm never going to let that child see me take a drink."

INTERVIEWER

But your father made that deal with God—vowed he wouldn't drink again if you and your mother survived her perilous childbirth—before he knew he had a boy.

PRICE

Of course, whether he'd kept it if it'd been a girl, we don't know, do we?

INTERVIEWER

Do you think your father's own alcoholism continues to fuel your imagination? I'm thinking again of Blue Calhoun.

PRICE

He began stopping the day I was born, and he was totally abstinent from the time I was about two or two and a half. So I never saw my father take a drink.

INTERVIEWER

Did I read somewhere that your father helped found a chapter of AA in Warrenton?

PRICE

No. Alcoholics Anonymous wasn't even organized until something like 1934. I was born in 1933. And it certainly didn't reach rural North Carolina until a while after that.

What you may have heard, when we went back to Warrenton to live when I was a teenager, he and mother went to an AA meeting one night that was held there. I remember my father saying, "If something like that had been around when I was drinking, it might have been easier for me."

But all he really had was one wonderful resource, which was a Baptist preacher named Mr. Robert Brickhouse. He and my mother were my father's main standbys. Both my families—the Prices and the Rodwells—all the men were "bad to drink."

INTERVIEWER

Alcoholism does seem to cluster in families. Do you subscribe to the theory that there's a gene for alcoholism?

PRICE

I was talking to Robert Coles, the [Harvard] psychiatrist, about it recently, and Bob says, "You know, now everyone is rather liberally throwing around the notion that there is a gene for alcoholism." He said, "There may be, but we're not at all sure that there is."

And God knows, all of us can think of families in which it's run haywire. All of my mother's three brothers had serious drinking problems. All of my mother's nephews had drinking problems. My father and one of his two brothers had serious drinking problems.

INTERVIEWER
And the women?

PRICE

On neither side of the family was there a woman who had the faintest problem with drinking, or, as it was called then, "doping." There was a fair amount of depression in my mother's family, male and female. And I've often wondered if the men weren't to some extent medicating themselves for a disease that was totally not understood at the time.

Now, when the women in the family got depressed, they just sat in the living room and felt miserable and then got up and cooked supper for the two millionth time in their lives. [Laughter.]

INTERVIEWER
It's an intriguing subject.

PRICE

When I was child, I could watch it in my cousins and my uncles. And I was both fascinated and terrified by it, because I thought it still constituted a temptation for my father, which it turns out it didn't.

When he finally got himself sober, I don't think he was ever really seriously tempted to go back to it. But elsewhere in the family, there were these charming cousins and uncles who were constantly sobering up and then falling off the wagon, and then sobering up and falling off the wagon. And I read a lot of it through, especially, my mother's heartbreak in seeing her brothers and some of her nephews—to whom she was very devoted and with whom she had been reared—and realizing how devastating it was in their lives and in the lives of their wives and children.

INTERVIEWER
Would you make any kind of leap between the craving for artistic expression and the craving for something that seems, temporarily at least, to be satisfied by alcohol?

PRICE

I don't know whether I would phrase it that way. I would certainly say that I think in my own life, though I've never had the faintest problem with chemical addiction of any sort, I've known since I was almost a teenager that I was potentially an addictive personality. So I was tremendously careful as a young man. I thought, "If I do this once, I'll be some sort of raving drunk by dark." [Laughter.]

But I do think that my writing has been for me a tremendous channel down which I think I've poured and let rush all kinds of potentially devastating energies, and I have felt tremendously lucky in that way.

Blue Calhoun seems to believe that his actions stirred the process that caused the cancer in both his wife and his daughter. Do you believe stunning emotional blows can interrupt health and encourage a breakdown in the immune system?

PRICE

Yes, I do. In the case of my own cancer— which I didn't discover until the spring of 1984, by which time it was very far advanced—I had had a really devastating break-in in my home in the summer of 1979.

I was in town getting the mail, and the men who broke in the house were all heavily armed. The burglar alarm alerted the police. The police came. There was a big shootout. Nobody was killed, but when I finally arrived at home, there were helicopters over my house and deputies with double-barreled shotguns in the front door. So it really just depressed the hell out of me.

And I went through the only period in my life when I just got really melancholy. I probably would have been much better off if I'd gone and seen a therapist a little bit. I would say that lasted two or three months and had no observable result, except I laid around in the bed and stared at the ceiling and felt miserable a lot.

But I've always told myself since that that might've been a time when a tumor, which no doubt was under way in my body already, might've gotten some kind of big start.

INTERVIEWER

What is your daily routine?

PRICE

My daily routine remains what it's been almost all my writing life, except more so. Gertrude Stein always said, "We don't get any older, we just get more so." I'm at work, at the desk, by nine in the morning.

INTERVIEWER

Back up. What's for breakfast?

PRICE

Now for breakfast I have a big cup of strong coffee and low-fat Dannon yogurt. It can have fruit in it, but it's got to have ninety to a hundred calories only. [Laughter.]

And then I go to the desk, and I just word-process the rest of the morning. And then around twelve-thirty, I have a mineral-vitamin drink and fruit juice. It's called All-One. I can give you the 800 number in Santa Barbara, California, where you can order it: 1-800-235-5727. It's wonderful stuff. [Singer] James Taylor and his wife put me onto it. It's marvelous. That's my lunch.

Then I lie down. Like most paraplegics, I have a problem with my legs swelling, because they stay down all the time. So I have these kind of pressure blowup stockings I put on. My brother says I look like the Michelin boy.

I lie down for about an hour and a half, and I read, and I watch "The Young and the Restless." And then I get up, and I work the rest of the afternoon, and then we eat supper around six-thirty or seven. And then, after supper, I like to see friends, watch a movie, work a little bit more if I'm particularly into it that day.

I usually go to bed around eleven at night. That goes on about six days a week, except for the semester when I teach, which is always January until early May. Then I teach all day on Tuesdays and Thursdays, and I have office hours on Wednesdays. So I don't keep that tight a writing schedule while I'm teaching. But the rest of the time I do.

INTERVIEWER

What can you teach students about writing? You once quoted Ben Johnson as saying, "Don't tell a young poet all his faults."

PRICE

I think I can tell them two basic things. I can tell them the kind of thing that my only writing teacher, William Blackburn, told me, as he told his other students he thought were gifted enough to be writers. I can tell them that I, with my experienced eye, think that they have the ability to do this if they want and need to, which is a big if. An enormous number of students I've known who are talented enough to write—from a point of view of linguistics or a narrative talent of their own or intelligence—turn out not to need to do this bizarre thing of staying alone in a room typing all day.

And then I think I can tell them one other thing that Blackburn was not able to tell us, because he himself was not a writer. I can just tell them a lot about everything from the value of routine, the values of health—because young people absolutely never believe that their work is done by their body and that they have to be good to their bodies if they're going to have good work.

I can tell them little individual ways I've solved this or that technical problem. In the last four years, I guess I've made myself a contributing member of my writing class, and I think that's the single most valuable thing I've ever done for my writing students. Because I simply put my work up in early drafts for them to criticize in the way I criticize their work.

INTERVIEWER

Aren't the students too intimidated by your work to offer any criticism?

PRICE

There's always a little bit of edginess right at the beginning: "Can we tell the teacher what we really think?" But I just urge them to do so. I say, "Look, we've got to be adults here. Don't worry about your grade, because I'm not going to tell you the whole-hog truth about your work, and you don't have to tell me the whole-hog truth about mine." We wind up being truthful, within the bounds of civility.

I try to teach them as much civility and courtesy in their work as I possibly can. And by courtesy in their work, I really to a large extent mean clarity. Making the work as accessible to a reasonably intelligent reader as they can possibly make it. You don't want to oversimplify. You certainly don't want to convert it into some kind of pap because you think the readers are children or babies. But I think you have to guard very much also against the dangers of obscurity or overcomplication.

INTERVIEWER

What about your famous course on John Milton?

PRICE

It's the course I most love. I just teach the hell out of *Paradise Lost* and the great poems of Milton, and we talk about all those deathless ideas of free will and predestination and human choice and the fall of man and woman and the relationship of husband and wife, and all the topics that are so totally and completely dealt with in Milton.

INTERVIEWER

Wesley Beavers in your 1988 novel, *Good Hearts*, and Blue Calhoun in this new novel are each beset by psychic fires. Do you believe some people long for something big that will transform them—something bigger than love or sex or money or power or religion?

PRICE

Yes. There's something very big out there that an enormous number of human beings are blindly in love with. And I don't know what we can call it. Part of it is some reckless dream of perfect freedom, perfect pleasure—that we can be perfectly free, and that we can also be perfectly satisfied by whatever life we are leading.

Wesley really bolts, you see, for unknown reasons. He just gets the heebie-jeebies and bolts, in his early forties, when a lot of men get nervous. Blue bolts when he's thirty-six, which is also pretty much getting into that late-thirties

and early-forties early menopause for men, when they suddenly begin to realize that things are seizing up on them. And I think Blue has a bigger sense of what he wants. He just suddenly sees somehow this unformed dream of his whole life crystallized in this one young girl, who I think is an extraordinary girl. She's not just some dream. She's a very complicated and real and resourceful woman, and proves to be throughout the whole length of the story.

What the end of that dream is, I don't know. Nothing could've satisfied Wesley and Blue. But as somebody says in one of my books, "Sweet Jesus in tights wouldn't satisfy you."

They're just pursuing some idea of perfect bliss, of being used up by life in a way that would leave them smiling. I saw that dream on all the older men in my family, because none of the men had a job or a profession which he really loved.

INTERVIEWER

In a 1991 *Paris Review* interview, you talked about writers taking good care of their physical selves and their brains. Are you talking about sleep, exercise, vitamins, or what?

PRICE

I've been so aware, as an American novelist and poet and dramatist, of how many of our heroes, our icons, were tremendous physical destroyers of themselves. Faulkner. Hemingway. Thomas Wolfe. Tennessee Williams. Truman Capote. It doesn't really get started in American literature until the twentieth century. Our nineteenth-century writers—the really great ones—tended to be terribly solid citizens. Like

Hawthorne. I mean, Melville is a little psychically tormented, but he was a solid citizen.

But the World War I generation, for perhaps understandable reasons, got off on a bad foot with liquor and drugs and women or men, or whatever their proclivities were.

It's kind of appalling to look at the work of all these great men—Faulkner, Fitzgerald, Hemingway, etc.—and realize they were either dead by their early forties or they had basically written and drunk themselves off the air. Their best work was behind them.

Not only my own family's problems with addiction have impressed upon me the need for a sound mind in a sound body, but also the great American heroic writers that the young men of my generation looked to as our models. And when I think now of how many of my own colleagues as a student at Duke—and later when I came back to teach—how just the general notion that a writer was supposed to be somebody who was drunk all the time, or drunk at least once a day, and the marriage was disorderly, and the children were on food stamps or whatever. And I think I just figured out very early this never happened in world literature until Baudelaire and Rimbaud in France, and then that got translated to America in the 1920s. It's a very bad idea and should be stopped in its tracks.

So I really do try to remind my students, if they don't know, that writing is done by a physical organ called the human brain, and the human brain has needs that are just as ascertainable as the needs of your liver or your kidneys or your heart, and they are basically nutritional. And in terms of nutrition: Exercise, rest, self-respect. Which doesn't mean I don't like to have a nice drink now and then and relax.

INTERVIEWER
In the new novel, Mattie and Myra, Catholics each, were great believers in prayer. Do you yourself believe deeply in prayer?

PRICE
Oh, I do tremendously. And I think the whole atmosphere around Mattie and Myra in the novel—which is grounded in their Catholicism and in the Catholic Cathedral in Raleigh and Cathedral High School in Raleigh—all that springs a lot from my deep childhood friendship with Pat Cowden, who's now Patricia Boyd, Ty Boyd's wife in Charlotte.

Pat was a Roman Catholic, and we lived next door the whole way through my teenaged years and right on through college and have remained in touch ever since. And Pat's own intelligent, very witty, and realistic piety impressed me a lot when I was a young man.

She certainly didn't introduce me to religion or to the idea of prayer. But it impressed me that someone who was as beautiful and bright and funny and loving as she also had this very deep investment in the whole idea that life was a gift, that it was a gift from a giver, and that our acceptance of that gift and our agreeing to go on living implied that we had some sort of duty to that giver.

And throughout my life, before I knew Pat and long after, certainly, and then certainly very intensely during the time I was going through sort of desperate health problems six or seven years ago, prayer has always been a very important part of my daily life.

It's so much a part of my daily life I don't even think of it as prayer. It just seems like the same thing as making the coffee and answering the phone and doing the work. I don't have elaborate, ceremonial ways that I do it. I am not a churchgoing person. But I think I'm an intensely religious person.

INTERVIEWER

In the same *Paris Review* interview, you described yourself as a deep-dyed hedonist.

PRICE

I think hedonist in the literal sense that I don't think I have an even normal liking for pain or suffering. I think especially as a Southerner, you're supposed to have a kind of gene for suffering—moaning and regretting the old order, and that we lost the war, and that the house was burned by the Yankees.

I just don't like to hurt. So I really lack that kind of masochistic equipment that seems to go with being both a Southerner and especially being a Southern writer.

I love—and here again I'm tremendously the child of my mother and father—I love fun. I love to laugh. I love the companionship of interesting, generous-hearted, entertaining people. I dread bores and will tell any lie to avoid spending more than two seconds with one.

INTERVIEWER

You've compared writing to rolling a hand grenade in a room.

PRICE

I think what I largely mean is that I get some kind of fragmentary idea, which is what I think of as the live grenade. I say, "It's going to be this man who meets a teenage girl accidentally one day on Fayetteville Street in Raleigh, and it totally alters his life and the lives of everyone else he knows for the rest of his life."

Okay. That's the grenade. Pull the pin out. Roll it into the room. Here they are, in the middle of Atkinson Music Company on Fayetteville Street on such and such an afternoon in 1956. She walks in the door. What happens next? And I watch the explosion go off. And I follow the bits and pieces where they fly.

And if that sounds idiotically simple . . . Frankly, I think for a person who's a born writer and who's written virtually every day of his working life for more than forty years now, it *is* sort of idiotically simple to do. Not idiotically. But it feels wonderful. It feels wonderful in the way that I'm sure Michael Jordan feels wonderful when he goes up for a magnificent slam-dunk shot. I *can* do it. I *do* it. I know it's good. And I'm tickled to death.

Born February 1, 1933, in Macon, North Carolina, Reynolds Price is the older of two sons of William Solomon and Elizabeth Rodwell Price. He graduated from Needham Broughton High School in Raleigh in 1951 and graduated summa cum laude from Duke University in 1955. He was a Rhodes scholar to Merton College, Oxford University, in 1958. That year, he joined the English faculty at Duke University, rising in 1977 to his current position of James B. Duke Professor.

His novels include *A Long and Happy Life* (1962), *A Generous Man* (1966), *Love and Work* (1968), *The Surface of Earth* (1975), *The Source of Light* (1981), *Kate Vaiden* (1986), *Good Hearts* (1988), *The Tongues of Angels* (1990), and *Blue Calhoun* (1992).

His memoirs are *Clear Pictures* (1989) and *A Whole New Life* (1994).

His short-story collections are *The Names and Faces of Heroes* (1963), *Permanent Errors* (1970), *The Foreseeable Future* (1990), and *The Collected Stories* (1993).

His poetry collections include *Late Warnings* (1968), *Lessons Learned* (1977), *Vital Provisions* (1982), *Private Contentment* (1984), *The Laws of Ice* (1985), and *The Use of Fire* (1990).

His plays are *Early Dark* (1978) and *New Music* (1989).

His collected essays are *Things Themselves* (1972) and *A Common Room: New and Selected Essays* (1987).

His awards include the William Faulkner Foundation Award (1962); the Sir Walter Raleigh Award (1962, 1976, 1981, 1984, 1986); a Guggenheim fellowship (1964–65); a National Association of Independent Schools Award (1964); a National Endowment for the Arts fellowship (1967–68); a National Institute of Arts and Letters Award (1971); the Bellamann Foundation Award (1972); the Lillian Smith Award (1976); the Roanoke-Chowan Poetry Award (1982); the National Book Critics Circle Award (1986); the Elmer H. Bobst Award (1988); and the R. Hunt Parker Award from the North Carolina Literary and Historical Society (1991).

In 1994, *The Collected Stories* was a finalist for a Pulitzer Prize.

He was been awarded honorary doctorates from St. Andrews Presbyterian College, Wake Forest University, Washington and Lee University, and Davidson College.

Reynolds Price lives in Durham, North Carolina, where he is working on a new novel.

April 3, 1994

DORI SANDERS

*A*t Sanders Peach Stand in Filbert, South Carolina, two squint-eyed women finger the plump, rosy peaches, their pale arms dimpling and wobbling.

"This one's no good," says one, smacking a brown-spotted peach on the wooden counter. "This here one is rotten, too. So's this one."

"We'll get you more," Dori Sanders tells her customers, gently rolling the peaches from basket to cardboard box. "Hail got some of my babies this summer. They don't look good as usual. But we'll make sure none of yours have spots," she says evenly.

When the women have lumbered off in the white dust, Sanders explains why it's easy for her to turn the other cheek to prickly customers.

"There's a little writerly thing about it," she says. "I just pretend. I play-act at my stand. I play a role that makes me kind."

This same "writerly thing" prompted Dori Sanders's first novel, *Clover*, set on a South Carolina peach farm in the late 1980s. It's the loving, hopeful story of a ten-year-old black girl who finds herself suddenly in the hands of a brand-new stepmother—a white one.

Now in its fourth printing, *Clover* has made a radio and TV star of the willowy peach grower, the baby in a family of eight. She recently landed—with photo—in the July 30 issue of *Time* magazine.

Sanders keeps the magazine, along with a few copies of *Clover*, in a cabinet of the open-air shed where she and brother Orestus Sanders sell the produce they grow on land inherited from their father.

The summer's glory, baskets of Elberta peaches picked at dawn, line the wooden table. Other baskets brim with okra, Silver Queen corn, crowder peas. Behind these, pungent Burpee Ambrosia cantaloupe and watermelon—old-fashioned Stoney Mountain and striped Crimson Sweets.

"Our first pulling," says Sanders proudly, thumping the Crimson Sweets. "Have we got watermelons, or what?"

Early on a midsummer morning, the tin-roofed stand trapping the night's cool air, Sanders talks about her novel, about her grandfather's being sold into slavery, and about her "reasoning heart," which she says will not allow her to hate white people.

━━━━━

INTERVIEWER

You got into the head of ten-year-old Clover so perfectly it felt like you must have memorized your whole tenth year.

SANDERS

I have this impressionable mind. My mind is a sponge, and that's the truth. Ten years from today, if you would walk up here, I guarantee you, I would tell you what you had on. It's almost like a camera, my mind is, because every little thing I see, it means so much to me, and that's the way it has been since I was a child.

INTERVIEWER

Your family has been in this area a long time.

SANDERS

Right down the road as we look that way is a little place called Sharon. All I know is that the Hills put it on the map because they had that tremendous department store way before its time and had a bank that went into bankruptcy. What a fascinating family! That's where my father grew up, in the Sharon area, in a little area called Hoodtown.

INTERVIEWER

Mr. Sanders was a teacher and principal, so he must have gone to college.

SANDERS

He went to Clinton College, and then when he returned from Clinton, he got a post in Bowling Green, a one-room schoolhouse. He drove a horse and buggy every day up this road to his little school.

He was an imposing man. He had good cheekbones and a good nose. If I had only got my father's nose! I might've been beautiful!

He used to drive through the little community of Filbert and he saw the soil—sandy—and he thought, "Wonderful for Elberta peaches and sweet potatoes!"

Well, that man, about 1915 or 1916, bought eighty-one acres, used all of his savings—twenty-six hundred dollars—plus the rest to pay off. My father saved every dime, every penny. He had a brother who was away working in Philadelphia who helped him, too. Helped him get through school. He was the baby child of nine or ten children—seven or eight boys and one girl.

If your father was the baby, then his parents were born way back. Your family history spans a number of years.

SANDERS

Ooh, such a long time. My grandfather could not read or write, but he made markings. He made a 4 and drew a scythe. I'll bet he meant down in Forsythe [Georgia].

The only thing my grandfather remembered of his childhood was hearing his mother being auctioned off, and he does not have any idea where. She could sew. A woman who could *sew*! And a little boy who would be a wonderful water boy! That's how old we are.

INTERVIEWER

Your grandfather didn't even remember his own name. He only remembered that the man who bought his mother had the name Sanders.

SANDERS

When I was little, my grandfather told me a story, and I half put it out of my head, because I didn't want to remember it. It is so sad.

It was in the fall of the year, and in the old days whenever you hoed the cotton, the women carried watermelon seeds in their apron pocket. And when there was a skip in the cotton, you'd plant the watermelon seeds, so that in the fall of the year, hopefully, you would have watermelons to eat, because they would grow in and around the cotton.

It was your way of sneaking them in where the landowners couldn't see them, and making sure you'd have watermelons by the end of September.

But anyway, my grandfather said he was a little water boy, and that he was in the field where the other people were picking the cotton, and he was bringing the water to the cotton pickers, and he found a watermelon. A great big one.

Little Sam, they called him. Little Sam was a beautiful man. Sharp features and beautiful, straight, dark hair. So he found a watermelon and was, he said, foolish enough to show it.

When the master's son was riding through, Little Sam ran to him and said, "Look at my watermelon!" And then my grandfather said the master's son asked him for it. Little Sam said, "Noooo." So when he wouldn't give it to him, the master's son took his riding crop, with a little metal thing on it, and cracked Little Sam on his head.

This, I wasn't sure I believed, but he said he had a wound in his head, and his mother was told by another older woman that if she put a silver dollar in his head and closed it together really, really tight and bound it up, he would heal.

Growing up, every time I looked at my grandfather's head, I would walk around to see that. He would say, "It's there." I would say, "I don't see it." He would say, "It's all growed over."

In my heart, I didn't believe it. And in my heart, I wanted to believe it. I went to the Smithsonian and looked at the mummies and asked some of the people how they healed the wounds in the bloodletting days. And they said they put a metal thing on somebody, and I said, "Ooh."

My whole life, I tried to put distance between me and that story. Torn between not wanting to believe it, and yet wanting to know.

Doesn't that story make you hate white people?

That's something I never, ever wanted to do in my life. Because if I started to hate, I figured in my head, I would meld the innocent with the guilty. I felt that would be such an injustice.

So I said, "Let go of the injustice so that you will not harm the good." And that has always been my philosophy. Because in my little head, I knew then that if that did happen to my grandfather, that would not have been true of every landowner.

So when I was starting to grow up—right here in Filbert—I didn't want to have in my head that everyone was the same as the people on the plantation where my grandfather lived. So I sort of let it die in my mind. I put it down. And for that reason, I have always been happy here. Because I only look for the good in you.

You had some favorite people—white people—in Filbert, too, growing up.

I was so fond, really, of the man who ran the little store right through the woods. I figured if I started hating everybody, I would have to hate him, too. A white man, of course. I would walk in there. He knew in his heart, and I knew in my heart, that those eggs I had only covered what my mother sent me for.

But I'm looking at the candy . . .

Some days, Mother would say, "You can get a cinnamon bun." Or "Today, you can get some BB Bats." Or "Today, we don't have any extra. My old Dominique hen ran off into the woods." So today she doesn't have any extra for candy. Tomorrow she will because she's going to find that nest. But today I can only get what she sent me for.

So I'm looking at the candy . . .

And I ask, "Is there anything left over?" knowing in my head nothing is left over. "Anything left over for a couple of BB Bats?"

And he'd say, "Well, maybe I figured it wrong. Let's see. Yes, I believe you have enough left over for a couple of BB Bats."

Now, you tell me. How in the world can I sit here and trace up some kind of hate? You can't do it if you have any reasoning in your heart. You just can't. How can I lump that man with everybody else, and say he's no good because he's white?

Didn't you get the idea for *Clover* right here at this stand?

I saw a couple—an interracial couple. All right. An interracial couple. And a little black girl here says, "If they have kids, they will be checkerboard kids."

And I just thought to myself, "It's true. If they

April 3, 1994

had children, there the children would be. A mixed race." And I thought, "Ooh, I wonder . . ." And this is my imagination beginning to soar. I just thought, "What would life be like for a woman or a child faced with the situation?"

So imagination is set in motion. There I went. But I took it from what I thought people would do. Real life comes down not so much to a prejudice of a little girl looking across and saying, "My stepmama is white." But rather, "The woman sure can cook grits."

Because let me tell you: I am a strong believer, and I know well that children are not born with prejudices. Generational prejudices come because they are passed down. Children have to acquire that. Whatever environment you place them in, that's what they will adjust to.

Obviously, from the setting in *Clover*, this little girl didn't have the basis for those generational prejudices, because after all, if her father was going to marry this woman, certainly he didn't tell her that they were all bad. So therefore she could only look at it from her own little view.

INTERVIEWER
I don't see how you even have time to think here at the stand.

SANDERS
Hey! I got some customers!
Come and buy us out! Hey, Thelma. Hi-ya-do. Hi-ya-do.
We don't hurry up 'em. We don't put soda near the watermelons, or nitrogen. We don't do

anything to enhance their growth. What we do is let them grow long and slow, the way our fathers and grandparents did. And that's why they're so good!

April 21, 1993

Dori Sanders is squealing, her words squirming like piglets. She is talking about her book tour, which started in April and will run through June, with time off for her to work at the family peach stand.

"I'll go out weeeest!" she says. "Up noooorth! Indiaaana. Iowa. Boston. Seaaaattle. San Franciiisco. New York. Philadelphia. Memphis. New Orleeeeans!"

She's up to it. Her clothes are ironed and ready. Her chin is up. Spirits high.

Sanders's acclaimed 1990 novel, *Clover*, won the Lillian Smith Book Award and stayed ten weeks on the *Washington Post* bestseller list.

Her latest, *Her Own Place*, is the story of Mae Lee Barnes—mother, realist, survivor—who loves her kids, the Braves, and her own place.

Sanders herself has recently discovered her own place. Most of her life, she's lived among eight brothers and sisters. Now, she's surprised to find how much she enjoys solitude, how essential it is to her spirit.

In this interview, Sanders, tall and lean and "sort of sixtyish," talks about privacy, about never having been a mother, and about loneliness, play-acting, and the writerly life.

INTERVIEWER

Last year, you did something fairly bold for a woman who's almost always lived among family. Even though your sister had built a big house on Highway 321 near Filbert, South Carolina, complete with a writing studio for you, and even though the family home was available for your use, you rented an apartment in Charlotte, North Carolina, to use as a writing studio.

SANDERS

I was trying to finish *Her Own Place*, and I couldn't handle it the way it was going. It was more like I was down to the stage to where I had too many seams in the garment. I needed to smooth this thing out, and in order to do that I had to really concentrate.

INTERVIEWER

Why can't you concentrate in Filbert?

SANDERS

It was the fishing business that did me in. Friends would say, "Dori, want to go fishing?" We say "feeshing" in Filbert. Well, I don't really like to fish, but if you don't go, you end up losing all your friends. Soooo. I have to come out and face up. And I say, "I'll go in ten or fifteen minutes." And they say, "Dori, how long is it going to take you to finish this book?" And I say, "In a few days or a few weeks, I should be all finished."

I don't want them to feel that I'm rejecting them, because I'm not. But I can't get a thing done when I'm there. So I decided to get a little place so I could write.

INTERVIEWER

We'll keep the location a secret. But please describe your apartment—two rooms, plus kitchen and bath.

SANDERS

I call it my hideaway. It's a garden apartment. Almost cottagelike. It's out in a big field, and there are trees and everything. I have a wonderful fireplace. I have one chair and a cot. There's a straight-backed chair and a bright, bright-colored rust tablecloth and beautiful floral napkins.

Then I have the reminders of little things of the past that I've had to pull in here. They remind me of how things were in the country, how my life was earlier.

I have a very old clay jug from my grandmother's, with a wonderful marbling effect—copper and rust, burnt tones with a little trace of yellow—which was probably made by Catawba Indians.

I have a portion of our old churn, and I have as many smoothing irons as I dare have, and more hidden away. They were my grandmother's and others' in my family. I used to like to use them so much. We did what everyone else in the area did. We'd gather cedar branches, and after you removed the iron from in front of the fireplace, you'd run it over the cedar branches, and that's how you'd give your clothes a wonderful fragrance.

INTERVIEWER

You have an unusual method of writing. It involves taking scraps of paper, on which you've written notes for whatever novel is in progress, and putting those scraps in a big box. Then you go through the scraps and arrange them in piles chronologically in a circle on the floor. Chapter 1 scraps go here. Chapter 2 scraps there. And so on. How do you work from there?

SANDERS

As I walk around the circle—or go on bended knee inside the circle—the story that's in my head starts coming out. I stop in front of a pile of paper, and I get a single 8½-by-11-inch piece of paper, and in the center of the page I write what's on the scrap. If my thoughts give me more ideas, I will continue writing. Sometimes I'm just flooded with words, and I write pages and pages. If my well runs dry, I then go back to yet another section.

INTERVIEWER

You've mentioned that the one drawback to this writing-on-bended-knee procedure is that you sometimes tend to get ahead of yourself. Maybe you'll jump to chapter 6 when you really need to be working on chapter 2.

SANDERS

That's when I get all tangled up. I have to say, "Dori, whoa! You can't pick the beans before the plants are even out of the ground!" Then I have to pull myself in check. I have to say, "Dori, you plant the seed. You wait for the plant. You tend. Then you harvest."

INTERVIEWER

What do you do while you're waiting?

SANDERS

I have to leave out of that room where everything is scattered. I have to go away and sit in that little area by my fireplace, overlooking my patio. I tend to think best then. When I'm there with those few things visual, I can pull in my thoughts from my farming past. I like to have a small fire in the fireplace. If there is the least hint of it not being eighty-three degrees, or even if it is just cloudy, I will have a fire. Then my thoughts can flow back to the past, and I can forget where I am, and suddenly I can be almost anywhere on the farm.

INTERVIEWER

What's your writing schedule in your hideaway?

SANDERS

I'm still cursed with the farming alarm clock. I wish it would turn off. Usually about four-thirty I'm awake. And I'm going to have some breakfast as soon as I hit the floor. Ooh. You got to have some grits. My thoughts won't even flow if I don't have grits. I have to have my butter—butter and a biscuit and a little dab of my homemade jellies or jams and a cup of coffee or orange juice.

Then I sit there and just wait. I just sit there thinking. I call that my imaginative hour.

If it's warm enough, I open the patio doors. It's woodsy outside. I hear the morning sounds. That is just about all I need to get me going and get my thoughts flowing.

By the time it's light, I'm ready to hit my day. I really work and work and work, and then I

have to have a break. And I go to bed with the sunset.

INTERVIEWER

You've begun a new novel, which you say is not yet focused enough to talk about. And you're also writing a farm-stand cookbook, using many of your childhood recipes.

SANDERS

I remember so well the things we had at one time on the farm. Our cooking depended solely on what was in the jars in the pantry, and what was in the root cellar that we had grown, and what potatoes were in the sweet-potato house, and what was in the Ball Mason jars, and also what was left of the brown sugar we always made every year from the molasses.

Some days I will walk into the kitchen, and I'll make sweet-potato salad. I'll have a cooked version of it, and I'll have a raw version of it. Then I'll go buy my raisins and apples. (We didn't buy our apples. We had them wrapped in newspapers in wooden whiskey barrels.) And then I will create, by using measurements this time, some of the things I grew up with, and try to work for a taste.

INTERVIEWER

So you're in this wonderful hideaway, cooking and writing to your heart's content, not bothered by a soul. It must be heaven.

SANDERS

I feel so free to be able to spend the time cooking and experimenting, testing this recipe and that recipe.

And I guess I'm a child at heart. One day, I made without a doubt—and I will have this in my recipe book—one of the most delicious meals I think I have ever tasted: Roast pork, creasy greens, sweet-potato salad, cornbread, sweet iced tea, and stickies for dessert. I think I could have served it at the White House and it would have gotten rave reviews.

The table was set perfectly for it. I'd gone out and picked what wildflowers I could find. It was beautiful.

And I'm all alone sitting down for my dinner, and I tasted the food and I felt so lonely. I missed my brothers and sisters so much. Do you know what I did? I cut out little stand-up paper dolls and put a paper doll at each place and carried on an imaginary conversation with my brothers and sisters.

INTERVIEWER

Somewhere, I read that you created the character Clover to relive your tenth year. Did you perhaps create Mae Lee in your new novel to see what it would have been like to have children?

SANDERS

Yes. Oh, yes! Absolutely! I got so attached to those kids. I especially loved Taylor. I had my pick among my four girls which one of those girls I liked best. I found myself not making her do anything that was terrible and defending her when she was up for criticism.

People say, "Dori, you never had any children?" I say, "No, not ever, really. But I created five. If only in fiction. I have five children now."

It's a wonderful feeling. I don't feel so deprived anymore.

INTERVIEWER

I noticed something about you when I visited your vegetable stand a year or so ago. No matter how hateful and mean some of your customers acted, you were so consistently nice. You told me then that you play-act at your stand. In fact, you said, "I think I've play-acted all my life."

SANDERS

I have to play-act to go on this tour I'm getting ready to go on. That's the best example. How do you think I fit in when I'm being interviewed? There is nothing that has prepared me for the things that I've been exposed to. Meeting Louis Rubin, Shelby Foote, Ernest Gaines.

How do I handle that? I play-act. I pretend I'm not Dori Sanders. I usually will pick a character, and usually they're all faded movie stars. They had a manner. . . . I'm Lena Horne, and I have been asked to say a few words and thank everybody. She had the most wonderful "Thaaaaank you."

Or I'm Joan Crawford playing Mildred Pierce [in the movie *Mildred Pierce*]. Oh, yes. The way she just held her body straight, held her head high. That's where I get the courage to go on the stage. If I didn't play-act, I couldn't do it.

Sometimes I play myself. See, what I do is, I take off my glasses. I'm farsighted. I can't see anyone sitting up close to me. So since I cannot see them, I pretend every person there is a customer at my peach stand. I say, "Dori, you've got to sell them okra, crowder peas, or peaches before they leave here." So then I sort of detach myself. It relaxes me.

INTERVIEWER

Dori, I have never interviewed anyone who talked as fast as you talk.

SANDERS

You know about my speech problem, don't you?

INTERVIEWER

I had no idea you had a speech problem.

SANDERS

Oh, my goodness. I have to make a conscious effort to say certain words. I press my tongue against my cheek. That's why I come up with these different accents.

When I was a child, they called me terribly tongue-tied. Oh, yes. The true story is that one of my sisters offered to clip my tongue, and she and my brother put a little pin to my arm and tested it with a little tiny prick. They said, "That's all you're going to feel, and you won't be tongue-tied anymore."

I said, "Okay." This little girl was holding my tongue, and I let her, because to me that wasn't much pain to feel in order to talk plain.

I had an older sister, and about this time she came around the barn, and she saw what was happening, and she screamed, "Stop!" They dropped the shears. If they'd done it, I would've died. I would have had gangrene.

One of my sisters said, "You know why you can't talk plain? That tongue of yours gets in the way. If you press your tongue against your bottom teeth, you can say almost anything."

So I started doing it. I would practice in the evening washing the dishes. I would say, "Arm and Hammer Baking Soda. Arm and Hammer Baking Soda. Arm and Hammer Baking Soda." I was so happy. It was almost like *My Fair Lady*. I can say it! I can do it! And the next year I won the county-wide speech contest.

INTERVIEWER

The farm you grew up on means so much to you to this day. No matter how many novels you write, I can't imagine your ever leaving that sweet little peach stand on Highway 321.

SANDERS

The stand means so much to me it's hard for me to put it into words. It's a way of life. As many times as I have said, "This is my last summer out here in this hot sun," I find myself quitting in the fall and cranking up again in the spring. And it's the same for my brother.

Sometimes you think, "It's not rewarding anymore. The weather is against the farming life." You're always holding your breath. If we have a good crop, there's always the threat of a hailstorm, and that can wipe it all out in the space of a few good minutes.

This afternoon I heard severe thunderstorm

and hail warnings for Iredell County [North Carolina]. That's today. Tomorrow, it could be York. It's so iffy, it's almost frightening. But I know I'll be there. You get that dirt under your fingernails. I think it's something that's a part of you. Sometimes I can't rightly help myself.

Born in Filbert, South Carolina, Dori Sanders was the seventh of ten children of Marion Sylvester and Cazetta Sylvia Patton Sanders. She graduated from Roosevelt High School in Clover, South Carolina, and attended community colleges in Prince George's and Montgomery counties, Maryland.

Summers, Sanders worked on her family's 150-acre peach farm, selling the produce in a family-owned open-air stand. Winters she spent in Maryland, living with her sister and working as a banquet manager at a motel near Andrews Air Force Base.

Her novels are *Clover* (1989) and *Her Own Place* (1993).

Her awards include the Lillian Smith Award, sponsored by the Southern Regional Council (1990). She was also a finalist for an Image Award, sponsored by the NAACP (1994). She received an honorary doctorate from Newberry College in Newberry, South Carolina, and she was a judge of the Robert F. Kennedy Awards in 1994.

She was married once and divorced.

Sanders lives in Clover, where she is working on a farm cookbook.

April 17, 1994

LEE SMITH

January 19, 1990

*I*n a 1985 *Newsweek* article, "The South Rises Again: A New Generation of Writers Has Emerged in Dixie," the author tried to render unto Dixie what was Southern about Southern writers, and unto the suburbs what was not. Novelist and short-story writer Lee Smith of Chapel Hill, North Carolina, fell cleanly into the Dixie camp—one of the writers who's never lost her distinctively regional roots.

Three years later, in 1988, Smith's seventh novel, *Fair and Tender Ladies*, propelled her headlong into the mainstream of American literature. Although her main character, Ivy Rowe, is definitely Southern—Smith used her native Virginia Appalachia and told Ivy's life story through a series of letters—the book soared above her other works.

The novel exhausted her, and she returned to a favorite form, the short story. Her second collection, *Me and My Baby View the Eclipse*, is due in bookstores this week.

This late-January morning, Smith's six-week-old Christmas tree languishes on the deck. In her kitchen, an electric string of red chili peppers blinks off and on. From her living room, Smith can see beyond the wooded slopes in the backyard to the pen that inspired the story "Bob, a Dog" in her new collection.

"But his name wasn't Bob," she says. "It was Ralph. And finally he was removed from this neighborhood—at the request of a large number of people."

Today, Lee Smith talks about the packet of letters she found that inspired *Fair and Tender Ladies*, about the difference between writing short stories and novels, about losing her mother, and about the necessity for writers to spend long hours gazing out the window.

INTERVIEWER

When you finished your last novel, *Fair and Tender Ladies*, you said you thought you'd do short stories for a while. Why short stories instead of another novel?

SMITH

Because Ivy Rowe just wore me out. You always read other writers saying the character took over and wrote the book. That never happened to me before. I always felt like I wrote the book.

But with *Fair and Tender Ladies*, after the first couple of letters, you see, I just started writing, and it was never even like writing a novel. It was like every day I would just sit down and write a letter. I didn't take any time off from teaching. I didn't do anything that would upset the way it was going, because I just got real sort of spooked and superstitious, and I didn't even admit to myself I was writing a novel. I would just sit down and this stuff would come out. It was amazing. It really was like a character taking over.

INTERVIEWER

That must've been exhilarating.

SMITH

It was very exhilarating and very terrifying and also very deeply satisfying. At the time I was writing, my mother was really sick. She was dying. I think one thing I was doing was creating a really strong role model. You know, everything happens to Ivy, but she can handle it. And I think a lot of times we write for reasons we don't understand, and there was a reason I needed to create Ivy at that particular point in my life.

But I think that's one reason she was so necessary to me, and she sort of came on so strong. At the time, I was having trouble with my teenagers, and everything was happening at once. So somehow to be able to go and close the door and do Ivy was the best thing that happened to me for those two years. It was just wonderful, because when you're at somebody's bedside you know you can't go away to Florida and feel better. And so for me the writing of it was absolutely wonderful, because it was like a place to go in my head apart from the things that were going on with our family.

INTERVIEWER

You were teaching during that time, and you were writing before school, after school, at night.

SMITH

Any old time. And I write longhand, so I do it everywhere. I have a desk downstairs, so I do it down there, or I do it in the kitchen. I do it in the car. I did it everywhere. I did it in a million motels, particularly when she [Smith's mother] was sick in Bristol, Tennessee.

That's the thing about a novel, too. You can do it anytime you want, and you can take it anywhere you are. See, that's one thing that's always attracted me about writing fiction, is just the freedom of that. Being able to do it. I always write a lot at the Chapel Hill Public Library.

Before you wrote *Fair and Tender Ladies*, before Ivy more or less dictated her story to you, what had been your experience with fiction?

SMITH

The same kind of thing but lesser. [Laughter.] This was to a major degree. Always when you're writing you are transported, you're carried away, you're something beyond yourself, which is, I think, really why we do it. To transcend ourselves, our bodies. We all want to do that. But this was the first time that happened to me in such a sustained fashion. I think particularly it had to do with the nature of the book. It was the first time in a long time that I had written something with a single voice throughout the whole book, rather than a cast of characters, each with his or her chapter. So therefore it really did have the opportunity to take off. I loved that material so much.

INTERVIEWER

At a yard sale in Greensboro, you found a packet of letters that inspired the novel.

SMITH

It was a whole bunch of letters that were being sold in a big box, along with a lot of other things, as an old lady's house was being cleaned out by her relatives. They were selling everything. They were selling Tupperware bowls, and they were selling chairs, and they were selling her letters, which nobody much seemed to be interested in, especially the family. [Laughter.] So I just bought them and brought them home.

INTERVIEWER

What interested you about the letters?

SMITH

I love the way we express ourselves in letters. And so when I saw all these letters I just scooped them up, and I brought them back and read them for an entire weekend. And it was amazing. One sister was writing to another. And the letters were not so hot, but what I realized was, once you've read thirty or forty letters, you really feel like you know these people.

And I began to think of a collection of letters as a vehicle for a story or a novel, because what you end up with is something much greater than what is actually on the page. Because of people that are alluded to but that you don't have to put in your novel, because of time that has passed. And it just seemed to me like a great device.

I had wanted very much to write a book about an ordinary woman's whole life, and I couldn't ever figure out how to handle the time passing in it. As soon as I realized about the letters, I realized I could keep it short enough to use the novel as the genre if I did it that way—skipping a lot of time in between. It sort of fell into place.

INTERVIEWER

How does it feel to take a break from something so sustained like that and do these short, vigorous stories?

SMITH

I love short stories. I remember at one point right in the middle of writing *Fair and Tender*

Ladies, I went to the outlet mall in Burlington and nobody would wait on me in Linens 'n' Things, because they had this book, and they were all in there interpreting each other's dreams. It was hysterical. So I came home and wrote the story "The Interpretation of Dreams," right then, that weekend. It was the Fourth of July weekend, when I was right in the middle of writing *Fair and Tender Ladies*. But short stories just hit you. I think it's a great delight to write a short story. I just finished one yesterday.

INTERVIEWER

Writing a short story sounds more like you're taking a shower than a bath. At least there's some different feel to it.

SMITH

It's a real rush to write a short story. I've never been a poet, but I think it's somewhat the same impulse. Whereas when you settle in for a novel, it's like you're setting off on a really long trip, and you have no idea if you'll make it or not. And you don't even know quite where you're going.

But a short story, it's like you can hold it in your mind while you're writing it, and when you finish it you just feel great. A novel is like striking off into the wild blue yonder.

INTERVIEWER

Eudora Welty once said that for her, a short story is like a splinter that festers in her thumb. When it's ready to come out, she just plucks it.

And she knows from the beginning how it's going to end.

SMITH

I'm that way, too. I'll think about them sometimes for years. The one I just finished is one that I've been thinking about writing for about two and a half years, and just suddenly I was ready to write it, and then you just go crazy if that happens at a point when you can't write, when you have too many papers to grade or something else you have to do. I was lucky, because suddenly Christmas was over with and I just realized that, "Okay, I'm ready to write this."

INTERVIEWER

Have you ever lost stories because you couldn't sit down to write them?

SMITH

I've lost several stories. I cannot go back and find them. It's just like they gather in my head, and they get to a point . . . That's when I have to write. And so the biggest problem with my writing is arranging the rest of my days around that time. Because I can say, "I can write this in the summer." But it would not be the same story. It would be a different story.

INTERVIEWER

It's clear from your stories certain things tickle you. Like Fabric World. Like Vienna sausages and Velveeta cheese. Like panty girdles and Oil of Olay. Like people meeting at Xerox machines.

SMITH

I'm simply delighted by the things of the world. And I have a very hard time thinking in or dealing in abstractions. But I can think for hours about fabric. [Laughter.] I know writers are not supposed to say that, but I really am interested in fabric or makeup or just stuff. I always have been. Which is a kind of lowlife approach to literature, but I can't help it.

There's nothing abstract or holy about writing, as far as I'm concerned. It's very linked to the physical world. It involves real people and real details. And when I make up a character, I draw their house, and I draw their room. And I have maps for every story. I know where they live. Like "Bob, a Dog," I had a map. And for "Intensive Care," I know where the ex-wife lived and where the farm is.

INTERVIEWER

Who are these people in your stories? They aren't like you.

SMITH

I don't know. But I do know that for me to write well, I have to be writing about something that is not too immediate. I could not possibly write a novel now set in an English Department at North Carolina State, interesting though that might be, especially if I put Jim Valvano in the college. But the thing is, I can't do that.

You have to write about people that you understand, but who are at enough remove from you so that you can manipulate the events of their lives and the characteristics of their per-

sonalities enough to make it fiction. Because fiction is not life. Fiction is a contrivance. It's a made-up, artificial, highly concentrated version of life.

Anne Tyler once said—and I always thought it was the best remark I ever heard about writing—somebody asked her why she likes to write, and she said, "I write because I want to have more than one life." And I think many of us go at it for that reason. I mean, we wonder. We go in Linens 'n' Things and there's a girl interpreting dreams, and we wonder what it would be like to be that girl.

INTERVIEWER

I've heard so much about life at Hollins College when you were there—1963 to 1967—in the writing program with Annie Dillard. It sounds as it if was a very free-spirited place.

SMITH

It was just an absolutely wonderful place to go to school for anybody who wanted to be a writer. Louis Rubin was our teacher. Lots and lots of us were just drunk on books and writing, and we all happened to fall in together at the same time, and it was just absolutely like falling into a womb. [Laughter.] I think Annie said once that the best thing about Hollins was that they made you think you could do anything.

INTERVIEWER

You must tell about the trip you and some other Hollins students took down the Mississippi River after your junior year.

SMITH

It was in Louis Rubin's American lit class, where several of the people just got really interested—after reading *Huck Finn*—in going down the river on the raft. And we had one very, very enterprising young woman, who is now a lawyer, and she sort of organized us. Right after school was out that year, twelve of us went to Paducah, Kentucky, and built a raft—lumber on oil drums in a shipyard there—and got on it and went sixteen hundred miles down the Mississippi.

As it turned out, one of the first things that happened was, as soon as we got the thing built, these people from the River Authority came and said, "Well, it's two feet longer than it can be for a pleasure craft. You'll have to have a licensed riverboat captain."

And of course we all burst into tears because we didn't have one, and we thought, "Oh, no! Now we won't get to go!" And at that point the most wonderful thing happened, which was that the door to the Irvin S. Cobb Hotel popped open and out came, dressed in his three-piece white suit, Mr. Gordon Cooper, who was a retired riverboat captain living in the hotel. And he said, "I will take the girls down the river." And he did. He was wonderful. He was seventy-three. And he knew everything. He had a story to tell about every bend in the river.

But anyway, so we went, and we had a lot of trouble. We wrecked. We ran into the revetments at Cairo, Illinois, and had to rebuild. And that night was funny actually, because this terrible, huge, redneck sheriff came and said, "Well, I don't like these girls sleeping on the levee by

themselves." So he got some trusties out of the jail to come guard us, and we were so scared of the trusties that we all stayed up all night long, terrified.

But we got bored floating, so we painted roses all over the raft. So by the time we got to New Orleans, we had attracted a lot of media attention, and we were showered with roses out of planes, and we were met by the jazz band from Preservation Hall on a tugboat, and we got the keys to the city, and we got free rooms, and we were on Huntley-Brinkley. Remember them? It was wonderful!

INTERVIEWER

You've said play is creativity. Is writing a form of play?

SMITH

I suppose one reason I really like writing— and although a lot of what I write is very, very serious—what you do when you write is you let your mind play. You let yourself go to make connections. You let yourself not do the dishes or get the oil changed in your car. I think a lot of just fooling around is necessary for a writer.

A lot of times I will have adult students who are returning to writing or just beginning to write in the middle of their busy lives. And the hardest part for them is justifying—to whomever they happen to live with—what they're doing when they're just sitting in their chair looking out the window.

You've got to do that if you're going to write. It's play. It's creative thinking. You have to wander around the mall. You have to just let yourself go with an idea. This is the kind of time that writers have to have, and it's very hard for people who begin writing in their forties or their fifties to justify this time to themselves and their companions. Because nothing is produced. But it's absolutely necessary.

INTERVIEWER

How do you get this time for yourself?

SMITH

I just take it. I don't do other things I ought to do. I just sit around. [Laughter.] I watch TV. I spend a lot of time just doodling or walking around in public places looking at people. Just thinking about stuff.

And *play* is in a sense the wrong term, because a lot of this play is very serious. But it's very necessary. And I've taught enough to have run into people who are wonderful writers, and the circumstances of their lives are not allowing them to write right now. And it kills me.

I do not believe the theory that somebody who's going to be a writer is going to write no matter what. People have responsibilities. And if they are responsible people they have to fulfill those responsibilities. That's why figuring out how to get the time is one of the most important things for a writer.

Some people at a girls' school last year got really mad at me, because they asked me on this panel what these girls should do if they wanted to be writers, and I said, "Marry a surgeon." [Laughter.] They all got furious. But it's true. Or else teach. That's why we all teach, because

we can get semesters off, we have summers off. Hell, we have three weeks at Christmas!

INTERVIEWER

Right now, you're wealthy with time. The wealthiest you've ever been. Your children are in college or on their own. You're not teaching. You're rolling in time.

SMITH

Yes. I'm going to have a lot of time. And I'm just going to play around a lot of it. I'm very interested in writing a novel that has to do with women in the early days of country music, and I'm going to have a lot of time to read up and listen to music and travel around a little bit and go to Nashville and just mess around.

I've just always been extremely interested in country music. That's the music I heard growing up. I listen to it all the time. I just love it. There's something about it. It's about real stuff.

INTERVIEWER

Your mother died last year. How are you different?

SMITH

It was an enormous loss for me, and it has made a big difference, and I'm still trying to sort out what that difference is. Sometimes things will happen, and I'll reach for the phone to call her up. And it just astonishes me that she's not there.

It has certainly brought home the notion of mortality to me. I think all writers are death-haunted anyway. I mean, that's one reason they write. You just have a sense of the passing of things, and that's why you want to get them down. And I think, if anything, it's maybe intensified that, because when somebody you love so much dies, then you just know it's happening. It's going to happen to everybody. It's going to happen to you. And that's something you never know when you're in your twenties or even your thirties. You don't know it in the same way, or on the same level.

I was so close to her, but I don't think she ever read any books I wrote. All the ways in which we were close were sort of aspects of myself that in a lot of ways I'm afraid I'll lose now. It's fabric. Okay? Or recipes. Or just gossip about the neighbors sitting on the back porch. It's talking about what's in the *National Enquirer*. I don't have a lot of other people around me to keep that part alive. A lot of the friends I have want to talk about books instead of Tina Turner. And I just hate that.

June 24, 1992

April 17, 1994

A few years ago, Chapel Hill novelist Lee Smith was interviewing a man who told her he needed some mountains to rest his eyes against.

His words struck a chord. Last January, Smith and husband Hal Crowther found a cabin in Ashe County, North Carolina. Elevation: Four thousand feet. View: Mountains to rest their eyes against.

Smith's eighth novel, *The Devil's Dream*, about country-music families, is due this week from

Putnam's. Now, she's at work on a novella, writing by hand on yellow legal pads for a couple of hours each morning.

After she writes, she tends her mountain garden of basil, mint, chives, parsley, peppers, radishes, pumpkins, squash, carrots, and tomatoes. And blue hollyhocks, which grow close to the cabin. This morning, she talks about country singers, sin, sex, guilt, and ambition.

INTERVIEWER

You've said writing is really a physical thing for you. What do you mean?

SMITH

I have to gear up, like you'd get ready to run a marathon. Once I start writing something, it's an endurance test.

My writing is not at all intellectual. It's not at all abstract. It's very physical. I have to rely totally on the senses, because that's all I know. I think it's a lack in my writing that it's not thematic, not intellectually complicated. What I do is people. The only way to get at them is through the senses, which is the only way we can experience the world.

INTERVIEWER

I've never asked you about your ideal writing day.

SMITH

An ideal writing day for me is anywhere I could write for two hours. I would get up and not have to talk on the telephone and not have to do anything except drink a cup of coffee or a Coke and just sit down and write for a couple of hours. If I can do it fresh like that, it goes so much better. Then I'm wrung out.

After that, I like to do things that are physical or that put me in touch with other people, because I don't like to get too far out of the real world. I might do the laundry or take Gracie [the dog] for a walk. Dig in the yard. Talk to somebody on the telephone. Go to the post office or go to the grocery store. If I write too long, I fly off to Harris Teeter and see people that you know and stuff.

INTERVIEWER

Where did this idea come from—to write a book of fiction about country singers?

SMITH

I've had the idea for years, because I have loved country music all my life, and I have always wanted to write fiction that would have something to do with it. One of my biggest regrets has always been that when I lived in Nashville I didn't try to get a job on Music Row, instead of teaching school.

I think probably my first impulse toward country music is that the songs tell a story, and all the performers are so colorful. Also, the first music I heard growing up—from a baby—was country music. My mother had the radio on all day long, and it was always country music.

INTERVIEWER

A Lyndhurst Foundation Prize allowed you to take at least a couple of years off from teaching to research and write. How did you go about the research?

SMITH

Mike Casey in the Wilson Library [at UNC-Chapel Hill] was wonderful. He's a wonderful musician himself. I would say, "Okay, Mike, I want to see everything you have on sister acts in the 1930s." Or I would say, "I want to see everything on barn dances in Richmond or Charlotte in the 1940s."

I love facts. The hardest thing for me in writing this kind of book is always to stop doing the research and just write.

INTERVIEWER

And you actually went to performances, didn't you? And interviewed singers?

SMITH

I went to a lot of performances. I listened to a lot of music. I drove all around, listening to tapes. Went up to the Carter family home in Poor Valley, Virginia. I drove over to Nashville and talked to a lot of people. Drove over to Grundy [Virginia]. Drove over toward Kentucky, where the Ritchie family lived.

INTERVIEWER

Are there still a lot of country-music families, and are they well-documented?

SMITH

There are the Carters. Johnny Cash married June Carter. And the Stonemans. And the Whites. Another family that is well-documented is the Ritchie family. Jean Ritchie has done so much work to preserve that whole heritage. And the Arthur Smith family from Charlotte. Country music is very much a family tradition.

INTERVIEWER

I like to think of Dolly Parton picking up this book and saying, "That's exactly how it is."

SMITH

I would love it if Dolly Parton would read it and like it. I would love it! I have some fear about the reception the book will get among certain country-music people. The information that is published about the Opry stars is highly moral. I did try to give a real honest portrayal of that life, and it does include elements many people have tried to whitewash out of country music. It was a hard, hard, hard-as-hell life.

When you read the biographies and autobiographies of these people, you get quite a different picture than you do from the sanitized promo stuff you get in brochures.

As everybody knows, there is another side. It is very complex. It's very, very much a dark side. Just like with the early groups who had two different names—one of them doing gospel and sacred songs and one of them doing honky-tonk. There's always this split—which is so profoundly interesting—between Saturday night and Sunday morning, between "looking on the sunny side of life" and "tears in your beer." This makes a perfect breeding ground for fiction.

INTERVIEWER

Are there any other aspects of that conflict?

SMITH

There's the conflict between the ideal of home and the lure of the road. The road is such a part of this life. Yet so many of the songs are about home. But once you leave, and you take up that kind of life, you can never go back home.

INTERVIEWER

Your characters may not go back home exactly, but many do eventually return to religion.

SMITH

In almost every biography of the different stars, there's a point at which people come back to church. And it's usually a different church from that old naysaying church of their childhood. But they definitely come back to God.

INTERVIEWER

In your last novel, *Fair and Tender Ladies*, you homed in on one voice and stayed there, with one person, Ivy Rowe, through her whole life. Here, you went in and out of a number of voices. A few men. A lot of women.

SMITH

I love to do that. Plus, you see, as a writer, frankly, it's both my great strength and my weakness, because as I say I'm not a historian. So if I want to write a novel that attempts to show the history of country music, I doubt my ability to do that accurately. So the most I can hope for is to catch accurately one person's story, rather than the truth of the whole.

INTERVIEWER

Your modern-day character Katie Cocker overcomes all kinds of obstacles. But she also depended on men a lot. Do you find women still depend too much on men?

SMITH

In the end, Katie was singing her own song. Appalachian women, or rural women in general—all of us—have been apt for generations to hitch our wagons to somebody else's star and let other people dictate to us. Now, that's changing. It's been hard. It's taken awhile for us to figure out our own lives. Katie Cocker gets to the point where she can become self-realized and determine her own life. But there's a price. There's always a cost. There's no free ride.

INTERVIEWER

In these country-music families, there seems to be a lot of religion, a lot of repression, and a lot of violence and out-of-control passion.

SMITH

All those things are like vines climbing up the same fence. That's one of the functions that the early churches served—both to repress and to release. It's still true in many denominations today. Speaking in tongues gives an emotional release that these people do not have in their lives. Their lives are hard. Real hard.

And singing is a release, particularly in the early days. To sing in a way is to release yourself, just as sex is a release. But the singing happened in church. The repressed fervor for expression had to come through that music.

INTERVIEWER

So this early church singing, thrumming with all that emotion, was a rich source of country music?

SMITH

It's as much a source as the ballad tradition. And that's the split. The Saturday night–Sunday morning split. The sacred and the profane. It's still there.

INTERVIEWER

Do you think singing runs like DNA through some families?

SMITH

You see it in all these different singing families. It's something you do. One of the people I got to be really good friends with when I was researching the early songs was Sheila Barnhill from Sodom, North Carolina, above Asheville. She is a seventh-generation ballad singer. She says you couldn't grow up in her family without singing. She has children who are twenty, eleven, and nine, and they're all singing and playing instruments. It still happens.

INTERVIEWER

Let's go back to the women singers. They had a hard time admitting their own ambition. Do you think women, maybe particularly Southern women, are still wrestling with ambition?

SMITH

Absolutely. We really have a hard time admitting we have ambition and articulating that we have desires. Each one of us has to find a way to sing our own song.

But for many of us, for many of us women in the South, society's expectations for us, and consequently our expectations for ourselves, are very limiting and very rigid. Guilt is the great disease of Southern women. Just free-floating guilt that will attach to anything.

I have a friend who said he never even considered guilt until he came to the South. He didn't realize it was any kind of *deal*. It's such a motivating factor for Southern women, who think they should be and do all these things for other people. It hasn't changed fast enough, actually.

INTERVIEWER

There's a Melungeon in your novel. Another character says the Melungeons are "a race of people which nobody knows where they came from, with real pale light eyes and dark skin and frizzy hair like sheep's wool." Are there really such people?

SMITH

Oh, hell yes. They all live in Tennessee on Newman's Ridge, outside of Elizabethton. A lot of people have studied them and written about them. They're only one of a number of very strange, isolated pockets of people who intermarry and develop for a couple of generations. My father used to tell me that if I didn't behave, he would give me to the Melungeons. Some people believe they're descendants of the Lost Colony. They are probably a mixture of Portuguese, African-American, and Indian.

INTERVIEWER

At the beginning of your novel, it was a sin, in a way, to be creative. At the end, it's a sin not to be creative.

SMITH

As I say, the whole country-music thing provides a perfect literal metaphor for talking about that. In the beginning, there were no women stars. None. Now, it's a field in which women are just as important as men.

INTERVIEWER

One of your narrators comments that some

people say that what we will do is buried deep inside us all anyway, like a dark seed. Do you agree with your narrator?

Lord, I don't know. I keep writing these books trying to find out.

═══

The only child of Ernest and Virginia Marshall Smith, Lee Marshall Smith was born November 1, 1944, in Grundy, Virginia. She graduated from St. Catherine's School in Richmond, Virginia, in 1963 and from Hollins College in 1967. She also studied at the Sorbonne, University of Paris.

From 1968 to 1969, she wrote for the *Tuscaloosa News* in Tuscaloosa, Alabama. From 1971 to 1977, she taught seventh-grade English in Nashville, Tennessee, and Durham, North Carolina.

From 1977 to 1981, she was a lecturer in fiction writing at UNC-Chapel Hill. Since 1981, she has taught creative writing at North Carolina State University. In 1989, she was visiting professor at Virginia Commonwealth University, and from 1990 to 1992, she was a fellow at the Center for Documentary Studies at Duke University.

Her novels are *The Last Day the Dogbushes Bloomed* (1968), *Something in the Wind* (1971), *Fancy Strut* (1973), *Black Mountain Breakdown* (1980), *Oral History* (1983), *Family Linen* (1985), *Fair and Tender Ladies* (1988), and *The Devil's Dream* (1992).

Her short-story collections are *Cakewalk* and *Me and My Baby View the Eclipse.*

Her awards include two O. Henry Awards, two Sir Walter Raleigh Awards, the North Carolina Award for Fiction, the John Dos Passos Award, the Weatherford Award for Appalachian Literature, the Robert Penn Warren Prize for Fiction, and a Lyndhurst Foundation Prize.

Smith married the poet James Seay on June 17, 1967. They have two sons: Josh, born December 23, 1969; and Page, born May 22, 1971.

On June 29, 1985, Smith married journalist and critic Hal Crowther.

Smith and her husband live in Chapel Hill, where she is at work on her ninth novel.

April 29, 1979

WILLIAM STYRON

*I*n 1979, when an affable William Styron visited Davidson College to talk about his best-selling novel *Sophie's Choice*, few could have predicted what lay ahead. Within five years, Styron would be besieged by a depression so severe he felt himself slipping to the icy edge of suicide.

Over the years, Styron had talked little about depression, which had shadowed him since adolescence. But in 1984, the onslaught was so severe that he committed himself to Connecticut's Yale–New Haven Hospital. Within hours, he felt better. Within a day or two, his self-destructive impulses came close to evaporating.

After seven weeks, able again to laugh, he went home to his wife and resumed work on a novel he'd abandoned the summer before. He began enjoying life again—food, music, conversation.

Still, Styron might not have gone public if a 1988 event had not so enraged him he felt he must speak out.

A year earlier, eminent Italian writer and Auschwitz survivor Primo Levi had killed himself. The next year, New York University sponsored a seminar dedicated to Levi. At the seminar, it became apparent some people believed Levi's suicide was a "puzzling failure of moral strength."

Styron was stunned. Moral failure, Styron well knew, had nothing to do with Levi's suicide. Depression probably had everything to do with it. Styron poured out his rage in a piece for the *New York Times*, describing his own despair and near-suicide. The response was so overwhelming that he followed it with a memoir of his depression, *Darkness Visible*.

Today, Styron is just back from a two-week visit to St. Lucia. From his rambling yellow farmhouse in Roxbury, Connecticut, he talks about depression, about what writing means to him, and about the origin of the oppression that dominates his novels, from *Lie Down in Darkness* to *The Confessions of Nat Turner* to *Sophie's Choice*.

———

INTERVIEWER

You went to Davidson before transferring to Duke. According to hints in *Sophie's Choice*, while a student at Davidson, you lost your virginity in a two-dollar-a-night walk-up fleabag hotel in Charlotte, North Carolina. Was it a memorable experience?

STYRON

[Laughter.] I can't remember the street, but I know it was the Green Hotel. It was a walk-up. It was memorable. And I was with my friend Charlie Capps. He's from Cleveland, Mississippi, and is the chief Republican in the Mississippi legislature. I don't think it was his first time. But it was mine. Quite frankly, we'd been first to the Barringer Hotel, and we had been drinking vast amounts of beer. So to be quite honest, I was so filled with beer that I don't remember a great deal about it. I remember getting on the bus back to Davidson very fulfilled.

INTERVIEWER

In 1962, you covered Faulkner's funeral for *Life* magazine. You were among a handful of outsiders permitted into the Faulkner home.

STYRON

Faulkner's brother, John Faulkner, was barring the door and not permitting any strangers, and he didn't want me in there. But Bennett Cerf, who was Faulkner's publisher as well as mine, went up to Mrs. Faulkner, who was in seclusion upstairs. He said, "There's a young writer here named William Styron who would like to write this piece for *Life* magazine. He'll be very respectful."

"Let him in," Mrs. Faulkner said. "Bill read *Lie Down in Darkness*, and he loved it. Please welcome Mr. Styron."

I can't remember whether lunch came before or after the funeral. There were no more than a dozen members of the family and the brother from Mobile and the daughter from Charlottesville and a few others. After the service, we all followed the coffin to the cemetery.

INTERVIEWER

Several people I've talked to—you, Josephine Humphreys, Reynolds Price, Fred Chappell—studied under William Blackburn at Duke. You've said that for you, he was a spiritual anchor whose counsel was almost everything to one still floundering at the edge of a chancy and rather terrifying career. What was the man's gift as a mentor?

STYRON

He worshiped literature. He saw it as a sustaining force in life. He thought the world of young people who wanted to be writers—feeling, I suppose, they could carry on the continuity of literary tradition.

His field was Elizabethan prose and poetry. The Renaissance. He was extremely well-informed and certainly well-supplied as a teacher and had an enormous ability, emotional and intellectual, to transfer what he felt about great writing. And he just had this magnetic way of making you feel the grandeur of these texts, whether they were poetry or prose.

He was also a man of extraordinary personal charm. A man of deep, soulful pessimism, which is quite unusual in an optimistic society such as the United States. He was a melancholy man, but with a great underlying sense of wit. Although he didn't have the scathing quality of H. L. Mencken, he had the same sort of skepticism, the same sort of sly humor, about the follies that he saw around him.

He was a man who had very little tolerance for the status quo, especially at the university, with their pompous policies. He loved to puncture pomposity, and it was a wonderful corrective to a lot of the shibboleths that were floating around at that time. We revered him because he made us see things we hadn't seen before. He was an illuminator.

INTERVIEWER

In your twenties, as you were making your way in the publishing business in New York, you were fired from McGraw-Hill for not wearing a hat and for blowing bubbles out the window. Wasn't that a lucky day for you—being fired and set free to write?

STYRON

Those were just the capping blows to a series of blows that I think I had inflicted on McGraw-Hill. I don't think I was suited for editing. I didn't have enough discipline to read literally tons and tons of manuscripts. I wasn't really fit to do that. I think it was inevitable that a firing process was going to happen one way or another anyway. It did indeed free me to be a writer. Had I been encouraged to stay, I don't know what my career would have been. I suspect I would have given it up for writing.

INTERVIEWER

Another autobiographical question: When you were a reader at McGraw-Hill, did you really read the manuscript of *Kon Tiki* and turn it down?

STYRON

As a matter of fact, yes. I didn't do it myself. I did it in collaboration with a much older woman editor who felt, as I did, that it was rather boring. The piece I wrote about that in *Sophie's Choice*, I made up. Nonetheless, my [reader's] report was probably similar to that.

INTERVIEWER

When *Sophie's Choice* came out, you told an interviewer you made the novel autobiographical for dramatic impact. You said, "I had to back off and give the reader—from the very first page—a sense of who was talking." You said this dramatic device is "at the heart of storytelling and is the art of the novel—to establish oneself with a great authority as the narrator who's going to tell you a very interesting story, but who has not gotten around to telling you the story yet." What makes this device succeed?

STYRON

Certainly, not all novels succeed because of that device. A lot has to do with the authority with which the tale teller invests his voice. The authority and the skill. If you don't have much to say, or if the story is dull, it's not going to work. If it does, it's a wonderful way to tell a story.

INTERVIEWER

You and newspaper columnist Art Buchwald are good friends. Wouldn't you say that that kind of authority is essential to writing a strong column?

STYRON

Yes, I would say that the intimate voice is the key to such a thing. I don't think necessarily all columnists have that. There are some exceedingly dull columnists. But the ones that appeal most widely, it's because of that voice. Art has it wonderfully. It's unmistakable. An absolutely indelible sort of style.

INTERVIEWER

How did you and Buchwald become friends?

STYRON

I knew Art originally in Paris, when he was working on the *Herald-Tribune*. I was in the south of France with some friends, including my close friend Peter Matthiessen. Art had contacted Peter, knowing Peter was a bullfight aficionado, although he wouldn't claim it any longer. In France in those days, they had bullfights in the little town of Bayonne, near the Spanish border. They had to have a dispensation to have real bullfights, killing the bull and all that.

Peter and Art and I went to this bullfight, and Art wrote a very, very funny column for the *Herald-Tribune* about the bullfight. It was a parody of Hemingway's *Death in the Afternoon*. Obviously, Art did not find the bullfight all that appealing. That was my first encounter with Art. And I saw him over the years. Whenever I went back to Paris, I visited him. When he moved to the U.S., he came up to the Vineyard and bought a house there, and he's one of my closest friends over recent years.

INTERVIEWER

Your stories and novels seem to hatch for a long time. In the most recent case, *A Tidewater Morning: Three Tales from Youth*, for something upwards of fifty years. Would you see the mind—your mind, specifically—as a wonderful sort of incubator? Would you have been able to write those tales any earlier?

STYRON

Well, they plainly are linked to my memories of my boyhood and growing up in that part of Virginia. And my mind constantly goes back to that time. It's a very magnetic and compelling time for me. And I suppose they have hatched over the years, and I've been drawn back to the period.

Plainly, it was invented. But there was a large nub of truth, too. [As in the title story] my mother did die during the heat of the summer in that period, and I wanted to link various impressions of my childhood with her death. That story was not in any sense an exact rendition, and it had to do with other facets of that period of early adolescence. I did have a paper route. The store I described is very close to the real thing. Yet none of those events actually happened as I described them.

It's what you try to achieve. You take the various disparate elements of life and fit them into a mosaic that tries to cohere.

INTERVIEWER

You once referred to writer's block as being an insufficient understanding of the material. You were working on a novel about the marines when the idea for *Sophie's Choice* burst upon you. Do you now believe you thought you had an understanding of the marines subject, but your incubator simply wasn't finished with the material?

STYRON

I think you could say that probably. Yes. It's the way I work. I'm no more similar or no more different than other writers. I have my own way of doing things. For me to be able to complete something, I have to have a very coherent view of the whole thing.

INTERVIEWER

Consciously, though, you didn't yet know you had a very coherent view of *Sophie's Choice* when you woke that morning from your reverie about a Sophie you'd known years earlier in Brooklyn. Still, you called your editor and told him you were abandoning the novel about the marines and starting a new novel.

STYRON

Of course, a great deal does rely upon the subconscious. As you proceed through the story, you're constantly inventing and enriching your story with material that bubbles up from the subconscious. In this case, I did have a very put-together understanding of what I was trying to achieve. The choice. And I knew that I had these other themes at work, too—the conflict between Sophie and Nathan, the paranoia and suicidal impulses of Nathan. Quite a few elements I had in my command, so to speak, that worked as sort of strands of the story that I spun out the rest of the novel on. All sorts of things just popped up out of my subconscious that I had to deal with along the way.

I knew the word *holocaust*. But I don't think it's used in the entire book. Because I think I was writing at a time before the word *holocaust* came before the popular imagination. In 1978, a TV miniseries came out on the Holocaust. But when I began the book, the word *holocaust* was not part of my lexicon. I do think the book would have certainly succeeded on its own terms anyway. But it had the advantage of sort of being groundbreaking. It was the first American novel to deal with it.

INTERVIEWER

I'm interested in the Yale University study you participated in, "The Seasons of a Man's Life." The study confirmed that a mentor was essential to the smooth development into maturity, that a mentor gave the vision and the idealism necessary for a man to excel in his chosen vocation.

STYRON

"The Seasons of a Man's Life" was a project of the Department of Psychiatry at Yale University. They had a group of tradesmen, a group of academics, and a couple of creative people like myself. And they wanted to get a cross-section of relatively young men to see how they developed toward a goal.

As you alluded, they discovered that no matter what endeavor men were involved in—plumbers or academics or scientists or artists—in order for them to progress with some sense of self-assurance, they all had to have a mentor. Someone aside from their parents or their father. Someone who stepped in at one critical point and became their guru.

This is a very interesting insight. It applies to men no matter what the nature of their ambition or career was. And, of course, I mentioned Blackburn. I don't think they used his real name.

I mentioned that he had been a central figure in my life.

INTERVIEWER

In your study in Martha's Vineyard is a quote from Flaubert: "Be regular and orderly in your life like a Bourgeois, so that you can be violent and original in your work." How does that philosophy manifest itself in your life?

STYRON

In a letter that Flaubert wrote to his mistress, Louise Colet—among his many, many letters to her—I remembered that line, which stuck out prominently when I read it. It just arrested my imagination. I did indeed post it above my desk. It's become very famous in the literary world. I do claim that I was the first person to grab hold of it and make it a popular slogan.

INTERVIEWER

What does it mean to you?

STYRON

I think it's a cautionary sort of slogan, merely saying you don't have to perform any romantic tricks in order to become a writer. If you remain home and do your bourgeois duties, that's enough. You don't have to go out and become a pothead and an adventurer or a drug addict or an alcoholic. Just do your daily thing, and you'll write these books.

INTERVIEWER

And what is your daily thing?

April 29, 1979

STYRON

I try and get a certain amount done every day, usually in the afternoons.

INTERVIEWER

A 1979 essay by Robert Brustein describes you as something of a recluse, who once refused to come down for a dinner party because your wife hadn't checked the guest list with you. Are you antisocial and somewhat curmudgeonly?

STYRON

I have that side of me. I'm not antisocial, but I have to pick and choose very carefully about what I want to do and the people I want to do it with. Don't ask me. It's part of my nature. I'm bifurcated. Part of me is very gregarious and social, and probably the opposite is true. An irreconcilable duality. I'm both curmudgeon and recluse and open-hearted host. I think none of us is consistent. Some of us are. Most of us have schizoid qualities in our nature.

INTERVIEWER

What kept you humble enough to keep working hard at your craft after such early success — the Rome de Prix at twenty-six for *Lie Down in Darkness*?

STYRON

I cast my lot as a writer early on because I had no alternative. I had a calling. What priests call a vocation in the Catholic priesthood. There's this notion that God calls you to this, and that you can't do anything else. I early understood I had no alternative. That I couldn't become anything else. Not only because I was ill-equipped, but because I had no inclination. I wanted to be a writer and nothing else. The die was cast. My first novel was indeed quite successful. And I realized this is what I had to do with the rest of my life. So that's where I've been.

I've never been totally satisfied with myself as a writer. On the other hand, I feel glad I have done what I have done.

INTERVIEWER

Why wouldn't you be satisfied?

STYRON

I think there are many writers like myself who fall into some transcendental view of themselves and wish they had done a great deal more, rather than being satisfied with what they have done.

Instead of completion, you see incompletion. You see so many huge gaps that you feel should have been filled, and they are not filled. They remain gaps. And those, if you're a melancholy fellow like myself, dominate your sense of achievement, rather than what you have achieved.

Someone once asked Sartre what hell was. He said it was failure of self-fulfillment. And I think there is that. And it's foolish. But it's often a nagging misery for a lot of people who have demanded so much of themselves that they can see only what they haven't done. And I'm afraid that's what one of my curses is. I know on certain levels I've achieved what I had once set out to do in several very important instances. So basically, in order to console myself about the gaps, I fall back on that.

Early on, what were the symptoms you were a writer?

The absolute passion and delight in reading works that move you to raptures—a primitive like Thomas Wolfe or Shakespeare or Melville or even Crane or Scott Fitzgerald. And the concomitant need to say, "If they've done this, I've got to do something like it. If they've given us works that are so significant and soul-stirring, then I want to do the same. I have things to say, too. I have a view, a vision of life. If Virginia Woolf can move me so, then I can move readers, too."

That's what one's aim has always been, to distill one's own vision of what it's all about. A certain underlying truth one sees in existence and wants to put down on paper.

It's also just probably unconsciously carrying on the continuity of literature. It's a kind of a river to which you want to be a tributary.

Ultimately for me, life would really not be worth living unless I could be a writer. If you were to pick the brains of almost any writer, living or dead, I think they would say that's what made them write.

INTERVIEWER

As you mentioned in your memoir about your depression, *Darkness Visible*, the real onslaught of your depression began one summer's evening in 1985 when you suddenly, for no apparent reason, found you could no longer drink without becoming ill. In looking back, you've said you believe you unconsciously used alcohol as a buffer against depression for about forty years. The last time we talked, in 1989, you said you were not an alcoholic, and that you were able to drink a couple of glasses of wine with dinner. Has that changed or stayed the same?

STYRON

That's stayed the same. This is an important observation—to make a distinction between pure alcoholism and alcohol abuse. And I'm not an alcoholic. But I was an abuser. I was not. . . . I was. . . . It was complicated. Although I was dependent upon alcohol, I was not addicted in the sense that most alcoholics view alcohol as being an addiction. That's the reason, after the full year that I didn't drink a drop, I said to myself, "I'm going to test and see if I can drink." I like the taste of wine. I love wine. I love it as the complement to meals. So very cautiously I began to drink, and I was able to do it without feeling it was going to plunge me into trouble.

The strict alcoholic would be unable to do that. I'm fully capable of saying I was an abuser. But I can drink wine with no trouble. Not only no trouble, I'm an advocate of wine. I believe it's a very good thing for you. I recently wrote a plug for a book coming out from HarperCollins, and the thesis is, wine is good for your health. If you're not an alcoholic, it's very good for you. I fully believe that.

INTERVIEWER

In Donald Goodwin's book, *Alcohol and the Writer*, he puts forth a loner's theory of alcoholism. He compares children brought up in

Jewish and Japanese households with children brought up in Irish and French households. He says the Jewish and Japanese children learn a sense of dependency in the family, whereas the Irish and French tend to make their children independent before their time. Because he believes alcoholism is basically a disease of individualism, he says that a person who feels psychologically alone in the world can't gain emotional release through relationships with other people, so gets this emotional release by drinking. What do you make of this?

STYRON

It's a very provocative viewpoint. There's no doubt that Jewish families tend to encourage if not abstention, then very moderate tippling. I would say that the vast majority—and I have many, many Jewish friends—the vast majority are very abstemious. By contrast, there are some who pour the booze down.

INTERVIEWER

In *Darkness Visible* you wrote that the evening you decided to live, you were sitting bundled up in a cold house—the furnace was out—watching an old movie, out of which came a "sudden soaring passage from the Brahms Alto Rhapsody." You'd been unresponsive to music for months, but this sound pierced your heart like a dagger. I'm wondering if the music didn't finally pierce through to your pent-up grief for your mother, and sort of burst the cyst of that grief. From "A Tidewater Morning," I know how she loved Brahms, and how your father played

it at full volume on the Victrola the day before she died.

STYRON

There is certainly a connection. There's no doubt about it. If I were entirely candid about that period of my depression, I'd have to say that those days were horribly blurred, because of the agony I was going through. This particular moment of feeling salvation as a result of that music may be a generalized impression. Certainly at one point during that period, I remember that episode where I saw the movie and the music was played. But I'm not entirely sure if the experience that I wrote about was as direct as that.

Ultimately, that passage was wound up or bound up in my decision to go to the hospital and to sort of save myself. But I had to write that because all of that period in my depression was extremely confused. That moment of hearing that music—maybe that represented the reality I was trying to deal with.

INTERVIEWER

Do you still believe your depression was the result of that unexpressed grief over your mother's death all those years ago?

STYRON

I find it overwhelmingly convincing that the death of a parent at that moment in one's development—especially a mother—can be just absolutely catastrophic. And that if one somehow freezes out the need for mourning, it can get you much later in life.

INTERVIEWER

I've seen references to your stepmother and what an overbearing presence she was for you. I'm wondering if she could be the catalyst for the sense of oppression that runs through your novels—in Peyton, in Nat, in Sophie. In a sense, of course, you are Peyton and Sophie and Nat.

STYRON

Oppression. I think especially when it's coupled with a very profound antiauthoritarian spirit that I have—that I've always had, just by virtue of who I am, my nature. It could easily have been exacerbated by this other person appearing in my life. I've always been rebellious, and I have an inability to tolerate authority. And she was a rather oppressive presence. Deeply oppressive.

INTERVIEWER

Yet look what came of it.

STYRON

Blessings in disguise.

INTERVIEWER

Since your depression—or the breakthrough of your grief—have there been major and minor differences in your life? In other words, did you not only return to those things that gave you pleasure, but is the pleasure keener?

STYRON

I think it helped dissipate some fog, although to be quite honest I don't think one is entirely free ever of the depressive mood. I'm well out of the horrible traumatic experience of that major depression. But I think I've had it all my life, and I think I still have it. I'm free of it to the extent that I'm perfectly functional, to the extent I don't have the horribly psychosomatic symptoms of depression. But I think it's ingrained. I don't think I'll ever get rid of, entirely, the predilection of melancholia. I've learned how to deal with it. I have a safeguard now.

INTERVIEWER

What kind of safeguard?

STYRON

It's an ability to be able to fend it off in some philosophical way. It's approaching on me, I'll ward it off. When you first have this catastrophic experience, it comes at you unawares. It's a monster. It comes down on you. But later on, you learn how to deal with it with considerably more skill and with considerably more ability to fend it off. I've never suffered an episode since 1985 which was not entirely due to taking this awful pill Halcyon. I consider that a psychotic, drug-induced episode. With the exception of that, I've had no profound mood disorder since 1985. I've had many, many lows, and they continue to be part of my life. But they're manageable.

INTERVIEWER

Tell me about those years in Paris, when you and Donald Hall and Peter Matthiessen and George Plimpton and others were starting the *Paris Review*. Did you have fun?

STYRON

I really had a great time. It was very liberating for me to learn what it was like to just live in another country. I've always felt so at home in France. There's a part of my nature that is French, I guess, in the sense that I respond to life like French people do.

There's something in our own culture that I profoundly despise. I hate aspects of this culture, and those aspects are somehow corrected by living the way the French do. I despise our dour attitude toward the pleasures of life, our ability to just swallow junk food when you can eat well.

In France, they value leisure. Not that they don't love money, but they've learned how to apportion time so that money is not a prime concern twenty-four hours a day like it is here.

Also, to be quite honest, they have been very receptive to my own work, and that has been a pleasure to know that I'm well-received. A little book like mine on depression sold tens of thousands of copies in France. Just to know your work is appreciated somewhere else is very exhilarating.

I've always felt Americans are incredibly childish and pricklish about the French. They think the French are xenophobic. In reality, the French honor artists of all countries.

INTERVIEWER

Describe an ideal writing day for you.

STYRON

I can't.

INTERVIEWER

You end *Sophie's Choice* with four words which indicate Stingo is going to survive and live. Those words are, "Morning: Excellent and fair." In your own life, what have been the mornings, excellent and fair?

STYRON

I suppose, ultimately, the few times that I have written something that I knew I had achieved to the limit of the possibilities of my writing gifts, whatever they are. I haven't done it many times, but I've done it enough to know they were exceedingly satisfying. To finish a work of literature that fulfills every shred of my talent. I think that knowing that I had given my best to what I could do. That's the highest fulfillment.

The only child of William Clark Styron, Sr., and Pauline Margaret Abraham Styron, William Clark Styron, Jr., was born June 7, 1925, in Newport News, Virginia. He attended Warwick County High School before transferring to Christchurch School in Middlesex County, Virginia, where he graduated in 1942. He entered Davidson College in the fall of 1942 and left the following spring. In July 1943, he enrolled at Duke University. He graduated from Duke in 1947.

During World War II, he left Duke to join the United States Marine Corps, where he became a first lieutenant.

He worked as an editor at McGraw-Hill in New York in 1947.

In 1952, he was one of the founders of the *Paris Review*.

His novels are *Lie Down in Darkness* (1951), *The Long March* (1957), *Set This House on Fire* (1960), *The Confessions of Nat Turner* (1967), and *Sophie's Choice* (1979).

He is also the author of a play, *In the Clap Shack* (1972); a collection of essays, *This Quiet Dust* (1982); a memoir of depression, *Darkness Visible* (1990); and *A Tidewater Morning: Three Tales from Youth* (1993).

His awards include the American Academy of Arts and Letters Prix de Rome (1952), the Pulitzer Prize (1968), the Howells Medal of the American Academy of Arts and Letters (1970), the American Book Award (1980), the Connecticut Arts Award (1984), Commandeur Ordre des Arts et des Lettres (1987), and the Edward MacDowell Medal (1988).

He is a member of the National Institute of Arts and Letters, the American Academy of Arts and Sciences, and the American Academy of Arts and Letters.

On May 4, 1953, Styron married the poet Rose Burgunder. They have four children: Susanna, Paola, Thomas, and Alexandra.

Styron lives with his wife in Roxbury, Connecticut, and on Martha's Vineyard, Massachusetts. He is working on a semiautobiographical novel about the Marine Corps.

June 9, 1972

PETER AND ELEANOR ROSS TAYLOR

January 31, 1989

*T*he brawny arm of a four-hundred-year-old live oak tree thrusts through a wooden privacy fence in the side yard of the winter home of Peter and Eleanor Ross Taylor.

That strength is a testament to the creative spirit inside the brown-trimmed nest of a house—filled with antiques, books, photographs—on a quiet street near the University of Florida in Gainesville.

Taylor and his wife, the poet Eleanor Ross Taylor, have been publishing since the 1930s. But now they are each experiencing new creative highs.

Peter Taylor, in fact, was sixty-five before his public reputation reached its zenith. At sixty-one, he won the prestigious Gold Medal for Literature from the American Academy and Institute of Arts and Letters for his body of short stories. But he was sixty-nine before he published his second and most important novel, *A Summons to Memphis*, set in his native Tennessee. That book won both the Pulitzer Prize and the $50,000 Ritz-Hemingway Award.

He is at work on a novel about the passengers on a funeral train bearing the body of an illustrious senator back home to Nashville.

Taylor sets most of his fiction in Tennessee, and he draws heavily on family lore. His major themes involve family relationships and the ever-present power of the past.

Eleanor Taylor has written almost enough poems for a new collection, her fourth. Her poems also explore family relationships.

Over the years, the Taylors' friendships have included many of the most famous names in twentieth-century literature: Allen Tate, Robert Penn Warren, John Crowe Ransom, Robert Lowell, Randall Jarrell, Eudora Welty.

In 1946, when Peter Taylor went to UNC-Greensboro—then Woman's College—to teach, he continued his friendship with Jarrell, begun at Vanderbilt. The two couples, the Taylors and Jarrell and his first wife, Mackie Jarrell, bought a duplex together in Greensboro, the first of thirty houses the Taylors would buy and restore over the next forty years.

On a January afternoon, azaleas showy along Gainesville's streets, the Taylors talk about their courtship, about Randall Jarrell's upper lip, and about why insight is an essential ingredient in a writer's success.

INTERVIEWER

Eleanor, you were a graduate student at Vanderbilt, studying under Allen Tate—who had also taught Peter—and the Tates were just determined to make a match. Peter was on leave from his army post, and they invited you both to their house Easter weekend 1943. Then, boom. Six weeks later, you were married. What made you fall so head over heels in love?

PETER

We were opposites, really. I think that was one of the attractions. I'm much more gregarious and outgoing.

ELEANOR

I think it was partly because he thought I was a good deal like his sisters and his mother.

PETER

You looked sort of like my sister, but that wasn't it. Eleanor seemed wise, and I liked her looks. In fact, she wasn't like my family. They were all party, party, party and good times, and that was their life.

INTERVIEWER
You liked his looks, too, I'll bet.

ELEANOR
That's right, absolutely.

PETER
Are you kidding?

ELEANOR

We were expecting him that night [at the Tates'], but nobody saw him come to the door. I saw him through the glass, and I got up to let him in. And I said, "I guess you're Peter?"

PETER

I saw her through that glass door—that's my first memory—and I told Robert Lowell that day I was going to marry that girl.

ELEANOR

We did our courting partly in Centennial Park in Nashville. And one day he was smoking and out of matches. He went over across to some man in the park to get a match from him and stood there talking. When he came back, he said, "I'm sorry to be so long, but after I borrowed the match, I had to pass the time of day with him." And that just seemed to me so much like the sort of country ways I know.

PETER

Our families were very much alike in their backgrounds. My family had gone to the city long ago, but we were brought up to respect the country relatives more than anything. They would come to stay with us endlessly, but my father and mother would say, "You've got to be nice to Cud'n Rob."

INTERVIEWER

Why did you get married at the Tates' in Tennessee, and not at home in St. Louis or Norwood, North Carolina?

ELEANOR

It was so sudden, for one thing. And the Tates had just thrown themselves into the match and wanted the wedding right there. And the Lowells were there.

PETER

And the Tates loved such a thing as a wedding. You can say what you please. Both of them loved dramatic occasions.

ELEANOR

Allen specialized in giving brides away.

PETER

I've always said the wedding was sort of like a high-school play. But at any rate, the man who married us was Father Fly. He married us at his church at Saint Andrews School. He was a marvelous man, and we thought he was so old that day. Because what was he, sixty, maybe? And he lost you in places in the prayer book. But he lived on. We saw him in Charlottesville when he was over one hundred.

INTERVIEWER

What did your parents think about all this?

PETER

Our parents were just shocked by the suddenness of the thing. They couldn't believe it.

ELEANOR

Your parents weren't even coming. My parents were down on the farm and didn't come. I understand now how upset they must have been about the whole thing.

PETER

My parents *said* they weren't coming, but then my father and mother couldn't resist a party. So the day before the wedding, my father, my mother and sister, and her little girl all came driving up with a case of champagne.

ELEANOR

Well, don't forget that Dad Taylor had come

to Vanderbilt and checked me out. He took me to lunch at the Hermitage Hotel and discouraged me about Peter. He said, "I'll tell you what my father said about me: 'He's smart, but he's not as smart as he thinks he is.'"

INTERVIEWER

Now, it was after you married that you and the John Crowe Ransoms used to play bridge and keep score on the closet door? And Eleanor and Mrs. Ransom usually won?

PETER

They were marvelous people. And fun. And you know, we weren't avid bridge players always, but when you get people that you have a lot of other things in common with, then it's fun. I don't like to play a game of bridge or anything with people that I don't have anything else in common with, just for the sake of the game.

And Mrs. Ransom was so intellectual about the game. When she got the last three cards in a hand, she would say, "Eenie, meenie, minie, mo." And yet she was a wonderful—almost professional—bridge player. She got Eleanor taking lessons and all that, but the scores were not entirely in their full favor. We sort of played poker-bridge.

ELEANOR

I'm terrible, but I loved it. It was just fascinating.

INTERVIEWER

Eleanor, you were one of four children who grew up in Norwood, each of whom became a writer—the "Writing Rosses," you're called. There's your sister, Jean Ross Justice, the short-story writer who is married to the Pulitzer-winning poet Donald Justice. Your brothers, Fred Ross and James Ross, both novelists. And Fred's daughter, Heather Ross Miller, a novelist and a poet. Your own children, Ross Taylor and Katie, are publishing short stories and poems. How do you account for all these writers? What were your parents like?

ELEANOR

My father was studious and very hard-working. He explained my arithmetic problems to me, while Mama would just throw in the sponge. But Mama had much more imagination, and I think a real gift for words. I adored my mother. She was devoted to children. At the same time, there was nothing simple about her, really. She was a very grown-up sort of person, and always exploring people's motives. She'd go off and say, "Wonder if he didn't do that because so-and-so . . ."

INTERVIEWER

I read something recently that said when you, Peter, see the word *Tennessee* on a page, it will just lift right up. I wonder if you, Eleanor, feel that strongly about North Carolina?

ELEANOR

Oh, I'm very patriotic about North Carolina. And particularly in Virginia, where people are so snobbish about North Carolina and Tennessee and anywhere that's not Virginia.

PETER

She just fires up when people say things against North Carolina.

ELEANOR

I mark them off my list.

PETER

Your mother was chauvinistic about North Carolina.

ELEANOR

I wouldn't consider my mother chauvinistic about anything.

PETER

You know what I mean. She resented any slur on North Carolina. Or any slur on anything Southern, too.

INTERVIEWER

You-all have owned and restored a number of houses. It sounds as if you take the restoration process almost as seriously as the creative process.

PETER

Well, I don't think we do, really. It's our escape from writing, more than anything else.

INTERVIEWER

Both are creative.

PETER

Oh, it's a creative sort of thing. But there's not the pressure there is on you as when you're trying to write.

ELEANOR

If you stay married to the same person, it's nice to live in different houses pretty regularly.

INTERVIEWER

Why do you say that?

ELEANOR

It's just like a sort of unfaithfulness somehow, to be moving from one house to another.

PETER

It's like starting all over again. But I'm not the villain in this piece that people often accuse me. People are always saying, "Why are you always buying houses and moving about?" And the truth is that Eleanor is often . . .

I had put down some money to get a house in Greensboro, and she said, "It's in too good condition." And I found one down the street that was awful, and she said, "That's more like it."

ELEANOR

The other house was more expensive, of course.

PETER

But that's not what her objection was.

ELEANOR

I liked that other house.

PETER

One time in particular—and this is more typical—I came down for breakfast one morning in Charlottesville, and there was an advertisement for a house with a picture by my plate. It was a gorgeous eighteenth-century house with out-buildings and everything, out in Albemarle County. And before night, I'd gone out there. She's always pointing out these discoveries.

INTERVIEWER
But she acts sort of innocent, doesn't she?

PETER
Yes, she does. Everybody thinks I'm so absurd going out and buying these houses, but it's not all me. She gets carried away by these houses. Or she knows what I get carried away by and puts out the paper on the table.

INTERVIEWER
Tell about the house of Faulkner's you-all owned in Charlottesville.

ELEANOR
I don't think it entered very much into our buying of the house.

PETER
As a matter of fact, I said if we bought Faulkner's house, people like [Robert] Lowell and [Randall] Jarrell would say I was trying to step into Faulkner's shoes.

ELEANOR
And we didn't buy it from the Faulkners.

PETER
But Mrs. Faulkner did talk to us about it, and she said she loved the house. And we liked her very much.

ELEANOR
She did the garden at the back. She put in all that terrace.

PETER
She loved that house. But it really had nothing to do with Faulkner.

INTERVIEWER
Peter, when you were teaching at UNC-Greensboro, you and Eleanor and Randall Jarrell and his first wife, Mackie, bought a duplex together. Did you have qualms about living next door to good friends?

PETER
We were too young to know any better.

ELEANOR
We didn't know any better.

PETER
We wanted a place to live. They wanted a place to live. Randall was that way, though. He loved the idea of being . . . What was it Cal [Lowell] used to say about Randall?

ELEANOR
Allen's phrase was *sophomoric*.

PETER
That's not the word he used. Oh, Randall loved the idea of dormitory life. There was one front door and a little hall where you entered each apartment, and Randall would insist we leave both doors open all the time, so his cats could wander around.

ELEANOR

We kept our door firmly closed.

PETER

We got along. We didn't fall out. It was a dangerous thing to do.

ELEANOR

But it was awfully nice knowing them so well. You would go in and Randall would be sitting there at his oak desk that he loved, and he'd be listening to music and writing on his poem at the same time, and talking to us. I really took a shine to Randall right away. I really loved Randall's brilliant remarks.

PETER

He was just really devoted to Eleanor and to encouraging her, reading her poems over and over. He wrote the preface to her first book. If he liked Eleanor's poems or one of my stories, he could sit down with you and just talk for an hour about everything that's good in the story or poem.

ELEANOR

But if it was a poem he didn't like, his upper lip had a way of getting sort of . . . Well, it just seemed a little crooked-up. And he would put the poem aside. It was absolutely withered and charred after that. You couldn't do anything with it.

PETER

One of the things I remember is, I used to like to paint at Kenyon [College], and it was typical of him—Randall knew a great deal about painting, too. And he saw a painting I had done and said, "Oh!" He thought it was so good and just raved over it as only Randall could rave about it. And the next day he came in and looked at the painting and said, "No, I've decided I am wrong about that painting. I think it's pretty dull." It was very deflating.

ELEANOR

He could crush people.

INTERVIEWER

I understand that after you-all eat breakfast, you don't encourage conversation for fear you won't get back on track with your writing.

ELEANOR

I like to get up early, about six, and then I sit down with Peter when he gets up and has breakfast, about eight or eight-thirty.

PETER

What I like to do is get up and go to the back door and call outside to Eleanor where she's gardening and say, "Eleanor, breakfast is ready!" so the neighbors will think I have prepared breakfast.

INTERVIEWER

When you each finish some piece of writing, do you go right to the other and show it?

ELEANOR

Oh, we do.

INTERVIEWER

Eleanor, you learned to read Randall Jarrell's upper lip. So there must be signs in Peter you look for.

ELEANOR

If Peter doesn't like something I've written, he's apt to be just rather quiet about it. He'll just make general comments.

PETER

We usually like each other's work and are very encouraging. Well, no, there've been things . . . I wrote a story called "Heads of Houses," a longish story. And Eleanor read it, and she didn't like it. It's the only story I've ever just torn up and written over.

ELEANOR

I didn't know I did this. That's terrible.

PETER

Well, you did. It was a long time ago, but I changed the setting and I changed the characters.

INTERVIEWER

Peter, you've talked about your stories beginning with events and experiences that worry you. I hear a lot of writers say that something obsesses them. But *worry* is a much more interesting word.

PETER

If something—a dream or a dirty joke or anything—if I keep remembering that thing, I de-

cide it must be a good subject for me, because it gets to me so much, and I care about it. I remember an anecdote someone told me, about the girl who cut off her hand, and I just couldn't forget it. It just stuck in my mind. And I thought, "Why? What does it mean to me?" And writing is a way for me of discovering what I think about something. I think that's the great delight in writing.

INTERVIEWER

Eleanor, your last volume of poetry, *New and Selected Poems*, was published in 1983. Now, your work is appearing everywhere: the *New Yorker, Grand Street, Ploughshares, Shenandoah*. What accounts for the new burst of creativity?

ELEANOR

It's been so long since I had any sort of a reputation, and I suddenly felt, "I want to be alive, and I want to print some poems." So I began sending poems out, and I just began working at it harder.

PETER

It's not just ambition that makes you do it. It's what you enjoy most in the world.

ELEANOR

But I think that I am working at it harder. And the funny thing is that lots of times now, in spite of my age, I feel as though I have all the time in the world.

INTERVIEWER

Peter, you suffered a stroke in 1986 that

June 9, 1972

affected the left side of your brain, and as a result you lost some use of your right hand. But you've said if the stroke had affected the right side of your brain, your imagination would've suffered.

PETER

I was awfully lucky in that I had begun a novel six months before I had my stroke. And so I could get right back into it. We had a friend who was a novelist who had a stroke, and it was on the right side. And I think it did affect her. Her imaginative process wasn't as it once was.

I'm right-handed, and my right hand is all that's affected.

INTERVIEWER

But there was a period when you were physically unable to write.

PETER

Oh, yes.

INTERVIEWER

That must have felt terrible.

PETER

It feels terrible still.

ELEANOR

He was so frustrated he had an ulcer.

PETER

Yes, I had an ulcer.

INTERVIEWER

Trying to get it down in longhand?

PETER

Yes. Everything was such a struggle and so frustrating.

INTERVIEWER

You still have difficulty using your right hand. How have you accommodated that?

PETER

I always had to write longhand and then type it. Well, I can't really write now. It's not legible for anybody else but me. But I do a scribble on a big legal pad and then I dictate it to somebody. And then I sort of revise it and go on. I've sort of gotten into doing that. But lately I can write some on the typewriter. It's very slow. If I could write a novel just using A, B, C, D, and F, I could do fine. My left hand can just fly.

INTERVIEWER

I bet you never thought you'd say your left hand could fly.

PETER

That's right, I didn't. I was very vain. That's why I say God strikes you where he knows you're vain.

INTERVIEWER

What are you working on now?

PETER

I've been writing a few little stories and making notes. This novel I'm writing now will take the rest of my life. It's not going to be long, but I just take forever writing it.

But I have fun rewriting it and doing it over

and over, and unlike other people who can't stand to give readings from things they haven't finished, I go about reading, and then I rewrite it and think, "Oh, it's much better this time." [Laughter.]

INTERVIEWER

And it's about a senator coming home to Tennessee on the train, in a coffin?

PETER

Well, it was originally to be just that. But I realize now that it's not just that. As I told Eleanor today, you change your themes as you come to understand what a piece is about, and then you go back and reshape it. That's great fun. I think that's why writing is so much more fun when you get older. You really know much more about what you're doing. In the early days, I would write a story, and I'd be so unsure what was good about it that I wouldn't dare change anything, because I was afraid that maybe that was what was good about it.

INTERVIEWER

For years, you wrote for the sheer joy of writing. You were well-respected, highly admired by your peers and colleagues. Then all of a sudden you won three very big prizes, snap, snap, snap. And your works got a wider audience. How did that make you feel?

PETER

I just felt like I had a good stroke of luck. I didn't feel any differently about my stories or about writing.

ELEANOR

It was partly just writing a novel.

PETER

It was, really, although the PEN/Faulkner was not for the novel. But Katherine Anne Porter was practically not known until she wrote a novel, and I had always known that, and I had cursed the situation.

ELEANOR

And Eudora Welty's stories came first, didn't they?

PETER

Yes. Her stories are her great work. But it's the novel that sells, and it gets attention. But I had always survived on having such wonderful writers for friends. I felt if I had their respect, then that really meant a lot more to me than having the big, wide audience.

But if a writer is good enough, he ought to have a wide audience. But I still much more cherish the good opinions I had from Robert Penn Warren and [Allen] Tate and [John Crowe] Ransom and all my literary friends.

INTERVIEWER

Everybody wanted their admiration, and you had it.

PETER

Well, I think that's true. But I think literary people and artists make friends among their peers. You can't be good friends with people whose work you don't admire. If someone is not a very good writer, sooner or later it comes to the front, and you have to tell the truth about what you think of people's writing.

INTERVIEWER

Why is that?

PETER

Because it's something very important to the person—maybe the most important thing in his life. And if you are dishonest about it, then sooner or later it will get in the way of the friendship.

I have a friend, a former student, who is a very good writer, who wrote several stories I thought were just extremely good. And then he wrote a novel I didn't think was good. I finally had to tell him. I didn't want to, but I said to myself, "I can't go on being friends with him, and when the subject comes up, saying to other people I don't like it, and then not saying it to him."

So I had to. And it was very painful, and he was a wonderful person and a marvelous friend. And he accepted that—didn't necessarily agree with it—but it made it possible to go on. He knows exactly what I think of it, and we are still good friends. But I know how good he's *capable* of being. I think a writer is as good as his best work.

ELEANOR

Well, you know what Randall said: "This man doesn't like my writing, but he likes me." And I always thought, "But I *am* my poems. If he doesn't like my poems, he doesn't like me."

INTERVIEWER

You-all read out loud to each other. What is your specific pleasure in doing this?

PETER

Eleanor usually reads to me. Especially, say, if something's funny, you enjoy it together much more.

ELEANOR

And now and then, just a sort of brilliant touch of writing—character or phrase or something.

PETER

And reading it together, you just catch the pleasure of it.

ELEANOR

Reading things out loud gives you a different feeling about it. Don't you think so?

PETER

I think it does. When I began writing in the earlier years, I had to read everything I wrote out loud to myself. Did you do that?

ELEANOR

Oh, never.

PETER

Everything I wrote, I had to go off somewhere where nobody could hear me, and I'd read it out loud. And then after enough years, I got so that I would just hear it.

ELEANOR

I think maybe I do the same thing now, because I tend to memorize my poems and to say them to myself, polishing them over at night.

INTERVIEWER

Peter, when you were nineteen, your teacher Allen Tate said you wrote better than most people who'd been writing nineteen years. Did any of your stories ever fall short of somebody's expectations?

PETER

Well, they fell short in my own estimation.

ELEANOR

Some of your best stories were turned down by the *New Yorker*, and that feels like a rejection.

PETER

Yes, that's right. It's bad for a magazine editor to write to a young writer and say, "This is not a good story." He ought to write him and say, "These are not the stories for us. We don't like it." Because it is so discouraging.

I had an experience with an editor—not at the *New Yorker*. I sent him a story and wrote a note saying I thought this was the best thing I'd done. He wrote me back a letter—he was obviously drunk when he wrote it—saying, "Naturally, *you* think it's the best thing you've ever done." Then he went on to write a long letter about how bad it was.

INTERVIEWER

Is it true, Peter, your father once got very up-set about a great-aunt you had put in a story, one who seemed a little too true-to-life for comfort?

PETER

Yes. We were living in Hillsborough [North Carolina], and I went to meet his plane at Durham. And when he got off the plane, before he was really on the ground, he said, "If you had been home when that story about Katty came out, I would've knocked you down."

INTERVIEWER

What would you-all say to young people interested in writing?

ELEANOR

Allen Tate used to say that the writing of poetry cannot be taught; it only can be permitted. And I feel that writing just has to go ahead and take place. Even if the world says you're no good, if you have to write, you go ahead and do it.

PETER

I think it's compulsive. If you have to write, you have to write.

ELEANOR

If I had to live my life over, I would say, "Write while you are young, and write every day if you can, even if it is just a paragraph or a page. Just a little something. The more you write, the more you learn."

PETER

I think that's true, but then I didn't know enough when I was under forty. You learn writing, but your real writing may come later. Chekhov died at forty. But on the other hand, [Thomas] Hardy wrote most of his after he was fifty.

INTERVIEWER

But if you're working on craft or technique all along, when you reach your mature powers, you're ahead.

PETER

But I don't know that I think you can just work on your technique. It's your subject that's controlling your technique. You can't set any rules about it. Like everything else, there's luck and experience and insight. I've known young people who had just the most marvelous insight and understanding, and they never wrote. Others didn't have much insight, but then by the hardest effort they found it and learned it. So it's amazing what the human being can learn and what he can do with his life if he has a drive to do. But it's no good having all the drive and ambition if you don't have some kind of insight.

INTERVIEWER

Would you say, then, that insight is more important than talent for words?

PETER

I think so. Think how few words Hemingway has in his vocabulary.

ELEANOR

And what [Henry] James said: "The superficial person can only write a superficial novel."

PETER

And "The profound person can only write a profound novel."

Eleanor Ross Taylor

Born June 30, 1920, in Stanly County, North Carolina, Eleanor Ross Taylor is the third of four children of Fred Elbert and Jennie Catherine Lilly Ross. She graduated from Norwood High School in Norwood, North Carolina, in 1936 and from Woman's College, now UNC-Greensboro, in 1940. She did graduate work at Vanderbilt University until 1943.

Her collections of poetry are *Wilderness of Ladies* (1960), *Welcome Eumedides* (1972), *New and Selected Poems* (1983), and *Days Going, Days Coming Back* (1991).

She is the recipient of a literature award from the National Academy and Institute of Arts and Letters (1964) and a prize from the *Kenyon Review* for a group of poems (1990).

She was poetry editor of the literary magazine *Shenandoah* in 1977.

On June 4, 1943, Eleanor Ross married Peter Taylor in Sewanee, Tennessee. They have two children: Katherine Baird, born in 1948; and Peter Ross, born in 1955.

The Taylors live in St. Augustine, Florida; Charlottesville, Virginia; and Sewanee, Tennessee.

Eleanor Ross Taylor is at work on a new collection of poems.

Peter Taylor

Born January 8, 1917, in Trenton, Tennessee, Peter Hillsman Taylor is the youngest of four children of Matthew Hillsman and Katherine Baird Taylor Taylor. He attended Country Day School in St. Louis, Missouri, and graduated from Central High School in Memphis, Tennessee, in 1936. He attended Vanderbilt University from 1936 to 1937 and Southwestern College, now Rhodes College, in Memphis, Tennessee, from 1937 to 1938. He received his B.A. from Kenyon College in 1940. He also studied at Louisiana State University.

From 1946 to 1967, Taylor taught at the University of Virginia, where he is a professor of English. He also taught intermittently at Woman's College, now UNC-Greensboro, from 1946 to 1966. He has served as a visiting lecturer at Indiana University (1949), the University of Chicago (1951), Kenyon College (1952 to 1957), Oxford University (1955), Ohio State University (1957 to 1963), and Harvard University (1964 and 1972 to 1973).

From 1941 to 1945, he was a sergeant in the United States Army.

His novels are *A Woman of Means* (1950) and *A Summons to Memphis* (1988).

His short-story collections are *A Long Fourth and Other Stories* (1948), *The Widows of Thornton* (1954), *Happy Families Are All Alike* (1959), *Miss Leonora When Last Seen* (1963), *The Collected Stories of Peter Taylor* (1969), *In the Miro District* (1977), and *The Old Forest and Other Stories* (1984).

His plays include *Tennessee Day in St. Louis* (1959), *A Stand in the Mountains* (1971), and *Presences: Seven Dramatic Pieces* (1973).

His awards include a Guggenheim Fellowship in fiction (1950), a literature grant from the National Institute of Arts and Letters (1952), a Fulbright Fellowship to France (1955), an O. Henry Memorial Award (1959), an Ohioana Book Award (1960), a Ford Foundation Fellowship (1961), a Rockefeller Foundation Grant (1964), the gold medal for literature from the National Academy and Institute of Arts and Letters (1979), the Ritz-Hemingway Award (1989), the PEN/Faulkner Award (1986), and the Pulitzer Prize (1987).

He is at work on a novel.

May 1, 1972

EUDORA WELTY

August 29, 1988

*E*udora Welty has opened wide her bank of living-room windows to welcome any stray late-summer breeze. On the hearth are two small electric fans, ready to be plugged in should the afternoon grow too hot or too muggy.

Welty's parents, Chestina and Christian Welty, built this two-story Tudor house on Pinehurst Street in Jackson, Mississippi, in 1925, when Eudora was sixteen, brother Edward thirteen, and brother Walter ten. Only five minutes from town, it was considered country property. Today, tree-shaded Belhaven College across the street still provides a cool curtain of green. But even in midafternoon, Pinehurst Street rumbles with traffic. Since her mother's death in 1966, Welty, who never married, has lived alone in the house.

Until arthritis struck, she made her office in her upstairs bedroom. It was to that room she returned—with a Bachelor of Arts degree from the University of Wisconsin and a degree from the Columbia University Graduate School of Business—to write the short stories that have become classics: "Death of a Traveling Salesman," "A Worn Path," "A Piece of News."

In fact, all her short stories and novels have been evoked in this house and in this town where she was born.

The most autobiographical of her novels, *The Optimist's Daughter*, was written after her mother's death and published first in the *New Yorker* in 1969. After it was published in book form in 1972, it won the Pulitzer Prize. Most of her work is set in Mississippi and concerns the strange and mysterious workings of the human heart.

In 1983, Harvard University Press published Welty's *One Writer's Beginnings*. That autobiography—to her surprise, and to Harvard's— became a longstanding bestseller.

Welty has moved her office downstairs, to a room opposite the living room. To her frustration, she says, every flat surface in that room is stacked with mail she must answer and manuscripts she must read. But as she settles on the couch—making certain her guest is comfortable and at right angles to her good ear—she leans happily into her subject: The writing life and the imagination.

———

INTERVIEWER

It seems so many people who grew up to be writers—you, Walker Percy, Anne Tyler—spent some time in bed as children or youths with an illness. As a child, you spent time in bed with a "fast-beating heart." Do you think that that leisure enriched your already fertile imagination?

WELTY

It did give me a glorious opportunity to do what I loved to do: Read. 'Cause I lay on the bed with books all around me, like Robert Louis Stevenson's [poem] "In the Land of Counterpane." So that really was a feeling of being perfectly free to read to my heart's content. Or look out the window to my heart's content. I suppose anything that leads to, or even panders to, the habit of uninterrupted meditation, uninterrupted enjoyment of your imagination. I can't say I've meditated, but I've imagined.

Another thing: I used to—I think at the same time—enact plays I'd made with dolls, which you could do in bed. You could make a stage and a landscape. That may have played into my dramatic instinct, which storytelling is.

INTERVIEWER

I'd like to talk about your parents. You were fortunate your own mother passed along her passion for reading to you. Do you believe there's something magically contagious about passion? Do you think it's the best way to teach?

WELTY

Maybe it's the inevitable way to teach. And it certainly is the effective, it's the *critical*, thing in learning. It's sort of the essence. But it has to be real. I don't think it would come through if it were not true.

INTERVIEWER

Your mother couldn't help herself. But what would you advise parents who aren't themselves passionate, but still want to nurture their children's creativity?

WELTY

Even if you didn't have that, and you instigated a love of reading in the children, then it could follow. What worries me so much about now is that people grow up without having read anything. *Anything*! And the sense of the language is getting so muddied and imprecise. The poetry of the language is being lost. I can tell that also from letters I get. I think that's the most important thing in the world in education: The written word.

It can't come in cassettes—not all of it. That helps. But if you don't have a base knowledge of the word and of the existence of the word, the indelibility of the word, which you don't get from hearing. I don't mean not to hear anything. But that the other should be primary.

INTERVIEWER

With your father, it wasn't so much a passion that I sense in him. But it was his unselfishness. His ability to put his children ahead of himself.

WELTY

Absolutely. They both had that. I suppose a lot of it, at least to some extent, was because both of them came from families without much money. You know, everything had to be earned. They were educated, as it turned out, through their own efforts. And it had meant so much to them that they were determined that their children . . . Of course, that's the great story of America. Never, never did we get the idea that our family was sacrificing for our education, although I'm sure they were.

It wasn't this burden like, "I'm paying for this year at college, and you ought to study." That never happened. I guess we really studied anyway. But they didn't make us feel that they were suffering deprivation for us to be educated. They weren't, actually. But they would have. In some ways, I know they did give up things. But we were always comfortable in our family. We were small-town comfortable. They did everything they could for us.

INTERVIEWER

You just fell into the right hands, didn't you?

WELTY

I'll say I did. I realize it more all the time.

INTERVIEWER

You've taught writing from time to time, and I understand you taught Ellen Gilchrist in your workshop at Millsaps College.

WELTY

I never was a teacher, I'll tell you that. I needed to earn some money, and I couldn't leave home. My usual way was to go to colleges, when invited. But I needed to get some money because of illness in the house, and I couldn't leave. So I thought maybe I could do something at Millsaps College. What we really had was a workshop. And I told them right in the beginning that I didn't believe I could teach writing. We could have a workshop and have a back-and-forth among ourselves and see what came of it. We worked it out as we went. And I would say I learned more than any of the students, by the things we did.

INTERVIEWER

What did you do?

Well, the method I set out was to have each student read when and if they felt like it. Whatever was natural to them. Every day, or once a month, or whatever, to bring their story to class and for them themselves to read the story aloud and see how it sounded objectively. And then the class would ask questions, comment as a whole.

And I did that, too. I'd read before. But it was only when I read my work aloud that I saw for the first time all its weaknesses, and I could objectively judge it. In writing, that had never happened to me. But in reading it out loud, I learned so much.

INTERVIEWER

But you've also said you don't believe in teaching writing. That it's something people have to learn for themselves.

WELTY

I've felt that way. But I know that there are things that you can learn that you wouldn't have to learn by yourself. You can learn pitfalls and how to avoid them. You can be guided and learn something about form and things like that, just from the practice of it. And I will say that the stories I've read in different colleges and universities in the country—where I go there to visit and I read a bunch of manuscripts—they are all very accomplished. And I know I could never have written like that in college myself. They are very competent.

INTERVIEWER

How do you account for that?

WELTY

They are very accomplished in that they don't do anything wrong. But that isn't to say that they will go on even being writers, because that has to come from inside. You have to really *want* to do it and want to do nothing else.

It couldn't hurt anyone to learn to write in an accomplished way. You learn the language, and so on. But after they went out of college and decided they wanted to do something that would earn a living better—and God knows, most anything would do it better—then they might not ever come back to writing.

It's just like people who are good at dancing, painting, music when they are young. But it isn't sustained. And I do think that depends on what you were born with, which you can't help, and you can't get it. You've got to have that if you're really going to go on with it. You've got to have a talent for it, a gift, whatever, and be willing to work hard to develop that. That is, it can't all come from outside.

INTERVIEWER

Do you ever come across people you feel have the inside thing but don't yet have the appropriate skills?

WELTY

Sure. That's exactly the way I must have been for most of my young life. Because I think I had some kind of gift—I know I must have, or I wouldn't have kept on to be this old and still doing it—but I did teach myself. And it probably took longer. I don't do anything very well in a group.

You've always said your writing talent was a visual writing talent. I've never heard you mention your excellent ear, which I'm wondering if you think you might have inherited from your very musical West Virginia uncles. I'm wondering if that ear for dialogue has anything to do with that musical ear.

I don't know. I had a brother who was very musical. I was interested in dialogue after I started writing, I think. That got me interested, and then I started listening. I love dialogue, and when I read something or write something, I can hear it. So that's a good test for it. It also helps you remember, something you hear. But I think it's apart from the visual sense. Some stories are all one thing, and some are all the other.

Talk about the visual, too. When you read a letter, for instance, part of the experience for you must be visualizing what you read.

I see anything I read. The longer you live, the more you have seen things, so you can call up the image that is literally familiar to you. That you literally have seen. It's been on your retina.

But also as a child, reading fairy tales and happenings—Ali Baba and all those *Arabian Nights* and King Arthur.

In all the interviews I've read with you, you were getting letters from people who took it upon themselves to analyze the symbols in your stories. Does that amuse you?

By now, it kind of baffles and tires me, because I think, "What can I do about this?" There are some things now I don't even try to answer. Every room in my house has got stacks. The room across the hall—every flat surface has unanswered mail. Sometimes, I just feel like giving up the ghost. It's nice to know that people think they can connect with you. And I'm very moved by that fact. But what can I physically do about it? I just don't know. I just don't know what to say. They don't understand. I'm sure it hasn't occurred to them that someone else might be doing the same thing. I'm sure it doesn't occur to them.

I hope you keep your own writing room free of those stacks.

That's my trouble. I've had to move downstairs. My own room is directly above this one—my workroom where I have files and drawers and my desk and my typewriter. But I have arthritis in my knee, which means that going up and down stairs is not good. So I just moved downstairs a little at a time. Trying to switch books and things. So every room has got stacks. It's just awful to look at. I'm nowhere, really. I've been doing some work right in here, right in the living room. That's so inhospitable.

INTERVIEWER

I'd like you to describe—in as much detail as you will—your ideal daily writing routine.

WELTY

Oh, boy!

INTERVIEWER

I say ideal, because on an ideal day, you would've had all your mail answered yesterday.

WELTY

Oh, boy. Nobody's ever given me this chance before. Okay. Wake up early. I'm one of the people who think best in the morning. I like to wake up ready to go, and to know that during that whole day the phone wouldn't ring, the doorbell wouldn't ring—even with good news—and that nobody would drop in. This all sounds so rude. But you know, things that just make a normally nice day are not what I want. I don't care what the weather is. I don't care what the temperature is. I don't care where I am or what room I'm in. I'd just get up and get my coffee and an ordinary breakfast and get to work. And just have that whole day! And at the end of the day, about five or six o'clock, I'd stop for good that day. And I'd have a drink, a bourbon and water, watch the evening news—"MacNeil-Lehrer News Hour"—and then I could do anything I wanted to.

I would like to see a friend for dinner or something, or go out. You know, completely cut off, and have the river start going the other way again. And then part of the perfect day would be to have the next day to follow also perfect. Not to think, "I'd better make the best of it, because tomorrow . . ." I'd like to think, "I can do it tomorrow, too." And I'd also like to think, "Yesterday was a pretty good day." I'd like to have it work at both ends, toward the past and toward the future.

It used to be easy to do that, strange to say. When my family was living here, I would just go upstairs and shut the door, and I could do that work. And I was doing jobs at this time, too. Like book reviews or going to colleges. But I could shut it on and off better than I can now. And also, it didn't occur to me that there might be a time when I couldn't find that freedom to write. Part of it now is the experience of knowing that you really can't get that situation. It's just not to be had.

Life is different now. Pinehurst Street is different. Big traffic thing. Lots of noise. Also, everybody thinks it's okay to send all the mail by Express Mail, which means you have to go to the door and sign for it. All of those things life is just full of. It's just made with intrusions now. It's nobody's fault. It's just the way it is.

Sometimes, I think that maybe this partial deafness I have is brought about by my wishing I didn't have to hear so much. I hope not. But it could be.

During your ideal day, wouldn't you stop to eat lunch?

Oh, yeah. Yeah, I'd stop and eat. Yeah. But I would pick a good minute to do it, and I would fix something I could just slap together—a sandwich and a Coke. I wouldn't stop and cook something and all that.

And I wouldn't have any set time for it that I'd have to look forward to. Because it wouldn't matter. That would be wonderful. I feel as if I've had a day like that.

Even if I found out the next day that what I had done was really not very good, I would know it was important, because it was a bridge to something. I would know where to go from there.

I don't think any writing is ever really lost, because it all teaches you something. Even the bad teaches you something that you wouldn't have known otherwise. So I would like to be working on something sustained, to be writing a short story which is sustained and all of a piece.

I wouldn't be writing at all without the idea of what I wanted to do. I wouldn't just sit down and type. That would never do. It would be toward an end. That's a lovely question. Nobody ever asked me that before.

I know the act of writing, and even revising, makes you very happy. Please talk about how you feel or the state you're in when you're hard at work on a story or a novel.

I think you're unconscious of the state you're in, because you're not thinking about yourself. You're thinking about the piece of work. Totally absorbing. I guess if you stopped to think about yourself, it would stop you in your tracks. What am I doing here? [Laughter.] It's the act of being totally absorbed, I think, which seems to give you direction. The work teaches you about the work ahead, and that teaches you what's ahead, and so on. That's the reason you don't want to drop the thread of it. It is a lovely way to be.

And there was a time when I drove my car every other day—I was going to see my mother, who was away at that time—and on the trip, I wouldn't try to be thinking of my work, but it's sort of hypnotic to be behind the wheel of a car and take a well-known road you've done many times. Everything would start flowing into my head about the story [*Losing Battles*], and I would think, "This is the word I was trying to think about yesterday!" And so I'd write it down. I had a shorthand notebook with a hard back, you know, so I could write with one hand without taking my eyes off the road. Of course, I'd have to transcribe it pretty quickly when I got home, or I couldn't make sense of it. But all these things, it was just like your mind was saying, "All right. I've got you now, and I'm going to fill in these things that you missed yesterday."

It wasn't a note of direction. It was a piece of work. Sometimes it was the wrong idea.

INTERVIEWER

That's just amazing.

WELTY

What your mind does is so peculiar.

INTERVIEWER

Especially when your mind is on automatic.

WELTY

That's right. It was on automatic drive.

INTERVIEWER

Aren't you glad you were a broken left-hander, so you could write with your right hand?

WELTY

I certainly was. I would've had to get an English drive.

INTERVIEWER

You had started *Losing Battles*, and it was under way, and your mind was just supplying.

WELTY

I'd been working on it a long time, but never in a sustained way. I can't remember now—I have so many different versions of things.

INTERVIEWER

Do you save them all?

WELTY

I had saved them all. Then when I wrote the novel, I went back and put all these things together, looked at them all together, and selected what I could use. They were all in the shape of scenes. The scene was to tell you something about the character or the action. But I might have thought of another way to do it and have another scene. You didn't want both of them. So you would say, "Which one did it best?"

INTERVIEWER

It was as if, at some level in you, the whole thing was there, and pieces were just floating up, but not in any order.

WELTY

It was really weird. The mind is very strange. And I suppose everybody's mind has its own whatever it is—strangeness or method.

INTERVIEWER

Or its own way of focus or order.

WELTY

Focus. That's right. Because not in that novel, but in other stories I've written, which I've done in pieces of things, I've suddenly realized while doing something else—like riding on a train or washing the dishes—that the focus had been wrong in something. It was like I had the wrong spotlight on it. And instead, it should've been from this character or this year. But the story was there all the time, and I had seen it in the wrong light.

Isn't that strange? I guess I must be very slow-witted in lots of ways to be so belatedly aware of things.

INTERVIEWER

I think you trust your unconscious more. You don't feel the need to rush.

WELTY

I think so, too. I know what to trust. When I get an idea like that, I know it's right. You don't get a wrong idea like that. At least, I don't think so. It's a correction when you get a better idea. Just like, "Correction, please," in a Japanese accent: "Collec-shun, preeze."

INTERVIEWER

Let's go back to revision a minute. You've said your ideal way to write a short story is to write the whole draft through in one sitting, then to revise, then rewrite the final draft in one sitting. Talk about your method of revision. It's with scissors and pins, isn't it?

WELTY

That's right.

INTERVIEWER

Your mind predates computers, because we have a way to "block-save" on our computers. You can take this piece of material and "block-save" it and put it down here.

WELTY

Oh, you save the block.

INTERVIEWER

That's right. That's exactly what you're doing with pins and scissors, right? You're doing what the computer has finally learned to do.

WELTY

Except that with a computer, I don't know whether it stays in view.

INTERVIEWER

Well, that's the trick. You have to scroll it up. Your method has the advantage.

WELTY

I think it's an advantage, too, because then if you don't like what you've done, you can put it back. All you have to do is unpin it. You can try things. But you can with a computer, I suppose.

INTERVIEWER

Well, you still don't have it all in view at once.

WELTY

I have to have things in view. That's one of my troubles. Someone showed me a darling little typewriter. They said it was so lightweight, and it was wonderful. I said, "Oh, let me try it!" I went over there, and I saw that you did not see—it was not visible—the line you were typing. I said, "I couldn't even write a sentence that way."

INTERVIEWER

Let's get real specific about your pins-and-scissors method.

May 1, 1972

WELTY

Did you ever cut out and make dresses from patterns? Well, I guess it's that that made me think of it. Anyway, I think probably also it goes back to newspaper days. When you write copy, as you know, you're in a room with a lot of people. But there's a space bar on your typewriter, and if you don't like something, you rip it off. And so you have this long roll of paper. I think in a way it was to use that lesson. If it's not good, throw it away. Then write it again and use that.

Except I was too prudent, I guess, to really throw it away. I would save it in case I might need it after all. So I had these strips. But you do that in a newspaper office.

INTERVIEWER

We used to.

WELTY

Now you use computers. I could never work on it.

INTERVIEWER

I think you could. But your way sounds better.

WELTY

I have to have something under my hand to write on. I know at the *New York Times Book Review*, you never touch anything. Ever. There are no galleys. I'd be incapable . . .

INTERVIEWER

You wouldn't.

WELTY

Yes, I would. Maybe touch is part of it, along with seeing and hearing. All of this about one draft, of course, means it's a very short story— the kind I used to write. I couldn't do that now. I couldn't possibly do it all in one day. But that is my ideal way of writing a short story. Really.

INTERVIEWER

Can you say why?

WELTY

Because you then see it as a whole. You conceive it as a whole. And it's easy to follow its plan of action in a straight line that way. You know, well, it is a straight line. It's a tense line. It has tension in it. You can't relax it. It goes together with writing in one spurt. But of course it's been years since I wrote anything I could do like that, because I write so much more lengthily—too lengthily. It's a different kind of story now.

I do know this much: Everybody has a different way. And you have to figure out that way.

INTERVIEWER

You've said you must know exactly what's in a character's heart and mind before he ever sets visible foot on stage. You've also said a story grows like a thorn under your skin, festering, until it's ready to be plucked, or written. This means you've already done a lot of work before you start writing.

WELTY

Oh, yeah. I didn't know I'd ever said that

about the thorn. Heavens! It sounds so painful. I don't really feel pain in this. Anyway, I think maybe my perception of the character would be something else than the kind of thing we put in words or outlines. I think of the character as a whole. But really, the only way I know how to express the character is in the story. So that I couldn't make an outline and say, "Enter, so-and-so."

I think of them in the whole from the start, but as to how it's to work out, that does come in the writing. Or if I change my mind of what I thought was a good way and see if there's a better way.

INTERVIEWER

But the knowing of the character, what does that feel like? Does that come upon you silently? Do you even consider it work? You've also said that the story smolders until you're ready to light it. But that process that goes on inside you at some level—maybe you're not even conscious of it. Maybe you only know it when it festers.

WELTY

I think now, on looking back, that since I'm interested in human relationships, I think of the character as within a relationship also from the beginning. So it's more than just a single, lone creature there. It's the pattern of relationships, all affecting each other and causing things in each other and creating a development, making its own pattern.

But I don't know. Because it's not very self-conscious. I'm trying to be honest, but it may be different in different stories. I could not be-

gin a story if I did not have the whole clear intention as a single thing in my mind to what this story should exist as. Sometimes, I can find a better way to work it out than I had thought of in the beginning. But it's what I wanted to do in the beginning.

INTERVIEWER

But that part before you start writing is, as far as you know, effortless?

WELTY

I don't know. I don't feel strain about it. I can't be sure. It's not very conscious of itself. If it were, I probably couldn't do it at all. It is a mysterious thing. As I say, I'm sure it's different in different people, which makes it even more mysterious.

INTERVIEWER

You talked about memory in *One Writer's Beginnings* as a source and a force. I find the force really intriguing.

WELTY

I've forgotten how I used it.

INTERVIEWER

That by getting in there and getting those memories going, a person could do something very positive. Maybe even revitalize ourselves.

WELTY

Yeah. I think so, too. It's very illuminating. I think it's a great corrective force.

INTERVIEWER

What do you mean?

WELTY

Well, it sets you straight. You know, "I think that must be so-and-so." Then, "No . . ." And you start thinking about it. And it sets you straight. You can remember things wrongly. You assume something through the years, and then you realize you probably tinted that up a little bit.

INTERVIEWER

In your essay "Words into Fiction," you talk about a writer choosing his subject and a subject choosing a writer. You say, "He has taken the fatal step when he puts himself into the subject's hands." That line makes me think of the writer standing at the edge of a cliff.

WELTY

That was very dramatic of me, wasn't it, to put it that way? That's true with me, always. I mean, that's my true thought: That once you have committed yourself to a story, if you're embarked on it or if you're jumping on it, you can't go back on it. There's no way to unimagine something once you've imagined it. I don't mean it's going to be a success, but the act of imagining has its own velocity, its own power, its own . . . It calls up what it needs as it goes on. I know I'm sounding too fancy. But you can't unthink something, just as you can't disremember something. Or you can't snatch back a dream you've had. It has its own arrow. Like time. That does sound too fancy. If

you're really committed—if it's a strong idea you're committed to—I think you'll carry it on. Whether it succeeds or not is another matter. It doesn't guarantee anything.

You can't halfway start something. You can't put one foot over. You've got to jump. I don't know why I think of everything as diving and jumping. I'm a very unathletic person.

INTERVIEWER

And what about subjects choosing a writer?

WELTY

Certainly, when I wrote *One Writer's Beginnings*, it got hold of me. It was suggested to me as a subject, but no one could've done it but myself. And I really was in its grip when I was writing that very book. I thought about it night and day. And each thing would suggest something else and something else, and everything linked up. Connections appeared everywhere that I hadn't realized before. But if that isn't choosing you, I don't know what is.

INTERVIEWER

Did *One Writer's Beginnings* surprise you when it became a bestseller?

WELTY

Oh, of course. It surprised Harvard University off their nuts. They couldn't imagine it. A university press!

INTERVIEWER

Are you writing short stories again?

WELTY

I haven't found that beautiful consecutive time yet. The uninterrupted time. That's what I'm waiting for. I had some stories on the way and stopped to write *One Writer's Beginnings*, and I haven't gone back to see if they're alive. To see if their vitality is still there. I'm kind of scared to. I don't want to pick it up and immediately have to drop it again. So I want to wait until I have clear time again, which may be forever away. I want to very much. It's the only kind of writing that I really, really love to do.

INTERVIEWER

There's a story I've heard about how you came to Duke University to lecture, and Reynolds Price, who was an undergraduate at the time, met you at the train station in a white suit. Didn't you discover him as a writer even before he had published *A Long and Happy Life*?

WELTY

I wouldn't say I discovered him. No, I couldn't. He was in Mr. [William] Blackburn's class, and he was the editor of the magazine at that point. I think [novelist] Elizabeth Bowen had read his stuff. A lot of people had. Anybody who read him knew that here it was, the real thing. All I did that maybe the others wouldn't have had any way to do was to introduce him to my literary agent, Diarmuid Russell, who was such an unusual and sensitive man and just really an extraordinary agent that I thought good would come of that, and I think it did. But that would have happened, too.

INTERVIEWER

But you and Reynolds had an immediate affinity for each other, didn't you?

WELTY

We became friends right from the beginning. And he has meant a great deal to me.

INTERVIEWER

And how did he look in that white suit? I've heard Josephine Humphreys say that she went to Duke because she'd been so impressed with Reynolds Price in his blue seersucker suit during her interview there.

WELTY

Oh, he's a marvelous dresser. A wonderful dresser. Well, when I saw him, it was in just the glimmer of whatever early hours of the morning it was. Just one light at the station. Of course, I wasn't expecting to see anybody. He was very slender and youthful. Very dark. Of course, his hair's gray now. But then it was very dark. He was very romantic-looking. But I couldn't see anything that night except a savior dressed in white.

INTERVIEWER

You were doing a workshop at Duke?

WELTY

I think I did some readings. I was there a week, I believe.

INTERVIEWER

Your uncle—or your relative—is Walter Hines Page, for whom Duke's Page Auditorium is named.

WELTY

My grandfather's mother and Walter Hines Page's mother were sisters. He was a first cousin of my grandmother's. I've had some letters from some of the people that connected us—by the name of Robbiteau, a French Huguenot name. I was at Randolph-Macon [College] earlier this year for something, and I was given a book to sign—to Page Robbiteau somebody—and I wrote on the book, "Whoever you are, man or woman"—I didn't know who it was—"you're bound to be kin to me." And it is a woman. She wrote to me after I got home, and she said she'd been too shy to appear in person, but she knew we were kin.

INTERVIEWER

I read a *Paris Review* interview with you in which you told about the first time you met William Faulkner in Oxford, Mississippi. You said you were at a dinner party where there was a lot of hymn singing.

WELTY

There was some hymn singing.

INTERVIEWER

And ballad singing. And then you said, "He invited me to go sailing the next day." Did you go?

WELTY

Yeah. Faulkner and a bunch of his cronies had spent a long time making this sailboat. And he would go sailing on Sardis Lake. I think it was still new to him then. There was a man from home who was up there with me, and he invited us both. We went down to where the lake was, and the lake was so new that there were all these stobs—or what we called stobs. Stumps and stobs. It was like a cypress swamp standing there in the lake, and it was just mud. And the boat came up sort of far out. And Faulkner said, "Well, come on!" So we had to wade out.

INTERVIEWER

What did you have on?

WELTY

I guess I had on a cotton dress and probably my white pumps. I don't know what I had on. I had on clothes. I didn't have on pants, I know. So we walked out there and got into the boat, climbed in. I was so petrified, sailing. I don't think anybody said a word the whole time. Faulkner just placidly drove—steered, sailed—the boat. I sat behind, and John [the friend from Jackson] sat behind. It just felt like a dream going all around. And then he brought us back, and we went to his house and talked a little while. He was as kind as he could be. He didn't have to invite me to go sailing.

INTERVIEWER

What did you think of Faulkner when you met him the night before?

341

WELTY

I just thought he was fine. Of course, I was scared to meet him. I was surprised he was small—or compared to me—because I think of him as a giant. He was very quiet and small. He always spoke in a low voice. He did his part in the conversation. But I have seen him in company where he didn't say anything. Not that night. I was thrilled.

INTERVIEWER

Whose idea was the hymn singing?

WELTY

Oh, it was a bunch of cronies. That's who I ate dinner with. I was a friend of Miss Ella Summerville, who was one of the grand ladies of Oxford. She'd invited me to stay with her. So the Faulkners and two other couples were old friends that met all the time. I was meeting the Faulkners for the first time. I knew some of the others already. So it was the best way. Just a small dinner party—the two Faulkners and Bob Farley, who was dean of the law school, and I can't remember who else. I think they often did this way. I don't know whose idea this was.

INTERVIEWER

You'll be eighty in April. I remember Winston Churchill said when he turned eighty that it got there much faster than he thought it would. Do you feel that way?

WELTY

I don't know. It seems impossible. Ask me after the fact. If I'm still here, ask me after the fact.

It's always a shock to think of your age in any way. I'd like to just be in England and doing something I enjoyed. In Jackson, since I've lived here all my life, everybody just loves to celebrate things with me. They're very sweet about it. But I don't know if I could stand to have that celebrated. It's too much. The other day, I said I thought I was going to be in France or England. It struck me like a blow: They just can't do anything. They've done it all. There's nothing left. Too much. Too much.

INTERVIEWER

You've said you write from a feeling of praise and celebration for life, and that your wish would be not to point a finger in judgment, but to part the curtain.

WELTY

I think a writer of short stories writes to let their characters reveal human nature. That's what I mean by parting curtains. In writing a story, it's not *I* as a writer who wants to appear to be doing this, but the people of the story. The way you feel when you read a wonderful story by Chekhov or somebody: You feel you've been present at something.

———

Born April 13, 1909, in Jackson, Mississippi, Eudora Welty was the first of three children of Christian Webb and Mary Chestina Andrews Welty. She graduated from Jackson Central High School in 1925 and entered Mississippi State College for Women that fall. In 1929, she received her B.A. from the University of Wisconsin at Madison. From 1930 to 1931, she studied advertising at the Columbia University Graduate School of Business in New York City.

Welty returned to Jackson during the Depression and worked for local newspapers and radio stations until 1933, when she landed a job as publicity agent for the Works Progress Administration, traveling Mississippi, writing feature stories, and taking photographs.

Her novels are *Delta Wedding* (1946), *The Ponder Heart* (1954), *Losing Battles* (1970), and *The Optimist's Daughter* (1972). She has also written a novella, *The Robber Bridegroom* (1942).

Her short-story collections are *A Curtain of Green* (1941), *The Wide Net and Other Stories* (1943), *Short Stories* (1949), *The Golden Apples* (1949), *The Bride of Innisfallen and Other Stories* (1955), *Thirteen Stories* (1965), *The Collected Stories of Eudora Welty* (1980), and *Morgana: Two Stories from* The Golden Apples (1988).

Her nonfiction works include *Place in Fiction*, a collection of lectures for the Conference on American Studies in Cambridge, England (1957); *Three Papers on Fiction*, a collection of ad-dresses at Smith College (1964); *A Sweet Devouring* (1969); *One Time, One Place: Mississippi in the Depression—A Snapshot Album* (1971); *The Eye of the Story* (1978); *One Writer's Beginnings* (1984); *Photographs* (1989); and *Collected Book Reviews* (1994).

Welty's awards include Guggenheim Fellowships (1942, 1949); O. Henry Awards (1942, 1943, 1968); the William Dean Howells Medal of the American Academy (1952); the Creative Arts Medal, from Brandeis University (1966); election to the American Academy of Arts and Letters (1971); the William Gold Medal for Fiction, from the National Institute of Arts and Letters (1972); the Pulitzer Prize in fiction (1973); the National Medal for Literature (1980); the Presidential Medal of Freedom (1980); the American Book Award (1981, 1984); the Commonwealth Award for Distinguished Service in Literature, from the Modern Language Association of America (1984); the National Medal of Arts (1987); and the Chevalier de l'Ordre des Arts et Lettres (1987).

Bruce Schwartz of Palos Verdes, California, a literature professor at Marymount College, is making a thirty-minute movie of Welty's short story "A Worn Path," starring Cora Lee Day, to be shown on Mississippi ETV in 1994.

Welty lives in Jackson, Mississippi, where she continues to write book reviews, essays, and short stories.

Index